EMERGING COMMUNICATIONS FOR WIRELESS SENSOR NETWORKS

Edited by **Anna Förster and Alexander Förster**

Emerging Communications for Wireless Sensor Networks
Edited by Anna Förster and Alexander Förster

Published by InTech
Janeza Trdine 9, 51000 Rijeka, Croatia

Technical Editor Sonja Mujacic

Cover Designer InTech Design Team

Additional hard copies can be obtained from orders@intechopen.com

Emerging Communications for Wireless Sensor Networks,
Edited by Anna Förster and Alexander Förster
p. cm.
ISBN 978-953-307-082-7

For EU product safety concerns:
IN TECH d.o.o., Prolaz Marije Krucifikse Kozulić 3, 51000 Rijeka, Croatia,
info@intechopen.com or visit our website at intechopen.com.

Meet the editor

I am currently a Professor at the University of Bremen in Germany and leading the Sustainable Communication Networks group. I have received my PhD in Computer Science from the University of Lugano in Switzerland in 2009 and my Master degree in Computer Science and Aerospace Engineering from the Free University of Berlin, Germany, in 2004. After my MSc graduation I have spent an year as a junior consultant at the Business Technology Office of McKinsey & Company, before dedicating myself completely to research. Before joining the University of Bremen in early 2015, I have spent several years as researcher at the University of Applied Sciences of Southern Switzerland. My research goal is to enable a sustainable future for computer networking. I am interested both in the usage of computer networking techniques for enabling sustainability and vice versa: enabling more sustainable and flexible computer networks. I am mainly concentrating on wireless networks, cyber physical systems and networks, internet of things, opportunistic networks and computing, massively distributed clouds, participatory sensing, wireless underground sensor networks, smart grids, etc. Furthermore, I am exploring the usage and further development and adaption of machine learning techniques in these areas.

Contents

Preface

Wireless Sensor Networking is one of the most important new technologies of the century and has been identified to see significant grow in the next decades. Wireless sensor networks are power-efficient, small-size and communicate wirelessly among each other to cooperatively monitor and access the properties of their targeted environments. Applications reach from health monitoring, through industrial and environmental monitoring to safety applications.

In this book we present some recent exciting developments of software communication technologies and some novel applications. We hope you will enjoy reading the book as much as we have enjoyed bringing it together for you. The book presents efforts by a number of people. We would like to thank all the researchers and especially the chapter authors who entrusted us with their best work and it is their work that enabled us to collect the material for this book.

Anna Förster
Networking Laboratory, SUPSI,
Switzerland

Alexander Förster
IDSIA,
Switzerland

1

Wireless Sensor Networks: from Application Specific to Modular Design

Liang Song, and Dimitrios Hatzinakos
Dept. of Electrical and Computer Engineering, University of Toronto
Toronto, ON Canada

1. Introduction

The success of modular design and architecture has been observed in many fields. For examples, in the world of computer systems, the Von Neumann architecture set forth the fundamentals of modern computers. Equally important in computer networks is the Open System Interconnect (OSI) architecture, where the hierarchy of layers abstracts network functionalities and hides implementation complexities. In the multiple layers of OSI, the physical layer defines the actual waveform being transmitted in communication medium and the conversion of digital information bits (modulation/demodulation). The data link layer provides the abstraction of communication channel where packets are transmitted. The networking layer routes data packets across the network, and the transport layer defines an end-to-end tunnel hiding the complexity of communications from high layers. A related success story is the Internet.

Generally speaking, the benefits of modular design and architecture are: 1) it converts complicated system into simplified layers (modules); 2) methods developed for particular layers (modules) would benefit overall system as well; 3) modifications on a single layer (module) would not need a system re-design. Therefore, system modular abstractions have been important for any industrial proliferation, for example in both computer and communication engineering.

The rapid convergence of advances in digital circuitry, wireless transceiver, and micro electro-mechanical systems, has made it possible to integrate sensing, data processing, wireless communication, and power supply into a low-cost inch scale device. Thus, the potential of collaborative, robust, easily deploying, wireless sensor networks with thousands of these inch-scale nodes have been attracting a great deal of attention. For wireless communications and networking, the unique nature of sensor networks, which are application-specific and resource limited, pose unique challenges.

First, the applications of wireless sensor networks need mass collaboration of a large number of sensor nodes. Such applications, e.g., enviroment monitoring, object/asset surveillance and tracking, utility/energy management, generate very different network traffic patterns, and require different sets of application Qualtiy of Services (QoS). Before the emerging of wireless sensor networks, the research and development in communications and networking had been ususally focused on delivering more packets under bandwidth/power/latency constraints. Introduced by wireless sensor networks, such research and development are, for the first time, completely exposed to and closely correlated with the details of applications.

Second, inch-scale sensor devices are usually subject to tight resource limitations. For example, compared to portable devices such as smart phones and laptops that can have battery recharge frequently, wireless sensor nodes usually do not have such privileges due to cost constraints. Therefore, sensor nodes are usually relying on a small amount of battery energy storagy, while at the same time are expected to operate over years. The power constraints also introduce other resource limitions on hardware such as computing, memory, and communication capabilities.

Consequently, the tradeoff between application QoS requirements and the resource limitations of wireless sensor nodes has been unfound in traditional (wireless) communciations and networking. Traditional layered architecture of communication protocol stack has also been identified as insufficient in addressing the new challenges, where cross-layer optimizations are needed. More specifically, the research and development in wireless sensor networks have been calling for application specific design, where application details determine the optimization of lower-layer protocol stack. However, the introduction of application specific design has also been causing the loss of architectural modularity in wireless sensor networks.

In the following, we first review the need for application specific design in wireless sensor networks, in Section 2. We then further introduce a non-application-specific architecture, Embedded Wireless Interconnect (EWI), which was generalized from the studies of application specific design, but could also provide a universal platform with modular abstractions. The abstractions of EWI are then described in Section 3. Although a single sensor node is subject to tight resource limitations, a wireless network with thounds of wireless sensor nodes can exploit a wealth of dynamic resources in terms of nodes/radios and spectrum bandwidth. In Section 4, a cognitive-networking method is further introduced to best utilize resources in large-scael wireless systems, being ideally implemented in the abstracted modules of EWI.

From application specific to modular design, we aim to provide: an architecture with a set of Application Programming Interface (API) functions that can decouple application developments from the details of wireless communication/networking; an architecture with a set of modules that can best utilize dyanmic resources in large-scale wireless systems. Both have been prelimiarly achieved by the work of EWI.

2. Application Specific Design

The need for application specific design and cross-layer optimization can be illustrated by a simple example of wireless sensor networks. As shown in Figure 1, two sensor nodes *A* and *B* are collecting data and sending it to the sink *S* in real-time.

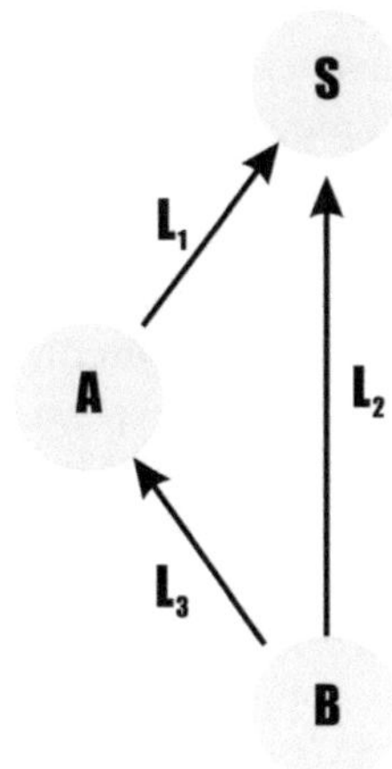

Fig. 1. A Simplified Illustrative Example

There can be three links in this simplified network: *L1* between nodes *A* and *S*; *L2* between nodes *B* and *S*; *L3* between nodes *B* and *A*. Given a constant data transmission rate, it is further assumed that the sum of packet power consumption on *L1* and *L3* is less than the packet power consumption on *L2*. Here, "packet power consumption" denotes the power consumption of transmitting/receiving one data packet on the corresponding wireless linkage.

Let's first assume that the design objective is to minimize the sum of energy consumption on nodes *A* and *B*. A simple think shows that application requirements decide the network topology. For example, if data packets arrive only sporadically, link *L2* can be removed, since node *B* should always take the multi-hop transmission, and have node *A* forward the packet, so as to minimize the total energy consumption. However, if data packets arrive continuously in time on both nodes *A* and *B*, e.g., multimedia streaming, the "multihop" topology will require a higher transmission data-rate on link *L1*. Since link power consumption could increase exponentially with the data-rate under Gaussian assumption, according to Shannon, C. E., 1948, it may turn out that a "star network" is more preferable, where link *L3* can be removed. However, if some processing capability, such as data fusion, is available on sensor nodes, node *A* might then compress two packets originated from the two sensor nodes, *A* and *B*, into one single packet. Since the high data-rate problem no longer exists, the "multihop" topology can be more favorable again.

If the network lifetime ends when either one of the two sensors runs out of energy, designers should balance the energy consumption between the two sensor nodes. This lifetime would be reduced by the "multi-hop" topology, since node *A* becomes a "hot spot", and would die much faster than node *B*. As one possible solution, node *B* might probabilistically decide between the switching between the multi-hop and the direct transmissions. The optimal value of this probability is decided by the source data-rate on both nodes *A* and *B*.

Furthermore, due to the broadcast nature of wireless medium, when node *B* transmits on link *L2*, node *A* is also able to decode the packet. If the transmission fails and is rescheduled, many possibilities of cooperative transmission exist even among two sensor nodes. Under our simplified channel model, node *A* may re-transmit the lost packet, on link *L1*, in order to save energy.

The above simplified example can already demonstrated numerous ways of cross-layer optimization in accordance with application requirements. Application specific design have been found necessary in wireless sensor networks for dealing with sensor-device resource limitations. Similar to what we have identified in the above simplified example, research literatures have already identified two basic approaches to the cross-layer optimization for wireless sensor networks.

Top down approach: it is to apply the application details to deciding network topology and packet routing. More specifically, data/message exchanges in sensor networks are event-centric, location-centric, and data-centric. A number of research works have been concentrated on adapting the ad-hoc routing and network management paradigm to accommodate the new application-specific features. For example, [Intanagonwiwat, C. et al., 2002] developed a data-centric routing paradigm for wireless sensor networks: Directed Diffusion; [Madden, S. et al., 2005] developed the TinyDB system which uses semantic routing and agregration trees to set up database applications in wireless sensor networks; similarly [Abdelzaher, T. et al., 2004] developed EnviroTrack as an applicaiton-specific network design for environmental tracking sensor networks.

Bottom up approach: it is to utilize the broadcasting nature of wireless medium to improve the quality and efficiency of wireless communications. For example, physical layer inter-node cooperation is usually neglected in traditional wireless (ad-hoc) networks, but can offer a large performance margin in terms of reliability and energy efficiency. Both features are of key importance in sensor-network applications. [Scaglione, A. et al., 2003] designed Opportunistic Large Array to utilize physical-layer cooperative transmisison; [Barriac, G. et al., 2004] studied a scheme of distributed beamforming where wireless sensor nodes can act as elements of virtual antenna array; [Song, L. et al., 2006] was using cooperative transmission to achieve better communicaiton reliability in wireless sensor networks.

However, both approaches need the cross-layer optimization of communication protocol stack, therefore have caused an issue at the same time: the lost of modularity. It could be concluded that traditional network architecture (primarily based on OSI) is not appropriate for meeting the challengs of wireless sensor networks, and a new modular network architecture needs to be identified from application specific designs.

3. Modular Abstraction and Architecture

Embedded Wireless Interconnect is one of the first modular architecture for wireless sensor networks. The key architectural differentiation is based on the abstract wireless linkage, where wireless links are now redefined as arbitrary mutual cooperation among a set of neighboring (proximity) wireless nodes. In comparison, traditional wireless networking relies on point-to-point "virtual-wired links" with a predetermined pair of wireless nodes and allotted spectrum. The architectural diagram of EWI is illustrated in Figure 2.

The concept of EWI was firstly proposed in some application specific studies of wireless sensor networks, including [Song, L. et al., 2007a, 2007b]. A protocol for target tracking in wireless sensor networks has been the first example to demonstrate the EWI architecture in [Song, L. et al., 2007a].

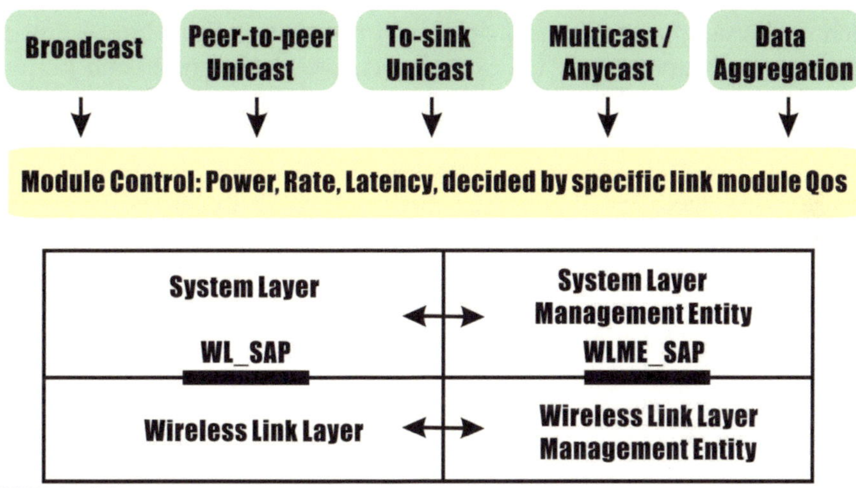

Fig. 2. EWI Architecture

Three principles about the EWI architecture have been generalized from application specific studies:

1. *Functional linkage abstraction:* By the functional abstractions, wireless linkage is redefined as arbitrary functional abstraction of proximity node cooperation. Therefore, "wireless link modules" are the building blocks for individual wireless nodes, so as to establish different types of abstract wireless links. For example, categories of wireless links (modules) can include: broadcast, unicast, multicast and data aggregation, etc. At the architecture level, this results in two hierarchical layers: the upper system layer and the lower wireless link layer. The wireless link layer offers a library of wireless link modules to the system layer; the system layer organizes the provided wireless link modules and API to achieve effective application implementation.

2. *Opportunistic wireless links:* In the formation of abstract wireless links, both the occupied spectrum and participating wireless nodes are opportunistically decided by their instantaneous availability. This largely differentiates from traditional wireless networking where both types of resources (spectrum and radio) are predetermined for point-to-point wireless links. The resulting system performance shall improve with larger network scale, since higher network density provides more redundancy for the opportunistic utilization. This also introduces the concept of large-scale cognitive networking that will be further described in Section 4.

3. *Global QoS decoupling:* Global QoS requirements at both application and network levels are statistically decoupled into local wireless link QoS, which are local requirements of proximity node cooperation. By decoupling global network QoS such as throughput, end-to-end delay and delay jitter, the wireless link module design such as unicast or multicast can achieve global end-to-end performance requirements. Similarly by decoupling global application QoS, the system layer can better organize the wireless link modules that are provided by the wireless link layer. Since wireless networking complexities are well encapsulated in the wireless link modules, the implementation complexity at individual wireless nodes shall be independent of network scale/size.

Like the merits of any modular architecture, the defined wireless link modules can provide system designers with reusable open network abstractions, where the modules can be individually updated or added in the wireless link layer. Five different wireless link modules are illustrated in Figure 2, which are broadcast, peer-to-peer unicast, multicast, to-sink unicast and data aggregation, respectively. Other types of wireless link modules can be added, subject to other system design consideration. The broadcast module simply broadcasts data to neighboring nodes; the peer-to-peer unicast module [Song, L. et al., 2008] can reliably send data from source to destination over long distance (multiple wireless hops); the multicast module sends data to multiple destinations; the to-sink unicast module [Song, L. et al., 2007b] can utilize higher power of data collectors (sinks) to achieve better data collecting; and the data-aggregation module [Song, L. et al., 2007a] can opportunistically collect and aggregate data from neighboring wireless sensor nodes.

EWI is an organizing-style architecture, where the system layer can manage and organize the wireless link modules. Peer wireless link modules can exchange module management information by putting it in the packet headers to system-layer information units. As illustrated in Figure 2, the interface between the system layer and the wireless link layer is defined by two service access points (SAP): the wireless link SAP (WL SAP) and wireless link management SAP (WLME SAP) that are utilized for the data plane and the management plane respectively. Each SAP is composed of a set of API functions [Song, L. et al., 2009] to control the state of the wireless link layer and link QoS.

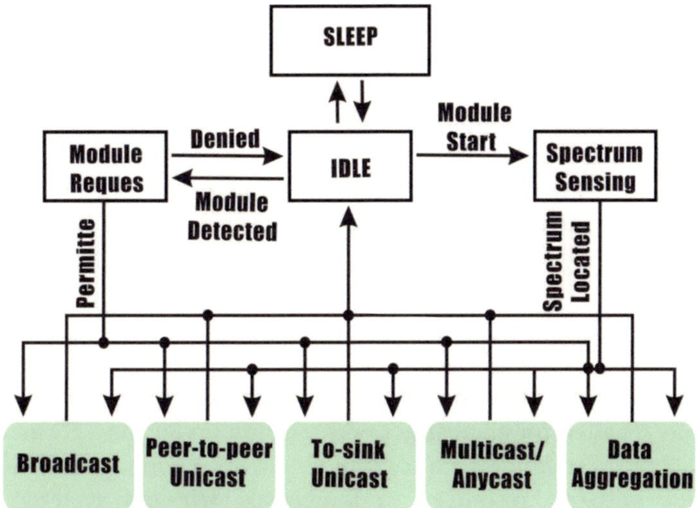

Fig. 3. State Diagram of the Wireless Link Layer

A state diagram of the wireless link layer can be illustrated in Figure 3. The wireless link layer remains in the IDLE state, when no wireless link module is invoked. A pair of primitives (API functions) can be utilized for the switching between the IDLE state and the SLEEP state (power-saving mode). In the IDLE state, the wireless link layer keeps monitoring if there are new abstract wireless links being initiated. Once an initiation from any neighboring nodes is detected, the wireless link layer transfers from the IDLE state to the Module Request state. This provides the system layer with the control of wireless link activities, so that the wireless link layer would either transfer back to the IDLE state or join in the new abstract wireless link, as decided by the system response. On the other hand, once receiving a command to initiate an abstract wireless link, the wireless link layer transfers from the IDLE state to the Spectrum Sensing state; a wireless link module would be then started after available spectrum resource being opportunistically located.

Fig. 4. Commercial Hardware/SDK based on EWI

An implementation of the EWI architecture for wireless sensor networks, including hardware platform and SDK (Software Development Kits), is now commercially offered by OMESH Networks Inc. (Toronto, Canada URL: www.omeshnet.com). The system has been used in commercial applications including wireless location and monitoring/controlling sensor networks in agriculture, mining, electricity, environmental monitoring, and industrial controlling. It has also been used for sensor network test-bed in academic research including a number of projects in the University of Toronto.

4. Cognitive Networking Method

As described previously, both the operating spectrum and participating nodes are opportunistically decided for an abstract wireless link under the EWI architecture. This introduces the concept of large-scale cognitive networking [Song, L. et al., 2009] which can best utilize network resources in large-scale wireless systems, such as the applications of wireless sensor networks. The networking concept is one-step further of cognitive radio [Zhao, Q. et al., 2007], and creates dynamic and real-time network with unlimited scalability.

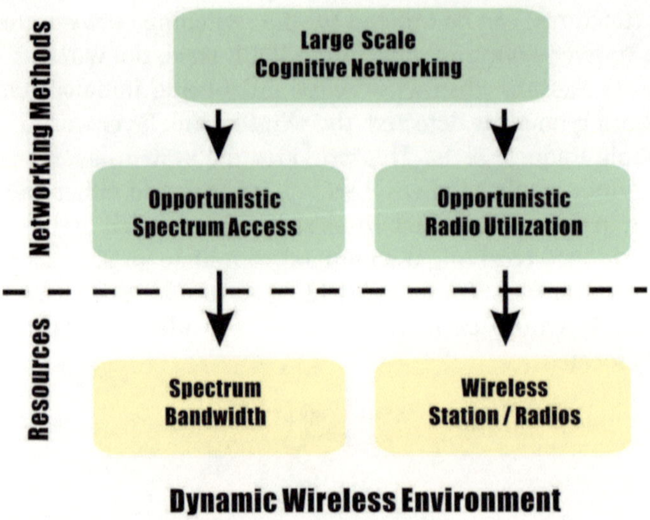

Fig. 5. Cognitive Networking Concept

In principle, large-scale cognitive networking is highly differentiated from traditional wireless networking, by its opportunistic network resource utilization of both spectrum bandwidth and wireless node/radio availability. On the contrary, traditional wireless networking assumes that those resources can be predetermined.

The cognitive-networking method creates a dynamic (fluid) wireless network without predetermined topology and spectrum allocation. For example, in multi-hop wireless communications, every packet takes opportunistically available paths in the wireless network, and with opportunistically available spectrum on every hop. The network-resource utilization can thereby reach its instantaneous maximum, disregarding volatile changes and the demand placed on the network. In large-scale wireless networks such as wireless sensor networks, the problem of volatile spectrum availability is typical in unlicensed bands where interference prevails. Similarly, the problem of random radio availability is also often encountered due to the dynamic traffic load and other factors such as radio failure. In dynamic wireless environment, traditional wireless networking seldom functions properly, given its assumption of predetermined "virtual-wired" links and network topology for (ad-hoc) network routing protocols. As a result, almost every today's real-world wireless network is based on single-hop wireless (e.g., cellular networks, WLAN - wireless local area networks) rather than a true multi-hop mesh.

A set of key comparative advantages of the cognitive-networking method is further explained as follows:

Dynamic network planning and deployment model:
No deterministic network topology has to be maintained, because the wireless node/radio resource is opportunistically utilized. The wireless sensor nodes, when implemented with the cognitive-networking method, become "drop-and-play" in the network deployment. Inserting more radios/nodes can improve the radio resource to be opportunistically exploited, and therefore increase the network capacity. Likewise removing any individual radio/node does not create bottlenecks in the network. This fluid "drop-and-play" nature offers the potential of vast cost-saving in network planning and deployments. The setup of wireless radio/node does not need expensive planning and calibration, as multi-tier new deployments (for example introduced by operators) guarantee improved network capacity. High mobility of the nodes/radios can be supported.

Better network resource utilization:
The network resource in large-scale wireless networks includes: the amount of spectrum bandwidth and the number of wireless nodes/radios. Theoretical network capacity is decided by the network resources, and the multiplication of these two factors. Traditional wireless networking depends on a deterministic network topology. It is therefore difficult to efficiently utilize the network resources, subject to a dynamic wireless networking environment where both spectrum bandwidth and radio availability cannot be predetermined. The cognitive networking method offers a means of better network-resource utilization, approaching the information-theoretical limit on wireless-network capacity.

Supporting guaranteed real-time services:
Due to the opportunistic network-resource utilization, reliable wireless communications with specified dataflow throughput, end-to-end delay, and delay variance can be supported over multiple wireless hops. Therefore, real-time services,

including multimedia streaming, can be supported by the cognitive-networking method. In order to better understand this, note that the opportunistic exploitation of local random-networking environment can result in overall-reliable end-to-end communications. Dataflow throughput is independent of the number of wireless hops; end-to-end delay and delay variance only increase linearly with the number of wireless hops; and delay variance can also diminish to zero with higher network density. Therefore, network operators only need to assure that sufficient network resources are deployed to support their applications, so as to provide guaranteed services of real-time communications, where the resources, e.g., gateway capacity and nodes/radios, can be deployed with low cost.

Robust to wireless interferences:
Due to the opportunistic network-resource utilization of spectrum bandwidth, the network is very robust to interferences which can be substantial in unlicensed spectrum bands (e.g., ISM bands). For example, viable operation within unlicensed bands can bring large free bandwidth to wireless sensor networks, which results in large network capacity with virtually zero cost.

Compatibility with current industrial standards:
The cognitive-networking method can be compatible with all established wireless radio standards, so that the implementation can be independent of physical radios. Therefore, the radio modules (with cognitive-networking capabilities) can use off-the-shelf RF chips which offer relatively low cost. The implementation can also be seamlessly integrated with all network-layer protocols, including for example Internet Protocols.

Supporting scalable radio complexity (low power):
The complexity of individual radio modules (with cognitive-networking capabilities) is low and independent of network scale/size. The low radio complexity results in lower power consumption, lower cost, and longer battery life. When needed, it also makes it possible to power the wireless node by cost-effective solar panel, which will further reduce installation cost by removing any cable attachment.

Better economics and business case (low cost):
As explained above, the cognitive-networking method can offer excellent economics in large-scale wireless systems including wireless sensor networks, by which 1) the costs of deploying network resources could be vastly reduced by the utilization of unlicensed spectrum bands and drop-and-play (mobile) wireless nodes; 2) much higher efficiency in network-resource utilization results in excellent performance with all the available resources being used to their instantaneous maximum.

5. Conclusion

In this chapter, we have not only reviewed the need for application-specific network design in the current research of wireless sensor networks, but also have pointed out the need for appropriate modular abstractions or network architecture. System modular abstractions are important for any industrial proliferation of computer and communication systems, where any modification and improvement of one layer or module would not need a system re-design.

We then introduced one of the first modular architecture for wireless sensor networks, Embedded Wireless Interconnect. The abstractions of EWI take a layered architecture, and hide networking complexities from application design in large-scale wireless systems, by the redefinition of wireless linkage. Modular abstractions are given on wireless links, and a set of API functions can be provided for the system to organize and manage the wireless link modules. Major resources in large-scale wireless networks, including both spectrum bandwidth and wireless nodes (radios) are opportunistically utilized in the construction of abstract wireless links, according to the cognitive-networking method. Therefore, the modular architecture of EWI creates low-complexity wireless sensor networks that can efficiently deal with dynamic changes typically in large-scale wireless environment, and ensure reliable application-level QoS at the same time, addressing the major challenges in wireless sensor networks.

6. References

Shannon, C. E. (1948). A Mathematical Theory of Communications, *Bell Syst. Tech. Journal*, Vol. 27, pp. 379-423, 623-656.

Intanagonwiwat, C.; Govindan, R., Estrin, D., Heidemann, J. & Silva, F. (2002). Directed Diffusion for Wireless Sensor Networking, *ACM/IEEE Transactions on Networking*, Vol. 11, No. 1, pp. 2-16.

Madden, S.; Franklin, M. J.; Hellerstein, J. M. & Hong, W. (2005). "TinyDB: An Acquisitional Query Processing System for Sensor Networks", *ACM Trans. on Database Systems*, Vol. 30, No. 1, pp. 122-173.

Abdelzaher, T.; Blum, B.; Cao, Q.; Chen, Y.; Evans, D.; George, J.; George, S.; Gu, L.; He, T.; Luo, L.; Son, S.; Stoleru, R.; Stankovic, J. & Wood, A. (2004). EnviroTrack: Toward an Environmental Computing Paradigm for Distributed Sensor Networks, in Proc. *24th International Conference on Distributed Computing Systems (ICDCS)*, pp. 582-589.

Scaglione, A. & Hong, Y. W. (2003). Opportunistic Large Arrays: Cooperative Transmission in Wireless Multihop Ad hoc Networks to Reach Far Distances, *IEEE Trans. on Signal Processing*, Vol. 51, No. 8, pp. 2082-2092.

Barriac, G.; Mudumbai, R. & Madhow, U. (2004). Distributed Beamforming for Information Transfer in Sensor Networks, in Proc. *the Third International Symposium on Information Processing in Sensor Networks*, pp. 81-88, Berkeley, CA.

Song, L. & Hatzinakos, D. (2006). Cooperative Transmission in Poisson Distributed Wireless Sensor Networks: Protocol and Outage Probability, *IEEE Trans. on Wireless Communications*,Vol. 5, No. 10, pp. 2834-2843.

Song, L. & Hatzinakos, D. (2007a). A Cross-layer Architecture of Wireless Sensor Networks for Target Tracking, *IEEE/ACM Trans. on Networking,* Vol. 15, No. 1, pp. 145-158.

Song, L. & Hatzinakos, D. (2007b). Architecture of Wireless Sensor Networks with Mobile Sinks: Sparsely Deployed Sensors, *IEEE Trans. on Vehicular Technology,* Vol. 56, No. 4, Part 1, pp. 1826-1836.

Song, L. & Hatzinakos, D. (2008). Real Time Communications in Large Scale Wireless Networks, *International Journal of Digital Multimedia Broadcasting,* ID 586067, DOI: 10.1155/2008/586067.

Song, L. & Hatzinakos, D. (2009). Cognitive Networking of Large Scale Wireless Systems, *International Journal of Communication Networks and Distributed Systems,* Vol. 2, No. 4, pp. 452-475.

Zhao, Q. & Sadler, B. (2007). A Survey of Dynamic Spectrum Access, *IEEE Signal Processing Magazine,* Vol. 24, No. 3.

2

Wireless Sensor Networks Applications via High Altitude Systems

Zhe Yang and Abbas Mohammed
Blekinge Institute of Technology
Sweden

1. Introduction

Wireless sensor networking is a fast emerging subfield in the field of wireless networking. It is a key technology for the future ad has been identified as one of the most important technologies for this century (Akyildiz et al., 2002; Business Week, 1999; Technology Review, 2003). These sensors are generally equipped with data processing, communication, and information collecting capabilities. They can detect the variation of ambient conditions in the environment surrounding the sensors and transform them into electric signal (e.g., temperature, sound, image). Interests in sensor networks have motivated intensive research in the past few years emphasizing the potential of collaboration among sensors in data collecting and processing, coordination and management of the sensing activity and date flow to the sink.

Depending on application to reveal some characteristics about phenomena in the area, sensor nodes can be deployed on the ground, in the air, under water, on bodies, in vehicles and inside buildings (Akyildiz et al., 2002). Thus, these connected sensor nodes have many promising applications in many fields (e.g., consumer, military, health, environment, security). Deployment of these sensor nodes can be in random fashion like dropping from a helicopter (a disaster management setup), or manual (deploying nodes in a building to detect the movement of human) (Akyildiz et al., 2002).

Sensor nodes are usually constrained in energy and bandwidth (Akyildiz et al., 2002). Such constraints combined with the deployment of a large number of sensor nodes are challenges to the design and maintenance of sensor networks. Energy-awareness has to be considered at all layers of networking protocol stack. It is also related to physical and link layers which are generally common for all kind of sensor applications. Research on these layers has been focused on radio communication hardware, energy-aware media access control (MAC) protocols (Demirkol et al., 2006; Hill et al., 2000; Intel, 2004; Jiang et al., 2006). The main aim at the network layer is to find ways for energy-efficient and reliable route setup from sensor nodes to the sink in order to maximally extend the lifetime of network.

HAPs are either aircraft or airships operating at an altitude of 17 km above the ground. They have been suggested by the International Telecommunication Union (ITU) for providing communications in mm-wave broadband wireless access (BWA) and the third generation (3G) communication frequency bands (Elabdin et al., 2006; Thornton et al., 2003;

Tozer & Grace, 2001). Currently, investigations on HAPs have been carried on in the 3G telecommunication and broadband wireless services. These platforms are regarded to be based on lighter-than-air vehicles or conventional aircraft proposed at various stages of development (Tozer & Grace, 2001). Employing unpiloted, solar-powered platforms in different altitudes can ultimately make the systems more reliable and competitive in the future.

HAP systems have many characteristics to make it competitive to be adopted in different telecommunication and wireless communication applications, e.g. a mobile sink in WSN. HAPs can provide high receiver elevation angle, line of sight (LOS) transmission, large coverage area and mobile deployment etc. The system combines the advantages of terrestrial and satellite systems, and furthermore contributes to a better overall system performance, greater system capacity and cost-effective deployment (Mohammed et al., 2008). Many countries have made significant efforts in the research of HAP systems and their potential applications. A company *StratXX®* in Switzerland has started to develop three different platforms operating from 3 km to 17 km above the ground to provide various services, e.g. mobile multimedia transmission, local navigation and remote sensing (StratXX, 2008). A similar scenario of using unmanned autonomous vehicle (UAV) to transfer information in the distributed wireless sensor system has been proposed (Vincent et al., 2006) and shown to be an energy-efficient solution.

In this chapter, we explore and analyze the potential of using HAPs in WSN applications to establish a HAP-WSN system. The HAP-WSN system is composed of a large number of sensor nodes, which can monitor and collect information about the physical environment and transmit the data to another location for processing in an ad-hoc manner, and a HAP, which collects information from sensor nodes as a remote sink above the ground. Reliable communication links are analyzed between sensor nodes and HAPs to achieve LOS in most cases based on the height of the platform. The HAP-WSN can be deployed in inaccessible or disaster environments, where sensor nodes and HAPs are both powered by battery, which means energy consumption is the key concept in the system design. The chapter is organized as follows: in section 2, an introduction to WSN and HAP-WSN system is given. Two scenarios of HAP-WSN are proposed based on the cell formation of the HAP system and sensor node radio link. In section 3, the configuration and simulation results in the system level of HAP-WSN are presented. In section 4, the configuration and simulation results in the physical layer are presented. In section 5, conclusions and future research are given.

2. High Altitude Platform-Wireless Sensor Network System

2.1 WSN communication scenarios and design issues

A typical sensor network contains a large number of sensor nodes with data processing and communication capabilities. The sensor nodes send collected data via radio transmitter, to a sink either directly or through other nodes in a multi-hop fashion. The technological advances in this field result in the decrease of the size and cost of sensors and enabled the development of smart disposable micro sensors, which can be networked through wireless links. Fig. 1 shows the communication architecture of a WSN. Sensor nodes organize themselves to collect highly reliable information about the phenomenon, and route data via other sensors to the sink. The sink in Fig. 1 could be either a fixed or mobile node with the capability of connecting sensor networks to the outer existing communication infrastructure, e.g. internet, cellular and satellite networks.

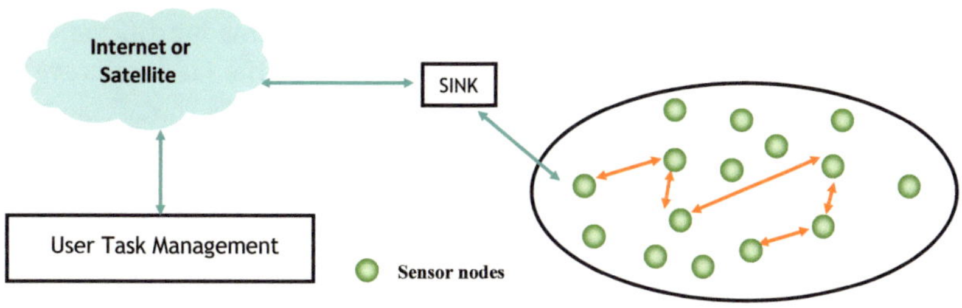

Fig. 1. General communication scenarios of a WSN

Due to the number of sensor nodes and the dynamics of their operating environment, it poses unique challenges in the design of sensor network architecture.
Dynamic network: Basically a WSN consists of three components: sensor node, sink and event. Sensor nodes and sink are assumed to be fixed and mobile. Although currently sensor nodes in most applications are assumed to be stationary, it is still necessary to support the mobility of sinks or gateway in the network. Thus the stability of data transferring is an important design factor, in addition to energy, bandwidth etc (Akyildiz et al., 2002). Moreover the phenomenon could also be dynamic, which requires periodic report to the sink.

- Energy constrains: The process of data routing in the network is greatly affected by energy considerations, routing path and radio link. Since the radio transmission in practical scenarios degrades with distance much faster than transmission in free space, means that communication distance and energy must be well managed (Chong & Kumar, 2003). Directed routing would perform well enough if all the sensor nodes are close to the sink. However, most of the time, it is necessary to use multi-hop routing to consume less power than directed routing, since sensors are randomly scattered in the area.
- Propagation environment: Sensor nodes are deployed on the ground which leads to a relative low height of antenna on a sensor node and a small distance to the radio horizon. Non line of sight (NLOS) signal transmission in WSN is predominant in most directions since the complicated environment of deployment can cause severe attenuations. Signal power at a distance d away from the transmitter may be estimated as $1/d^n$, where n=2 for propagation in free space, but n is between 2 and 4 for low lying antenna deployments in practical WSNs (Vincent et al., 2006).

There are other issues such as coverage area, scalability, transmission media, routing protocols, which could also affect the design and performance of the network (Akyildiz et al., 2002; Chong & Kumar, 2003). All the solutions to these issues need to reduce the energy-consumption and prolong the lifetime of WSN in most applications.

2.2 HAP-WSN System Scenarios and Advantages

Current research in HAPs has widely adopted two proposed types of cell planning in HAP system. By subdividing the coverage area of the HAP into one or multiple cells, the HAP antenna payload has potential to provide a high gain in each cell planning scenario. In (Thornton et al., 2003; Yang et al., 2007), the coverage area has been divided into 121 and 19 cells in order to improve the capacity of HAP system. Based on the architecture of HAPs and WSN, we propose two configurations for HAP-WSN systems for different applications. The first scenario is shown in Fig. 2. The sensor nodes inside the HAP cells are transmitting information directly to the HAP. The main aim of the scenario is to reduce the complexity and remove energy-consumption of multi-hop transmissions in WSN. It is suitable for WSN applications with low data transmission in large coverage area.

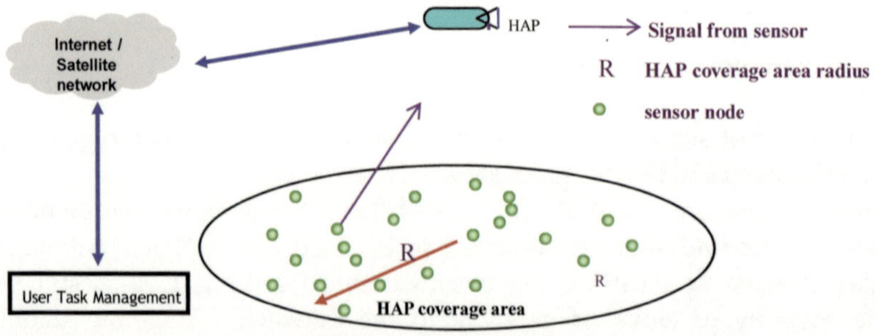

Fig. 2. A HAP-WSN system in a single cell configuration.

Fig. 3 shows the second system configuration of the HAP-WSN. The sensor nodes inside the HAP cell are organized into a cluster, where one node with the higher-energy is selected as the cluster head. Senor nodes as cluster members collect information and send to the cluster head, which is responsible to send all data to the HAP. The cluster formation in WSNs is typically based on the energy reserve of sensors and their distances to the cluster head (Akyildiz et al., 2002). The main aim of the scenario is to reduce the complexity of a multi-hop WSN and maintain the energy consumption of all sensor nodes. It can be employed in WSN applications with high data transmission requirement, e.g. multimedia.

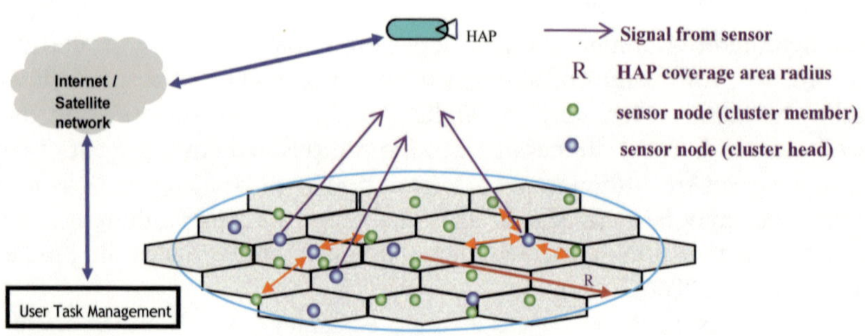

Fig. 3. A HAP-WSN system in a multi-cell configuration

The HAP-WSN system has advantages of HAP system which is employed as a sink in the WSN:

- Reducing complexity of multi-hop transmission and achieving energy-efficiency: A multi-hop routing has been under investigations because the radio link is usually constrained by obstructions on the ground. HAPs are often considered to be located a few kilometers above the ground, where it can establish a LOS link between the sensor node and the HAP sink. Therefore HAPs offer a potential of reducing or removing transmission burden in WSN, organize communications based multiple access schemes, e.g. TDMA, CDMA, to reduce energy consumption in sensor nodes.

- Low cost and rapid mobile deployment: It is believed that the cost of HAP is considerably cheaper than that of a satellite because HAPs do not require expensive launch and maintenance (Tozer & Grace, 2001). The HAP as a sink, can be reused, repaired and replaced quickly for applications of WSNs, e.g. disaster and emergency surveillance where it has clear advantages. It may stay in the sky for a long period, which can prolong the life of the WSN.

3. System Level Configuration and Simulation Performance

3.1 HAP system antenna and propagation issues

In this work we employ a directive antenna payload on HAPs, which can ensure more power radiated in the desired directions. The HAP antenna payload is assumed to be composed of either a single or multiple antennas according to the cell formation. The antenna radiation model is presented in (Thornton et al., 2003). The gain of the antenna of HAP $A_H(\varphi)$, at an angle φ with respect to its boresight, is approximated by a cosine function raised to a power roll-off factor n and a notional flat sidelobe level S_f. G_H represents the boresight gain of the HAP antenna.

$$A_H(\varphi) = G_H(\max[\cos(\varphi)^{n_H}, s_f]) \tag{1}$$

The antenna peak gain is accordingly achieved at the centre of the HAP cell. The HAP antenna beamwidth is initially defined by its φ_{10dB} set to be equal to the subtended angle away from the antenna boresight of the central cell to the edge of the HAP coverage area or the central HAP cell corresponding to the single and multi-cell formations. After defining the beamwidth, the boresight gain is calculated as (Thornton et al., 2003):

$$G_{boresight} = \frac{32 \ln 2}{2\theta^2{}_{3dB}} \tag{2}$$

We select the roll-off factor n to let the radiation curve falling to 10 dB lower than the maximum value. Fig. 4 shows the two HAP antenna radiation masks corresponding to the single or multiple cell structures in the system.

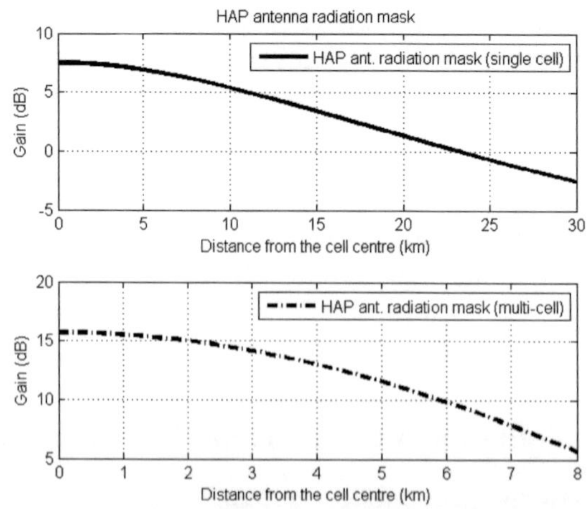

Fig. 4. HAP antenna radiation masks in a single cell and multi-cell formation.

Distance attenuation is the empirically observed long-term trend in signal loss as a function distance, which is typically proportional to the range raised to some power. A shadowing fading is used to represent the shadowing effect, which considers the surrounding environmental clutter that may be different at two locations with the same separation distance. In our scenario, the pathloss between HAP and sensor node is expressed as the log-distance pathloss and log-normal shadowing model:

$$PL(d)[dB] = \overline{PL}(d_0)[dB] + 10n\log(\frac{d}{d_0}) + X_\sigma \tag{3}$$

where n is the pathloss exponent, d_0 is the reference distance and d is the separation distance between HAP and sensor node. The value of n is between 2 and 6 depending on the propagation environment. $X\sigma$ denotes a zero mean Gaussian random variable with a standard deviation σ (in dB). The model shows that the pathloss at the particular location is random and log-normally distributed about the mean distance dependent value.

3.2 System evaluation criteria and parameters

Considering a sensor node in the location *(x,y) to* communicate with the HAP, performance can be evaluated by energy bit to noise spectral density ratio in (4):

$$\frac{E_b}{N_0}(x,y) = \frac{P_s A_s A_H PL_{SH}}{N_0 R_b} \tag{4}$$

where,

P_s is the transmission power of a sensor node in the target HAP cell.

A_s and A_u are antenna gains of a sensor node and HAP respectively.

PL_{SH} is the signal pathloss due to distance attenuation and shadowing effect depending on the location of sensor node.

R_b is the data rate of senor node.
N_0 is the noise power spectral density.

Evaluation parameters are shown in Table 1. The physical later (PHY) parameters, e.g. data rate, sensor node transmit power, are referred to product data sheets of the company *Crossbow®* specializing on the sensor network technology (Crossbow, 2008). Parameters of the low speed (R_b=38.4 kbps) and high speed (R_b=250 kbps) senor nodes are referred for different applications.

Parameters	Settings
Data Rate (R_b)	250 kbps / 38.4 kbps
Tx Power (P_s)	3 dBm / 5 dBm
Tx Antenna Gain Rx (A_s)	1
HAP Antenna Boresight (G_H)	7 dB / 16 dB
HAP Height	17 km (typical)
Coverage Radius (R)	30 km (typical)
Cell Radius	30 km/8km (multi-cell)
Pathloss Exponent (n)	2
Propagation Model	Free space
Shadowing Std. Deviation (σ)	2 dB (Log-normal)
ISM Frequency Band	2.4 GHz /868 MHz
Noise Power Spectral Density (N_0)	3.98e-21 W/Hz

Table 1. System level simulation parameters

3.3 System level evaluation results

The cumulative distribution function (CDF) of E_b/N_0 is used to evaluate the system performance. Fig. 5 shows the CDF of E_b/N_0 of the received signal in single cell and multi cell scenario with different transmission rate. According to the product data sheet in (Crossbow, 2008), industrial-scientific-medical (ISM) band at 868 MHz and 2.4 GHz is selected, respectively. It can be seen that transmission from sensor node to HAP at 17 km in two scenarios is possible under the coverage area of 30 km in radius. The performance of sensors in multi cell scenario is enhanced compared to the single cell HAP-WSN system with the same transmission rate due to improved HAP cellular antenna radiation profile.

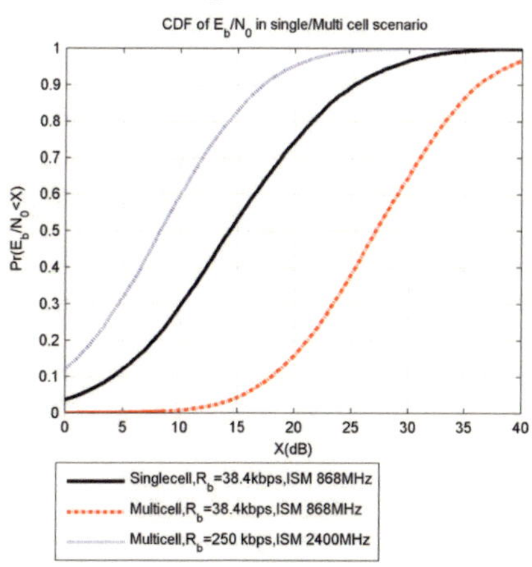

Fig. 5. E_b/N_0 of sensor node with different transmission rate in the single cell and multi cell HAP-WSN scenario

4. Physical Layer Configuration and Simulation

Reliable communication links are needed to be established between sensor nodes and HAPs to achieve a LOS in most cases based on the height of the platform. Our investigations in section 3 show the possibility of establishing a radio link between HAPs and sensor nodes. In this section, we investigate the performance of the promising multiple access scheme based on OFDM in conjunction with the HAP served as a mobile sink to communicate with multiple sensor nodes.

4.1 Time-varying HAP channel characteristics

The HAP communications channel exhibits time-varying characteristics due to the motion of the platform or receivers and frequency selectivity due to the multipath propagation. Doppler spectrum can be used to characterize a fading channel and determine if the fading is fast or slow. A simpler parameter, the maximum Doppler spread f_m, can be used to determine the channel coherence time T_c as (Rappaport, 1996):

$$T_c = \frac{9}{16\pi f_m} \tag{5}$$

where the maximum Doppler spread f_m at the carrier frequency f_o is:

$$f_m = f_{d,HAP} + f_{d,sensor} = [v_{HAP} + v_{sensor}]\frac{f_0}{c} \tag{6}$$

where v_{HAP} and v_{sensor} is the speed of HAP and sensor node, respectively. According to (Papathanassiou et al., 2001), the Doppler shift exhibits a well-behaved and rather deterministic variation with time. If we assume the HAP station is not moving, the multipath signals arriving at the HAP demonstrate unequal but relative small Doppler shifts, which illustrates that the second Doppler spread component exhibits a relatively small value and can be modeled in accordance to the typical techniques employed in terrestrial mobile radio system (Palma-Lazgare & Delgado-Penin, 2006; Papathanassiou et al., 2001).

In HAP-WSN applications, sensor nodes are mostly not capable of mobility and thus we don't take account of the movement of sensor nodes. It is one of advantages of using aerial platform compared to UAV since platforms can be more stably deployed upon the area of interest with a long duration.

The selectivity of channel is evaluated by the coherence bandwidth B_c of the channel, where B_c is approximately equal to the inverse of the maximum delay spread τ_m. In time domain, if the bandwidth of a signal is larger than the reciprocal of the maximum delay spread τ_m, each multipath signal can be modelled separately since different paths are resolvable. For a typical LEO channel, the τ_m ranges from 250 to 800 ns (Papathanassiou et al., 2001). Due to similarities of HAP and LEO satellites, we model the HAP channel as a slow-varying and frequency-selective fading channel. We assume the HAP is relatively stationary, thus the Doppler shift due to the motion of the HAP is assumed to be eliminated. The channel is

regarded to be a quasi-stationary, and so the fading profile can be regarded to be invariant during the period of one symbol.
The HAP channel is modelled as an impulse channel response *h(t)* with a sequence of discrete-time complex valued components. This sequence of discrete-time complex valued taps of a channel can be generally expressed by the vector $\boldsymbol{h}$, which is equal to $[h_1 h_2 \ldots h_l]$, where l is the length of discrete-time channel length, and h_l is the complex value of the lth tap. HAP channel modelling parameters are listed in Table 2.

HAP Speed (v_{HAP})	stationary
Node Speed (v_{sensor})	stationary
System bandwidth (B)	5 MHz
Carrier Frequency	ISM band 2.4GHz
Channel Model	Time-Flat Frequency-Selective
Max delay spread (τ_m)	500 ns
Power delay profile	exponential with τ_m
Fading	Ricean Rayleigh

Table 2. HAP channel characteristics

4.2 Multiple access schemes of OFDM

Orthogonal frequency-division multiplexing/Time division multiple access (OFDM/TDMA) is based on OFDM transmission scheme and time-division multiple access. Usually the overall bandwidth in OFDM/TDMA is divided into N subcarriers, and each subcarrier is carrying relatively small signalling rate. It has to be noticed that a precise synchronization between sensor nodes and HAP is required in order to have the flexibility and multiple node accessing. Furthermore the situation leads to a high implementation complexity both in sensor nodes and HAP. In this chapter, we consider a light version of OFDM/TDMA, where a single sensor node uses a full time slot to transmit, and the data rate stream is split into a number of low rate signals modulated in each subcarrier.
Consider the equation for the baseband complex signal of one OFDM symbol in the discrete-time domain:

$$x_{data}(n) = \sum_{k=0}^{N-1} X_k \exp(j\frac{2\pi}{N}kn) \quad \mathrm{n} \in (0,1,2,\cdots,\mathrm{N-1}) \tag{7}$$

We use N-long vector X_{data} to denote the total OFDM data to be part of the IFFT output:

$$X_{data} = \left[x_{data,1}, x_{data,2}, \ldots, x_{data,N}\right] \tag{8}$$

Furthermore, let X_{GI} be an N_{GI}-long vector expressing the guard interval (GI) precursor signal of X_{data}. X_{GI} is chosen to be equal the last N_{GI} elements of X_{data}, and is denoted as cyclic prefix (CP). So a completed transmitted OFDM symbol is given by:

$$X = [X_{GI} X_{data}] \tag{9}$$

Adjacent orthogonal subcarrier frequency separation B_{sub} is equal to B/N, and is chosen to let each subcarrier experience a favourable frequency non-selective fading based on N. Usually N is chosen to make the minimum coherence bandwidth B_c, which is approximately equal to the inverse of the maximum delay spread τ_m, 10 times higher than the B_{sub} (Papathanassiou et al., 2001).

$$B_{sub} = (B/N) < \frac{B_c}{10} \approx \frac{1}{10\tau_m} \tag{10}$$

4.3 Simulation setup and results

For a HAP channel at a carrier frequency of 2.4 GHz with τ_m equal to 500 ns, the minimum coherence bandwidth is equal to 2 MHz. Therefore, if we choose N equal to 64, the bandwidth of an individual carrier frequency is equal to 78.125 kHz. Each subcarrier can be guaranteed to be nonselective. In order to keep the orthogonality of the OFDM symbol, CP is inserted and the N_{GI} is equal to 3. Therefore, the duration of CP is equal to 0.6 ms, which is larger than the τ_m. In an individual OFDM symbol, CP occupies 4.4 percentage of the symbol X and can be regarded to be high-efficient transmission. The channel estimation is performed base on pilot symbols with a data interval at 8 in one OFDM symbol (Cai & Giannakis, 2004). In order to reduce the complexity of the problem, we have adopted a simplified but valuable approach purely based on BER performance, which can be achieved by a single sensor node. In other words, multiple sensor transmission scenario is not considered in our simulations since it usually requires a precise synchronization when a large number of sensor nodes transmitting at the same time. No coding schemes are considered in the simulation. Binary phase-shift keying (BPSK) is used to modulate sensor node data rate R_b at 250 kbps. The system is assumed to be perfectly synchronized.

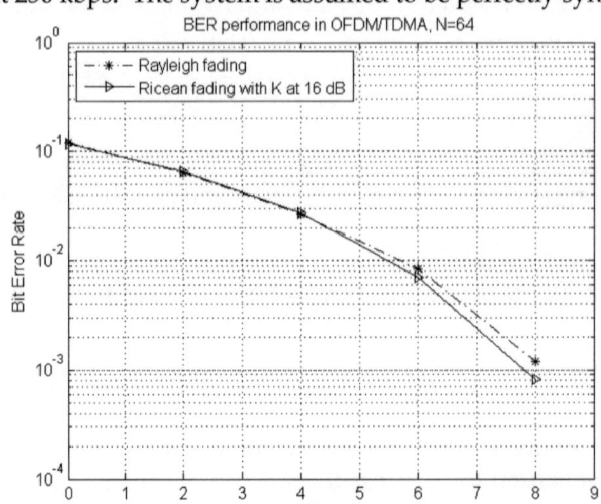

Fig. 6. BER performance of OFDM/TDMA in HAP-WSN

Simulation results in Fig. 6 show the bit error rate (BER) for N at 64. Generally, multipath can degrade the system performance due to severe signal attenuation. However, one of the main advantages of OFDM scheme is its improved performance and robustness in multipath environments, which is predominant in signal transmission of WSN. Consequently, it can be seen from Fig. 6 that there is a little difference in the BER performance under Rayleigh and Ricean fading in the investigated scenario.

5. Conclusion and Future Research

In this chapter, we have shown the scenarios of using HAP as a sink in the WSN in ISM band for different data rate transmission and examined the performance in the system level and physical layer. The HAP-WSN system can reduce complexity of the WSN and prolong the lifetime of sensor node by effectively decreasing or removing the multi-hop transmission. The HAP-WSN has a great potential in extending coverage area of WSN due to the unique height of the HAP. A LOS free space pathloss and log-normal shadowing model has been employed to examine the radio link between HAP and sensor nodes. It can be seen that employing HAP as a sink is possible and a promising application of WSN. In future work, a study of multiple access scheme based CDMA for HAP-WSN is promising. Furthermore, a comparison study of multiple access techniques based on OFDMA and CDMA using comparable system parameters can also be investigated to show the advantages of each scheme.

6. References

Akyildiz, I. F., Weilian Su, Sankarasubramaniam, Y., & Cayirci, E. (2002). A Survey on Sensor Network. *IEEE Communications Magazine,* Vol. 40, No. 8, August 2002, 102-114.

Business Week. (1999, August 30). 21 Ideas for the 21st Century. *Business Week,* 78-167.

Cai, X., & Giannakis, G. B. (2004). Error Probability Minimizing Pilots for OFDM with M-PSK Modulation over Rayleigh Fading Channels. *IEEE Transactions on Vehicular Technology, 53*(1), 146-155.

Chong, C.-Y., & Kumar, S. P. (2003). Sensor Networks: Evolution, Opportunities, and Challenges. *Proceedings of the IEEE, 91.*

Crossbow. (2008). Product Reference Guide. from http://www.lindstrand.co.uk

Demirkol, I., Ersoy, C., & Alagöz, F. (2006). MAC Protocols for Wireless Sensor Networks: A Survey. *IEEE Communications Magazine*

Elabdin, Z., Elshaikh, O., Islam, R., Ismail, A. P., & Khalifa, O. O. (2006). *High Altitude Platform for Wireless Communications and Other Services.* International Conference on Electrical and Computer Engineering, 2006, ICECE '06

Hill, J., Szewczyk, R., Woo, A., Hollar, S., E.Culler, D., & Pister, K. S. J. (2000). System Architecture Directions for Networked Sensors. *In Architectural Support for Programming Languages and Operations Systems,* 93-104.

Intel. (2004). Instrumenting the Word-An introduction to Wireless Sensor Networks.

Jiang, P., Wen, Y., Wang, J., Shen, X., & Xue, A. (2006, June 21-23). *A Study of Routing protocols in Wireless Sensor Networks.* 6th World Congress On Intelligent Control and Automation, Dalian, China.

Mohammed, A., Arnon, S., Grace, D., Mondin, M., & Miura, R. (2008). Advanced Communications Techniques and Applications for High-Altitude Platforms. *Editorial for a Special Issue, EURASIP Journal on Wireless Communications and Networking, 2008.*

Palma-Lazgare, I. R., & Delgado-Penin, J. A. (2006). *HAP-based Broadband Communications under WiMAX Standards - A first approach to physical layer performance assessment.* First COST 297 - HAPCOS Workshop, 26-27 October 2006, York, UK.

Papathanassiou, A., Salkintzis, A. K., & Mathiopoulos, P. T. (2001). A comparison study of the uplink performance of W-CDMA and OFDM for mobile multimedia communications via LEO satellites. *Personal Communications, IEEE [see also IEEE Wireless Communications], 8*(3), 35-43.

Rappaport, T. S. (1996). *Wirless Communications: Principles and Practice*. Englewood Cliffs, NJ: Prentice-Hall.

StratXX. (2008). StratXX near space technology. from http://www.lindstrand.co.uk

Technology Review. (2003, Feb.). 10 Emerging Technologies That Will Change the World. *Technology Review 106,* 33-49.

Thornton, J., Grace, D., Capstick, M. H., & Tozer, T. C. (2003). Optimizing an Array of Antennas for Cellular Coverage from a High Altitude Platform. *IEEE Transactions on Wireless Communications, 2, No. 3,* 484-492.

Tozer, T. C., & Grace, D. (2001). High-Altitude Platforms for Wireless Communications. *IEE Electronics and Communications Engineering Journal, 13*(3), 127-137.

Vincent, P. J., Tummala, M., & McEachen, J. (2006, April 2006). *An Energy-Efficient Approach for Information Transfer from Distributed Wireless Sensor Systems.* IEEE/SMC International Conference on System of System Engineering, Los Angeles, CA, USA.

Yang, Z., Mohammed, A., Hult, T., & Grace, D. (2007). *Assessment of Coexistence Performance for WiMAX Broadband in High Altitude Platform Cellular System and Multiple-Operator Terrestrial Deployments*. Paper presented at the 4th IEEE International Symposium on Wireless Communication Systems (ISWCS'07), Trondheim, Norway.

3

Wireless sensor network for monitoring thermal evolution of the fluid traveling inside ground heat exchangers

Julio Martos, Álvaro Montero (*), José Torres and Jesús Soret
Universitat de València
(*) Universidad Politécnica de Valencia
Spain

1. Introduction

Ground-Coupled Heat Pump (GCHP) systems are an attractive choice of system for heating and cooling buildings (Genchi, 2002; Sanner, 2003; Omer, 2008; Urchueguía, 2008). By comparison with standard technologies, these heat pumps offer competitive levels of comfort, reduced noise levels, lower greenhouse gas emissions, and reasonable environmental safety. Furthermore, their electrical consumption and maintenance requirements are lower than those required by conventional systems and, consequently, they have a lower annual operating cost (Lund, 2000). Ground source systems are recognized by the U.S. Environmental Protection Agency as being among the most efficient and comfortable heating and cooling systems available today (US EPA, 2008). The European Community and other international agencies, such as the DOE or the American International Energy Agency, are considering GCHP in the field of "heat production from renewable sources". In 2002, the growth in the number of air conditioning systems driven by ground coupled (geothermal) heat pumps was estimated in the range from 10% to 30% each year (Bose 2002). The number of installed units worldwide, around 1.1 million (Spitler, 2005), illustrates the high acceptance of this emerging technology in the Heating, Ventilation & Air Conditioning (HVAC) market.

A Ground Coupled Heat Pump is a heat pump that uses soil as source or sink of heat. A GCHP exchanges heat with the ground through a buried U-tube loop. Since this exchange strongly depends on the thermal properties of the ground, it is very important to have knowledge of these properties when designing GCHP air-conditioning systems. The length of Borehole Heat Exchangers (BHE) needed for a given output power greatly depends on soil characteristics, such as temperature, particle size and shape, moisture content, and heat transfer coefficients. Correct sizing of the BHEs is a cause for design concern. Key points are building load, borehole spacing, borehole fill material, and site characterization. Over-sizing carries a much higher penalty than in conventional applications. Methods to estimate ground properties include literature searches, conducting laboratory experiments on soil/rock samples and/or performing field tests. Due to these factors, the completion of a thermal response test (TRT), which determines the thermal parameters of the underground, is very important.

The standard TRT consists in injecting or extracting a constant heat load inside the BHE and measuring changes in temperature of the circulating fluid. The outputs of the thermal response test are the inlet and outlet temperature of the heat-carrier fluid as a function of time. From these experimental data, and with an appropriate model describing the heat transfer between the fluid and the ground, the thermal conductivity of the surroundings is inferred. A delicate aspect of the measuring process is to maintain constant the heat injection or extraction because a 5% of power fluctuation can lead to errors of around 40% for thermal conductivity (Witte 2002).

Thermal response tests with mobile measurement devices were first introduced in Sweden and the USA in 1995 (Eklöf and Gehlin, 1996; Austin, 1998). Since then, the method has been further developed, and its use has spread to several other countries. Kelvin's infinite line-source model is commonly used for evaluation of response test data because of its simplicity and speed (Mogensen, 1983; Eskilson, 1987; Hellström, 1991). This model is dominant in Europe, while the use of the cylindrical-source model (Carslaw and Jaeger, 1959) with parameter-estimating techniques is common in North America (Austin, 1998; Beier, 2008).

Other works have explored alternative methods to perform TRT and obtain ground thermal properties. There is a procedure based on fiber optic thermometers (Hurtig 2000) to determine the dynamic behavior of the heat exchanging medium inside a borehole heat exchanger. Another procedure attempts to determine the ground conductivity based on prior knowledge of the local geothermal flow (Rohner 2005). The importance of having TRT techniques is illustrated by the initiative of the Energy Conservation through Energy Storage (ECES), a Implementing Agreement (IA) of the International Energy Agency (IEA), to launch in 2006 the Annex 21, Thermal Response Test (Nordell 2006).

Most of the models for analyzing data from thermal response tests are constrained by the fact that only two measures are available, the inlet and outlet temperature of the heat-carrier fluid as a function of time. Thus, the analysis procedure arrives at the question of what is the right comparison between these two measures of fluid temperatures and the ground modelled temperatures that depend on spatial coordinates. Different aproaches are followed in the literature, such as comparing the average fluid temperature with the ground temperature at the mid-depth of the borehole heat exchanger, or comparing it with the average ground temperature in the neigbourghood of the heat exchangers. To avoid this ambiguity, it is desirable to know the evolution of the fluid temperature along its way through the U- pipe. Then, it will be possible to compare the fluid temperature at a spatial position with the corresponding ground modelled temperature at the correponding spatial point. The purpose of the instrument presented here is to measure the fluid temperature evolution and to improve the procedure to estimate thermal properties of ground heat exchangers.

Inspired by the implementations of wireless sensor networks, we have designed a new instrument to measure the temperature of the heat transfer fluid along the borehole exchanger by autonomous wireless sensor. The instrument consists of a device that inserts and extracts miniaturized wireless sensors in the borehole with a mechanical subsystem that is composed of a circulating pump and two valves. This device transmits the acquisition configuration to the sensors, and downloads the temperature data measured by the sensor along its way through the borehole heat exchanger. Each sensor is included in a sphere of 25 mm in diameter and contains a transceiver, a microcontroller, a temperature sensor, and a power supply. This instrument allows the collection of information about the thermal characteristics of the geological structure of soil and its influence on borehole thermal behavior in dynamic regime, and it facilitates an easier and more reliable implementation of the thermal response test.

This chapter is organized as follows. Section 2 discuses the relevance of monitoring the fluid temperature evolution along the BHE. Sections 3, 4 and 5 present the considerations adopted for design, firmware, and time synchronization, respectively. Section 6 presents other implementations, and section 7 presents energy harvesting considerations. Finally, section 8 presents the conclusions of this work.

2. Monitoring relevance in BHE

The knowledge of the heat transfer properties of a ground heat exchanger is the key to calculating the number and depth of wells needed in a plant; these parameters have a strong dependence on the local characteristics of soil. The conventional TRT makes an approach to the knowledge of the thermal characteristics of the environment surrounding the heat exchanger based on two parameters: the soil effective thermal conductivity and the borehole thermal resistance. Nevertheless, it cannot measure other important factors such as the effects of geological structure, humidity, and water currents. These aspects can be observed during drilling, but they cannot be quantified with a weighting factor by the conventional TRT. Furthermore, new TRT developments are trying to indirectly measure the effects of these factors by performing tests at different injected or extracted powers, and explaining the differences between the values obtained for each injected or extracted power as coming from geological structure, humidity, and water currents. This approach to obtain this information is constrained by the fact that only the inlet and outlet temperature of the heat-carrier fluid are available.

If all these effects and circumstances can be directly quantified, the design methodology could be modified to establish, in the implementation phase of drilling, the optimal balance between depth and number of drilling holes to maximize heat transfer and minimize the total drilling cost. This may be one of the key points in the expansion of the HVAC systems based on GCHP, especially in countries with moderate climates. For these reasons, the developed instrument, which is aimed at directly measuring the evolution of the temperature of the thermal fluid flowing inside a ground heat exchanger, attempts to monitor the heat exchange that occurs between the thermal fluid and the ground as a function of space and time.

3. Design considerations

The difficulty of this goal lies in the placement of temperature sensors at the desired points, without increasing the costs of installation or affecting the operation of the exchanger. In addition, the measure of temperatures is only necessary during the final stage of implementation, when the ground coupled heat exchanger is just being built, and is not necessary during operation time.

Other authors have proposed alternative systems to obtain the thermal evolution of the GCHE, from the standard TRT based on the Kelvin´s theory of infinite line source, which

has the advantage that only requires two measurements of temperature, to fiber-optic thermometers, requiring laser interferometer equipment.
The developed instrument is based on nodes of wireless sensor networks (Martos 2008), which are adapted to the functions and working conditions that occur in the BHE used in HVAC equipment with GCHP.

3.1 Working principle

The way to make the most accurate measure is to take the temperature of the same volume of thermal fluid at successive points, thus not masking the dynamics of the system in times of sudden changes in temperature. The working principle used by the instrument, which is shown in Figure 1. The measure of the temperature of the fluid along the tube exchanger, is performed by autonomous wireless sensors, which are carried by the thermal fluid. These probes are smaller than the diameter of the pipe and contain all the electronics needed to complete a set of measures along the pipeline and to download them to a central node.

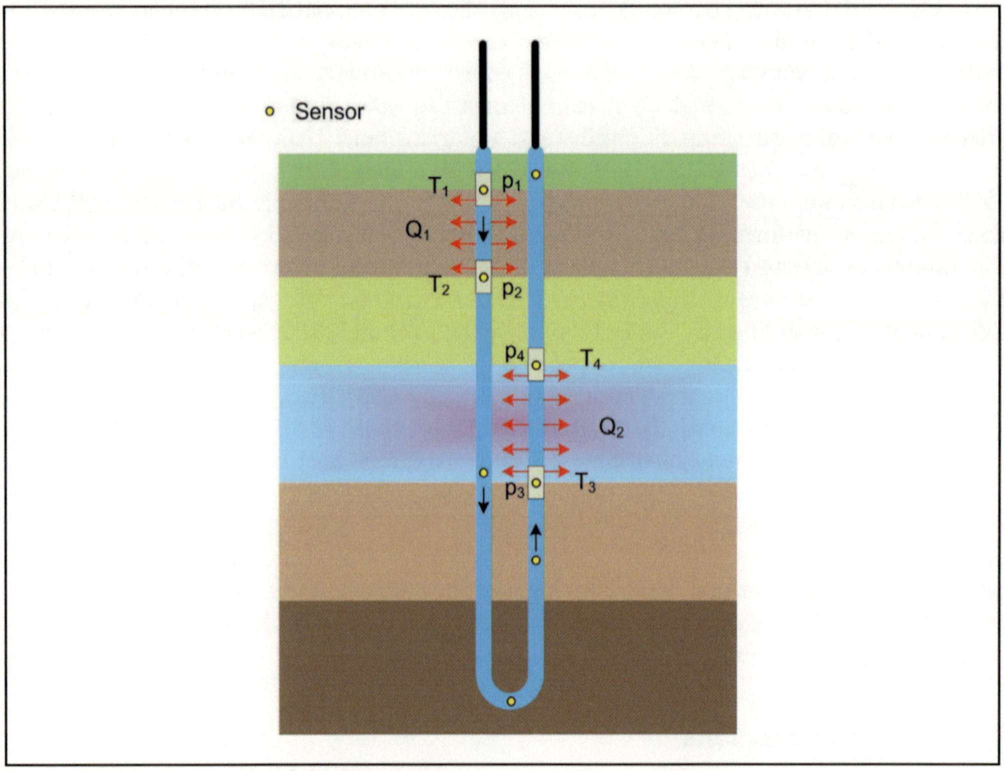

Fig. 1. Working principle of the instrument

The heat transferred (Q) between the thermal fluid and soil between two points p1 and p2, can be calculated using the expression:

$$Q = (T2 - T1) * C_p * S * (p2 - p1)*\rho \tag{1}$$

Where T1 and T2 is the temperature of the fluid at points p1 and p2, respectively, Cp is the specific heat of the thermal fluid, S is the section of the tube exchanger, p2-p1 is the distance between the points of measurement, and r is the fluid density.
The probes of the instrument developed should be able to simultaneously obtain three magnitudes (position, temperature and time) to perform the desired analysis. Time is easy to measure because any system based on microprocessors incorporates clock circuitry. To measure the temperature, the probe must incorporate a conditioning circuit that meets the constraints of volume and consumption. To determine the position, there are two possible options: direct or indirect measurement. Direct measurement could be carried out by inclusion of a pressure sensor that measures the pressure changes while the probe is traveling along the pipe. Indirect measurement could be carried out by correlating the distance with another parameter. The first method requires additional circuitry, which negatively affects consumption and miniaturization. We have chosen the second method, calculating the position based on the time between successive samplings of the temperature and the speed of thermal fluid. Among other advantages, this method offers the following: minimizes the necessary circuitry, it reduces consumption, it can be used in heat exchangers that are buried in vertical or horizontal configuration.
The relationship between the distance (l) and the time between samples (if the probe is carried without sliding) is:

$$l = F * t_s / S \qquad (2)$$

Where, F is the flow of thermal fluid, t_s is the time between two consecutive samples, and S is the section of pipe. If the density of the sphere that constitutes the probe is close to the density of the thermal fluid, it will be carried both vertical configurations and horizontal configurations. To verify this, we have completed a set of measures of transit time of a set of spheres throughout the interior of a 10 m-long pipe. Table 1 summarizes the results of this verification, showing the difference between the measured transit time and the expected transit time (Diff), and this error in per cent, for some values of water flows.

				Flow					
				700 l/h		1000 l/h		1300 l/h	
Ball	Type	Diameter (mm)	Density (g/cm³)	Diff (s)	Error	Diff (s)	Error	Diff (s)	Error
1	Acrilic	25	1,3	0,96	1,94%	0,03	0,09%	0,58	2,26%
2	Acrilic	25	1,3	1,05	2,11%	0,05	0,16%	0,77	2,97%
3	Acrilic	25	1	-0,44	0,88%	0,62	1,57%	0,04	0,14%
4	Acrilic	25	1	-0,64	1,27%	0,24	0,76%	0,11	0,38%
5	Acrilic	20	1	-0,55	1,09%	0,23	0,73%	0,24	0,91%
6	Acrilic	20	1	0,34	0,67%	0,36	1,13%	0,07	0,29%
7	Wood	25	1	-0,39	0,75%	0,20	0,62%	0,05	0,21%
8	Wood	25	1	0,70	1,35%	0,11	0,34%	0,04	0,17%
9	Wood	20	1	0,72	1,38%	0,14	0,44%	0,11	0,44%
10	Wood	20	1	1,08	2,07%	0,13	0,39%	0,06	0,18%
		Average	ρ=1	0,10	0,19%	0,02	0,05%	0,01	0,03%

Table 1. Travelling times along pipes for different sensors

As this table shows, this is a technique with small error, and you can trust it to deduce the position. You can also make an individual adjustment to correct the position proportionally to the difference between the expected time and the transit time measured.

3.2 System Architecture

In order to achieve the spatial and temporal behavior of the fluid temperature along the BHE, the instrument has been divided into three parts:

- A set of autonomous sensors
- A device for control, recording, and analysis
- A hydraulic system

In Figure 2, we present the logic diagram of the instrument; the hydraulic system comprises a water tank, a circulation pump, a flow meter, and two special valves for the insertion and extraction of the autonomous temperature probes. A laptop is the device that supports the control and human interface by a Windows program for TRT configuration, acquisition, and analysis of the values of measured temperature. Finally, a set of small balls 25 mm in diameter, contain the electronic circuitry of the autonomous temperature probes.
Also, a set of sensors monitors several variables during the running of TRT, such as the inlet and outlet water temperature of BHE, the temperature of the tank, as well as the pressure in the pipes.

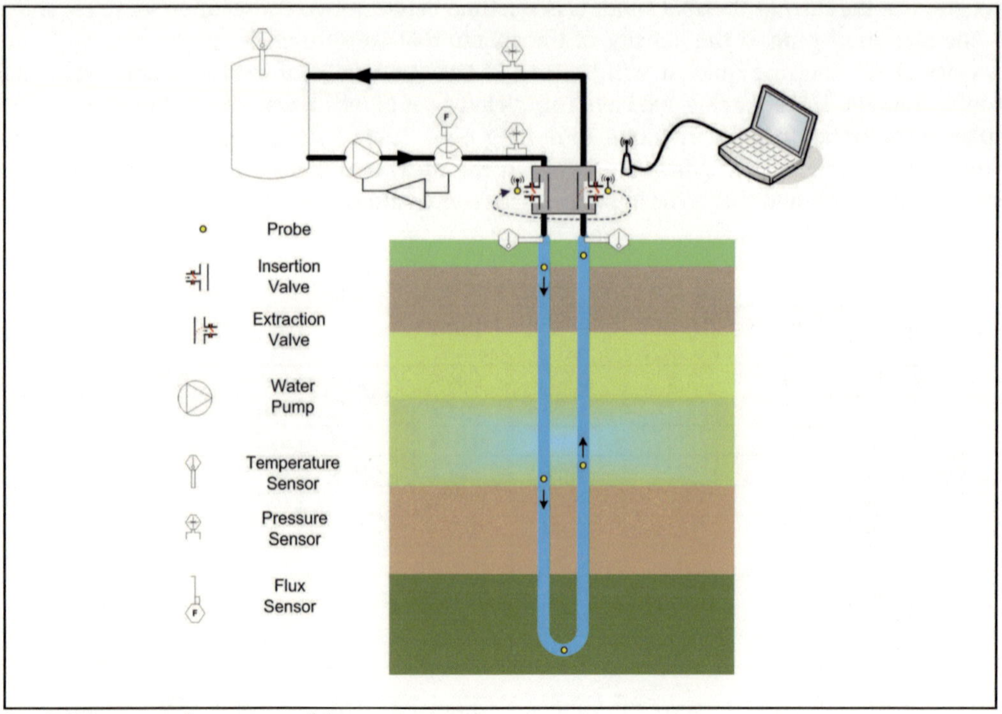

Fig. 2. Diagram of system architecture

The hydraulic circuit comprises a water tank, as buffer for the thermal fluid, an electronically controlled circulation pump, a flow meter, and two valves, one for inserting probes and another for their extraction. The water temperature can be set through an electric heater that is controlled by the program that runs on the PC, which also controls the flow of water that is injected into the BHE pipe. The insertion of the probes is performed with selected time intervals in terms of realizing the TRT, controlled by the PC. When extracted, the probe is situated at the point of data discharge and, once it is completed, the data contained in the probe is deleted and, then, it is prepared for the next insertion.
A program for PC that controls the configuration, execution, and analysis of a TRT has been developed. The graphical user interface (GUI) has been done in Matlab GUI.
The program performs the following tasks:

- Setting TRT parameters: allows to be introduced the values for the test, water flow, spatial resolution, and time insertion.
- Setting of BHE parameters: allows the BHE characteristics to be introduced.
- Control of acquisitions: begins and ends TRT and shows the number of introduced and recovered probes.
- Control of hydraulics devices: adjust in closed loop the water flow and the temperature of tank, it also controls the probe insertion and extraction.
- Recording data: saves a file with the data to disk, in Excel format or csv format.
- Real time display: presents the monitored temperature of fluid in graphical form.
- Communications management: the PC assumes the role of wireless network coordinator.

The autonomous sensors are key components of the instrument. They are devices that measure the thermal evolution of an elementary volume of water along the BHE pipe. Its sizes must be as small as possible so they can move easily through the pipes carried by the water flow, and at the same time be able to contain an acquisition system, temporary storage, and unloading of temperature data. To achieve these functions and capabilities, a circuit has been designed based on the CC1010 transceiver that allows you to include it in a sphere with a diameter that is smaller than 25 mm. A 4-layer PCBs has been designed to mount all the necessary components, (see Figure 3). The characteristics of each autonomous sensor are:

- Temperature range: 0-40 °C
- Resolution temperature:< 0.05 °C
- Accuracy temperature:< 0.05 °C
- Rank sampling: 0.1-25 s
- Capacity sampling: 1000 samples

The mode of operation of the autonomous sensors is as follows:

- The control system selects an available probe and puts it in the status of test run
- It transfers the parameters of sampling
- It insert the probe into the BHE water flow
- The probe starts the process of acquiring, storing temperatures at fixed intervals
- After the tour, the temperature data are downloaded to the control system
- The probe goes into low-power mode

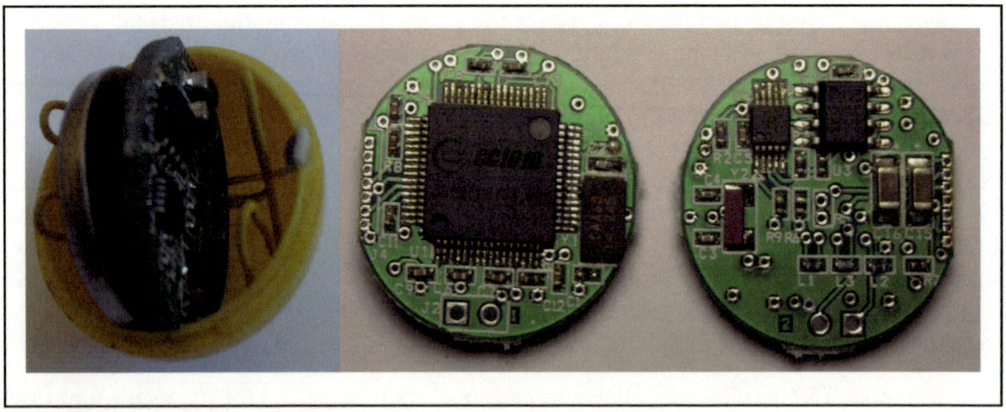

Fig. 3. Design and view of sensor

The final probe is enclosed in a sphere of 23 mm in diameter, which protects circuitry and allows the density of the probe to be equal to the water density.
The circuit for measuring the temperature has been designed based on a miniature Pt100 element that is located on the surface of the sphere. The conditioning circuit is designed to satisfy the size and consumption specifications. The Pt100 sensor is polarized by a current source that is integrated in an ultra low power consumption circuit and an instrumentation amplifier. This amplifier is also ultra low power, and the output signal is adjusted to the desired measurement range. Both components have a shut down signal that only switched on at the moment of measurement. The current consumption is 10uA in off mode and 1.58mA in on mode.

4. Firmware considerations

The microcontroller containing each autonomous probe is responsible for the smooth running of the probe. It properly manages wireless communications, acquisition and storage of data, and the states of work of the circuit. To achieve the requirements of energy saving, the firmware developed for each of the autonomous probe has been structured in four states:

- Power down
- Configuration
- In acquisition
- Down load

The "Power down" state is the key to achieving that the probes have a long life. It is the state that stays in longer, and the state the probe enters at the end of each data collection cycle or if it exceeds a certain amount of time without communication with the control system. To escape the "Power down" state, a reset signal is applied to the microcontroller, which becomes active and enters to "Configuration" mode. This mode begins a communication with the coordinator node, where the probe is identified (ID) and receives the configuration of the monitoring and the actual clock. After a timeout, the sensor initiates the acquisition and the temporal buffering of temperatures, i.e., it switches to the "In acquisition" state. In

this state, the microcontroller is sleeping between two acquisitions and is characterized by using the secondary oscillator, which only drives the peripheral that remains in operation: the timer that sets the sampling period. The circuit that conditions the signal from the Pt100 is activated moments before the measurement, and immediately returns to the low power state. At the conclusion of the scheduled number of acquisitions, the probe goes to the "Down load" state, recovering the main oscillator and establishing communication with the control system to transfer data. When the transfer is finished, it is passed to the "Power down" state.
The communications protocol is a simple design because it is during the wireless communications that thee consumption is higher Therefore, the fewer bits are transmitted more energy savings are achieved. All the messages that are exchanged between the transceivers are 6 bytes of data, a CRC-16, plus a header of 7 bytes for synchronization. The only exception is in the downloading of data, where the number of bytes transmitted is twice the number of acquisitions. The transfer rate is set at the highest rate possible, 76.8 kbs. The transmission power is also set at the minimum because the distance between transceivers is less than a meter, and the CC1010 can reach 100 meters at full power.

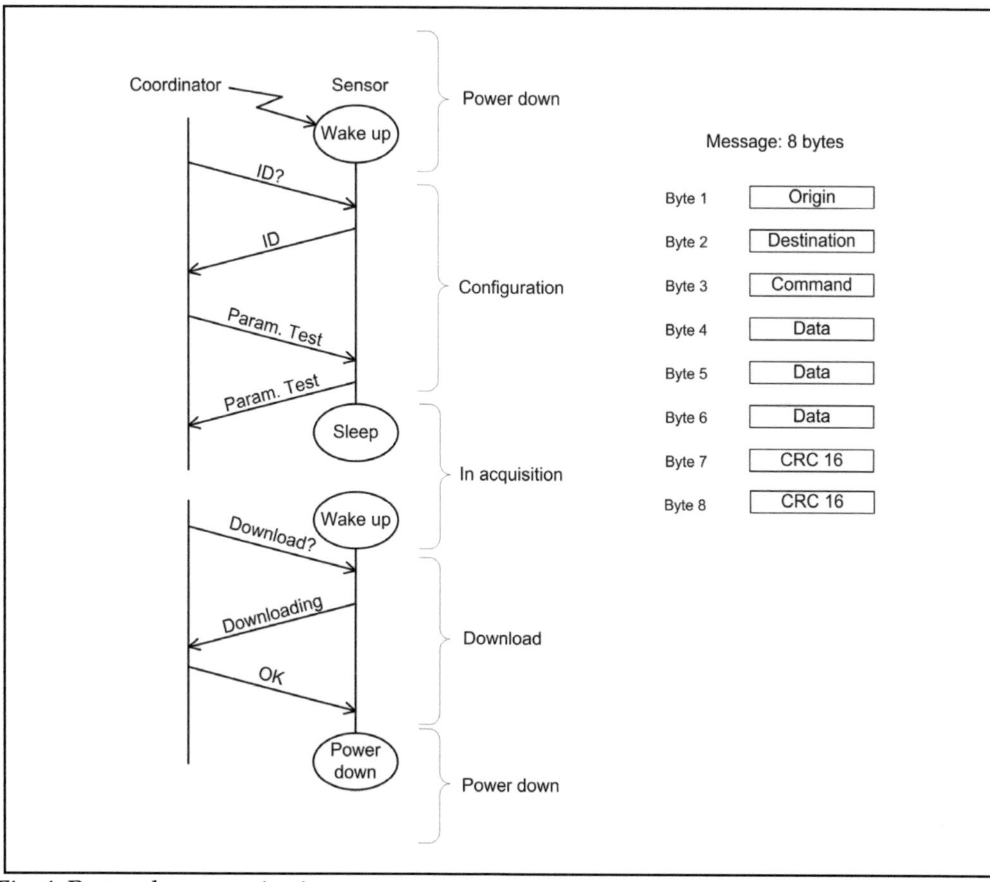

Fig. 4. Protocol communication

5. Time synchronization considerations

Another key to the reliability of the obtained data is the time synchronization: all probes must have the same clock as a reference for the estimated time of acquisition. Since the evolution of temperature on the heat exchanger is slow, the accuracy in time between all the probes must be better than 100ms. There are different synchronization techniques in wireless sensor networks (Sundararaman 2005, Jones 2001), but to meet the energy restrictions of the instrument, the so-called Synchronization Reference Broadcasts (Elson 2002) was used for its ease of implementation and the low power consumption added.
The coordinator node is responsible for sending the reference clock to the probe, which has just been removed from the "Power Down" state, and requests its identification. Together with the command to start the acquisition, the current value of the clock is sent, and the probe will take this as its initial value of local clock. All subsequent acquisitions are referenced to this clock, thereby completing the synchronization. Although there will be a time delay between the clock sent by the coordinator and the sensor, due to the time of transmission and processing of messages (since all probes have the same latency) the time between two consecutive samples is well known. The confirmation of the correct initialization of the local clock of each sensor is done via the sensor's response message to the coordinator.
The frame of data downloaded from the sensor includes the clock that was posted at the beginning of the acquisition, which allows the synchronization of data with on accuracy of better than 100 ms. Spatial synchronization is simpler; it depends of the moment in which the sensor is inserted into the flow of water, and this is controlled by the coordinator node, which performs the insertion of a certain time after receiving confirmation of the message startup acquisition. Since the flow rate and the section of the pipe are known, the point at which each temperature measurement is being made can be estimated perfectly.

6. Other implementations

The hardware solution adopted was taken after valuing other existing alternatives in the market that, still complying with the basic requirements, did not completely satisfy our needs. When we speak of RF communications, we have to always keep in mind the range, the charge, the need to use a standard, the price… In the current market, there are devices that work under the GHz, devices that work above the GHz, and devices that use a standard protocol (ZigBee, Wireless HART, Bluetooth...).
Our solution is from the first group due to the need to find an intermediate point among frequency of work, reach, power at the outset, environment, and consumption. Besides, we have an indispensable requirement, the size.
A success factor for the instrument is to obtain good quality communication while still maintaining very low consumption; the factors of propagation, attenuation, and shielding must be balanced to do this. Figure 5 shows the relationship between transmission quality and carrier frequency; the best choice is to work in the sub-Gigahertz range.

Of the options under the GHz that use no standard protocol, the followings families of devices can be found:

- ADF70XX of Analog Devices
- MC33XXX of Freescale
- TDAXXXX of Infineon
- CC11XX of Texas Instruments
- rfPIC12XXXX of Microchip
- MAXXXX of Maxim

Table 2 summarizes the main characteristics of these families.

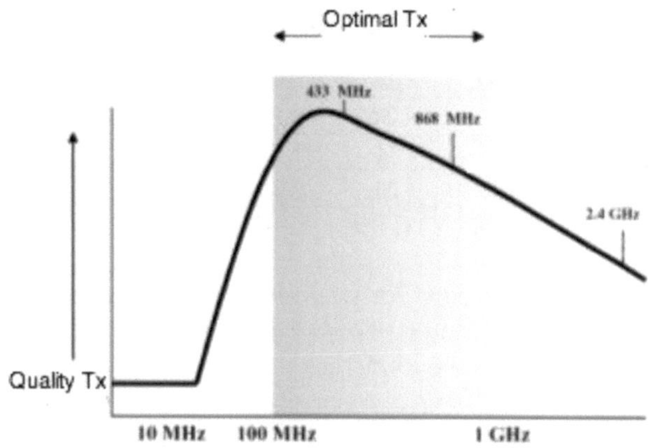

Fig. 5. Quality Tx versus frequency

Device	Band (MHz)	Modulation	Current (mA)	Voltag e (V)	Baudrate (kbps)	Power (dBm)	Package
ADF70XX	433-915	FSK/ASK	30	2-3,6	76/384	13	TSSOP
MC33XXX	304-915	OOK/FSK	25	2,1-5,5	20	7	LQFP
TDAXXXX	434-870	ASK/FSK	35	2,1-5,5	100	13	TSSOP
CC11XX	315-915	FSK/OOK	16	2-3,6	500	13	QFN
rfPIC12XXXX	310-480	ASK/FSK	20	2,7-5	80	6	SSOP
MAXXXX	300-450	ASK/FSK	5,3	3,3-5	70	10	QFN

Table 2. Main characteristics for devices < 1 GHz

As can be observed, the Analog Devices solution complies with the broadcast velocity requirements, power, and package. However, it does not comply with the consumption nor does it incorporate the transmitter and the microcontroller in the same device. The same occurs with the families of Freescale, Infineon, and Maxim; although Maxim has the lowest consumption.

The families of Texas Instruments and of Microchip meet the requirement of having a single chip for both components, although the price was higher than that of the solution adopted.

If we go to solutions above the GHz that do not require a standard, the following families can be found:

- MC13XXX of Freescale
- CC25XX of Texas Instruments
- CYWMXXXX of Cypress
- CyFi of Cypress
- MRF24JXX of Microchip

Table 3 summarizes the main characteristics of these families.

Device	Band (GHz)	Modulation	Current (mA)	Voltag e (V)	Baudrate (kbps)	Power (dBm)	Package
MC13XXX	2,4	GFSK/MSK	35	1,8-3,6	250	4	QFN
CC25XX	2,4	GFSK/MSK	23	2-3,6	500	10	QLP
CYWMXXXX	2,4	GFSK	20	2,7-3,6	64	17	QFN
CyFi	2,4	GFSK	12	1,8-3,6	1000	12	QFN
MRF24JXX	2,4	GFSK/MSK	22	2,3-3,6	250	3	QFN

Table 3. Main characteristics for devices > 1 GHz

The family of Freescale with these circuits for wireless communications, together with the microcontrollers of very low consumption of 8 bits of the family S08, allow ready point and point-to-multipoint communications to be implemented. This family is not of interest due to the high consumption and the need to have two components.

Texas Instruments acquired Chipcon to complete its range of wireless products including the Zigbee. Since the transceiver CC25XX has very few components, it does not need an electric antenna switch or a filter, providing great benefits and low consumption. It also offers programmable power sensibility at the outset. The CC25XX is a circuit of very low consumption that includes the transmitter and a microcontroller based on the core 8051 at 32MHz.

Cypress began with RF solutions to 2,4GHz for PC and the USB markets. It has several characteristics that distinguish it from other competitors such as very low consumption, immunity to interferences, generation of CRC, an auto transactions sequencer, etc. The advantages of this technology is that it has entered the consumer market (mice, keyboards, joysticks, ...) as well as the industrial market at a very low cost for ready point or point-to-multipoint applications. This technology can also be used even though the price is a lot higher than the solution adopted.

Cypress also presents a solution called CyFi to 2,4 GHz optimized for control since it has a PSoC microcontroller and a DSSS transmitter with, with a protocol that is easy to use for a network in star and with optimized consumption. The RF solution CyFi, of low consumption, is extremely dependable and easy to use to 2,4 GHz within an extensive range of applications. It allows designers to create high reliability systems in wireless communication, reducing the complexity of development and ensuring low power consumption. The CyFi networks vary the channel of work dynamically, the velocity of broadcast and the real-time power at the outset in order to maintain dependable communications in the presence of interferences. Besides having very low activity and a sleep mode, the CyFi solution greatly improves low consumption. CyFi networks minimize periods of peak consumption and maximize the periods of low power state. This solution was not adopted due to the difficulty of integrating it into the size of our system when using two components.

Microchip offers a solution based on its microcontrollers and a proprietary protocol called Miwi™ (Microchip Wireless). It is directed to low cost devices and networks that do not need high transfer of data, over short distances (100 meters without obstacles), and with minimum energy consumption. As occurs with CyFi, the reduced space of our system forces us to reject this solution. We can conclude that within the market of wireless technologies, there is an extensive range of possibilities. Some of them may improve and change continuously, and we must keep them in mind for a new generation of instrument.

7. Energy harvesting

European legislation imposes restrictions on the use of batteries in electronic devices (European Parliament and Council, Directives 2006/66/EC and 2008/103/EC) and their recycling. The instrument developed uses button batteries to supply the autonomous probes; its final design must meet current legislation. While this directive covers exceptions to the restrictions on the use of batteries, one way of reducing their presence, without compromising the design, is to completely dispense with batteries or reduce the needs of replacing them by increasing the lifetime of the sensors. The most convenient way to achieve this is to use energy that can be collected in the environment, i.e., using techniques of "energy harvesting". Energy harvesting has become an important emerging area of low power technology (Cymbet 2009, Mateu 2007) that can provide energy for smaller-scale needs such as sensor networks, utilizing the vibrations inherent in structures, vehicles, and machinery or from wind and solar systems. These can drive sensors while eliminating the need for wires and batteries.

The energy sources that are most commonly used in energy harvesting are mechanical energy (vibration), light, electromagnetic, thermal and piezoelectric (Paradiso 2005). The power that can be captured from these sources is summarized in Table 4.

Source	Power	Harvesting technologies
Light	100uW/cm2 to 100 mW/cm2	Photovoltaic
Vibrational	4 uW/cm3 to 800uW/cm3	Piezoelectric cantilever
Thermoelectric	60uW/cm2	Thermogenerator
Radio frequency	~1uW/cm2	Antenna
Push button	50uJ/N	Electromagnetic, piezoelectric

Table 4. Capabilities of energy harvesting

In our instrument, we estimate that energy harvesting can be applied to power the sensors, using light or heat as an energy source or heat. With light, we can embed small photovoltaic cells in the cover of the sensor. With heat, we can incorporate small thermo generators based on Seebeck effect in the cover of the sensor. A circuit for power conversion and energy storage should be added. The device for storage can be a secondary battery or a capacitor (supercapacitor, Goldcap, etc.). The first method allows more energy density, but has limited life due to charge-discharge cycles and presents a small discharge current. The second method has an infinite life that is not affected by charge- discharge cycles, and presents a discharge curve that is non constant and has a small density of energy.

8. Conclusions

Achieving GCHP designs that are more accurate and tailored to soil conditions requires new tools and methods for calculating thermal soil properties. For the expansion of GCHP, it is essential to develop simpler and more economic methods in time and cost for BHE sizing. The instrument under development contributes to this goal by providing a device that offers easy transportation and installation, small size, and the possibility of operation by non-specialists.

We have verified that it is possible to insert and extract small probes, which contain a miniaturized acquisition system, for temperature monitoring of the water flowing along the pipes of the BHE. It is possible to configure each probe with the desired parameters for monitoring temperature inside the pipes by wireless transmission. In autonomous mode, each probe completes the acquisition and, once the probe is extracted, downloads automatically the acquired data also by wireless transmission. The data collected and recorded on a PC, allows the design of a new analysis that takes into account the dynamics of the BHE. Some as yet untapped possibilities should be studied and quantified, such as groundwater flows, the effects of convective wet layers, etc. Accurate assessment of soil thermal recovery, and hence, the effects of saturation and thermal degradation of the efficiency that can occur in a particular installation must also be studied and quantified.

9. Acknowledgments

This work has been supported by the Spanish Government under projects "Modelado y simulación de sistemas energéticos complejos" (2005 Ramón y Cajal Program), "Modelado, simulación y validación experimental de la transferencia de calor en el entorno de la edificación" (ENE2008-0059/CON) and by the Valencian Government under project "Diseño y desarrollo de un instrumento de medida para la caracterización de intercambiadores de calor." (GV/2007/058).

The instrument has been patent pending since November of 2008.

10. References

Austin, W. A. (1998). Development of an in-situ system for measuring ground thermal properties. *M.S. thesis, Oklahoma State University*, Stillwater, OK, USA, 177 pp.

Beier, R.A. (2008). Equivalent Time for Interrupted Tests on Borehole Heat Exchangers. *International Journal of HVAC & R Research* 14, 489-503.

Bose, J.E.; Smith, M.D.; Spitler, J.D. (2002). Advances in ground source heat pump systems. An international overview. *7th IEA Conference on Heat Pump Technologies*, Beijing (China)

Carslaw, H.S.; Jaeger, J.C. (1959). *Conduction of Heat in Solids*, Oxford University Press, New York, NY, USA, 510 pp.

Cymbet Corporation (2009). White *paper: Zero power wireless sensor* http://www.cymbet.com

Elson, J.; Girod, L.; Estrin, D. (2002). Fine-Grained network time synchronization using reference broadcasts. *Proceedings Fifth Symposium on Operating Systems Design and Implementation (OSDI 2002)* Vol. 36, 147-163.

Eskilson P. (1987). Thermal Analysis of Heat Extraction Boreholes. *PhD. Thesis, Dept. of Mathematical Physics*, University of Lund, Lund, Sweden, 264 pp.

Eklöf, F.; Gehlin, S. (1996). A mobile equipment for Geothermal Response Test. *M.S. thesis, Lulea University of Technology*, Lulea, Sweden, 65 pp.

European Parliament and Council, Directive 2008/103/EC, *Batteries and accumulators and waste batteries and accumulators as regards placing batteries and accumulators on the market*

European Parliament and Council, Directive 2006/66/EC, *Batteries and accumulators and waste batteries and accumulators and repealing Directive*

Genchi, Y.; Kikegawa, Y.; Inaba, A. (2002) CO2 payback-time assessment of a regional-scale heating and cooling system using a ground source heat-pump in a high energy-consumption area in Tokyo. *Applied Energy* Vol.71, 147-160

Hellström, G. (1991). Thermal Analysis of Duct Storage System. *Dep. of Mathematical Physics*, University of Lund, Lund, Sweden, 262 pp.

Hurtig, E.; Ache, B.; Großwig, S.; Hänsel, K. (2000). Fiber optic temperature measurements: a new approach to determine the dynamic behavior of the heat exchanging medium inside a borehole heat exchange. *TERRASTOCK 2000, 8th International Conference on Thermal Energy Storage Stuttgart*. August 28th to September 1st, 2000.

Jones, C.E.; Sivalingam, K.M.; Agrawal, P.; Chen, J. (2001). A survey of energy efficient network protocols for wireless networks. *Wireless networks* 7, 343-358

Lund, J.W. (2000). Ground source (geothermal) heat pumps. In: *Course on heating with geothermal energy: conventional and new schemes.* Lineau P.J. (editor). World Geothermal Congress 2000 Short Courses. Kazuno, Japan, pp. 209-236.

Martos, J.; Torres, J.; Soret, J.; Montero, A. (2008). Wireless sensor network for measuring thermal properties of borehole heat exchangers. *Proceedings IEEE International Conference on Sustainable Energy Technologies (ICSET 2008)*, Singapur

Mateu, L.; Codrea, C.; Lucas, N.; Pollack, M.; Spies, P. (2007). Human body energy harvesting thermogenerator for sensing applications. *International Conference on Sensor Technologies and Applications SENSORCOMM 2007*,Valencia, Spain

Mogensen, P. (1983). Fluid to duct wall heat transfer in duct system heat storage. *Proceedings of the International Conference on Surface Heat Storage in Theory and Practice*, Sweden, Stockholm, pp. 652-657.

Nordell, B.; Reuss, M.; G. Hellström, G. (2006). Annex 21: Thermal Response Test. Draft.

Omer, A M. (2008). Ground-source heat pump systems and applications. *Renewable and Sustainable Energy Reviews* 12, 344-371.

Paradiso, J.A.; Starner, T. (2005). Energy scavenging for mobile and wireless electronics. *IEEE Pervasive Computing* Vol 4, Issue 1, 18-27

Rohner, E.; Rybach, L.; Schaärli, U. (2005). A new, small, wireless instrument to determine ground thermal conductivity In-Situ for borehole heat exchange design. *Proceedings World Geothermal Congress 2005*, Antalya, Turkey.

Sanner, B.; Karytsas, C.; Mendrinos, D.; Rybach, L. (2003). Current status of ground source heat pumps and underground thermal storage in Europe. *Geothermics* 32, 579-588.

Spitler, J.D. (2005). Ground-Source heat Pump System Research - Past, Present and Future. *International Journal of HVAC & R Research* 11, 165-167.

Sundararaman, B.; Buy, U.; Kshemkalyani, A.D. (2005). Clock synchronization for wireless sensor networks: a survey, *Ad-Hoc network*, 3(3): 282-323

Urchueguía, J.F.; Zacarés, M.; Corberán, J.M.; Montero, Á.; Martos, J.; Witte, H. (2008). Comparison between the energy performance of a ground-coupled water to water heat pump system and an air to water heat pump system for heating and cooling in typical conditions of the European Mediterranean Coast. *Energy Conversion and Management* 49, 2917-2923.

U.S. EPA, (2008). Energy Star Program, US Environmental Protection Agency. http://www.energystar.gov.

Witte, H.J.L.; van Gelder, G.J.; Spitler, J.D. (2002). In Situ measurement of ground thermal conductivity: a Dutch perspective. *ASHRAE Transactions* 108, 1-10.

4

Automated Testing and Development of WSN Applications

Mohammad Al Saad, Jochen Schiller and Elfriede Fehr
Freie Universität Berlin
Germany

1. Introduction

Over the course of time the application range of Wireless Sensor Networks will become more varied and complex. A WSN may consist of several hundred sensor nodes, which are independent processing units equipped with various sensors and which communicate wirelessly. WSNs can be compared to wireless ad-hoc networks, but the sensor nodes are constrained by very limited resources and suit the purpose of collecting and processing sensory data.

Therefore it is increasingly important to programme it with the corresponding efficiency. Programming can become more productive and robust, if it is subject to a systematic and structured software development process, which enhances application and accommodates for the sensor network's operating conditions. The pivotal approach for this can be found in the automated Software development process, during which administrational functionalities, which are suitable for the operation of the Sensor Network, are integrated. This constitutes the approach of our proposed Tool-Chain ScatterClipse (Al Saad et al., 2008b). The architecture centric method of the model driven paradigm (Stahl et al., 2006) is used for the automation. New in this case is that the models are not only used for documentation or visualisation: The semantic and expressive formal models also act as a method to completely and concisely represent important concepts as well as the domain's (platform's) basic conditions. Such specific, yet technology neutral models, are inputted into the configurable code generator and after their validation the corresponding software artefact is generated and distributed to the appropriate platform (wireless sensors nodes).

The high degree of automation accelerates the development and testing of applications, which are already running on sensor nodes. Furthermore substitutability and reusability of the software artefacts are increased, because the artefacts, alongside the automated code generation, are represented by their respective models. Both increase the development process's productivity. The model driven code generation is used to furthermore generate a largely tailor made code, so that only the required amount of code is generated for the sensor node's intended roll. Thus the scarce memory space is not only optimised, but also unnecessary calculating and energy intensive software modules are avoided. The decreased portion of manually written code also reduces the possibility of a programmer's careless mistakes. In this process the validation on the model level plays an important role, because the earlier a mistake (bug) is discovered in the development process the more robust and reliant it will become.

For automation purposes an appropriate generative infrastructure was developed ScatterFactory (Al Saad et al., 2007a) and ScatterUnit (Al Saad et al., 2008a), which constitutes the backbone of our platform or Tool-Chain. For the modelling a graphical editor, based on the Eclipse Modelling Framework and the Graphical Modelling Framework (GMF), was developed. For the examination of the basic conditions, which are linked to the respective models, a real time validation was integrated into the editor, which also makes the development process more robust. OpenArchitectureWare (oAW) framework is used as the code generator, where the corresponding code is automatically generated from the inputted model and this code is then deployed onto the deployed sensor nodes. All frameworks are Eclipse platform open source projects.

Furthermore the emphasis lies on the integration of essential functionalities, which regard the administration and Management of the Wireless Sensor Network, with the model driven software development process. These shall not be isolated, but shall be seamlessly combined with attributes like configuration, bug fixing, monitoring, user interaction, over the air software updates as well as sensor status visualization (Al Saad et al., 2007b). This combination potential is an important character of the platform. The realisation of such combinations was achieved by the plug-in oriented architecture in accordance with the Eclipse platform. On the one hand the user can operate certain plug-ins (functionalities) independent from each other, so that a "separation of concerns" is achieved, and on the other hand the user can navigate the different plug-ins collaboratively at the same time, whereby coherence is achieved. In order to improve the platforms productivity, its main features can be accessed in local as well as in remote, or internet based, mode. For this reason one can, for example, operate the administration and configuration from a computer in one location (for instance in a development or test laboratory) while the sensors are deployed in real world conditions (for example an experiment field) in a different remote location. This was realized by an ordinary client/server architecture.

1.1 ScatterWeb WSN-Platform

ScatterWeb (Schiller et al., 2005) is a platform for teaching and prototyping WSN, which was developed by our Work Group Computer Systems and Telematics of the Free University Berlin. The hardware components of the ScatterWeb platform mainly consist of Embedded sensor boards (ESBs), the newly developed configurable Modular sensor boards (MSBs) and and the sink (eGate), which is connected to the PC via USB (see Figure 1). The sensor boards have in addition to a controller and transceiver many functions at its disposal, such as a sensor for luminosity, vibration, temperature and IR movement detection, a beeper, LEDS (red, yellow and green), as well as a microphone. Thus a prototype of a comprehensive monitoring sensor is created, which makes studying the insertion of WSNs in various areas and scenarios - like environmental monitoring, intelligent buildings, Ad hoc process control, etc. - possible. With this ability, various applications running on the computer can communicate with ScatterWeb sensor boards via the eGate, and vice versa, which makes data-gathering, debugging, monitoring, over the air software updates, etc. possible.

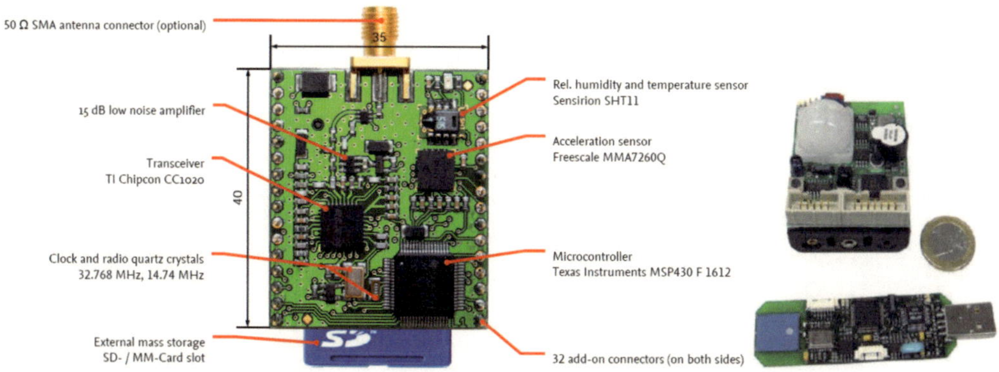

Fig. 1. ScatterWeb WSN-Platform: MSB left, ESB top right, eGate down right

1.2. Architecture Centric Model Driven Software Development (AC-MDSD)

While the main objectives of the OMG relative to the Model Driven Architecture (MDA) are the increase of the portability and interoperational ability of the software on a universal basis, the architecture centric model driven software development (AC-MDSD), as the name states, puts the focus on each an application domain. Instead of generating the same software for different platforms, the AC-MDSD has the goal of variations of software (software families) for a certain domain to automate as much as possible. This attempt is motivated with the observation that the (self repeating) infrastructure code has a considerable part of the entire code-basis in similar applications. With eBusiness applications, it lies around 70%, but with programming closer to the hardware, for instance with embedded systems, this share lies often between 90 and 100% (Eisenecker & Czarnecki., 2000). Consequently it is naturally preferred to create the part automatically so that the actual application specific logic can be concentrated on. In this way, the concentration is set on an application domain for a model language, which would allow the concepts for the underlying platform to be domain related and precisely expressed.

Such a domain specific language (DSL) has as advantage over the usually more complex UML-based models used in the MDA, that the models created in it have a more complete knowledge of the domain. Since the model elements of DSL stand for concrete architectural concepts or aspects of the domain, a model written in DSL offers a higher abstraction level, but is concrete at the same time. The semantic gap between model and code becomes smaller. As a side-effect this simplifies the transformation of the models to code, because the step-by-step refinement of the models to code can often be skipped, since the underlying platform is known and clearly restricted. Overall, the objective target of the paradigm of the AC-MDSD can be compared to the use of modern product lines in the automobile industry.

At the beginning stands the prototype (Reference Implementation), in which the most important concepts are included. The prototype shows what the vehicle that is to be produced is supposed to look like. The construction plans (Models) serve as the starting basis for the end product (Generated Artifact) and point out which units (Components) are required.

In order to simplify the construction of the product line (Generative Architecture), as well as the later production (Code-Generation), logical coherent Components are summarized to production units. Production units, which are not automated or are too complicated to automate, have to be done by hand (Manual Code). To offer a wide production palette (System Family), the components, as a rule, have to be varied during the production process, while the production platform as such is left unchanged. Thus in context of the AC-MDSD, this approach is also called Product Line Engineering (see Figure 2).

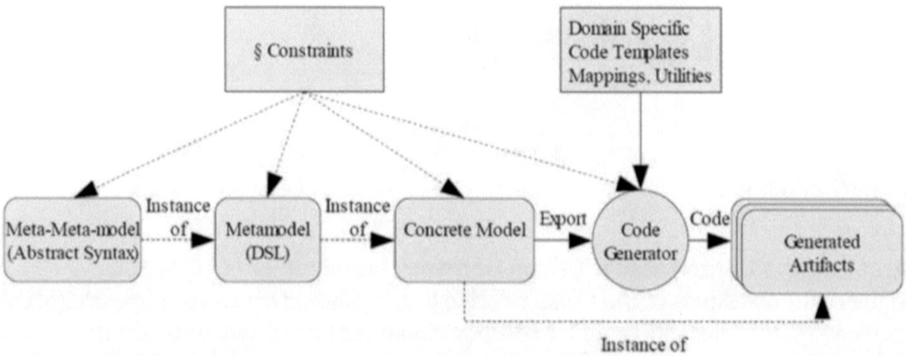

Fig. 2. AC-MDSD as product-line

2. Testing Track

In our research, we examined how tools can support the person who writes test cases. With this in mind, we particularly looked at automated testing of applications for wireless sensor networks (WSNs). A WSN may consist of several hundred sensor nodes, which are independent processing units equipped with various sensors and which communicate wirelessly. WSNs can be compared to wireless ad hoc networks, but the sensor nodes are constrained by very limited resources and suit the purpose of collecting and processing sensory data. To test WSN applications, many common services are needed, e.g. the simulation of sensor input. To provide those services, we implemented a testing framework for our WSN platform ScatterWeb, called ScatterUnit.

2.1 ScatterUnit

Our aim was to create a general-purpose testing frame-work that enables automated tests of WSN applications in respect to component, integration, and system tests. At first, we looked at the spectrum of WSN applications that will potentially be tested using our framework in order to elicit the requirements. A typical WSN application is to collect sensory data over a period of time, which is then evaluated on a PC connected to the WSN, e.g. to keep an eye on water pollution in a river (Akyildiz et al., 2002). A test scenario we may want to apply works as follows:

1. Five sensor nodes to form the WSN.
2. All sensor nodes collect sensory data.
3. The collected data is read out by a PC connected to the WSN.

To write an automated test case for this test scenario, we need a testing framework which is able to simulate sensor input, to invoke the functionality of the WSN application to read out the collected data, and to observe if the correct data is transmitted to the PC. Thus, the testing framework has to orchestrate the WSN application with mechanisms that in general enable the test case to control the actions and observe the behaviour of the application. When orchestrating the application with these mechanisms, we have to mind the intrusion effect (Cunha et al., 2001): Because the mechanisms allocate resources on the sensor nodes (e.g. processing time) they inevitably influence the execution of the application. This intrusion may cause the application to fail, which it would not have without the orchestration. This may be the case for applications which must react quickly and are orchestrated with mechanisms that allocate significant processing time. Thus, the mechanisms must not allocate resources that influence the execution of the application unfavourably. The mechanisms needed to test the WSN application we mentioned above allocate mainly processing time. This does not lead to an unfavourable intrusion since the application is not constrained by timeliness. Because our aim was to create a general-purpose testing framework, we do not consider WSN applications with stringent timeliness constraints.

However, we found an unfavourable influence the orchestration can have on the execution of the WSN application being tested when we looked at another typical test object: We may also want to test a service used by many WSN applications, such as a routing protocol. A simple test scenario is to establish a small multi-hop network and to send a data packet from one sensor node to another, whereas the routing protocol has to forward the data packet on one or more intermediate nodes. A test case for this scenario sends a data packet by using the functionality of the routing protocol, observes through which intermediate nodes the data packet is forwarded, and asserts that the data packet is received by the destination node. When we execute this test case, the routing protocol may fail to deliver the data packet because it was forwarded on a wrong route. To understand at which point the routing protocol actually failed, we have to reconstruct the route the data packet took. For that, we need the information of the observed forwarding actions on the intermediate nodes in the correct order. Because this information is retrieved on different sensor nodes we have to gather it at a central place for evaluation. A testing infrastructure that is able to do so is SeNeTs (Blumenthal et al., 2004): A base station sends commands to the nodes in the network - e.g. to initiate sending the data packet - and the nodes send information on all relevant events back to the base station, i.e. where the route the data packet took is reconstructed. However, this architecture was designed for wireless ad-hoc networks where resources are not as limited as in WSNs. For WSNs we noticed that the transfer of a data packet may fail if the radio channel was currently occupied by another sensor node (the reason may be the occurrence of too many collisions on the radio channel). Therefore, we cannot afford to establish a resource demanding communication between a base station and the sensor nodes as SeNeTs does. To avoid an unfavourable influence on the execution of the WSN application being tested, our testing frame-work must not use the radio channel too frequently. Thus, we decided not to use a centralized but a decentralized approach (Rafiq & Cacciar, 2003) for our testing framework ScatterUnit which meets the requirement to produce the least possible intrusion effect.

To avoid sending commands over the radio channel each sensor node is configured with its own set of actions before the execution of a test case is started. Those actions may call a method of the application being tested, e.g. to send a data packet using the routing protocol. They may also simulate an event, e.g. to simulate sensory data input. And they may be used to start waiting for a specific event, e.g. to wait for the reception of a data packet on the radio channel. All actions which will be executed on the same sensor node are implemented by a node script which also knows when to execute them. Thus, a node script has the responsibility to control the execution of the test case locally on its sensor node. To coordinate the actions executed on different sensor nodes, a command service is provided by ScatterUnit (Ulrich et al., 1999). Sending commands for coordination is the only reason to use the radio channel for testing purposes while the test case is running. During the execution of the test case, all relevant events are logged on the sensor node where they occur. Not until the execution of the test case was terminated the radio channel is used to send the logs of all sensor nodes to a PC connected to the WSN. The PC uses these logs to evaluate the behaviour of the application being tested and to decide whether a failure occurred or not.

How to implement a test case using ScatterUnit is well demonstrated by a test case to test a routing protocol. Especially in the field of WSNs, routing protocols must have the ability to adapt to changing network topologies. To test this feature we apply the following test scenario:

1. A WSN is set up with the topology shown in Figure 3 (left). (ScatterUnit provides a topology simulation service which filters out received data packets from nodes virtually out of range.)
2. Sensor node 1 sends a data packet to sensor node 4.
3. Sensor node 4 receives the data packet.
4. The WSN changes its topology in a way that the path between sensor node 1 and 4 changes: Sensor node 4 moves out of range of sensor node 3 and into range of sensor node 2 (see Figure 3 right).
5. Sensor node 1 sends a second data packet to sensor node 4.
6. Sensor node 4 receives the data packet.

Due to the changing topology of the WSN, the routing protocol has to choose a different path to redirect the second data packet. If sensor node 4 does not receive the second packet we would have shown that the routing protocol failed to adapt to the changed network topology.

This test case is implemented by four node scripts - one for each sensor node. ScatterUnit calls a set-up method of those node scripts before the execution of the test case is started. This gives us the chance to initialize the topology simulation service provided by ScatterUnit as depicted in Figure 3.

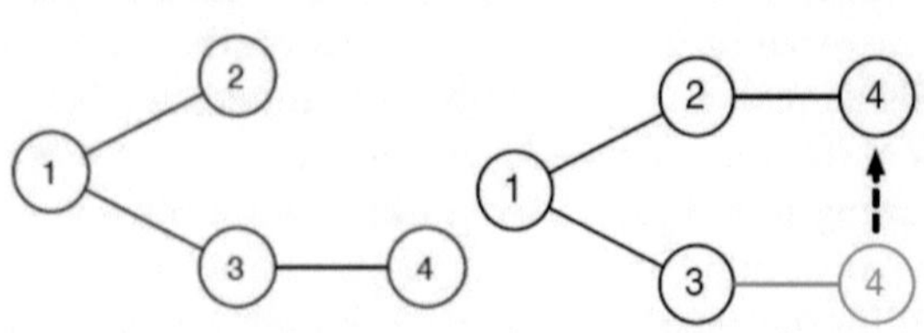

Fig. 3. WSN with four sensor nodes (left: nodes are within communication range of each other, right: simulative modification of the topology while running the test)

This is all we have to implement for the node scripts of sensor nodes 2 and 3. For the node script of sensor node 1, we additionally implement the following: In the start method, which is called by ScatterUnit once the execution of the test case is started, we prepare a data packet and send it by calling a method of our routing protocol. After the node script receives a command from the node script of sensor node 4 we send the second data packet. If sending one of the data packets fails, we abort the execution of the test case. For the node script of sensor node 4, we implement the following: In the start method we start waiting for the first data packet by using the waiting service provided by ScatterUnit. Once the data packet is received, we reconfigure the topology simulation service by virtually moving sensor node 4 out of range of sensor node 3 and into range of sensor node 2. After that, we send a command to the node script of sensor node 1 to let it send the second data packet and start waiting for it. Once the second data packet is received, we terminate the execution of the test case.

The logs of all sensor nodes which are accumulated during the execution of the test case are sent to a PC and merged into a single time ordered log which looks like this in case the routing protocol failed to send the second data packet:

- The execution of the test case is started.
- Sensor node 4 starts waiting.
- Sensor node 4 received the awaited data packet.
- Sensor node 4 leaves the range of sensor node 3.
- Sensor node 4 enters the range of sensor node 2.
- Sensor node 4 starts waiting.
- Sensor node 1 aborts the execution of the test case.

This log is analyzed by several routines which each check for a certain failure. One of them will report that sensor node 1 failed to send the second data packet. The evaluation of the test results is discussed later in more details.

The outline to implement a test case is a test scenario like the one we enumerated in six steps in the previous section. A test scenario consists of actions - like sending a data packet - and events that are expected to occur if the application being tested does not fail - like receiving a data packet. The first step towards the implementation of the test scenario is to convert each expected event into an action. For example, we have to convert the event of receiving a data packet into an action that starts waiting for the corresponding event to occur. Thus, we have several actions we need to implement in order to get an executable test case. Additionally, we have to specify the order in which these actions are executed. This order is directly given by the test scenario. But to write the code needed to guarantee this order is a complex task.

ScatterUnit requires us to implement a test case by several node scripts. Thus we have to answer two questions by recalling the test scenario:

1. Which actions are executed on the sensor node we want to implement the node script for?
2. After which action has each action to be executed?

If we implemented an action by a node script for one sensor node, we would possibly notice when answering the second question that the preceding action is executed on another sensor node. Actually, this is the case for the action of the test case we introduced in the previous section that sends the second data packet from sensor node 1. This action is executed after the last action to change the topology of the WSN. So, the action is executed on sensor node 1 and its preceding action is executed on sensor node 4. To guarantee the correct execution order of these actions, we have to use the command service provided by ScatterUnit: After the execution of the preceding action is finished, a command is sent to the sensor node where the other action will be executed once the command is received. The command service used to coordinate the execution of the node scripts is required because of the decentralized approach applied to ScatterUnit. To implement a test case we have to split the test scenario into chunks of consecutive actions which are executed on the same sensor node. We then have to implement all chunks that are associated to the same sensor node by a node script. And these chunks that are distributed throughout the node scripts have to be tied up again by using commands.

To split the test scenario into chunks and tie it up again is a complex task especially for more extensive test scenarios. Obviously, it is not easy to write a test case because the test scenario - which is our outline - cannot be implemented directly. In order to be able to implement a test scenario easily, we have to delegate the task to split and tie the actions. For that, we applied a model-driven approach to ScatterUnit, where we delegate this task to the code generator which generates the node scripts from a test case model whereat the test case model is a direct representation of the test scenario.

2.2 Model-Driven Visual ScatterUnit

Model-Driven Software Development (MDSD) is the field of automated code generation from formal models. A formal model describes a certain aspect of a system in an abstract way. The architecture centric method of the model-driven paradigm is used for the automation. In the context of ScatterUnit, the described system is a test case. Therefore, we model the test case formally and generate the code for the node scripts. The crucial part of the model-driven approach we applied to ScatterUnit is the choice of the aspect of the test case that is modeled in an abstract way: We model a direct representation of the test scenario wherein the corresponding actions, their assignment to a sensor node on which they will be executed, and the order in which they are executed is modeled. Given this information, the code generator can do the job to split the actions into chunks and tie them up by using commands - as we discussed previously - when it generates the code for the node scripts.

When modeling a test case with Model-Driven Visual ScatterUnit (Al Saad et al., 2008a), we start with a diagram like the one shown in Figure 4. It depicts the course of the test scenario we introduced in previously. The notation is very similar to UML Activity Diagrams. It only differs regarding the activities: An activity represents a group of actions which serve a single purpose, e.g. changing the topology of the WSN. Furthermore, the interior of an activity shows which sensor nodes the represented actions are executed on. Thus, the diagram reads as follows: Once the test case is started, two activities are executed in parallel. Sensor node 1 sends the first data packet, and sensor node 4 waits for reception of that packet. After the packet has arrived, the topology of the WSN is changed. Then, the second packet is sent from sensor node 1, while sensor node 4 waits for reception. If the data packet is received, the execution of the test case is terminated.

The purpose of this diagram is to represent the test scenario in an intuitive way. But to be able to generate the node script code from the model, we have to fill in more detail. Therefore, we add an additional diagram for each activity that models the actions that are represented by the activity. Figure 5 shows the diagram that details the activity Change Topology. We have two actions. One for virtually moving sensor node 4 out of range of sensor node 3; and one to enter the range of sensor node 2. These actions are modelled with all information needed to generate the respective calls of the topology simulation service.

Since the actions are inside the box of sensor node 4 - this is how actions are assigned to sensor nodes - the generated code is part of the node script for sensor node 4.

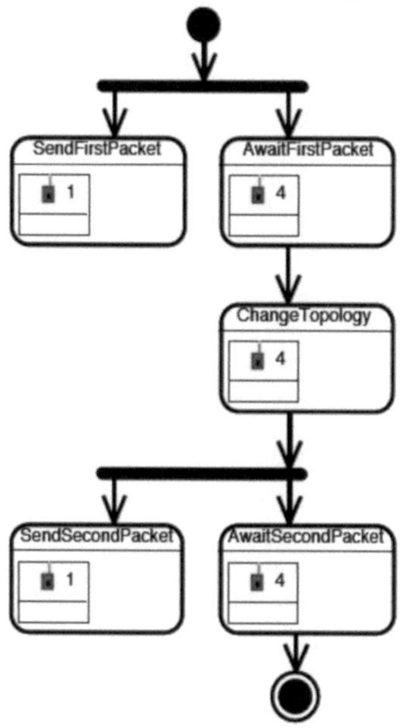

Fig. 4. Test scenario to test a routing protocol

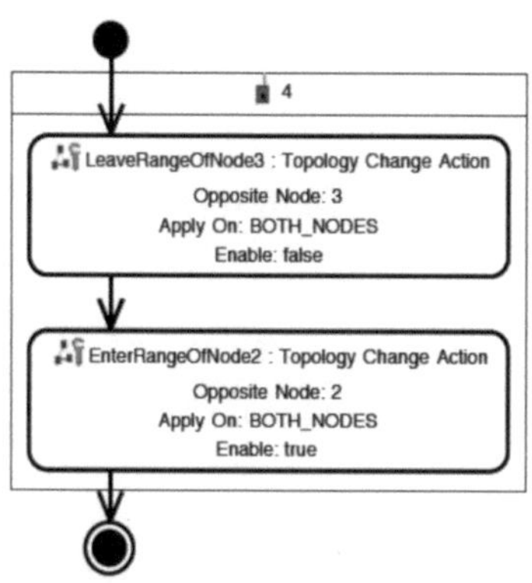

Fig. 5. Diagram that details the activity 'ChangeTopology' in Fig. 4

However, not all the code needed for the node scripts can be generated from the test case model. An action that requires manually written code is part of the diagram shown in Figure 6. This diagram models the actions represented by the activity SendSecondPacket. We actually see just one action with no further detail because the manually written code will do the work. In order to send a data packet over the radio channel using the routing protocol - which is the application being tested - we have to prepare the data packet and call a method of the routing protocol to send the packet. This action is very specific to the application being tested. That is why this action has to be implemented manually. There would be no benefit in trying to model every action in a way that no manually written code is needed, because the work done by actions varies extensively since we have a wide spectrum of WSN applications potentially being tested using ScatterUnit.

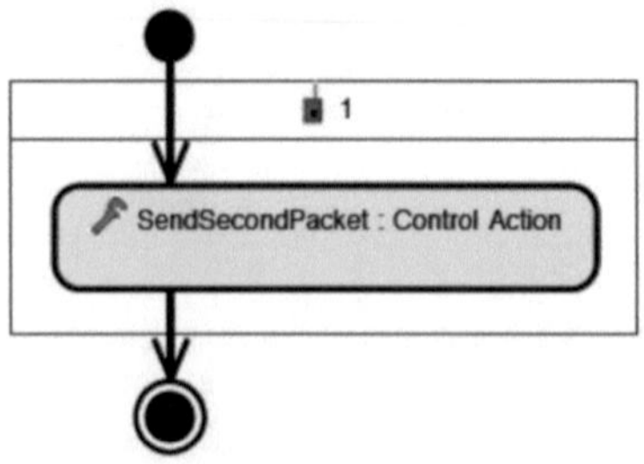

Fig. 6. Diagram that details the activity 'SendSecondPacket' in Fig. 4

Figure 7 shows the diagram which models the actions represented by the activity AwaitSecondPacket: First, the waiting service provided by ScatterUnit is asked to give a notification once the awaited data packet has been received. This notification is represented by the event SecondPacketReceived. Then follows the action AbortIfTimedOut for which we manually implement code to abort the execution of the test case in case the data packet was not received and the waiting job timed out. (Actions which are implemented manually are indicated by a gray background.) If no time out occurred, we actually received the data packet which is logged by the action LogRadioPacket.

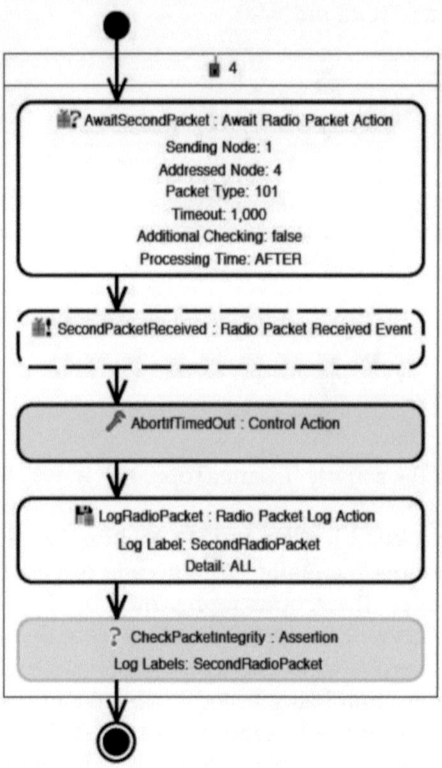

Fig. 7. Diagram that details the activity 'AwaitSecondPacket' in Fig. 4

Referring to this data packet by using the log label SecondRadioPacket, we check its integrity with the assertion CheckPacketIntegrity. Assertions are executed once the execution of the test case is terminated and analyze the log accumulated during the execution in order to check for failures of the application being tested. Since those assertions are application specific, they are manually implemented as well, i.e. we check if the payload of the data packet was not corrupted during transmission. When generating the node scripts from the test case model, the code generator splits up all actions and assigns them to the node script of the sensor node on which they are executed. To maintain the execution order of the actions, the command service provided by ScatterUnit is used. The execution order is modeled through the arrows in the diagrams. Since both actions linked by an arrow are assigned to a sensor node, the code generator is able to decide whether a command is needed to maintain the execution order of both actions, which is the case if the actions are executed on different sensor nodes. For the person who models the test case, it makes no difference if an arrow is drawn between two actions that are executed on the same or on different sensor nodes. Thus, the complex task to write code for coordination purposes is fully hidden from the user which makes modeling the execution order of the actions easy.

The code generated for maintaining the execution order is called infrastructure code because this code is needed in order to write a test case on the ScatterUnit platform. This technical term is used in the context of architecture centric model-driven software development (AC-MDSD, Stahl et al., 2006), which we applied to ScatterUnit: The main purpose of code generation is to generate infrastructure code - for coordination, that is - which is required by the platform, in this case ScatterUnit. As a result, the user can focus on the design of the test scenario rather than having to spend valuable development time on writing infrastructure code which is a complex and time consuming task.

Apart from infrastructure code for coordination purposes, we also enabled the generation of infrastructure code that is needed to evaluate the test results. Once the execution of a test case is terminated, we get a log of all relevant events that have been observed while the test case was running. This log is then analyzed by routines which individually check for a certain failure in order to decide whether the WSN application being tested failed or not. Those routines are represented by assertions in the test case model. For example, the assertion CheckPacketIntegrity shown in Figure 7 represents a routine that checks the payload of the second data packet. If the payload does not contain the expected data, the routine will report the failure that the payload was corrupted.

To run a routine that checks for a specific failure, we have to accomplish two tasks: First, during the execution of the test case, the data must be logged that indicates the absence or the presence of the failure we look at. Second, after the execution of the test case is terminated, the corresponding log entries must be picked out of the log in order to analyze them. We log the needed data by adding log actions to the test case model, i.e. the log action LogRadioPacket. (In contrast to LogRadio-Packet, which needs no manually written code, it is possible to implement application specific log actions manually as well.) To have the corresponding log entries right at hand when implementing a routine to check for a certain failure, log labels are used, i.e. the log action LogRadioPacket declares the log label Second-RadioPacket, which is referenced by the assertion CheckPacketIntegrity. Thus, we do not have to implement code for picking the needed log entries out of the log, because this can be done by the code generator which processes the log labels in the test case model.

Although the code for picking the log entries out can be generated, the routine represented by the assertion has to be implemented manually. The reason is the same as for most actions in the test case model: The routine to check for a certain failure is specific to the application being tested. However, there is one typical failure for which the routine can be generated without the need of manually written code. This type of failure requires the following reasonable assumption about the test case model: The modeled sequence of actions represents the test course that is expected in case the application being tested does not fail. Thus, if the execution of the test case is aborted, we conclude that a failure occurred. For example the action SendSecondPacket shown in Figure 6 may abort the execution of the test case to indicate that the routing protocol failed to send the data packet. A generated routine will report this failure by indicating that the action aborted the execution of the test case. Through aborting the execution of the test case a failure can be reported very easily because no manually written code is needed besides a single call by the action to abort. Since failures that can be reported in this way are of common interest we save significant time to implement code for reporting failures.

Altogether we accumulate the following test results: Failures reported by assertions, a failure reported by aborting the execution of the test case, and the data that has been logged by log actions. To facilitate the reading of these test results, we incorporated them into the diagrams of the test case model. The diagram in Figure 8 incorporates the test results indicating the failure reported by the assertion CheckPacketIntegrity. This failure is shown by the lightening icon in the lower left of the assertion. The tooltip of that icon prints: "The payload of the data packet was corrupted." Additionally, the i icon in the lower left of the log action LogRadioPacket indicates the logged data. The tooltip of that icon prints the data of the data packet. Thus, the test results are easily accessible in the diagrams, because each piece of information is assigned to a corresponding action in the test case model. Without the incorporation of the test results, the user would have to read a textual log, with no reference to the test case model. To understand the information given by the textual log the user would have to embed it into the context of the test scenario herself which is a difficult and time consuming task. The improved readability of the test results also makes it easier and less time consuming to use log actions to get insights on the cause of a reported failure. If we got the test results shown in Figure 8, we would look at the data logged by the log action LogRadioPacket and may notice that the payload was still intact but only the last byte was missing.

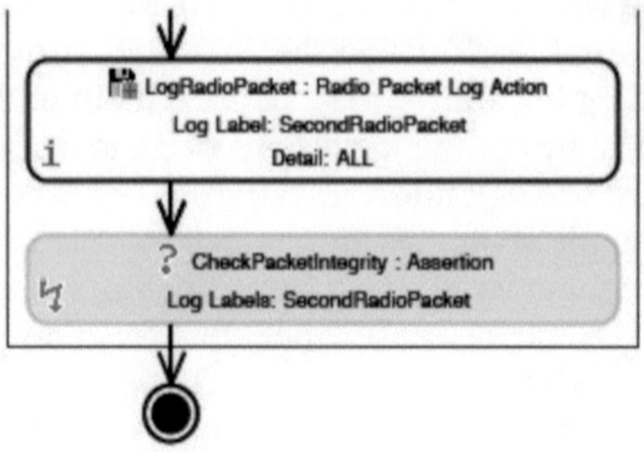

Fig. 8. Test results incorporated into the diagram by adding icons to the lower left of the actions

After we detected a failure by executing a test case, our next step is to fix the fault within the application being tested which caused it to fail. But before we can correct the application code, we have to locate the fault (see Figure 9).

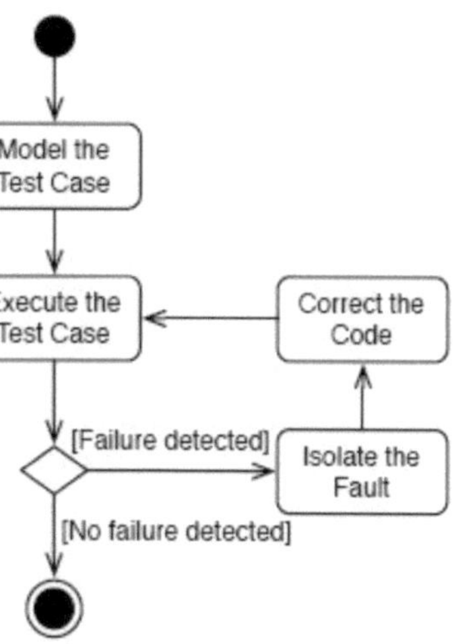

Fig. 9. The process of quality assurance in the context of a test case

In general, we do this by gradually isolating its code location until we can pinpoint the fault. Therefore, Agans recommends using a divide and conquer approach (Agans, 2002). To illustrate this approach, we shall use the test case for the application which measures the water pollution we introduced in Dection 2: Suppose that the test case reports a failure that not all sensory data was transmitted to the base station. The cause may lie within the activity of each sensor node to collect and store the sensory data, or it may lie within the task to transfer the stored data to the base station. To answer which case is true, we next check if all sensory data was stored on each sensor node as expected. If this is true, we have to look for a cause associated to the transmission of the data to the base station. Otherwise (the stored data is corrupted), the code for collecting and storing the sensory data is faulty. Now, we have identified the part of the code where we have to look for a fault. If the application failed to collect and store the sensory data, we may divide the location of the fault again by asking whether the collection task or the storing task went wrong. In general, we iteratively divide the code part where the fault is located and thus narrow our focus until we are able to locate the fault itself.

The process of isolating a fault is a very demanding cognitive task where hypotheses about the cause of a failure are suggested and verified iteratively (Xu & Rajlich, 2004). We do so when using the divide and conquer approach by suggesting a hypothesis that will help us - once verified - to divide the code where the fault is located: In the above example, we may have suggested the hypothesis that the cause of the failure lies within the activity to collect and store the sensory data. To verify this hypothesis, we need to gather information on the data that the sensor nodes actually store. This task to gather information on the behavior of the faulty application is mandatory to be able to suggest and verify hypotheses. Actually, information can be gathered by adding log actions to the test case model, which logs the needed information. Thus, we refine the test case model in order to get more insight on the cause of the failure reproduced by the test case.

In summary, altering a test case - which is done many times when isolating a fault - would involve writing and rewriting infrastructure code which is required by the platform ScatterUnit. This task is completely done by the code generator of Model-Driven Visual ScatterUnit, which makes the fault isolating process more efficient.

2.3 Model Checking

In order to ensure the generated code's and with it the test cases' quality, the test case model is checked with regard to its syntactic and semantic rules in the form of constraints. This happens not only before the node script's test case model is generated, but also during the modeling of the test case and is called for this reason Live-Validation. As the model validation is run with the help of openArchitectureWare Framework and as the visual editor was created with the help of the Graphical Modeling Framework, the components are combined with the help of the GMF2 Adapters to enable Live-Validation. For this purpose the visual editor embeds the GMF2 adapter, which allows access to the openArchitectureWare's model checking engine. This is repeatedly called to validate the test case model, which is momentarily being edited, based on the constraints. Figure 10 shows ScatterClipse's Architecture regarding the Live-Validation.

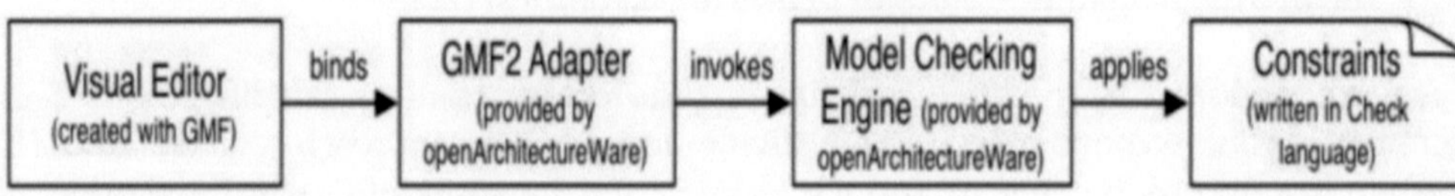

Fig. 10. Live-Validation Components

For instance the command names are used in the generated code's method names, they are not allowed to contain any special characters, so that the code can be compiled (see Fig. 11).

```
context testcase::ControlPath
ERROR "The name must only contain alphabetic and numeric letters." :
this.name.matches("[\\p{Alpha}\\p{Digit}]*");
```

A large number of syntactic rules can be compiled, but the true use of model validation unfurls when checking for semantic rules. For instance as it is defined that a test case model models a course of the test case, it is therefore sensible to check (see Fig. 12), if the test case model consists of a linear sequence of commands:

```
context testcase::ControlPath
        ERROR "A control path must have one incoming link." :
        this.incoming.size == 1;
context testcase::ControlPath
        ERROR "A control path must have at maximum one outgoing
link." : this.outgoing.size <= 1;
```

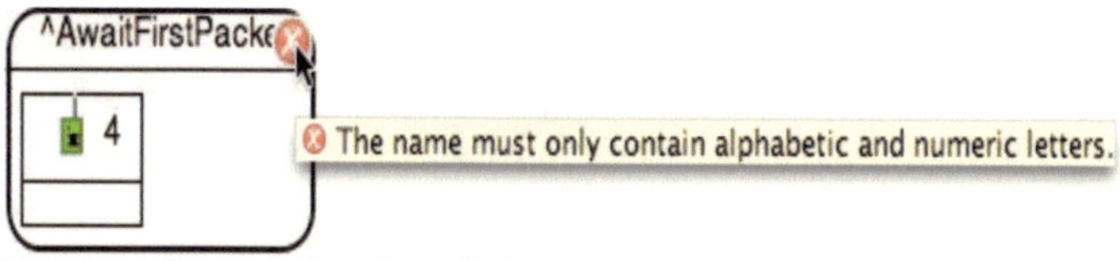

Fig. 11. Live-Validation detected an invalid name

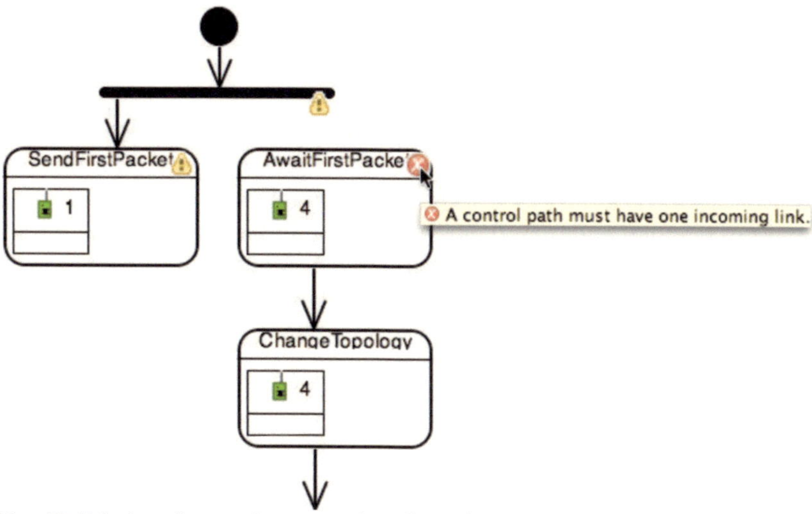

Fig. 12. Live-Validation detected a control path with no predecessor

Overall the model validation secures the quality of the executable test case and increases with it the robustness of the test case development. Furthermore the Live- Validation shows mistakes during the test case modeling, so that the user can correct them in a timely fashion.

3. Development Track

ScatterFactory (Al Saad et al., 2007a) - similar to Visual ScatterUnit - is a generative infrastructure for the model driven development of software for the Embedded sensor boards of the WSN-Platform ScatterWeb. The chosen architecture centric approach represents an instance of the Model Driven Development. The goal is the furthermost automated and standardized production of software system families for the ScatterWeb sensor boards. For this purpose, a component meta model was developed, which builds a basis for a complete tool chain, from the model platform all the way to the deployment of the generated code onto the sensor boards. To model a ScatterWeb network, a domain specific graphical editor was developed on the basis of the Eclipse Modeling Framework and the Graphical Modeling Framework. For the examination of static model constraints, a real time validation was integrated into the editor. The open ArchitectureWare framework was used for the transformation from models into code. The ScatterFactory framework was completed with additional components like assistants or flash-components for the automatic deployment of generated artefacts in an existing network. Our ScatterFactory tool chain was realized with the Eclipse Framework as a basis.

ScatterFactory was originally developed for the first generation ScatterWeb platform - eGate and ESB sensor nodes - and we wanted to keep the advantage of Scatterfactory also for the second generation ScatterWeb platform - MSB sensor nodes. So we developed ScatterFactory2, which was modelled on the principles of the original ScatterFactory. However ScatterFactory2 accommodates now for the innovations and improvements brought on by the second generation ScatterWeb. ScatterFactory was originally developed for the first generation ScatterWeb platform - eGate and ESB sensor nodes - and we wanted to keep the advantage of Scatterfactory also for the second generation ScatterWeb platform - MSB sensor nodes. So we developed ScatterFactory2, which was modelled on the principles of the original ScatterFactory. However ScatterFactory2 accommodates now for the innovations and improvements brought on by the second generation ScatterWeb.
The main difference between the first and second generation ScatterWeb platforms is the new modular design made up of available firmware, system services and hardware drivers, instead of the old monolithic design. Every driver and every algorithmic library has been made available as a library and can be inserted into the run time environment as needed. In this way only the necessary libraries for an application's operation need to be inserted. ScatterWeb's modular design facilitates the configuration of the run time environment enormously and thus lends itself to be represented with a model of an application's run time environment, created of course with the help of ScatterFactory2. Figure 13 shows a model that was drawn with the help of ScatterFactory2's graphical editor.

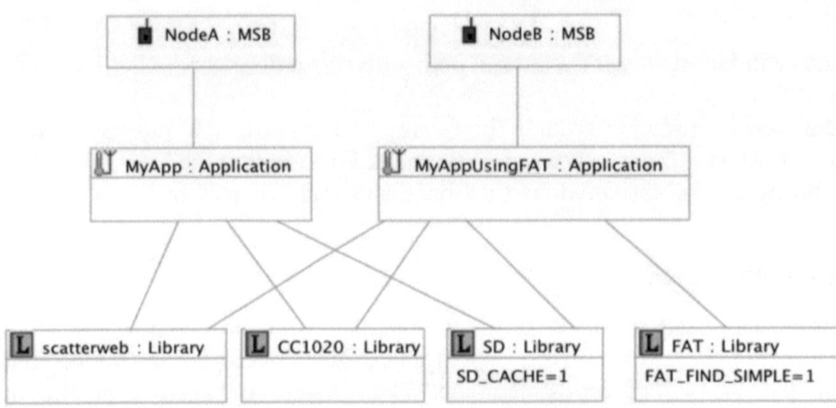

Fig. 13. Model of the run time environment of two applications

The model represents two applications, each with different run time environments: Both applications use the libraries scatterweb and CC1020, which represent the system core. Furthermore the library SD shall also be embedded into their run time environment. This library is a driver, which allows interaction with the sensor node's memory card. However only applications, which allow the management of the memory card's FAT file systems, also receive the library FAT. The diagram elements for the libraries SD and FAT consist, apart from the library's name, of more details, which allow the configuration of the respective library. If the library can be configured with 'Defines' ("#define" of the language "C"), then 'Defines' value can also be placed into the appropriate model. In the case of the SD library, caching for the memory card access has been activated. In the case of the FAT library a search function has been added. These details allow the customization of the individual libraries to fit the needs of the application. For example the activation or deactivation of the SD library's caching makes a big difference: If the caching is activated, then the data access to the memory card is on average faster. If the caching is deactivated though, then memory space can be saved, which would otherwise be used for the cache and which usually requires about ten percent of all main memory. ScatterFactory2 basically generates out of the model a Make file, which contains the information needed by the translator to insert the libraries as modelled. In order to use the same modelling and code generation tools as in ScatterFactory, the same technologies and tools were used here - especially EMF/GMF and oAW.

3.1 The Integration of Visual ScatterUnit and ScatterFactory2

In the previous examination of the testing process it was assumed that the soon to be tested application already existed and the preceding application development was ignored. An important reason though requires that the application development and the testing process are examined together: An application may need different configurations for different sensor nodes of the same sensor network. Therefore it needs to be taken into consideration with which configuration a sensor node modeled in a test case is associated with. For example it is possible, that not all sensor nodes in a sensor network also have the same sensors on board. A test case therefore, which simulates sensor measurements, may only simulate sensor measurements on sensor nodes which actually have these sensors on board. As the run time configuration needs to be examined, it lends itself to unite Visual ScatterUnit and ScatterFactory2, because in a sensor network the sensor node's configuration can be configured with the help of ScatterFactory2. The aim during the integration was to associate the sensor node modeled in the test case with the modeled application, which had its run time environment configured with the help of ScatterFactory2 (see Figure 14).

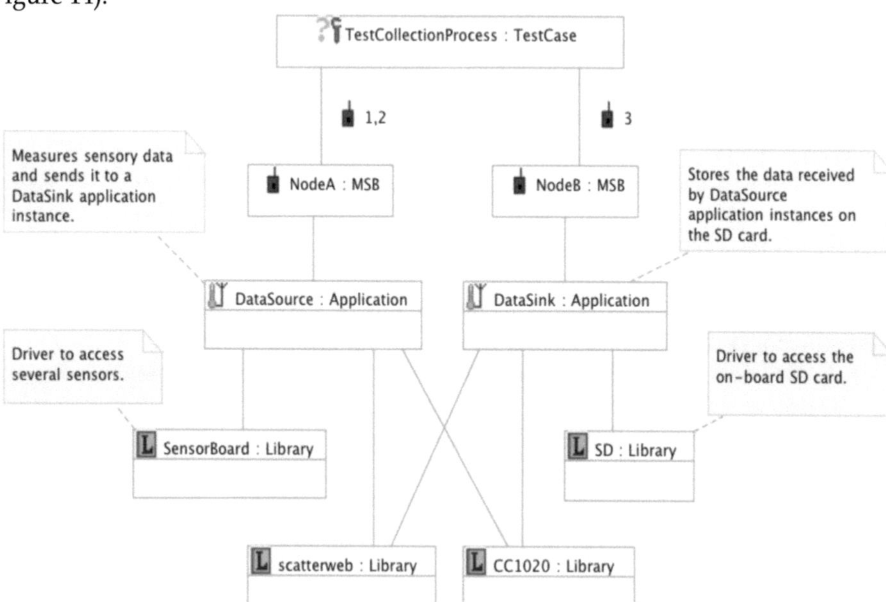

Fig. 14. Test case within an application

In order to make this association the model is supplemented with diagram elements, which represent test cases. The modeled test cases are connected with the modeled sensor nodes. The connection indicates which sensor nodes of the test case are mapped onto which modeled sensor nodes. The modeled test case TestCollectionProcess consists of three node scripts, whereby the node scripts for the sensor nodes 1 and 2 each run on one sensor node, which runs the application instance DataSource and the node script for sensor node 3 runs on one sensor node, which runs the application instance DataSink. If the node script is generated, one receives for each of the three modelled sensor nodes a Make file. Each Make file consists of instructions for the compiler, which makes sure that the correct node script is compiled with the right application instance and the right run time configuration.

4. Management and Monitoring Track

Nowadays apart from text editors, used for editing plain text files, there also exist many different types of editors, for example for the editing of audio and graphical files and of course for web pages. The more complex the edited item is, the higher the demand is for that editor. A good editor should simplify the user's work a lot. This principle can be transferred to WSN, which in the current ubiquitous and pervasive computing era plays a central roll and can be found in more and more areas of application. The challenges regarding programming, monitoring, managing and troubleshooting of WSN increase accordingly and with that the challenges for the corresponding tools as well. The Management Track of the ScatterClipse tool-suit is as an Eclipse based plugin of this manner, which provides the above mentioned services by illustrative means and in so doing, allows the user to utilize them interactively and thus to "edit" the WSN. With the Management plugin's design we attached great importance to the aspect of human-computer interfaces for WSN. Tabfolders, which enables easy user navigation, were used to represent the different features of the Management Plug-in. A supernode can be used as an alternative to the eGate. A supernode is a sensor board with special software, which offers the same functionality as an eGate and which is connected to the computer via serial cable. In this form the supernode can also act as a sink. The Management Plug-in's tabfolder oriented design offers the user the possibility of combining individually required features, so that the collaborating tabfolders function together as a coherent whole. Nevertheless the user can navigate between them at any time, so that a separation of concerns is ensured. The following list represents the Management Plug-in's different features or tabfolders and their functionality:

1. Connection: manages the connection between eGate or SuperNode and the sensor boards.
2. Property: manages the graphical representation of the sensors' status.
3. Terminal: receives and displays information. The user can enter commands in order to configure or control the sensor boards as well as the eGate.
4. Over The Air Flashing: flashes a selected code image Over the Air to the chosen sensor boards and also allows that deployed sensor boards can receive their software updates.

4.1 Connection

Given that the software that runs on the sensor boards is written entirely in the programming language C and given that the Eclipse Framework is written in Java, it has become necessary to develop a bridge between the two systems. This objective is achieved

by a ScatterWeb library for Java that is used to model the ScatterWeb platform into an object oriented paradigm on the basis of the language Java. Thus the communication in both directions between any Java based system and any ScatterWeb WSN, which has been deployed in the real world, is ensured. The connection is made uncomplicatedly by the method eGate.connect() using the javax.comm. Library. The serial port and its corresponding input and output data streams are determined by the parameter names (like Nr. of the COM Port) assigned to the method. Messages are sent to the network, which are necessary for its initialization, and the connection is made.
Figure 15 shows a screenshot of our connection window, through which the connection to the WSN is established, whereupon its components (eGate and all sensor boards) are determined. Firstly the communication type is selected (1). If the local communication type is chosen, the computer connects with the sensors via eGate or supernode. If the remote communication type is chosen, the computer connects as a client with the sensors through the server. When the local communication type is in use the user can determine if communication with the sensors via eGate or supernode is desired (2). In the next step the user selects the COM port's number (3), through which shall be communicated. If this computer acts as a server, then the other clients in the network can also access the sensors. If the local terminal is chosen, then the sensor data will only be shown on the local computer. If the remote terminal is chosen, then the sensor data is shown on the client computers (4). Information regarding the connection to the WSN (like connect time, sensor ID and sensor type) is shown in a table (5). All information of the sensors is stored in the background to memory. The connection is established and disconnected with a mouse click (6) and the WSN can be scanned again (7). Upon starting the Management Plug-in only the connection tabfolder can be seen. The remaining tabfolders are only shown after the connection with a port was successful and after the scanning of the WSN. This contributes to the clarity and eases the interaction with the user.

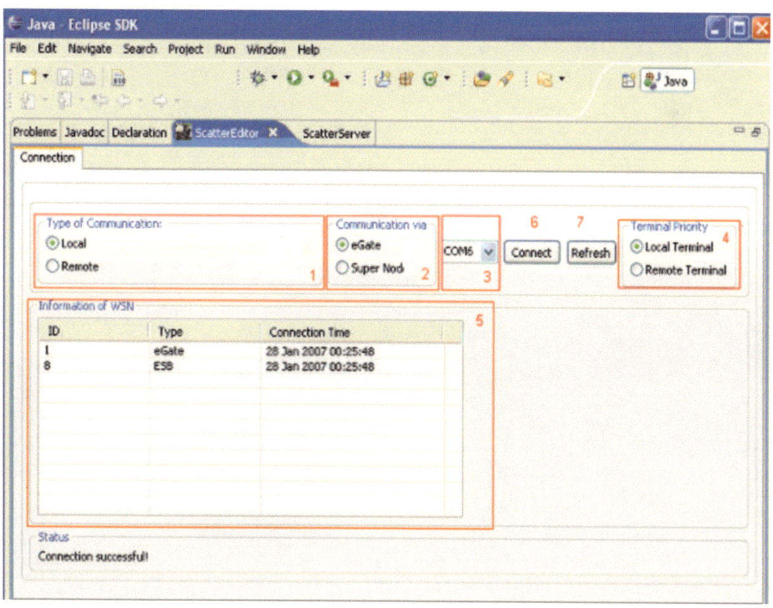

Fig. 15. Connection Tabfolder

4.2. Property

After the connection to the WSN has been established, it is possible to examine the properties of the sensor boards as well as of the eGate. The task of the program section "property" is of graphical representation of the sensor status. Every important sensor state is illustrated "on the fly" and can be configured and controlled through a transparent user interaction. Depending on the sensor's properties, functions can be activated or deactivated, and data, for example the temperature of the sensor's environment, can be shown in this tabfolder. The property tabfolder's visual oriented design is an example for how the aspect of human-computer interfaces for ScatterWeb-WSN is realised. Figure 16 shows a screenshot of property tabfolders. Firstly the user selects a sensor (1). The user updates the list of available sensors by pressing the refresh button and all available sensors are listed in the pull-down menu. In our example we chose the sensor with the ID 8. The IDs can be changed in the field "change sensor ID" (2). If applicable, information concerning the eGate or the supernode is shown (3). The LED's control panel on the sensor (4) can be switched on or off by pressing the appropriate button. The sensor can be restarted (reset) with the restart button, just as the beeper (6). The configuration of the Announce-Flags Serial and Radio (7) as well as the configuration of the Firmware-Flags Programmable and DCO-Checker (8) can be read out and changed. The data from the different measurements (like temperature, volume, movement and vibration) in the sensing field are shown (9). Also shown are the values for Transmit Power and Receive Limit (10), as well as the status of the battery voltage and the optional external power supply (11).

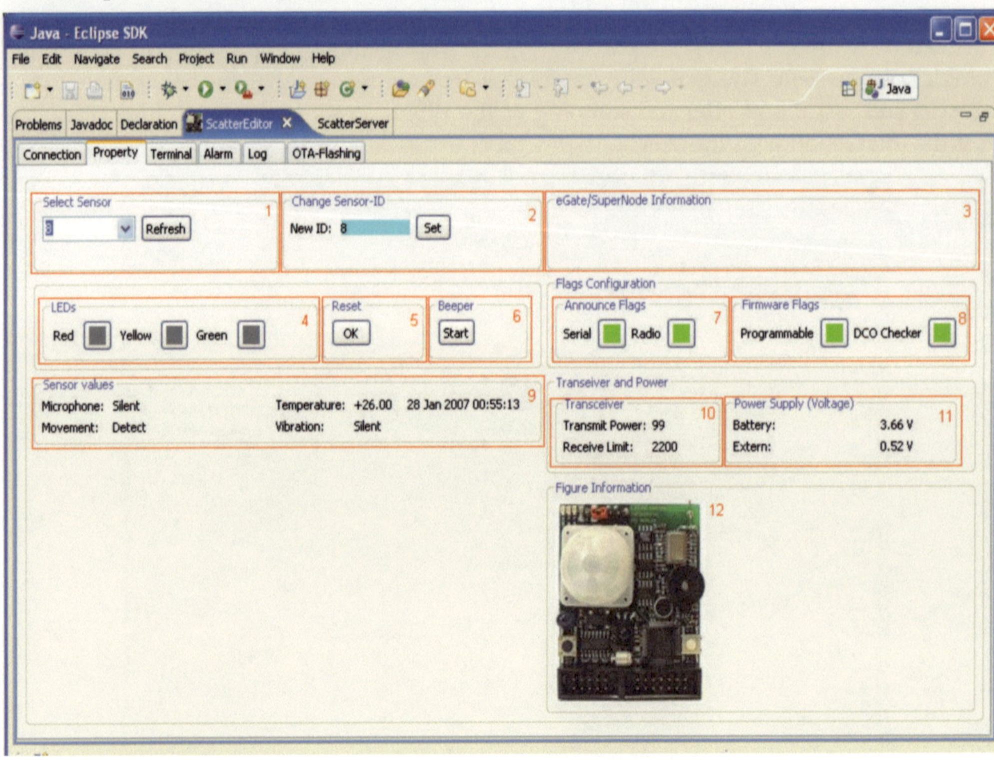

Fig. 16. Property Tabfolder

4.3. Terminal

The terminal offers an easy approach to configure and control the sensor boards through the eGate (see in fig. 17 a screenshot of our Terminal View). This is achieved by the input of terminal commands, which have a specific, but easy, format. In so doing the user can interactively operate the sensor boards. The following example demonstrates how terminal commands look and how they are used: @21 stp 99. The ID of the addressed sensor board always follows the @ character. If the @, and in so being also the ID, is missing, then the command refers to the eGate. After this the instruction follows. stp stands for set transmission power. Certain commands expect parameters like the command in the example above. In this case 99 stands for the transmission power.
If the commands are sent over the eGate, then they are sent in the form of a text with the help of Javax.comm library through the COM port to the eGate. The received string is then parsed by a specific parsing module in the eGate and interpreted. After this the interpreted string is processed by creating a package, which corresponds to the command, and sending it over the Air to the sensor board. The functionality of every terminal command is implemented by a C macro on the sensor's C level. With this one can flexibly define individual terminal commands and have them carried out by the corresponding implementation on the C level. This eases the conducting of experiments, as well as testing and debugging of newly implemented functions. The top output window (1) in Figure 24 shows the response of the queried sensor board. When the first letter of a command is pressed a list of commands appears above the command line (4) with the same starting letter and these commands are taken on in the command line when they are clicked on.

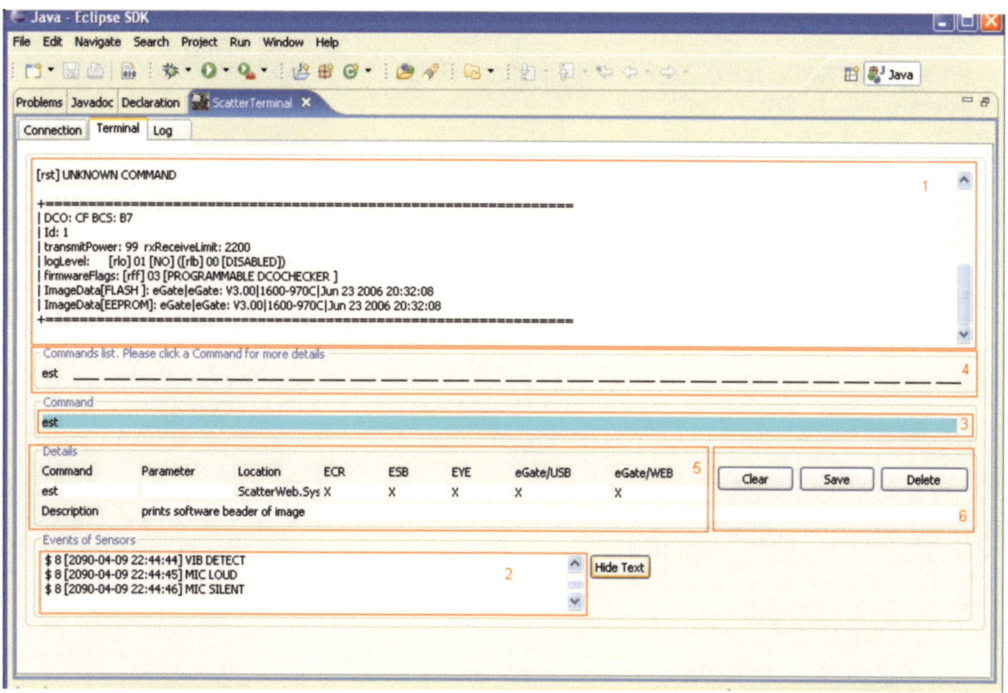

Fig. 17. Terminal Tabfolder

As an assistance the meaning and, where appropriate, the parameters of a clicked on command are displayed below the command line (5).

4.4. Over The Air Flashing

Mass flashing over the eGate is a little more complex when compared to serial flashing. First of all a serial connection to the eGate via Java COM Ports is made. For this task we use the Javax.comn package. Through this the software's binary image (Hex file) is loaded line for line into the eGate's EEPROM. Next the image is sent to all target nodes and at the same time errors, which have occurred, are listened for on the serial connection to the eGate. If necessary this will be announced by the respective dialog box. Another challenge lies in providing the user with the clear and easy interaction possibility with this process, which would improve the reliability and handling of the OTA flashing component in ScatterEditor. Figure 18 shows the GUI for OTA flashing as well as the of interaction with the user after the selection of the Hex file in the relevant folder. As shown in the Connection Tabfolder when the refresh button is pressed, all sensors within range of the eGate are determined and the IDs of the sensors are shown in the corresponding window. Scanning the WSN at the beginning has the effect that only live (non defect) sensor boards come into question for the OTA flashing process. The selected Hex file (1) is loaded into the eGate's EEPROM and the progression of this step is shown to the user by the progress bar (2). During the loading process the eGate sends its respective messages, which are shown in the window (4). When the loading process has been completed, the user can insert the IDs of the senor boards, which should be flashed (3).Thus it is also possible to select several sensors by inserting their IDs and to flash these at the same time with the same Hex file.

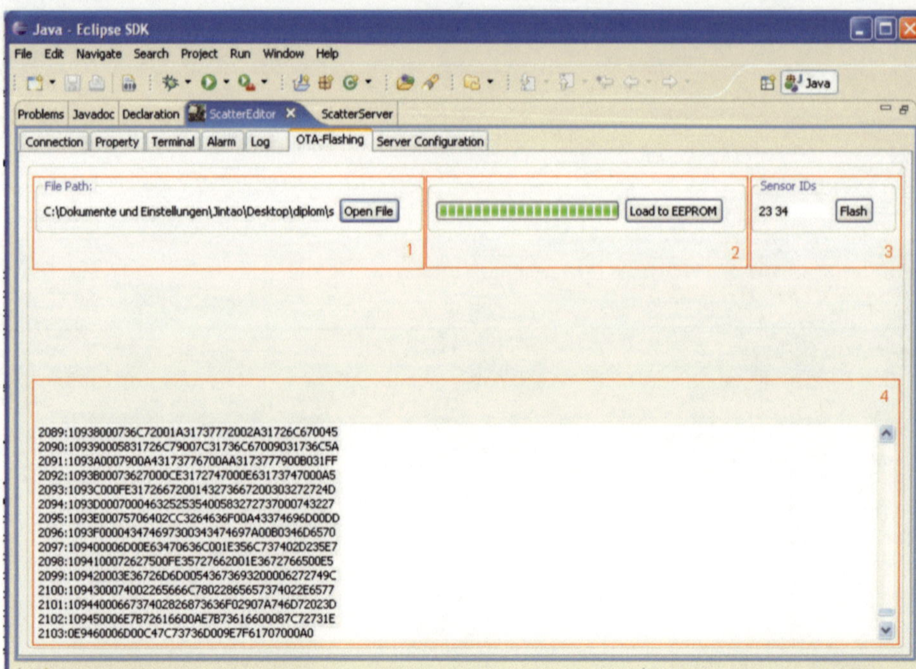

Fig. 18. OTA Flashing Tabfolder

The flashing process begins as soon as the Flash Sensors button is pressed (3). Alternatively one can also flash the eGate by typing "egate".

4.5. Internet Integration

Sensor networks are often deployed in areas, to which people normally have only a limited access, for instance a nature reserve or areas with an extreme climate etc. It stands therefore to reason to connect the management Plug-in with the internet, in order to offer access to Plug-ins's services and features from any, one or more, remote computers (clients). In this case there would not be an eGate connected to these computers (clients). To solve this problem the classical client/server approach was followed by using RMI (Remote Method Invocation, RMI) from Java (see Figure 19). We implemented an eGate server, which runs on the computer, to which the eGate is connected. This computer takes on the role of a server. The Server possesses an interface, which contains the methods, which are available to all clients. Only methods, which are defined on the server, are available to the Client.
The remote function's security is a vital issue. If one wishes to extend the remote option further, then it is important that the client's access rights are clearly defined. That is why the (server) Management Plug-in provides a generated public key during the first program start. The administrator is advised to change the key. Clients can not use old keys to access the server after the key has been changed. The client (user) must be contacted, in order to find out the new key. The procedure, with which the services of the server can be accessed, is, from the point of view of the client, as following: The first step in connecting with the server is the input of the server IP and key. Access to the server will be denied without the correct key. The key, as mentioned afore, can only be changed on the server side. The second security feature is the IP address list, which was set up on the server. From the server this list can be changed, enlarged or deleted at any time.

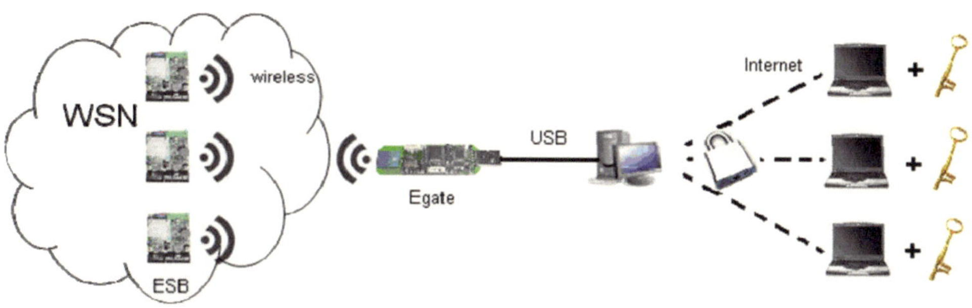

Fig. 19. Server Configuration

5. Conclusions: Putting It All Together

We presented ScatterClipse a model-driven Eclipse-based toolchain for developing, testing and managing Wireless Sensor Networks. The high degree of automation accelerates the development and testing of applications, which are already running on sensor nodes. Furthermore substitutability and reusability of the software artefacts are increased, because the artefacts, alongside the automated code generation, are represented by their respective models. Both increase the development process's productivity. The model driven code generation is used to furthermore generate a largely tailor made code, so that only the required amount of code is generated for the sensor node's intended roll. Thus the scarce memory space is not only optimized, but also unnecessary calculating and energy intensive software modules are avoided. The decreased portion of manually written code also reduces the possibility of a programmer's careless mistakes. However if the same code had been written manually, then a bug would be more probable. Such a bug results in the test case being defect, which is highly undesirable. This is why the use of a model-driven test environment gives a certain robustness against bugs made during the development of the test case. The model validation also makes a large contribution towards robustness by discovering certain bugs early on, which, if manually implemented, would only be discovered very late in the process.

Hence, several tasks of implementing an a test case and detecting a bug are delegated to the code generator. This is beneficial because these tasks are complex and time-consuming. Rather than performing these tasks himself, the user who tests a WSN application can concentrate on more important matters: Regarding the implementation that is the design of the test scenario; in case of the detection of a bug, that is the decision on an appropriate refinement of the test case to verify a hypothesis. A contribution that could be of general interest is our approach to incorporate the test results into formal models in the context of the Model-Driven paradigm. In so doing models are enhanced with the results of the test process, a method which is practical in other domains as well.

Apart from the interconnection between IP and ScatterClipse, another focus of the tool-suit lies with the aspect of human-computer interfaces for WSN. ScatterClipse provides the opportunity to manage and monitor different characteristics and properties of WSN illustratively and interactively. Since the tool-chain is based on Eclipse, it offers a plug-in oriented architecture and is comprised of free open source components. The tool's plug-in oriented architecture increases the adaptability for the end user and eases the updating of components. Furthermore the open architecture simplifies the tool's expansion, which increases the system's level of interoperability and flexibility.

Thus ScatterClipse is comprised of many tools for the development and operation of WSN applications, which offer a wide spectrum of functionality. This functionality can be used with the help of wizards, editors, views and menu items. However these can only be accessed from many different locations within Eclipse. Hence the user has been missing an overview of the total functionality at his disposal. In order to give the user this overview and a chance to directly access the functionality we developed an Eclipse view called ScatterClipse Assembly Line, which allows the access of all of ScatterClipse's functionality from one central location (see Figure 20).

Development: The Development stage allows access to all of ScatterFactory2's functions. With the first step a wizard is opened, which creates a model file or opens an already existing model file, which then can be used for modelling. The next step activates the code generation. First a project is chosen, in which code should be generated, and then the code generation is activated as pertaining to the model file chosen during the first step.

Testing: The Testing stage allows access to all functions of Visual ScatterUnit and ScatterUnit. Similar to the last stage the first two steps revolve around creating and editing a model file and the generation of test case code. During the third step a portion of test case code (code that will be executed on a sensor node) can be chosen, compiled and then installed onto a sensor node. During the final step, after all portions of test case code have been installed onto their respective sensor nodes, the test case can be run and the newly created resolution minutes loaded, so that the test results can be visualised in the test case model.

Deployment: The Development stage allows the application's installation and flashing onto the sensor nodes, not for testing purposes, but for actual service. This stage represents the transition between application development and application operation. Furthermore it has been taken into account that applications can be comprised of different parts. These application parts were modelled within the Development stage with the help of ScatterFactory2 and can be individually selected during this stage.

Troubleshooting and Configuration: The Sensor Network can be depicted by using the proper wizards and opening the respective file. Furthermore views supplied by Plugins regarding WSN Management and Monitoring can be opened directly. One is for instance the Terminal-View, which allows Configuration Commands to be sent directly to the sensor nodes.

Resulting from the collaboration between the several frameworks the user can, for example conduct model-driven software testing and development for the sensors with ScatterFactory2 and Visual ScatterUnit, while concurrently he can configure, control and carry out OTA software updates of the sensors with the support of the Management Plug-in and that not only locally but also remotely via the internet.

Overall the ScatterClipse Assembly Line represents the power of the tool chain, gives the user an overview of the available functionalities and facilitates the access of them. Furthermore the ease of access motivates using all tools from ScatterClipse in symbioses. This open architecture also eases the appropriate enhancement of the platform in response to newly arisen questions regarding WSN. A screen-cast of ScatterClipse can be found under (ScatterClipse).

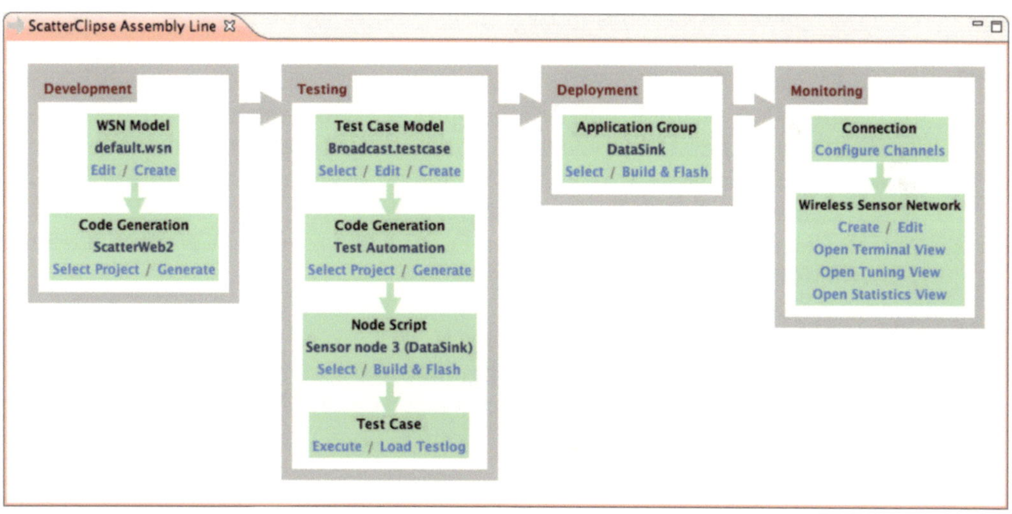

Fig. 20. The ScatterClipse Assembly Line

6. References

Agans, D. J. (2002). Debugging: The 9 Indispensable Rules for Finding Even the Most Elusive Software and Hardware Problems, Amacom, ISBN 0-8144-7168-4, New York.

Akyildiz, I. F.; Su, W.; Sankarasubramaniam, Y. & Cayirci, E. (2002). Wireless sensor networks: a Survey. Computer Networks, Vol. 38 No. 4 (2002), pp. 393–422

Al Saad, M., Hentrich, B. & Schiller, J. (2007a). ScatterFactory: An Architecture Centric Framework for Wireless Sensor Networks, Proceedings of the International Conference on New Technologies, Mobility and Security, pp. 12-31, ISBN 978-1-4020-6269-8, May 2007, Paris, Springer, Netherlands

Al Saad, M., Ding, J. & Schiller, J. (2007b). ScatterEditor: An Eclipse Based Tool for Programming, Testing and Managing Wireless Sensor Networks, Proceedings of the International Conference on Sensor Technologies and Applications, pp. 441-450, ISBN 978-0-7695-2988-2, October 2007, Valencia, Spain, IEEE CS Press

Al Saad, M.; Kamenzky, N. & Schiller, J. (2008a). Visual ScatterUnit: A Visual Model Driven Testing Framework of Wireless Sensor Networks Applications, Proceedings of ACM/IEEE 11th International Conference on Model Driven Engineering Languages and Systems, pp. 751-765, ISBN 978-3-540-87874-2, September/October 2008, Toulouse, France, LNCS Springer

Al Saad, M.; Fehr, E.; Kamenzky, N.; & Schiller, J. (2008b). ScatterClipse: A Model-Driven Tool-Chain for Developing, Testing, and Prototyping Wireless Sensor Networks, Proceedings of 6th IEEE International Symposium on Parallel and Distributed Processing and Applications, pp. 871-885, ISBN 978-0-7695-3471-8, Sydney, Australia, IEEE CS Press

Blumenthal, J.; Handy, M. & Timmermann D. (2004). Senets - test and validation environment for applications in large-scale wireless sensor networks, Proceedings of the 2nd IEEE Int. Con. on Industrial Informatics, pp. 69-73, ISBN 0-7803-8513-6, Berlin, Germany, June 2004, IEEE CS Press

Cunha, J. C.; Loureno J. & Duarte V. (2001). Debugging of parallel and distributed programs, In: Parallel program development for cluster computing: methodology, tools and integrated environments, Cunha, J.C.; Kacsuk, P. & Winter, S. C. (Eds.) pp. 97-129, Nova Science Pub. ISBN 978-1560728658, New York

Eisenecker U. & Czarnecki, K. (2000). Generative Programming. Addison-Wesley Longman, ISBN 978-0201309775, Amsterdam

GMF, http://www.eclipse.org/gmf

oAW, http://www.openarchitectureware.org

Rafiq O. & Cacciari, L. (2003). Coordination algorithm for distributed testing. Journal of Supercomputing, Vol. 24 , No. 2 (February 2003), pp. 203-211, ISSN 0920-8542

ScatterClipse, http://page.mi.fu-berlin.de/saad/ScatterClipse/video.htm

ScatterWeb, http://scatterweb.mi.fu-berlin.de

Remote Invocation Method, http://java.sun.com/javase/technologies/core/basic//rmi/index.jsp

Schiller, J.; Liers, A. & H. Ritter (2005). ScatterWeb: A wireless Sensornet Platform for Research and Teaching.Computer Communications, Vol. 28 (2005) pp. 1545-1551

Stahl, T.; Voelter M. & Czarnecki, K. (2006). Model-Driven Software Development: Technology, Engineering, Management, Wiley, ISBN 978-0470025703, Hoboken, New Jersey, USA

Ulrich, A. W.; Zimmerer, P. & Chrobok-Diening G. (1999). Test architectures for testing distributed systems, Proceedings of the 12th Int. Software Quality Week, pp. 24-26, San Jose, California, USA, May 1999

Xu S. & Rajlich, V. (2004). Cognitive process during program debugging, Proceedings of the 3rd IEEE Int. Conference on Cognitive Informatics, pp. 176-182, ISBN 0-7695-2190-8,Victoria, Canada, August 2004, IEEE Computer Society, Washington, DC, USA

5

A Survey of Low Duty Cycle MAC Protocols in Wireless Sensor Networks

M. Riduan Ahmad[1], Eryk Dutkiewicz[2] and Xiaojing Huang[3]
[1]*Universiti Teknikal Malaysia Melaka,* [2]*Macquarie University,* [3]*CSIRO ICT Centre*
[1]*Malaysia,* [2,3]*Australia*

1. Introduction

This chapter examines various important low duty cycle MAC protocols and the two most important MAC protocols designed specifically for cooperative Multiple-Input Multiple-Output (MIMO) transmission. In most cases, the low duty cycle MAC protocols trade off latency for energy efficient operation. Also, we can observe later that asynchronous MAC protocols are more scalable than synchronous MAC protocols.

On the one hand, when sensor nodes join or leave a group or a cluster, the MAC needs to re-synchronise the network over and over in such protocols as LEACH and S-MAC. Frequent re-synchronisation can lead to higher energy consumption. The situation becomes more complex when global synchronisation is required instead of local synchronisation. Thus a balance must be made between frequent synchronisation and scalability in synchronous MAC protocol design. On the other hand, in some cases with asynchronous MAC, the higher scalability comes at the cost of higher transmission energy due to the implementation of a long preamble and overhearing in such protocols as RF Wake-up and B-MAC. However, the burden of long preamble transmission is reduced gradually by the introduction of short packet techniques such in SpeckMAC and X-MAC. Moreover, it is important to note that little attention has been paid to increasing the link reliability in SISO systems. The only mechanism used is the ACK packet feedback in protocols such IEEE 802.15.4 MAC and WiseMAC.

The MIMO-LEACH and $CMAC_{ON}$ protocols provide measures to increase link reliability and at the same time reduce transmission power by exploiting spatial diversity gain. On the one hand, the MIMO-LEACH protocol employs a duty cycle mechanism through TDMA time slots assignments which reduces the total energy consumption. Furthermore, multi-hop communication between cluster heads is introduced to replace the direct communication which reduces further the total energy consumption. Also, collisions can be avoided with the distinct time slot assignment to each sensor node. The benefits come at the cost of higher latency (multi-hop communication). In addition, the scalability issue is not addressed at all.

$CMAC_{ON}$ is more scalable and does not require pre-selection of cooperative nodes. $CMAC_{ON}$ does not suffer from tight synchronisation and overhead of cluster formation. Also, collision avoidance is provided through RTS-CTS signalling. Moreover, an ACK mechanism is used as a double measure of link reliability. However, we note that all the sensor nodes are always on which makes the issues of idle listening and overhearing still need to be addressed. The $CMAC_{ON}$ protocol should deploy a duty cycle mechanism to reduce further the total energy consumption. Also, circuit energy must be included to get a better picture of the overall energy usage in the network.

The comparative study in this chapter provides a basis for further study to design an improved version of the $CMAC_{ON}$ protocol which employs a low duty cycle mechanism in cooperative MIMO communication. The improved MAC will be evaluated with a set of cooperative MIMO systems in terms of energy efficient operation and its trade-off relationship with packet latency.

The rest of the chapter is organized as follows. The concept of a low duty cycle is introduced in Section 2 to provide a basis of energy efficient MAC operation. We examine state-of-the-art duty cycle MAC protocols in Sections 3 and 4. We classify these protocols into synchronous and asynchronous. In Section 5, we explore existing MAC protocols designed specifically for cooperative Multiple-Input Multiple-Output (MIMO) transmissions. Finally the chapter is concluded in Section 6.

2. Low Duty Cycle Concepts

The basic idea of low duty cycle protocols is to reduce the time a node is idle or spends overhearing an unnecessary activity by putting the node in the sleep state. The most ideal condition of low duty cycle protocols is when a node is a sleep most of the time and wakes up only when to transmit or receive packets. In the literature, the concept of a low duty cycle is represented as a periodic wake-up scheme. A node wakes up periodically to transmit or receive packets from other nodes. Usually after a node wakes up, it listens to the channel for any activity before transmitting or receiving packets. If no packet is to be transmitted or received, the node returns to the sleep state. A whole cycle consisting of a sleep period and a listening period is called a sleep/wake-up period and is depicted in Figure 1.

Duty cycle is measured as the ratio of the listening period length to the wake-up period length which gives an indicator of how long a node spends in the listening period. A small duty cycle means that a node is asleep most of the time in order to avoid idle listening and overhearing. However, a balanced duty cycle size must be achieved in order to avoid higher latency and higher transient energy due to start-up costs.

There are various low duty cycle protocols proposed for WSNs which differ in aspects of synchronisation, the number of channels required, transmitter- or receiver-initiated operation etc. (Karl & Willig, 2007). We categorise the low duty cycle protocols into two major classes: namely synchronous and asynchronous schemes. The concept of synchronisation is related with data exchanges in WSNs (Kuorilehto et al., 2007). In asynchronous schemes, there are two basic approaches, namely transmitter-initiated and receiver-initiated. Using a transmitter-initiated approach, a node sends frequent request packets (preamble, control or even data packet themselves) until one of them "hits" the listening period of the destination node. On the other hand, the receiver-initiated approach is applicable when a node sends frequent packets (preamble, control, acknowledgment) to inform the neighbouring nodes about the willingness of the node to receive packets. The former approach puts the energy cost on the transmitter while the latter moves the cost to the receiver.

Another variation of low duty cycle protocols is a synchronous scheme where all the nodes in a group or cluster have the same wake-up phase. Usually each node sends frequent beacon frames to inform its neighbours about its wake-up cycle schedule and other information such as pending packets to be transmitted, etc. Thus a node schedules its transmission and reception time from the information obtained from the beacon frames. In another approach, a node becomes a group or cluster head and controls the data communications while maintaining the synchronisation between the nodes in the group or cluster. The former approach is more applicable for a distributed or flat topology while the latter is more applicable for a clustered or centralised topology. However, in both approaches, tight time synchronisation requires frequent resynchronisation with neighbouring nodes consuming a significant amount of energy (Karl & Willig, 2007; Kuorilehto et al., 2007).

In the following sections, we examine both synchronous and asynchronous low duty cycle protocols and compare both types of protocols in terms of four major design requirements, namely energy efficiency, latency, scalability and reliability.

3. Synchronous Low Duty Cycle MAC Protocols

Synchronised low duty cycle MAC protocols are typically equipped with predetermined periodic wake-up schedules for data exchanges which consist of a sleep period T_{sleep} and an active period, T_{active} repeated at T_{wakeup_period} intervals (Kuorilehto et al., 2007). A typical operation of synchronised low duty cycle MAC protocols is shown in Figure 2 where the synchronisation is achieved by means of frequent beacon frames transmissions. A node broadcasts its beacon frames once it enters the active period in order to share its current schedule and status information with its neighbouring nodes. This way, all the nodes can learn their neighbour's schedules and use this knowledge for data communication.

Consider a case when a node has a data packet to be transmitted. The node wakes up at the time of the active period of the destination node and then transmits its data packet. Clearly, we can observe that the operation of data transmission can be done in such a way due to the advanced timing knowledge of the destination node which was obtained from frequent beacon frames transmissions.

Moreover, synchronisation is typically maintained only within a small group or cluster due to the difficulty of global synchronisation in a large scale WSN deployment and also to ensure high scalability. In the following sub-sections, we examine the most important synchronous low duty cycle MAC protocols proposed in the literature which relate closely with the chapter direction.

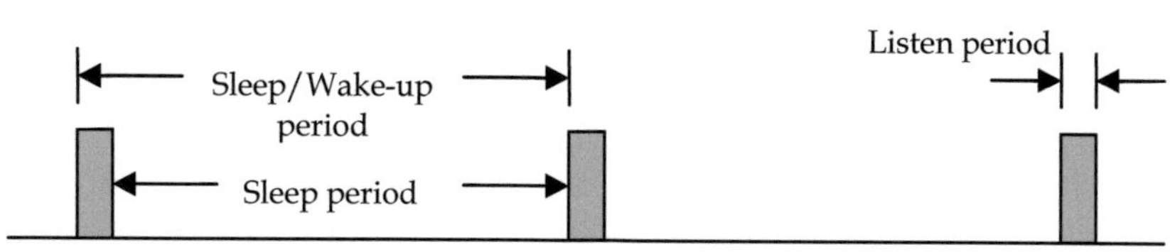

Fig. 1. A periodic wake-up scheme.

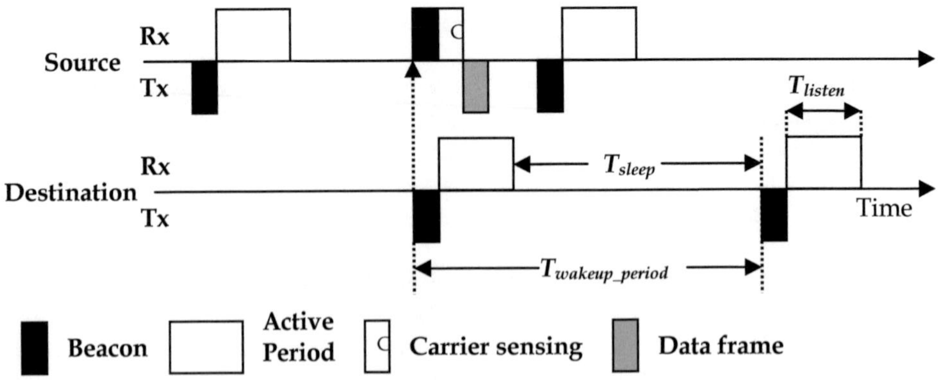

Fig. 2. A synchronous periodic wake-up scheme.

3.1 Power Aware Clustered TDMA (PACT)

Power Aware Clustered Time Division Multiple Access or PACT protocol (Pei & Chien, 2001) was proposed in 2001 for networks with a clustered multi-hop topology. PACT utilises the concept of passive clustering (Gerla et al., 2000) where nodes are allowed to take turns as the communication backbone.

Basically there are three types of nodes in a cluster, namely a cluster head, inter-cluster gateways and ordinary nodes. Gateway nodes are used to exchange traffic between clusters. A simple selection algorithm is used to select the gateway nodes in a cluster which is based on a criterion where a node with the highest number of distinct cluster heads is selected (Kuorilehto et al., 2007). In order to reduce energy consumption within a cluster, the role between cluster heads and gateway nodes is rotated. Furthermore, the duty cycle of each node is adapted to the traffic conditions in the network where the radios are turned off during inactive periods.

3.2 Low-Energy Adaptive Clustering Hierarchy (LEACH)

Low-Energy Adaptive Clustering Hierarchy or LEACH (Heinzelman et al., 2002) is a Time Division Multiple Access (TDMA-based) MAC protocol with clustering features. A network is formed as a star topology in two hierarchical levels as shown in Figure 3. A cluster consists of one cluster head and a number of ordinary nodes. All the ordinary nodes communicate with the cluster head directly. On the other hand, there is a single base station which communicates with all the cluster heads. Direct communication with high transmission power is used in order to ensure the cluster heads can reach the base station.

The LEACH protocol is organised in rounds and each round is subdivided into a setup phase and a steady-state phase. The setup phase begins with the self selection of nodes to become cluster heads. After a node properly sets up as a cluster head, it contends for the channel using a Carrier Sense Multiple Access (CSMA) mechanism and then broadcasts an advertisement packet to its neighbours if the channel is idle. Whenever an ordinary node receives an advertisement packet and in the case of multiple advertisement packets, the node selects a cluster head based on the received signal strength. Next, it contends for the channel using CSMA and sends back an acknowledgment to the selected cluster head in order to join the cluster. Immediately, the cluster head broadcasts a TDMA schedule to its cluster's members. The cluster is formed completely when all the cluster members are synchronised to the TDMA schedule. The cluster head creates and maintains the TDMA schedule.

The LEACH protocol implements two strategies to ensure energy efficient operation. The first strategy is to shift the total burden of energy consumption of a single cluster head by rotating the assignment of the cluster head to the other members in the cluster. The aim behind this strategy is to distribute evenly the energy usage between the members of the cluster. The second strategy is to switch the ordinary nodes in a cluster into the sleep mode whenever they enter inactive TDMA slots. In this way, we actually create a duty cycle mechanism through the implementation of an active and inactive TDMA time slots schedule. However, high transmission power during direct communication between cluster heads and the base station may dominate the total energy consumption in the network. Furthermore, the fixed clustering structure and the need for global synchronisation make the network not scalable whenever nodes join or leave the network. The condition becomes worse when we consider mobile nodes.

3.3 Self-Organizing Slot Allocation (SRSA)

The Self-Organising Slot Allocation or SRSA protocol (Wu & Biswas, 2005) was proposed to improve the LEACH MAC protocol in terms of energy efficiency and network scalability. The SRSA protocol is a TDMA-based MAC and has a similar network topology as LEACH. The strategy to increase energy efficiency is by utilising multiple base stations instead of only one base station as in the LEACH architecture. Thus, cluster heads can communicate directly with the nearest base station which reduces transmission energy significantly.

Moreover, in order to increase network scalability, SRSA provides local synchronisation where each cluster maintains its own local TDMA MAC frame. The main idea is to initiate communication with a random initial TDMA allocation and then adaptively change the slot allocation schedule locally based on feedback derived from collisions experienced by the local nodes within a cluster (Kuorilehto et al., 2007). Therefore the scalability that is achieved for large networks depends only on local synchronisation within a cluster. However, frequent local synchronisation may consume a significant amount of energy and may dominate the total energy consumption of the network.

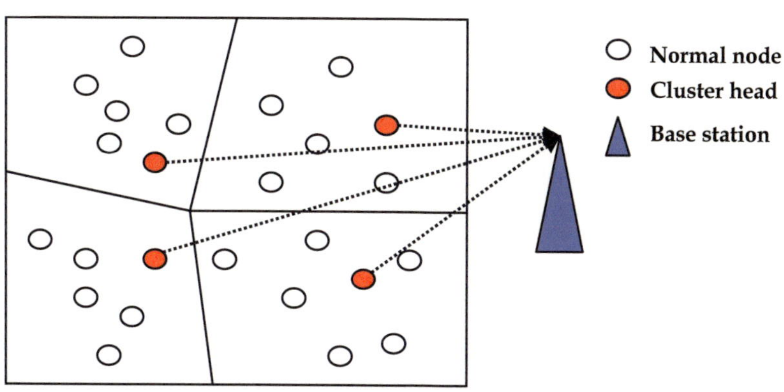

Fig. 3. Clustered LEACH MAC architecture.

3.4 Sensor-MAC (S-MAC)

S-MAC or Sensor MAC (Heidemann et al., 2002) was introduced and uses periodic sleep with virtual cluster features as shown in Figure 4. Basically a network is formed as a flat single-hop topology and S-MAC utilises only one frequency channel for communication.
The active period is fixed at 115 ms and the wake-up period can take up to hundreds of milliseconds. Thus the sleep period is adjustable. Within a cluster, all the nodes are synchronised such that all the nodes can wake up at the same time. The active period is divided into three phases, SYNC, RTS and CTS. Each phase is divided into time slots and each node uses the CSMA mechanism with random back-off to send its SYNC, RTS and CTS packets to its neighbours and the intended receiver. Also, each node shares and learns the sleep schedule with/from its neighbours. After the SYNC phase, any node that wants to transmit a data packet needs to contend for the channel.
A node listens to the channel and receives an RTS or CTS packet and if it is not the target receiver, it extracts and learns the duration of the data transmission from Network Allocation Vector (NAV), and then it enters the sleep mode. Moreover a node can perform both transmission and reception during the RTS and CTS phases.
The duty cycle mechanism in S-MAC leads to higher latency because a transmitter needs to wait for the next cycle to send its data. In order to reduce the latency, an improved S-MAC was introduced (Heidemann et al., 2004) which adopts an adaptive listening mechanism where nodes with NAV information wake up around the time when data transmission is expected to be finished and the nodes wait for a short time listening for any incoming packets. By introducing this method, the latency is cut in half. However, a significant amount of energy is still wasted when the active part remains idle due to no activity or due to overhearing an unnecessary activity in the network.

3.5 Timeout-MAC (T-MAC)

The T-MAC protocol (Dam & Langendoen, 2003) is a variation of SMAC with an adaptive listening mechanism. The main idea is to adjust or shorten the active period according to the traffic conditions in the network. Thus a node does not need to remain idle for the remaining duration of the active period after the SYNC phase, when there is no activity in the network. Basically, the network is formed as a flat single-hop topology and T-MAC utilises only one frequency channel for communication.
After the CTS phase and each received frame, a node waits for a short period of time which defines a timeout window. If no activity is detected, after the timeout the node enters the sleep mode. As observed in (Dam & Langendoen, 2003), T-MAC uses one-fifth of the power consumption of S-MAC. However, this method increases the latency, although the energy is reduced dramatically. Moreover T-MAC is not suitable for high load networks when we consider a lower latency requirement and also a short active period reduces the ability of T-MAC to adapt to changing network conditions.

3.6 Traffic-Adaptive Medium Access (TRAMA)

The Traffic-Adaptive Medium Access or TRAMA protocol (Rajendran et al., 2003) is a TDMA-based MAC with a flat-based network topology. The basic operation of the TRAMA protocol is to create and maintain a TDMA schedule for each node with its neighbouring nodes within the range of two hops from each node. Basically, sensor nodes share a list of node identifiers from a two-hop neighbourhood and then they exchange their schedules. The strategy to provide energy efficient operation is by implementing a duty cycle mechanism where the node goes to sleep when it enters inactive time slots. The knowledge of active and inactive timeslots is provided during the exchange of the nodes schedules. Moreover, the active timeslots can be adjusted according to traffic patterns in the network thus providing an adaptive duty cycle mechanism. However, the latency gets higher as the load gets higher in the network.

3.7 DMAC

The DMAC protocol (Lu et al., 2004) was proposed with the objective to provide energy efficient operation with low latency requirements. The network for DMAC is structured as a tree-based data gathering architecture where each node is equipped with a different duty cycle schedule according to the level of deepness in the tree structure. Thus nodes at the same depth in the tree have the same duty cycle schedule. Consequently, the nodes at the lowest level have the longest sleep period. Channel access is performed through CSMA and DMAC utilises only one frequency channel for communication. The DMAC protocol is energy efficient for low load; however it suffers higher latency when the load gets higher due to congestion at intermediate nodes.

3.8 IEEE 802.15.4 MAC

The Institute of Electrical and Electronics Engineers (IEEE) released the 802.15.4 MAC standard (IEEE Standard, 2006) for wireless personal area networks (WPANs) equipped with a duty cycle mechanism where the size of active and inactive parts can be adjustable during the PAN formation. The IEEE 802.15.4 MAC combines both the schedule-based and contention-based protocols and supports two network topologies, star and peer-to-peer as shown in Figure 5.

Basically, there are two special types of peer-to-peer topology (Kohvakka et al., 2006). The first type is known as a cluster-tree network which has been used extensively in ZigBee (Zigbee Alliance, 2004). The other type is known as a mesh network which has been used extensively in IEEE 802.15 WPAN Task Group 5 (TG5) (IEEE Standard, 2008).

The standard defines two types of nodes namely the Full Function Device (FFD) and Reduced Function Device (RFD). The FFD node can operate with three different roles as a PAN coordinator, a coordinator and a device while RFD can operate only as a device. The devices must be associated with a coordinator in all network conditions. The multiple coordinators can either operate in a peer-to-peer topology or star topology with a coordinator becoming the PAN coordinator.

The star topology is more suitable for delay critical applications and small network coverage while the peer-to-peer topology is more applicable for large networks with multi-hop requirements at the cost of higher network latency. Furthermore, the standard defines two modes on how data exchanges should be done, namely, the beacon mode and the non-beacon mode. The beacon mode provides networks with synchronisation measures while the non-beacon mode provides the asynchronous features to networks.

The beacon mode of IEEE 802.15.4 MAC defines a superframe structure to organise the channel access and data exchanges. The superframe structure is shown in Figure 6 with two main periods; the active period and inactive period. The active period is divided into 16 time slots. Typically the beacon frame is transmitted in the first time slot and it is followed by two other parts, Contention Access Period (CAP) and Contention-Free Period (CFP) which utilise the remaining time slots. The CFP part is also known as Guaranteed Time Slots (GTS) and can utilise up to 7 time slots.

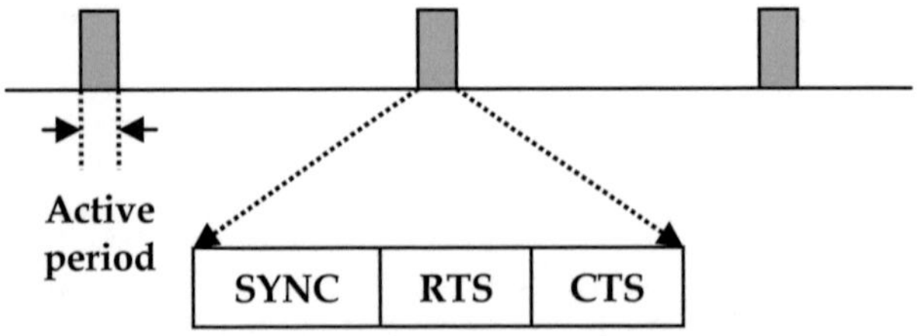

Fig. 4. S-MAC synchronous periodic wake-up scheme.

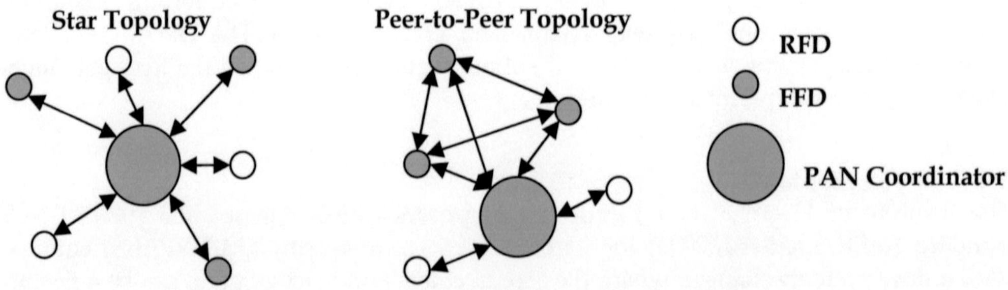

Fig. 5. Topology configurations supported by IEEE 802.15.4 standard.

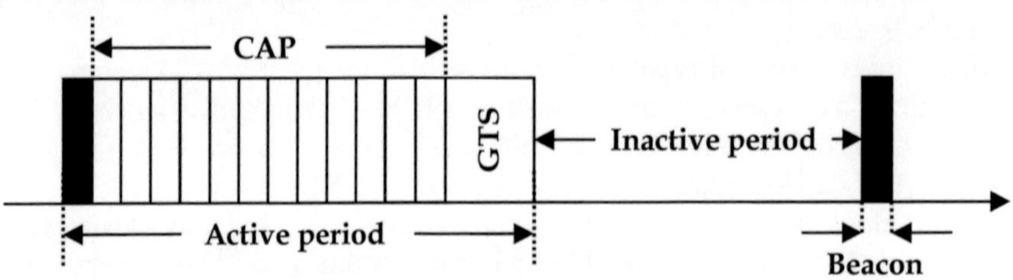

Fig. 6. Superframe structure in beaconed mode IEEE 802.15.4 MAC.

The length of the active and inactive periods as well as the length of a single time slot are configurable and traffic dependant. Data transmissions can occur either in CAP or GTS. In CAP, data communication is achieved by using slotted CSMA-CA while in GTS nodes are allocated fixed time slots for data communication.
The strategy to achieve energy efficient operations in IEEE 802.15.4 MAC is by putting the nodes to sleep during the inactive period and when there is neither data to be transmitted nor any data to be fetched from the coordinator. However, the burden of energy cost is put on the coordinator where the coordinator has to be active during the entire active period.

3.9 Zebra MAC (Z-MAC)

The Z-MAC (Rhee et al., 2005) protocol combines CSMA and TDMA advantages. The network is formed as a flat multi-hop topology. Nodes must be fixed in their locations. The setup phase is the most crucial part with neighbour discovery, local frame exchange of neighbours' lists and slots assignment. All the nodes are synchronised with a global time synchronisation feature. Each node is assigned a slot but it is not fixed. Any node can contend for the channel within any slot for data transmission but the assigned node will get the highest priority.

In a high contention situation, the slots assignment is enforced to reduce collisions. Any data transmission is preceded with a long preamble to increase the probability of hitting the receiver's active period. Z-MAC experiences high latency together with high transmission power for long preamble transmission. Also, all the nodes need to be fixed which limits the network scalability. If new nodes join the network, the setup phase needs to be repeated over and over.

4. Asynchronous Low Duty Cycle MAC Protocols

Unlike the synchronous case, asynchronous low duty cycle MAC protocols do not provide prior knowledge about the global or local timing information and schedules to the nodes in a network to assist with data communications. Thus the nodes do not need to remember the schedules of its neighbours which significantly reduce the usage of memory and energy cost due to schedule sharing between the nodes.

Asynchronous low duty cycle MAC provides a frequent channel sampling mechanism for detecting possible starting transmissions in the network. In the literature, the frequent channel sampling at the receiver is also known as a low power listening (LPL) mechanism. The concept of preamble packet transmission is used in order to hit the intended destination node. When the destination receives the preamble packet, it waits for the data to be transmitted. The transmission of a preamble packet is one of the examples of transmitter-initiated approach in asynchronous WSNs. However, the long preamble packet size contributes to higher transmission energy in the network. Other approaches such as receiver-initiated and redundant transmission of preamble packets are explored to reduce the burden on the transmitter. Furthermore, the very frequent channel sampling also can contribute to higher start-up costs where proper measures must be taken to ensure the optimal wake-up period is implemented.

In the following sub-sections, we examine the most important asynchronous low duty cycle MAC protocols proposed in the literature which relate closely with the chapter direction.

4.1 RF Wake-up Protocol

One of the earliest proposed preamble sampling protocols is the RF wake-up scheme (Hill & Culler, 2002). This protocol samples the channel every 4 seconds to check the channel activity. If it detects any activity, it waits for a short period of time for any incoming packets. At the sender side, the data is preceded with a long preamble with CSMA being performed. The size of the preamble packet must be at least the same as the wake-up period size in order to have a chance of hitting the receiver. This type of configuration has achieved a very low duty cycle, below 1% in a dense WSN with 800 nodes (Hill & Culler, 2002). However, this protocol is not suitable for latency-critical networks because of the overhead of long preamble packet transmission. Clearly, we can observe that latency is traded off with energy efficiency. Also transmission power gets higher when the size of the preamble packet gets longer, thus putting a constraint on the maximum length of the sleep period. Furthermore, the unintended nodes in the vicinity of the sender stay on for the remaining duration of the preamble packet transmission, resulting in the overhearing problem.

4.2 ALOHA with Preamble Sampling

Instead of using CSMA, ALOHA is used with preamble sampling in (El-Hoiydi, 2002a). An ACK packet is transmitted immediately after the data is received correctly. The protocol inherits the advantage of the RF wake-up protocol to reduce the idle listening cost and at the same time provides higher reliability. However, the protocol is not suitable for high contention networks and inherits the latency and overhearing problems from the RF wake-up protocol. Later the same authors improved the protocol by replacing the ALOHA scheme with CSMA and maintaining the ACK mechanism (El-Hoiydi, 2002b). The collision probability is reduced with higher reliability but still the latency and overhearing problems occur.

4.3 Wireless Sensor MAC (WiseMAC)

The Wireless Sensor MAC or WiseMAC protocol (El-Hoiydi et al., 2004) was proposed to reduce the burden of long preamble packet transmission at the sender side and to tackle the high collision probability in previous protocols. WiseMAC defines two types of nodes, the access point and the ordinary sensor nodes. All the ordinary sensor nodes must communicate only with the access point which basically forms a network with a star topology. WiseMAC utilises the same channel access method as the previous protocol where the ALOHA protocol is used before a preamble packet is transmitted. Unlike the previous protocol, only the access point can initiate data transmission which means that collisions can be avoided. Moreover, the access point learns the wake-up schedule of each sensor node where by knowing the schedule, the access point can make the preamble transmission time shorter. This knowledge is obtained from the ACK packet sent back by the sensor nodes after the data packet is received correctly. WiseMAC provides more energy efficient operation than the previous protocols but at the cost of low scalability due to the fixed star topology operation.

4.4 Asynchronous IEEE 802.15.4 MAC

In non-beacon mode, the IEEE 802.15.4 MAC standard defines a wake-up period or a sleep cycle for devices only and the coordinators are always on. Also no GTS mechanism is used which means that the asynchronous IEEE 802.15.4 MAC is a pure contention-based protocol. Data transmission is performed using an un-slotted CSMA-CA mechanism with a single CCA operation. No preamble sampling mechanism is deployed. Data is acknowledged immediately after the successful data reception to ensure reliability. The energy efficient operation is guaranteed for devices through a sleep cycle mechanism. As a comparison, most of the performance evaluation work on the IEEE 802.15.4 standard has suggested that the beacon MAC is more energy efficient than the non-beacon MAC (Kohvakka et al., 2006).

4.5 Berkeley MAC (B-MAC)

(Polastre et al., 2004) introduced B-MAC or Berkeley MAC. The protocol is a variant of CSMA with a preamble sampling mechanism. The preamble sampling is improved with a selective sampling method where only energy above the noise floor is considered as useful. This selective measure makes sure that the receiver is not wasting its energy just for an insignificant channel activity. The channel sampling interval is made adjustable at the receiver side when a significant activity is detected. If the channel is sensed busy and the energy is above the noise floor, the receiver turns on until the data packet is received or timeout occurs.

At the transmitter, CSMA is implemented before data and long preamble packets are transmitted. In order to ensure high reliability, an ACK mechanism can be used with the basic B-MAC operation. Furthermore, RTS-CTS can be implemented in high load networks to reduce the collision problem.

Figure 7 illustrates the basic operation of the B-MAC protocol. B-MAC defines the whole wake-up period of the LPL structure as a check interval, T_i. The check interval consists of two parts, the listen interval and the sleep interval. (Polastre et al., 2004) provides a framework for analysing the operations of B-MAC in a WSN. An analytical model for monitoring applications was developed where the B-MAC's parameters were calculated to optimise the application's overall power consumption. The impact of various application variables such as the check interval, duty cycle and sample rate were considered. Moreover, the authors considered a specific periodic monitoring application for a case of single cell analysis where the sensor data is streamed to a base station.

Although B-MAC is considered for a periodic monitoring application, the authors claim that the protocol is flexible to be realised efficiently with various kinds of applications. Furthermore, a Chipcon CC1000 transceiver was used as the hardware reference due to its low complexity when compared to other transceiver models, such as CC2420 and its primitive operations are given in (Polastre et al., 2004).

The energy model of a sensor node consists of five major consumers: transmitting energy E_{tx}, receiving energy E_{rx}, listening energy E_{listen}, sampling sensor data energy E_{sensor}, and energy of sleeping E_{sleep}. All the modelled energy components are defined in units of millijoules per second, or milliwatts. The total energy, E is given as:

$$E = E_{tx} + E_{rx} + E_{listen} + E_{sensor} + E_{sleep} \tag{1}$$

The energy of sampling sensor data is included in the model which is based on an application deployed by (Mainwaring et al., 2002). The related parameters are given in (Polastre et al., 2004). Each node takes 1100ms (T_{sensor}) to start its sensor, sample and collect data. If the data is sampled every T_s minutes, the sample rate can be given as:

$$r_s = \frac{1}{(T_s \times 60)} \tag{2}$$

The sample rate is chosen based on the application requirements and network conditions. The energy associated with sample data, E_{sensor} is given as:

$$\begin{aligned} T_d &= T_{sensor} \times r_s \\ E_{sensor} &= T_d \cdot c_{sensor} V \end{aligned} \tag{3}$$

where T_d is the frequency of sample data, c_{sensor} is the current consumption during the sample data and V is the supplied voltage.

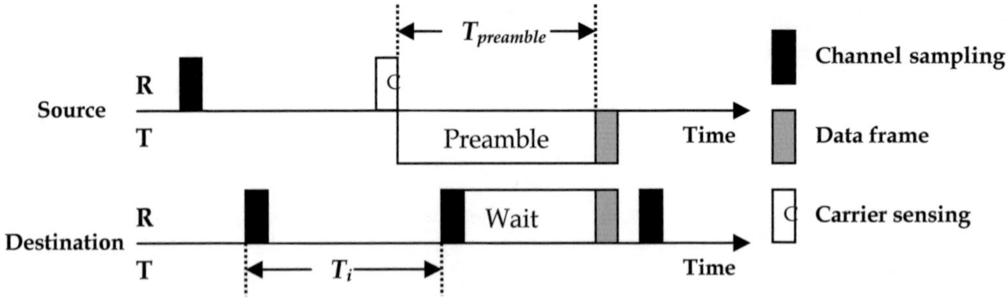

Fig. 7. Basic operation of unsynchronised Berkeley MAC.

The energy consumed during transmissions is simply the length of the preamble packet, $N_{preamble}$ and data packet, N_{data} times the rate the data packets are generated by the application and it is given as:

$$T_{tx} = r_s \times (N_{preamble} + N_{data}) \cdot T_{txb}$$
$$E_{tx} = T_{tx} \cdot c_{txb} V \tag{4}$$

where T_{tx} is the frequency of packet transmission, c_{txb} is the current consumption when transmitting 1 byte and T_{txb} is the time taken to transmit 1 byte. The receiving energy of a node is modelled as reception of packets from its n neighbours regardless of the packets' destinations. Thus the energy consumed during reception is given as:

$$T_{rx} \leq n \cdot r_s \times (N_{preamble} + N_{data}) \cdot T_{rxb}$$
$$E_{rx} = T_{rx} \cdot c_{rxb} V \tag{5}$$

where T_{rx} is the frequency of packet transmission, c_{rxb} is the current consumption when receiving 1 byte and T_{rxb} is the time taken to receive 1 byte. In order to make sure that the intended receiver receives the transmitted packet, a measure of reliability is implemented with the length of the preamble packet set to be equal or higher than the length of the check interval. Thus we have the constraint:

$$N_{preamble} \geq \left\lceil \frac{T_i}{T_{rxb}} \right\rceil \tag{6}$$

The power consumption of a single LPL CC100 radio sample was measured by the authors and the value is given as E_{sample} = 17.3 μJ. Thus the total energy spent listening to the channel can be defined as the energy of a single channel sample times the channel sample frequency:

$$E_{listen} \leq E_{sample} \times \frac{1}{T_i} \tag{7}$$

and the frequency of listening to the channel and the transient time are given as:

$$T_{listen} = \left(T_{rinit} + T_{ron} + T_{rx/tx} + T_{sr}\right) \times \frac{1}{T_i} \tag{8}$$

$$T_{transient} = T_{rinit} + T_{ron} + T_{rx/tx} \tag{9}$$

where T_{rinit} is the time taken to initialise the radio, T_{ron} is the time taken to turn on the radio and its oscillator, $T_{rx/tx}$ is the time taken to switch the radio to the receive mode and T_{sr} is the time taken to sample the channel. The sleep time is defined as the time remaining each second that is not consumed by other operations. Thus the total energy consumed during the sleep time is given as:

$$\begin{aligned} T_{sleep} &= 1 - T_{rx} - T_{tx} - T_d - T_{listen} \\ E_{sleep} &= T_{sleep} \cdot c_{sleep} V \end{aligned} \tag{10}$$

where c_{sleep} is the current consumption when a node is sleep B-MAC provides flexibility to the higher layer by allowing the important parameters to be adjusted, such as the sample rate and the check interval, based on the changing network conditions. However, some trade-off relationships must be considered before any changes take place. For example, increasing the sample rate actually increases the amount of traffic in the network. As a result, each node overhears more packets which leads to the overhearing problem. Moreover, lowering the check interval size can reduce the size of the preamble packet. On the one hand, the burden of long preamble packet transmission can be reduced. On the other hand, the radio is sampled more often which contributes to the increase of transient energy during the start-up period. Clearly, the trade-off relationship must be considered carefully before any changes to the parameters can be made.

4.6 Speck MAC (SpeckMAC)

SpeckMAC (Wong & Arvind, 2006) was introduced as a variation of the B-MAC protocol with the ideas of redundant transmission of short packets and an embedded destination address. The first idea is targeted to reduce the transmission energy and the second idea provides a measure of reducing the significant overhearing problem in heavy traffic conditions. Figure 8 illustrates the basic operation of the SpeckMAC protocol.

Basically there are 2 variants: SpeckMAC-Back-off (SpeckMAC-B) and SpeckMAC-Data (SpeckMAC-D). The first variant, SpeckMAC-B, sends a short wake-up frame preceded by carrier sensing with embedded target destination address and data transmission timing information. Any receiver that wakes up performs selective sampling and after that checks the address field of the received wake-up frame. If the address does not match, it goes to sleep immediately. In the case of matching, it sets its timer to wake up later in order to receive the data packet before going to sleep. The sender transmits the short wake-up frame till the moment the data packet is transmitted.

The problem with this scheme is that the sender wastes its transmission power by still sending the wake-up frames although the receiver has already received this frame. Although the burden at the transmitter is reduced and overhearing at the receiver is eliminated, SpeckMAC-B still inherits the excess latency problem. SpeckMAC-D, on the other hand, sends the data packet many times which is preceded by carrier sensing until one of the data packet hits the receiver. The method of retransmission of data packets reduces the energy at the receiver but still suffers from excess latency.

A comprehensive comparison study has been done (Wong & Arvind, 2007) between the SpeckMAC variants which is based on different traffic types in terms of energy efficient operation. The results demonstrated that SpeckMAC-D is more energy efficient than SpeckMAC-B when broadcast packets are transmitted. SpeckMAC-B, on the other hand, is more energy efficient when unicast packets are transmitted.

Later, the SpeckMAC Hybrid or SpeckMAC-H protocol (Wong & Arvind, 2007) was proposed combining the advantages of each of the SpeackMAC variants. SpeckMAC-H adopts an adaptive approach where the sender selects which SpeckMAC variant to be used depending on the current traffic type. In this way, the energy consumption can be reduced significantly but the excess latency problem is still not addressed.

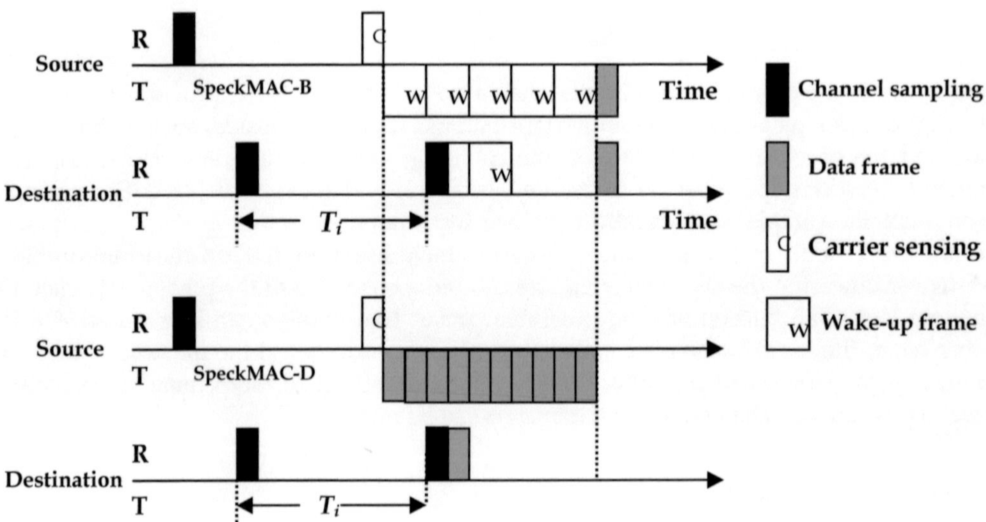

Fig. 8. Basic operation of unsynchronised SpeckMAC.

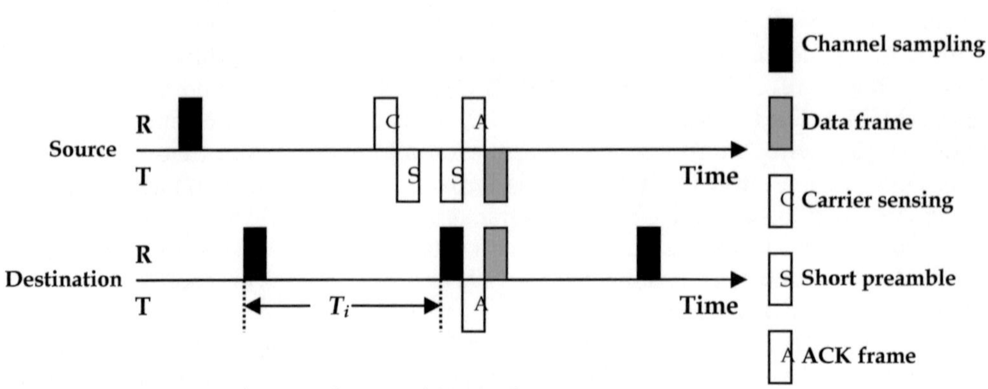

Fig. 9. Basic operation of unsynchronised X-MAC.

4.7 X-MAC

Further work by the X-MAC (Buettner et al., 2006) protocol proposed the use of a series of short preamble packets with the destination address embedded in the packet. Figure 9 illustrates the basic operation of the X-MAC protocol.

The idea of the ACK packet is used here but not after the data packet reception but, instead after the first preamble packet that hits the target receiver's active period. By doing that, the preamble packets transmission can be stopped and the data packet can be transmitted immediately. Also, the size of the preamble packet now can be made very short with redundant transmission of the same packet until the sender gets the ACK packet. Like in the previous protocol, CSMA is performed before the preamble packet is transmitted. After the data packet is received, the receiver waits for a short period to give a chance to any nodes that want to send packets.

The X-MAC protocol provides more energy efficient and lower latency operation by reducing the transmission energy and transmission period burdens, idle listening at the intended receiver and overhearing by the neighbouring nodes. One concern is that the gaps between the series of preamble packets transmission can be mistakenly understood by the other contending nodes as an idle channel and they would start to transmit their own preamble packets which can lead to collision. One solution is to ensure that the length of the gaps must be upper bounded by the length of the listening interval.

5. MAC Protocol for Cooperative MIMO Transmission

As already discussed, all the duty cycle MAC protocols were designed mainly to reduce the total energy consumption by reducing idle listening, overhearing and both transmission and reception energy consumption over a single link. We can observe that most of the protocols traded off latency for energy efficient operation. Also, some of them, such as the IEEE 802.15.4 MAC and the variants of the ALOHA with preamble sampling MAC protocols including CSMA and WiseMAC, provide certain measures to increase the reliability of WSNs with the feedback of the ACK packet. Furthermore, we observed that the asynchronous duty cycle MAC provides higher scalability than the synchronous duty cycle MAC.

To the best of our knowledge, little attention has been paid in the previous duty cycle MAC protocols to consider the impact of deep fading on the total energy consumption. As already discussed in the previous chapters, deep fading contributes to packet errors (if a portion of the packet is affected) or to packet loss (if the whole packet is totally lost). The consequences are severe with a higher retransmission rate and thus higher transmission and reception energy consumption. By utilising the collaborative nature of sensor nodes, the cooperative MIMO scheme provides a higher reliability link than the single link which significantly reduces the retransmission rate. Moreover, the cooperative MIMO scheme exploits the spatial diversity gain and reduces the transmission energy as the number of the transmitting nodes, M, gets higher.

5.1 MIMO-LEACH MAC

Perhaps among the first duty cycle MAC protocols introduced to accommodate cooperative MIMO transmission is the MIMO-LEACH protocol (Yuan et al., 2006) which is an improved version of the original LEACH MAC protocol (Heinzelmann et al., 2002). The cluster-based

MIMO-LEACH protocol is designed with multi-hop routing and incorporates a Space-Time Block Coding (STBC) scheme for inter-cluster communication. Figure 10 shows the architecture of the multi-hop MIMO-LEACH scheme.

In each cluster, a star topology is maintained with the cluster head managing the TDMA schedules for data transmissions. The selection of cooperative nodes is done by the cluster head within each cluster during the cluster formation phase. The selection is based on three major parameters: the remaining energy in the sensor nodes at the moment of measurement, the distance between the sensor nodes to the targeted cluster head and the distance between the sensor nodes and the current cluster head. The selection criterion is defined as the ratio of the remaining energy of a sensor node over the sum of communication energies for both distances. Thus a node with higher remaining energy and lower communication energy for both distances has a higher probability to be selected as one of the cooperative nodes.

When a cluster head has data packet to be transmitted, it broadcasts the data packet to the selected cooperative nodes. Then the cooperative nodes encode the data packet according to STBC and transmit the transmission sequence to the intended cluster head towards the sink. Clearly, in this way, the cost of high transmission power from a cluster head to the base station in original LEACH MAC can be reduced by using the multi-hop and cooperative MIMO transmission strategy. However, the excess latency and scalability issues are not addressed.

5.2 The Always On Cooperative MAC ($CMAC_{ON}$)

In 2007, a MAC with an always on transceiver or $CMAC_{ON}$ protocol was designed to accommodate cooperative MIMO transmission (Yang et al., 2007). Basically, the MAC is a variant of CSMA protocols with RTS-CTS signalling features. The RTS-CTS control packets are used as a measure to avoid collision due to hidden- and exposed-nodes during the cooperative transmission. Also an ACK packet is sent when the data packet is received correctly in order to guarantee reliable communication.

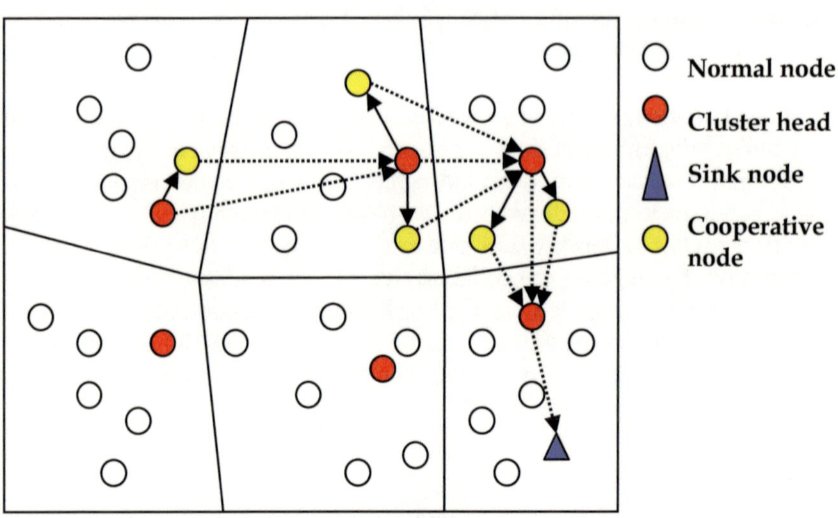

Fig. 10. Multi-hop clustered MIMO-LEACH MAC architecture.

Unlike MIMO-LEACH, the $CMAC_{ON}$ protocol does not provide pre-selection of cooperative nodes prior to data transmission. When a node has a data packet to be transmitted, the node starts to transmit an RTS packet to hit the intended destination. Once received the RTS packet, the destination broadcasts a packet with lower power to recruit its neighbours in order to cooperatively receive the data packet. The destination informs its neighbours about the estimated arrival time of the data packet. Following the broadcast packet, a CTS packet is sent to the source node. When the source node receives the CTS packet, it broadcasts the original data packet to its neighbours with lower power.

Any node within the vicinity of the source node which receives correctly the original data packet with the sending timer information automatically becomes a cooperative transmitting node. When the sending timer expires, all the M transmitting nodes send the data packet cooperatively to the N cooperatively receiving nodes. Each node in the receiving group receives the data packet and forwards it to the destination. To avoid collision, each receiving group performs CSMA with a random back-off before forwarding the data. The process of forwarding all the packets from the N-1 receiving nodes to the destination is denoted as a collection process.

The final decoding is done by the destination with a simple majority decision rule. The destination chooses the highest SNR among multiple received data packets. In case of a tie, the destination will take its own reception as the correct one. The basic operation of the MAC is shown in Figure 11. The algorithms of the $CMAC_{ON}$ protocol are presented in Algorithm 1 to Algorithm 5.

Performance evaluation of the $CMAC_{ON}$ protocol in terms of energy consumption and packet latency was done in (Yang et al., 2007). Performance of the $CMAC_{ON}$ protocol is compared to that of a SISO scheme. The SISO scheme employs RTS-CTS signalling prior to data transmission and feedback ACK to ensure reliability. Also the transceivers of the sensor nodes are always on. For simple notation, we denote the SISO scheme with such a MAC protocol as a SISO always on protocol or $SISO_{ON}$ protocol.

The energy model of a sensor node consists of two parts: successful and unsuccessful transmissions. The authors only consider transmission energy and neglect the impact of circuit energy on the MAC performance. The energy for an unsuccessful transmission attempt is given as:

$$E_u = E_{rts} + E_{Br} + E_{cts} + E_{Bs} + M \cdot E_{data} + (N-1) \cdot E_{col} \tag{11}$$

where E_{rts}, E_{cts}, E_{Bs}, E_{Br}, E_{data} and E_{col} are the energy consumption of RTS, CTS, broadcast packet at the transmitting side (BCASTdata), broadcast packet at the receiving side (BCASTrecv), DATA and collection energies. The energy for a successful transmission attempt is given as:

$$E_s = E_{rts} + E_{Br} + E_{cts} + E_{Bs} + M \cdot E_{data} + (N-1) \cdot E_{col} + E_{ack} \tag{12}$$

where E_{ack} is the energy consumption of ACK packet transmission. We can observe that the unsuccessful attempt occurs with the absence of the ACK packet. The total energy consumption is modelled as a function of the retransmission rate and it is given as:

$$E = \left(\frac{PER}{1 - PER}\right)E_u + E_s \tag{13}$$

where PER is the packet error rate of the cooperative MIMO system. Also the packet latency model consists of two parts: successful and unsuccessful transmission attempts. The duration of a successful transmission attempt is given as:

$$T_s = T_{rts} + T_{cts} + T_{Br} + T_{Bs} + T_{data} + T_{col} + T_{ack} \tag{14}$$

where T_{rts}, T_{cts}, T_{Br}, T_{Bs}, T_{data}, T_{col} and T_{ack} are the time required to send RTS, CTS, broadcast packet at the receiving side, broadcast packet at the transmitting side, DATA and ACK packets. The duration of an unsuccessful transmission attempt is given as:

$$T_u = T_{rts} + T_{cts} + T_{Br} + T_{Bs} + T_{data} + T_{col} + T_{wfack} \tag{15}$$

where T_{wfack} is the duration during which the sender waits for an ACK. The values used for the performance evaluation are given as T_{rts} = 0.353 ms, T_{cts} = 0.305 ms, T_{ack} = 0.32 ms, T_{data} = 6 ms, T_{wfack} = 70 ms, T_{Br} = 0.69 ms, T_{Bs} = 7.7 ms and T_{col} = 22.3 ms.

$CMAC_{ON}$ provides a less complex operation by eliminating the need to pre-select the cooperative nodes compared to the MIMO-LEACH MAC. $CMAC_{ON}$ is more scalable without any need for fixed cluster formation and synchronisation. The cooperative groups are formed when there is a data packet to be sent. Also, a collision avoidance mechanism is provided by RTS-CTS signalling. Furthermore, $CMAC_{ON}$ reduces transmission energy and increases link reliability by the exploitation of the spatial diversity gain when compared to the $SISO_{ON}$ protocol. However, we note that all the sensor nodes are always on which makes the issues of idle listening and overhearing still to be addressed. The $CMAC_{ON}$ protocol should deploy a duty cycle mechanism to reduce further the total energy consumption.

6. Conclusion

This chapter has examined various important low duty cycle MAC protocols and the two most important MAC protocols designed specifically for cooperative MIMO transmission. In most cases, the low duty cycle MAC protocols trade off latency for energy efficient operation. Also, we observed that asynchronous MAC protocols are more scalable than synchronous MAC protocols.

On the one hand, when sensor nodes join or leave a group or a cluster, the MAC needs to re-synchronise the network over and over in such protocols as LEACH and S-MAC. Frequent re-synchronisation can lead to higher energy consumption. The situation becomes more complex when global synchronisation is required instead of local synchronisation. Thus a balance must be made between frequent synchronisation and scalability in synchronous MAC protocol design. On the other hand, in some cases with asynchronous MAC, the higher scalability comes at the cost of higher transmission energy due to the implementation of a long preamble and overhearing in such protocols as RF Wake-up and B-MAC. However, the burden of long preamble transmission is reduced gradually by the introduction of short packet techniques such in SpeckMAC and X-MAC.

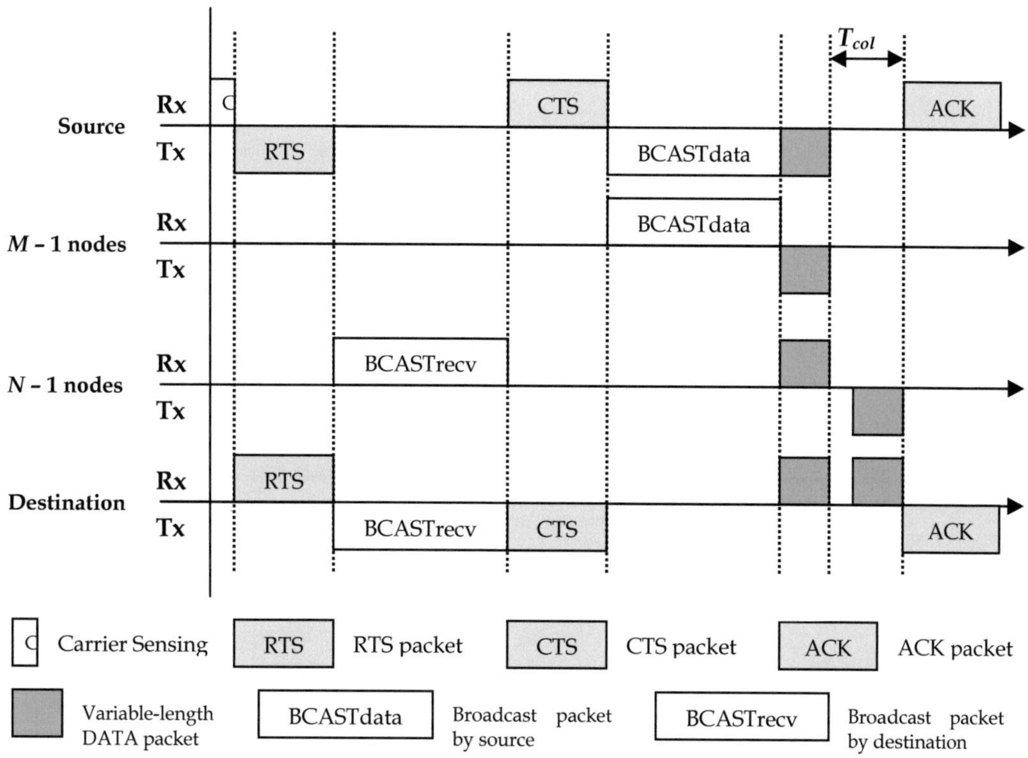

Fig. 11. Basic operation of $CMAC_{ON}$ with M transmitting and N receiving cooperative nodes.

Moreover, it is important to note that little attention has been paid to increasing the link reliability in SISO systems. The only mechanism used is the ACK packet feedback in protocols such IEEE 802.15.4 MAC and WiseMAC.

The MIMO-LEACH and $CMAC_{ON}$ protocols provide measures to increase link reliability and at the same time reduce transmission power by exploiting spatial diversity gain. On the one hand, the MIMO-LEACH protocol employs a duty cycle mechanism through TDMA time slots assignments which reduces the total energy consumption. Furthermore, multi-hop communication between cluster heads is introduced to replace the direct communication which reduces further the total energy consumption. Also, collisions can be avoided with the distinct time slot assignment to each sensor node. The benefits come at the cost of higher latency (multi-hop communication). In addition, the scalability issue is not addressed at all.

$CMAC_{ON}$ is more scalable and does not require pre-selection of cooperative nodes. $CMAC_{ON}$ does not suffer from tight synchronisation and overhead of cluster formation. Also, collision avoidance is provided through RTS-CTS signalling. Moreover, an ACK mechanism is used as a double measure of link reliability. However, we note that all the sensor nodes are always on which makes the issues of idle listening and overhearing still to be addressed. The $CMAC_{ON}$ protocol should deploy a duty cycle mechanism to reduce further the total energy consumption. Also, circuit energy must be included to get a better picture of the overall energy usage in the network.

Algorithm 1: Cooperative MIMO MAC Protocol

```
STATE: IDLE node is idle and listens to the channel
if Packet ready to be sent then
  go to algorithm 2
end if
if receive RTS packet then
  go to algorithm 3
end if
if receive BCASTdata packet then
  go to algorithm 4
end if
if receive BCASTrecv packet then
  go to algorithm 5
end if
```

Algorithm 2: Node is the source

```
STATE: RTS node sends RTS packet
if CTS not received then
   repeat STATE: RTS
end if
STATE: BCASTdata send data to transmitting group with low power, set sending timer
STATE: Data send MIMO data when the timer expires
if receive ACK packet then
   go to STATE: IDLE
else
   go to STATE: RTS
end if
```

Algorithm 3: Node is the destination

```
STATE: BCASTrecv broadcast recruiting packet with low power
STATE: CTS send CTS packet
if MISO data received then
   go to STATE: Collection
else if
   go to STATE: IDLE
end if
STATE: Collection set timer to wait for receiving group nodes to send packet
if packet not received correctly then
   go to STATE: IDLE
end if
STATE: ACK send ACK packet
go to STATE: IDLE
```

Algorithm 4: Cooperative sending node

```
STATE: Cooperative Sending nodes transmit data packet when sending timer expires
go to STATE: IDLE listens for channel activity
```

Algorithm 5: Cooperative receiving node

STATE: Cooperative Receiving set expiration timer
if MISO data packet received **then**
  go to **STATE: Collection**
else if
  go to **STATE: IDLE**
end if
STATE: Collection send data to destination after random back-off
go to **STATE: IDLE**

7. References

Buettner, M.; Yee, G.; Anderson, E. & Han, R. (2006). X-MAC: A Short Preamble MAC Protocol for Duty-Cycled Wireless Sensor Networks, *Proceedings of ACM Conference on Embedded Networked Sensor Systems (SENSYS)*, Baltimore, Maryland, USA, 2006.

Dam, T.V. & Langendoen, K. (2003). An Adaptive Energy-Efficient MAC Protocol for Wireless Sensor Networks, *Proceedings of ACM Conference on Embedded Networked Sensor Systems (SENSYS)*, Los Angeles, California, USA, 2003.

El-Hoiydi, A. (2002a). Aloha with Preamble Sampling for Sporadic Traffic in Ad-hoc Wireless Sensor Networks, *Proceedings of IEEE International Conference on Communications (ICC)*, New York City, USA, 2004.

El-Hoiydi, A. (2002b). Spatial TDMA and CSMA with Preamble Sampling for Low Power Ad-hoc Wireless Sensor Networks, *Proceedings of IEEE International Symposium on Computers and Communications (ISCC)*, Taromina, Italy, 2002.

El-Hoiydi, A.; Decotignie, J.D. & Hernandez, J. (2004). Low Power MAC Protocols for Infrastructure Wireless Sensor Networks, *Proceedings of European Wireless Conference*, Barcelona, Spain, 2004.

Gerla, M.; Kwon, T. & Pei, G. (2000). On Demand Routing in Large Ad-hoc Wireless Networks with Passive Clustering, *Proceedings of IEEE Wireless Communications and Networking (WCNC)*, Chicago, USA, 2000.

Heinzelman, W.B.; Chandrakasan, A.P.; & Balakrishnan, H. (2002). An Application-specific Protocol Architecture for Wireless Microsensor Network, *IEEE Journal on Wireless Communications*, Vol. 1.

Hill, J. & Culler, D. (2002). A Wireless Platform for Deeply Embedded Networks. *IEEE Journal on Micro*, Vol. 22, pp. 12-24.

IEEE Standard (2006). 802.15.4-2006 IEEE Standard for Information Technology-Part 15.4: Wireless Medium Access Control (MAC) and Physical Layer (PHY) specifications for Low Rate Wireless Personal Area Networks (LR-WPANs).

IEEE Standard (2008). IEEE 802.15 Wireless Personal Area Network (WPAN) Task Group 5 (TG5) electronic documents at http://ieee802.org/15/pub/TG5.html, 2008.

Karl, H. & Willig, A. (2007). MAC Protocols, In: *Protocols and Architectures for Wireless Sensor Networks*, pp. 111-148, John Wiley & Sons, 978-0-470-09510-2, West Sussex, England.

Kohvakka, M.; Kuorilehto, M.; Hannikainen, M. & Hamalainen, T.D. (2006). Performance Analysis of IEEE 802.15.4 and Zigbee for Large-scale Wireless Sensor Network Applications, *Proceedings of ACM International Workshop on Performance Evaluation of Wireless Ad hoc, Sensor, and Ubiquitous Networks,*, pp. 1-6, Malaga, Spain, 2006.

Kuorilehto, M.; Kohvakka, M.; Suhonen, J.; Hamalainen, P.; Hannikainen, M. & Hamalainen, T.D. (2007). MAC Protocols, In: *Ultra-Low Energy Wireless Sensor Networks in Practice*, pp. 73-88, John Wiley & Sons, 978-0-470-05786-5, West Sussex, England.

Lu, G.; Krishnamachari, B. & Raghavendra, C.S. (2004). An Adaptive Energy-Efficient and Low-latency MAC for Data Gathering in Wireless Sensor Networks, *Proceedings of Parallel and Distributed Processing Symposium (IPDPS)*, 2004.

Mainwaring, A.; Polastre, J.; Szewczyk, R.; Culler, D. & Anderson, J. (2002). Wireless Sensor Networks for Habitat Monitoring, *Proceedings of ACM International Workshop on Wireless Sensor Networks and Applications*, 2002.

Pei, G. & Chien, C. (2001). Low Power TDMA in Large Wireless Sensor Networks, *Proceedings of IEEE Military Communications Conference (MILCOM)*, Washington DC, USA, 2001.

Polastre, J.; Hill, J. & Culler, D. (2004). Versatile Low Power Media Access for Wireless Sensor Networks, *Proceedings of ACM Conference on Embedded Networked Sensor Systems (SENSYS)*, pp. 95-107, Baltimore, Maryland, USA, November 2004.

Rajendran, V.; Obraczka, K. & Gracia-Luna-Aceves (2003). Energy-efficient, Collision-free Medium Access Control for Wireless Sensor Networks, *Proceedings of International Conference on Embedded Networked Sensor Systems (SenSys)*, Los Angeles, USA, 2003.

Rhee, I.; Warrier, A.; Aia, M. & Min, J. (2005). A Hybrid MAC for Wireless Sensor Networks, *Proceedings of International Conference on Embedded Networked Sensor Systems (SENSYS)*, New York, USA, 2005.

Wong, K.J. & Arvind, D. (2006). Low Power Decentralized MAC Protocols for Low Data Rate Transmissions in Specknets, *Proceedings of ACM International Workshop on Multihop Ad-hoc Networks: From Theory to Reality*, Florence, Italy, 2006.

Wong, K.J. & Arvind, D. (2007). A Hybrid Wakeup Signalling Mechanism for Periodic-Listening MAC Algorithms, *Proceedings of IEEE International Conference on Networking (ICON)*, Adelaide, Australia, 2007.

Wu, T. & Biswas, S. (2005). Low Power TDMA in Large Wireless Sensor Networks, *Proceedings of International Conference on Information Processing in Sensor Networks (IPSN)*, Los Angeles, USA, 2005.

Yang, H.; Shen, H.-Y. & Sikdar, B. (2007). A MAC Protocol for Cooperative MIMO Transmissions in Sensor Networks, *Proceedings of IEEE Global Telecommunications Conference (GLOBECOM)*, pp. 636-640, Washington, USA, 26-30 November 2007.

Ye, W.; Heidemann, J. & Estrin, D. (2002). An Energy-Efficient MAC Protocol for Wireless Sensor Networks, *Proceedings of IEEE Infocomm*, New York, USA, 2002.

Ye, W.; Heidemann, J. & Estrin, D. (2004). Medium Access Control with Coordinated, Adaptive Sleeping for Wireless Sensor Networks, *Transactions of IEEE/ACM on Networking*, 2004.

Yuan, Y.; Chen, M. & Kwon, T. (2006). A Novel Cluster-based Cooperative MIMO Scheme for Multi-hop Wireless Sensor Networks. *EURASIP Journal on Wireless Communications and Networking*, Vol. 2006, pp. 1-9.

Zigbee Alliance Document 053474r06 (2004). Zigbee Specification, Version 1.0, 2004.

6

A new MAC Approach in Wireless Body Sensor Networks for Health Care

Begonya Otal[1], Luis Alonso[2] and Christos Verikoukis[1]
[1]*Centre Tecnològic de Telecomunicacions de Catalunya (CTTC),*
[2]*Signal Theory & Communications Dept., Universitat Politècnica de Catalunya (UPC)*
Barcelona, Spain

1. Introduction

Although the challenges faced by wireless body sensor networks (BSNs) in healthcare environments are in a certain way similar to those already existing in current wireless sensor networks (WSNs), there are intrinsic differences, which require special attention (Yang, 2006). For instance, human body monitoring may be achieved by attaching sensors to the body's surface as well as implanting them into tissues for a more accurate clinical practice. One of the major concerns is thereby that of extremely energy efficiency, which is the key to extend the lifetime of battery-powered body sensors, reduce maintenance costs and avoid invasive procedures to replace battery in the case of implantable devices. That is, BSNs in healthcare systems operate under conflicting requirements. These are the maintenance of the desired reliability and message latency of data transmissions, while simultaneously maximizing battery lifetime of individual body sensors. In doing so, the characteristics of the entire system, including physical (PHY), MAC and application (APP) layers have to be considered. In fact, the MAC layer is the one responsible for coordinating channel accesses, by avoiding collisions and scheduling data transmissions, to maximize throughput efficiency (and reliability) at an acceptable packet delay and minimal energy consumption. Now, the design of future MAC protocols for BSNs must tackle stringent quality of service (QoS) requirements, apart from the desired low power consumption. Hence, the right MAC approach is able to handle cross-layer PHY-MAC-APP features.

In order to consider all the aforementioned healthcare requirements, this chapter first concentrates on the analysis and evaluation of the energy consumption in a MAC level. Thereafter, novel cross-layer fuzzy-logic techniques are proposed to enhance QoS resource management in the here portrayed MAC approach for BSNs. Simulation results are achieved to validate the overall system performance, and its scalability, by increasing the number of wireless on-body sensors in the BSN (see Fig. 1).

In this context, among all IEEE 802 standards available today, the IEEE 802.15.4 (802.15.4, 2003) is regarded as the technology of choice for most BSN research studies (Yang, 2006); (Zhen et al., 2007); (Kumar et al., 2008). However, the 802.15.4 MAC is not actually intended to support any set of applications with stringent QoS, and, even though it consumes very low power, the figures do not reach the levels required in BSNs (Zhen et al., 2007); (Kumar et al., 2008). This is the reason why there exists the need to explore other MAC potential candidates for future BSNs that outperform 802.15.4 in the above-mentioned requirements. This chapter compares our newly proposed MAC approach for BSNs with 802.15.4 MAC. The 802.15.4 MAC accepts three network topologies: star, peer-to-peer and cluster-tree. Our focus is here on 1-hop star-based BSNs, where a body area network (BAN) coordinator is elected. In a hospital BSN, the BAN coordinator can be a central care unit linked to a number of ward-patients wearing several on-body sensors (see Fig. 1). Here a centralized architecture is appropriate, since the BAN coordinator is superior to the rest of the body sensors in terms of processing memory, storage and power resources. Note that if the traffic load in the BSN notably increases beyond saturation limits, a cluster-tree architecture with several BAN coordinators can be adopted, as also allowed in (802.15.4, 2003). Communication from body sensors to BAN coordinator (uplink), from BAN coordinator to body sensors (downlink), or even from body sensor to body sensor (ad hoc) is possible. In the following, we study uplink and downlink communication, which occurs more often than ad hoc communication for regular patient monitoring BSNs.

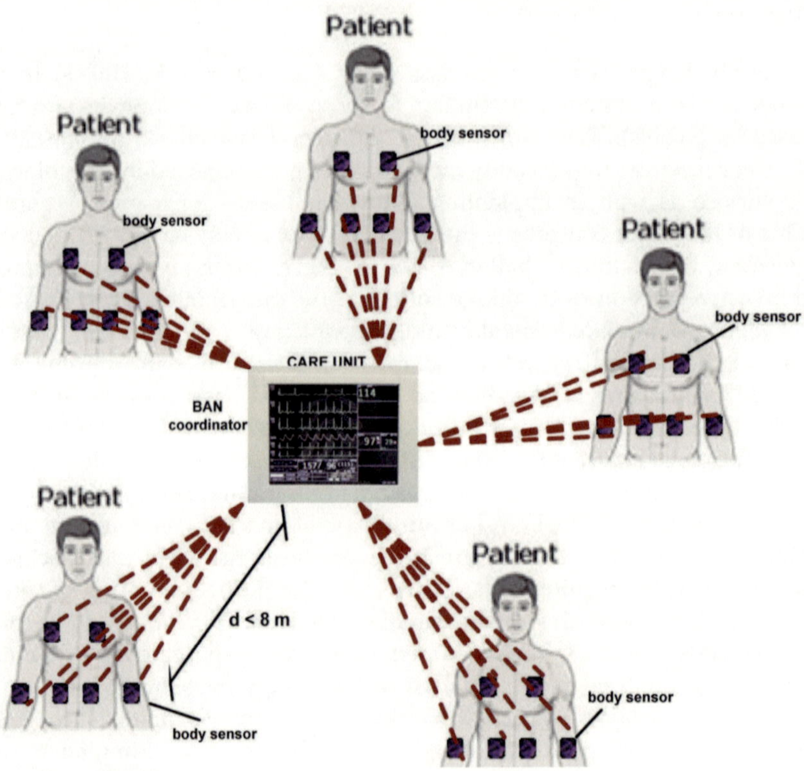

Fig. 1. A star-based BSN

2. The IEEE 802.15.4 MAC limitations in BSNs for healthcare

In a 802.15.4 star-based network, the beacon mode appears to allow for the greatest energy efficiency. Indeed, it allows the transceiver to be completely switched off up to 15/16 of the time when nothing is transmitted/received, while still allowing the transceiver to be synchronized to the network and able to transmit or receive a packet at any time (Bourgard et al., 2005). The beacon mode introduces the so-called superframe structure. The inter-beacon period is partially or entirely occupied by the superframe, which is divided into 16 slots. Among them, there are at most 7 guaranteed time slots (GTS), (i.e. they are dedicated to specific nodes), which form the contention free period (CFP) (802.15.4, 2003). This functionality targets very low latency applications, but it is not scalable in BSNs, since the number of dedicated slots is not sufficient (Zhen et al., 2007). In the medical field, where one illness usually boost-ups other illnesses, many body sensors should be able to reach the BAN coordinator via such guaranteed services. Further, the current protocol only supports first come first served based GTS allocation and does not take into account the traffic specification, delay requirements, and the energy resources. Again, in medical scenarios, many critical events may occur at a time, and some of them are more critical and need most urgent response (Kumar et al., 2008). An additional drawback with the current GTS allocation is the bandwidth under utilization. Most of the time, a device uses only a small portion of the allocated GTS slots, and the major portion remains unused, resulting in empty holes within the CFP. In such conditions, the use of the contention access period (CAP) is required; where channel accesses in the uplink are coordinated by a slotted carrier sense multiple access mechanism with collision avoidance (CSMA/CA). Nevertheless, in the literature (Bourgard et al., 2005); (Park et al., 2005); (Pollin et al., 2005), it has already been proved that the CSMA/CA mechanism has a significant negative impact on the overall energy consumption, as the traffic load in the network steadily increases.

Thus, the appraisal of other existing MAC protocols in terms of delivery ratio, end-to-end delay and effective energy per information bit introduces important challenges in BSNs. That is the reason why we here introduce energy-aware radio activation policies into a high-performance MAC protocol different from CSMA/CA, while analyzing and evaluating its QoS and energy-saving performance in BSNs.

3. Overview on distributed queuing MAC protocols

This section highlights the basic features related to distributed queuing (DQ) MAC protocols that are essential for the understanding of the new QoS and energy-saving enhancements proposed in this chapter. The introduction of the Distributed Queuing Random Access Protocol (DQRAP) for local wireless communications was already presented in (Lin & Campbell, 1993) and later in (Alonso et al., 2005) under the name of Distributed Queuing Collision Avoidance (DQCA), as an adaptation to IEEE 802.11b MAC environments. It has already been shown that the throughput performance of a DQ MAC protocol outperforms CSMA/CA in all studied scenarios. The main characteristic of a DQ MAC protocol is that it behaves as a random access mechanism under low traffic conditions, and switches smoothly and automatically to a reservation scheme when the traffic load grows. That is, DQ MAC protocols show a near-optimum performance independent of the amount of active terminals and traffic load.

Let us consider a star-based topology with several nodes and a network coordinator, following DQRAP original description (Xu & Campbell, 1992), the time axis is divided into an "access subslot" that is further divided into access *minislots* (m), and a "data subslot". The basic idea is to concentrate user access requests in the access *minislots*, while the "data subslot" is devoted to collision-free data transmissions. The DQRAP analytical model

approaches the delay and throughput performance of the theoretical optimum queuing systems M/M/1 or G/D/1, depending on the traffic distribution. Hence, DQ MAC protocols can be modelled as if every station in the system maintains two common logical distributed queues – the collision resolution queue (CRQ), and the data transmission queue (DTQ) –, physically implemented as four integers in each station; two station-dependant integers that represent the occupied position in each queue; and, two further integers shared among all stations in the system that visualize the total number of stations in each queue, CRQ and DTQ. The CRQ controls station accesses to the collision resolution server (the access *minislots*), while the DTQ is in charge of the data server (the "data subslot"). This provides a collision resolution tree algorithm that proves to be stable for every traffic load even over the system transmission capacity. Note that the number of access *minislots* is implementation dependant, but we are formally using 3 access *minislots*, following the original DQRAP structure and argumentation for maximizing its throughput performance (Xu & Campbell, 1992). A DQ MAC protocol consists of several strategic rules, independently performed by each station by managing the aforementioned four integers (i.e. corresponding to the two distributed queues, CRQ and DTQ) (Xu & Campbell, 1992), which answer:
i) 'who' transmits in the data slot and 'when',
ii) 'who' sends an access request sequence in the *minislots* (m) and 'when'; and
iii) 'how' to actualize their positions in the queues.
Hence, the promising behaviour of DQRAP in (Lin & Campbell, 1993) ; (Xu & Campbell, 1992), and similarly of DQCA in (Alonso et al., 2005), in terms of delay and near-optimum throughput achievements (i.e. allowing high reliability), evokes the idea to further explore DQ MAC protocols in terms of energy consumption under BSN healthcare scenarios. This favourable behaviour is especially achieved thanks to the inherent protocol performance at eliminating collisions in data transmissions and minimizing the overhead of contention procedures (i.e. carrier sensing and back-off periods) with respect to CSMA/CA. Based on that, we introduce energy-efficient enhancements to allow radio activation policies and power management solutions for the proper use of DQ MAC in BSNs, while comparing it to the standard de facto (802.15.4, 2003). Additionally, we propose here a new cross-layer fuzzy-logic scheduling algorithm to improve QoS features, and by means of computer simulations, we evaluate its overall performance.

4. DQ MAC energy-saving enhancements for BSNs

Fig. 2 shows the energy-saving superframe format of a DQ MAC protocol proposal for star-based BSNs. The complete energy-saving superframe structure comprises two differential parts; (a) from body sensors to BAN coordinator (uplink), with a CAP and a CFP. The CAP is further divided into m access *minislots*, whereas the CFP is devoted to collision-free data packet transmissions, and, (b) from BAN coordinator to body sensors (downlink) using the feedback frame, which contains several strategic fields. In fact, the DQ MAC superframe is bounded by the feedback packet (FBP) contained in the Fig. 2 portrayed feedback frame, which is broadcasted by the BAN coordinator. Similar to the 802.15.4 MAC superframe format, one of the main uses of the FBP is to synchronize the attached body sensors to the BAN coordinator. The FBP always contains relevant MAC control information (i.e. corresponding also to the protocol rules), which is essential for the right functioning of all body sensors in the BSN. When a body sensor wishes to transfer data, it first waits for the FBP. After synchronization, it independently actualizes the integer counters, by applying a set of rules that determine its position in the protocol distributed queues, CRQ and DTQ. At the appropriate time, the body sensor transmits either an access request sequence (ARS) in one of the randomly selected access *minislots* (within the CAP), or its data packet in the "data slot" (within the CFP). The BAN coordinator may acknowledge the successful reception of the data packet by sending an optional acknowledgment frame (ACK). This sequence is summarized in Fig. 1. The main differences of this energy-saving DQ MAC superframe format with respect to previous DQ MAC ones are the following; (a) a new preamble (PRE) between the ACK and the FBP is introduced to enable synchronization after power-sleep modus (i.e. idle or shutdown). That is to say that the body sensors, which are not supposed to be ACK recipients, are longer maintained in power-sleep modus, as later detailed, (b) further, the FBP is here of fixed length (i.e. independently of the number of body sensors in the BSN) and contains two strategic fields for specific energy-aware radio activation policies and power management solutions. These are the modulation and coding scheme (MCS) and the length of the data packet to be transmitted in the next CFP. This facilitates scalable power management processes for future multi-rate medical applications, and allows the use of a flexible CFP (i.e. data packets of different lengths for application-oriented medical body sensors).

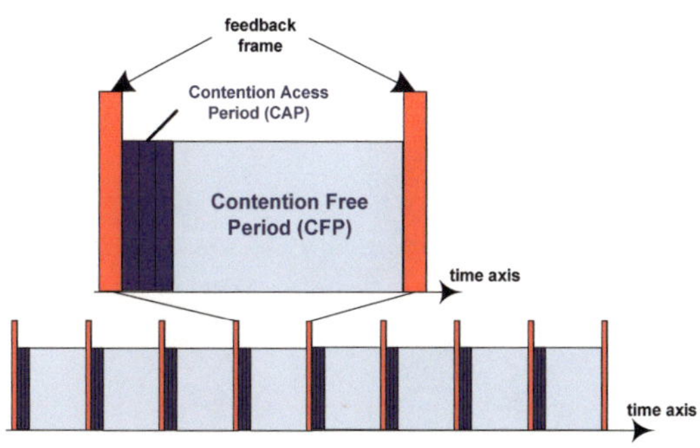

Fig. 2. A star-based BSN with DQ MAC energy-saving superframe format

4.1 Energy-aware radio activation policies

To be able to asses the average energy consumption of a body sensor in a BSN, we must first characterize the instantaneous power consumption of the transceiver, when operating in different states. Apart from the transmit and receive modes, a transceiver supports two further states: shutdown, when the clock is switched off and the chip is completely deactivated waiting for a start-up strobe; and, idle, when the clock is turned on and the chip can receive commands, for example, to turn on the radio circuitry (Bourgard et al., 2005). Fig. 3 illustrates our enhanced DQ MAC superframe format to allow different power management scenarios to body sensors using an energy-aware radio activation policy under BSNs. Note that each time slot is characterized by a different power consumption modus (i.e. transmit, receive, idle, and shutdown). As previously mentioned, each body sensor synchronizes to the BSN thanks to a newly introduced preamble sequence (PRE) of duration t_{PRE} after a period in idle mode. Thereafter, it receives the required system information via the FBP of duration t_{FBP} for updating the distributed queues, CRQ and DTQ (Xu & Campbell, 1992). After each FBP, a short inter-frame space t_{IFS} is left to allow the MAC layer to process the data received from the PHY layer, like in (802.15.4, 2003). Active body sensors involved in the access procedure like in scenarios (1) and (2) start by sending an ARS, here of duration length t_{ARS}, in one of the randomly selected access *minislots* (Alonso et al., 2005). Prior to that, these body sensors should have switched its radio from idle to transmit mode, which take them a transition time t_{ia} for body sensor radio wake-up (i.e. from idle to active modes (Bourgard et al., 2005)). Next, scenario (3) depicts the transmission of a previously granted packet of average duration length $\overline{t}_{DATA}$ preceded by the transition time t_{ia}. If the packet is received correctly, an acknowledgement (ACK) of duration t_{ACK} is sent back to the transmitting body sensor followed by the FBP (and PRE) after a maximum time $t_{aw} - t_{ACK}$, during which the receiver turns its radio to idle mode to save energy. In (802.15.4, 2003), t_{aw} is characterized as the maximum time to wait for an ACK. Scenario (4) shows how an active body sensor waiting in idle mode synchronizes through the PRE to receive the FBP. Finally, scenario (5) portrays how a body sensor in shutdown state wakes up and waits for some time in idle mode to synchronize through the PRE and get the FBP to update the state of the CRQ and DTQ queues (see Section 3).

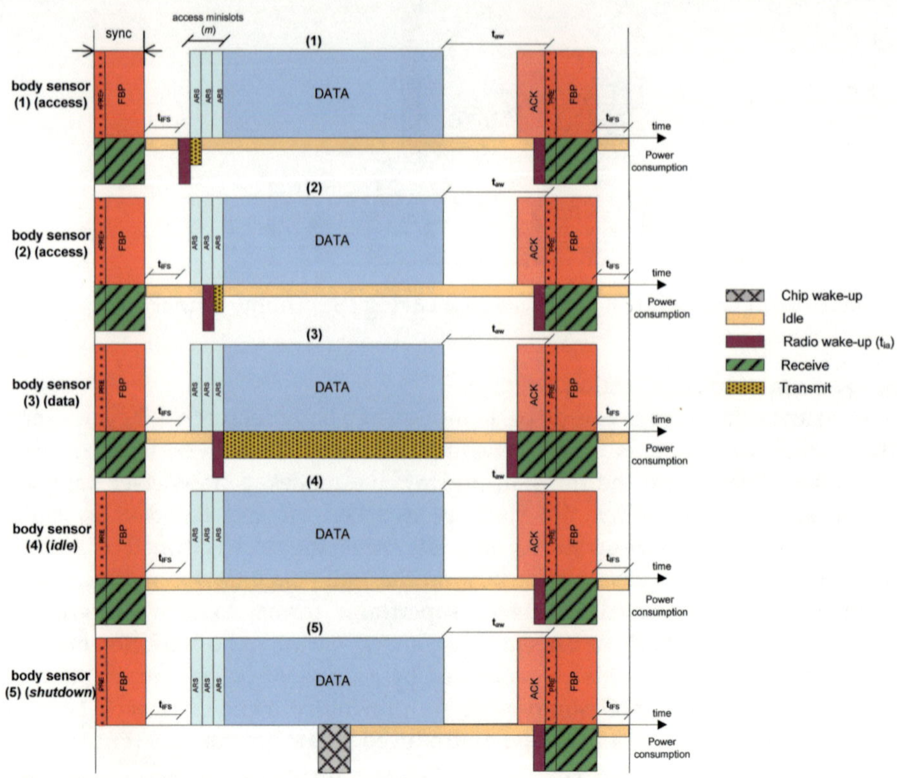

Fig. 3. Power management scenarios in BSNs

4.2 Energy-efficiency analysis

Let us now define P_{tx}, P_{rx} and P_{idle} as the power consumption in transmit, receive and idle modes respectively, and similarly, $\overline{T}_{tx}$, $\overline{T}_{rx}$ and $\overline{T}_{idle}$, as the average time a body sensor spends in each of the aforementioned modes within the queuing system (i.e. CRQ and DTQ). Thus, the average consumed energy per information bit for every active body sensor in the BSN can be expressed as $\overline{E}_{bit} = \overline{E}_{FRAME} / L_{bit}$, where L_{bit} corresponds to the payload data length in bits, and $\overline{E}_{FRAME}$ to

$$\overline{E}_{FRAME} = P_{tx} \cdot \overline{T}_{tx} + P_{rx} \cdot \overline{T}_{rx} + P_{idle} \cdot \overline{T}_{idle}. \tag{1}$$

The average time in transmit, receive and idle mode can be computed as,

$$\begin{aligned} \overline{T}_{tx} &= \overline{n}_{tx} \cdot (t_{ARS} + t_{ia}) + \overline{t}_{DATA} + t_{ia}, \\ \overline{T}_{rx} &= \overline{n}_{waiting} \cdot (t_{PRE} + t_{FBP} + t_{ia}) + t_{ACK}, \\ \overline{T}_{idle} &= \overline{n}_{waiting} \cdot [\overline{T}_{FRAME} - (t_{PRE} + t_{FBP})]. \end{aligned} \tag{2}$$

The average duration of the DQ MAC time superframe, $\overline{T}_{FRAME}$, derived from Fig. 2 is characterized as,

$$\overline{T}_{FRAME} = m \cdot t_{ARS} + \overline{t}_{DATA} + t_{aw} + t_{PRE} + t_{FBP} + t_{IFS}, \tag{3}$$

where m corresponds to the number of *minislots* used in the current DQ MAC superframe structure, and t_{ARS}, $\overline{t}_{DATA}$, t_{aw}, t_{ACK}, t_{PRE}, t_{FBP}, t_{IFS} and t_{ia} have been previously defined following the illustration example of power management scenarios in Fig. 2. Here, we specify $\overline{n}_{waiting}$ and $\overline{n}_{tx}$, as the total average number of slot time frames waiting in the whole queuing system (i.e. CRQ and DTQ), and, the average number of slot time frames used to transmit an ARS in the CRQ system, respectively. Their concrete characterization is not straightforward, but both numbers can be derived from DQRAP original delay theoretical analysis in (Zhang & Campbell, 1993). Fig. 4(a) portrays the analytical results of the energy consumption per information bit of DQ MAC versus the theoretical analysis of 802.15.4 MAC in (Bourgard et al., 2005), as the relative traffic load in the BSN increases. It can be seen, that the use of DQ MAC outperforms 802.15.4 MAC by reducing a 37% the energy consumption per information bit, when the relative traffic load is as high as 60%. The here presented DQ MAC energy-efficient analysis is corroborated by computer simulations in Fig. 4(b) and its description follows.

4.3 Energy-efficiency evaluation

The performance of the studied energy-efficiency analysis is validated via MATLAB computer simulations, by implementing the DQ MAC protocol (see Section 3), within a star-based BSN scenario, as the relative traffic load increases until saturation conditions. Relative traffic load is here defined, as the ratio of generated data packets per iteration. The traffic load rises by increasing the number of active body sensors in the BSN in each simulation. Note that all body sensors follow a Poisson traffic distribution, since we consider here a generalized case scenario. The energy consumption is computed considering every body sensor spent time and power consumption in each of the aforementioned states (i.e. transmit, receive and idle) following DQ MAC procedure in our simulated BSN scenario. Thus, the energy consumption per information bit is defined as the ratio of the total energy consumption per body sensor and per payload packet length (i.e. information bit). Every active body sensor is supposedly located at a random distance from the BAN coordinator, as portrayed in Fig.1. The channel link implementation is based on the path loss model of (802.15.4, 2003), where the average received power is expressed as a function of an arbitrary T-R separation distance of maximum 8 meters (i.e. within a hospital setting). In our simulations, the time-variant received signal also includes Additive White Gaussian Noise (AWGN) and the effect of log-normal shadowing, assuming the channel is coherent within the transmission of a DQ MAC superframe, like in indoor environments. The reference BSN scenario is characterised by the system parameters corresponding to the standardized 802.15.4 MAC default values in the upper frequency band 2.4 GHz at the fixed data rate 250 Kb/s (802.15.4, 2003). Following the illustration of DQ MAC superframe structure in Fig. 2, we choose the longest data payload lengths (L) of 80, 100 and 120 bytes, to minimize the PHY (6 bytes) and MAC (8 bytes) headers overhead per information bit. Further, a packet may be corrupted by bit errors due to noise. Hence, a body sensor waits for an ACK (11 bytes) for a maximum time of $t_{aw} - t_{ACK}$, where t_{aw} is limited to 864 μs, as defined in (802.15.4, 2003). The synchronization PRE corresponds to 4 bytes and it is followed by the FBP of 11 bytes, similar to a beacon (802.15.4, 2003). Additionally, we use 3 access *minislots*, like in the literature (Xu & Campbell, 1992), and an ARS occupies hereby the same size as a preamble sequence (i.e. 4 bytes), which is a worst case assumption. Power consumption values are formalized as in (Bourgard et al., 2005), (i.e. P_{rx} = 35.28 mW, P_{idle} = 712 μW, and, P_{tx} = 22.09 mW, for a transmit power of -5 dBm). The analytical and simulated results of DQ MAC energy consumption per information bit are depicted in Fig. 4(b).

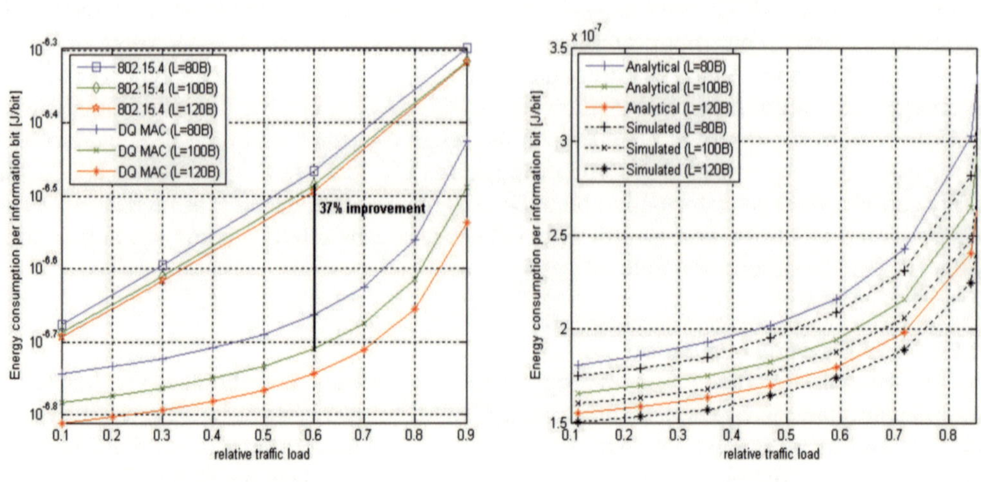

(a) (b)

Fig. 4(a). Energy consumption per information bit - Analytical results DQ vs. 802.15.4 MAC

(b). DQ MAC energy consumption per information bit - Analytical vs. Simulated
Here, it can be seen the excellent protocol performance even for the highest traffic load between 80% and 90%, which remains under 350 nJ/bit. Thus, the simulation results corroborate the accuracy of the newly introduced theoretical analysis in terms of energy efficiency. They also show the appropriate scalability of DQ MAC energy-saving performance for future BSN scenarios, while fulfilling healthcare stringent power consumption requirements

5. New DQBAN system modelling for QoS

Up to now, we mainly tackled energy-consumption per information bit and presented an enhanced energy-saving DQ MAC solution as a potential candidate to overcome 802.15.4 MAC deficit figures required in BSNs. However, the design of future MAC protocols for BSNs must also fulfill other stringent requirements, such as high reliability, fairness and low latency (i.e. QoS), apart from the desired low power consumption. For that purpose, a novel cross-layer fuzzy-rule scheduling algorithm is introduced for the first time within the use of a DQ MAC protocol (Otal et al., 2009). This operates on top of the energy-aware radio activation policies previously presented.

The main idea hereby is to integrate a fuzzy-logic system in each body sensor to deal with multiple cross-layer input variables of diverse nature in an independent manner. By being autonomously aware of their current condition and specific medical requirements, body sensors are able to demand a "collision-free" time slot, whenever they consider it strictly necessarily (e.g. high system packet delay or low body sensor residual battery lifetime). Similarly, they may refuse to transmit, if there is a bad channel link, thus permitting another body sensor to do so. This results in improving the system overall performance, while keeping the inherent distributed behavior of a DQ MAC protocol. Hence, the here proposed Distributed Queuing Body Area Network (DQBAN) protocol is an alternative enhancement to 802.15.4 MAC in all possible BSN scenarios. DQBAN corresponds to an enhanced MAC model specially modified by means of a novel cross-layer fuzzy-logic scheduling mechanism on top of the above described energy-aware activation policies to satisfy energy-efficient and stringent QoS demands in healthcare scenarios. Hence, DQBAN supports high application-dependant performance requirements in terms of reliability, message latency and power consumption, while being adaptable to changing conditions, such as heterogeneous traffic load, interferences, and the number of sensors in a hospital BSN.

DQBAN also utilizes the two common logical distributed queues CRQ and DTQ, for serving access requests (via the "access *minislots*") and data packets (via the "data slot"), respectively. In the new logic system model though, instead of keeping a first-come-first-served discipline in DTQ, a cross-layer fuzzy-rule based scheduler is introduced, as portrayed in Fig. 5. The use of the scheduler permits a body sensor, though not occupying the first position in DTQ, to transmit its data in the next frame collision-free "data slot" in order to achieve a far more reliable system performance for medical applications. Practically speaking, this is obtained by integrating a fuzzy-logic system in each body sensor in the BSN. As explained later, a fuzzy-logic approach allows each particular body sensor to individually deal with multiple cross-layer inputs of diverse nature (i.e. x_1, x_2, to x_k in Fig. 4). The basic idea is that body sensors consider their own QoS criteria, current channel quality and battery constraints, and make use of fuzzy-logic theory, as a control mechanism, to demand or refuse the next frame "data slot", according to their particular needs.

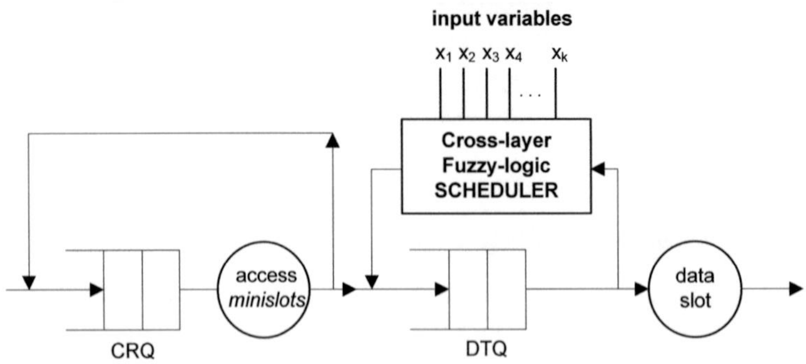

Fig. 5. New DQBAN logic system model

5.1 DQBAN body sensor flow chart

As illustrated in the DQBAN flow chart of Fig. 6 a body sensor willing to transmit a packet must first synchronize with the BAN coordinator through the broadcasted FBP to update the state of the system queues (CRQ & DTQ) (see Fig. 6,**(a)**). Note that when both queues are empty, the protocol uses an exception of slotted-Aloha (Xu & Campbell, 1992). However, if CRQ is empty - but DTQ is not -, the body sensor sends an access request - randomly selecting one of the "access *minislots*" - to grant its access into DTQ (see Fig. 6,**(b)**). If its access request collides with any of another body sensor in the selected "access *minislot*", these body sensors involved therein occupy the same position in CRQ (following the order of the selected *minislot* position), and wait for a future frame to compete for a free "access *minislot*" again to grant its access into a DTQ exclusive position. New body sensors, with a packet to send, are not allowed to enter the system until CRQ is empty (i.e. all current collisions are resolved) (see Fig. 6,**(c)**). When a body sensor selects successfully a free "access *minislot*" (known at the reception of the FBP), it takes immediately a place in DTQ up. If DTQ is now empty, it may be in the first position of DTQ, thus transmitting directly in the next DQBAN superframe "data slot" (see Fig. 6,**(d)**), DTQ Empty Case). If this is not the case, each body sensor applies its fuzzy-logic algorithm in order to demand a collision-free "data slot" (i.e. to be forwarded) or to refuse the next "data slot" (i.e. to be delayed) whenever it is required. As explained in the next section, this algorithm consists of a number of fuzzy-logic rules, which permit body sensors to find out 'how favorable' or 'how critical' their specific situation is, in a particular time frame. Every body sensor in DTQ has the chance to individually send its **Decision** (i.e. forward or delay) to the BAN coordinator via the "scheduling *minislots*". Otherwise, it remains in the same position and no decision is sent to the BAN coordinator. When having all different results, the BAN coordinator notifies — through the broadcasted FBP — about the specific changes to improve the system overall performance: i) if a body sensor requires the next collision-free "data slot", or ii) if a body sensor in the position to transmit indicated its refusal to do so (see Fig. 6,**(e)**). Upon reception of the FBP, each body sensor knows whether it may transmit in the next "data slot" or not, and updates the queue states consequently (see (Lin & Campbell, 1993); (Xu & Campbell, 1992)). Finally, the turn comes for the body sensor to transmit and wait for the reception of an ACK from the BAN coordinator (see Fig. 6, **(f)**).

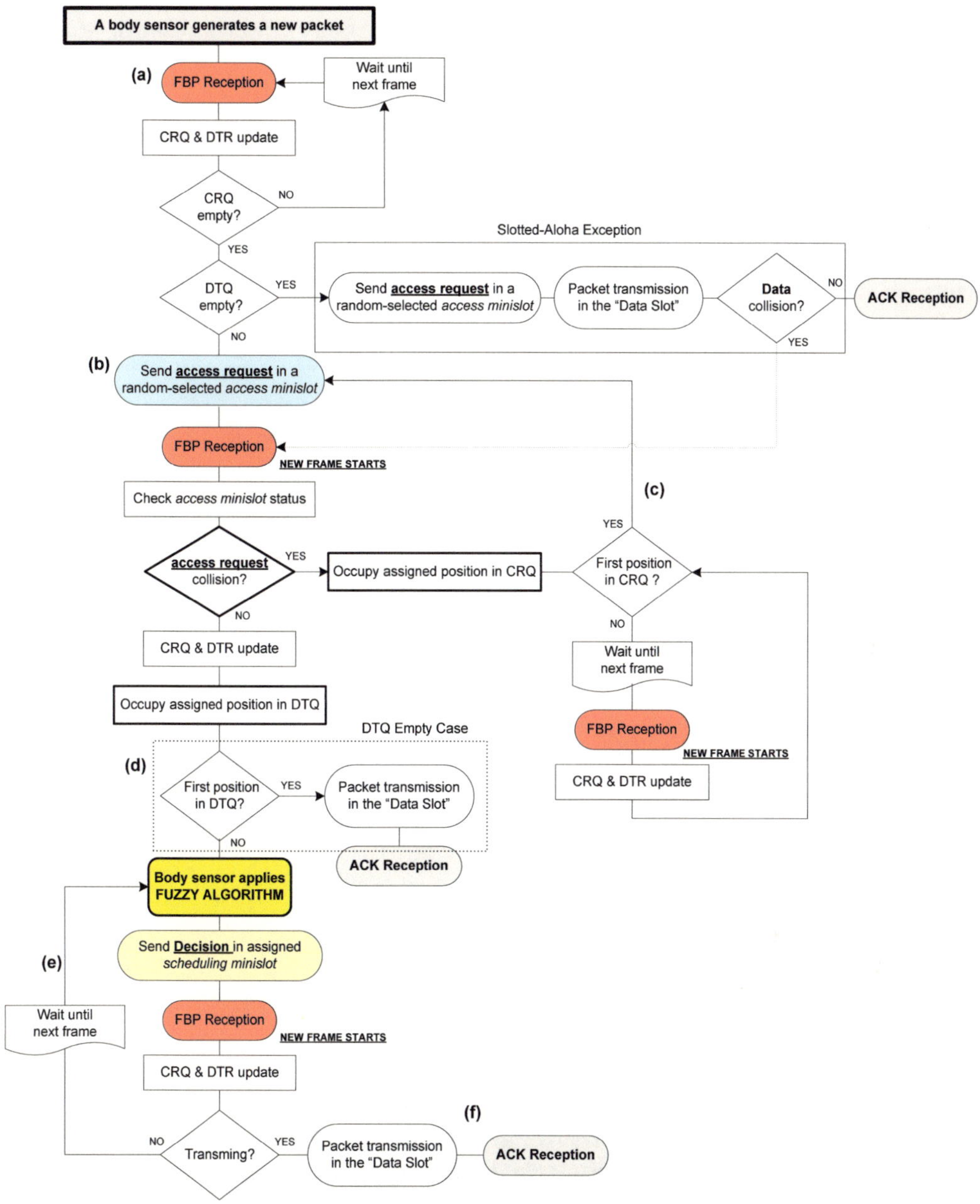

Fig. 6. DQBAN flow chart (with a fuzzy-logic scheduler)

5.2 DQBAN superframe structure

Fig. 7. illustrates the new conditioned DQBAN superframe structure to satisfy the aforementioned medical specific requirements. Body sensors use the following superframe format to communicate with the BAN coordinator:

i) m "access *minislots*" of duration t_{ARS} for access requests sequences,

ii) n "scheduling *minislots*" of duration t_{sch} for exceptional body sensor warnings,

iii) the collision-free "data slot" of variable duration t_{DATA} to send body sensor packets.

Similarly, the BAN coordinator communicates to the body sensors via the fields, already described in Section 4.1 and also illustrated in Fig. 7; (a) an ACK to acknowledge the packet of the transmitting body sensor that must arrive before t_{aw} elapses, as explained in (802.15.4, 2003); (b) the synchronization PRE, which permits the energy-aware radio activation policies previously proposed; and (c) the FBP of fixed duration broadcasted by the BAN coordinator.

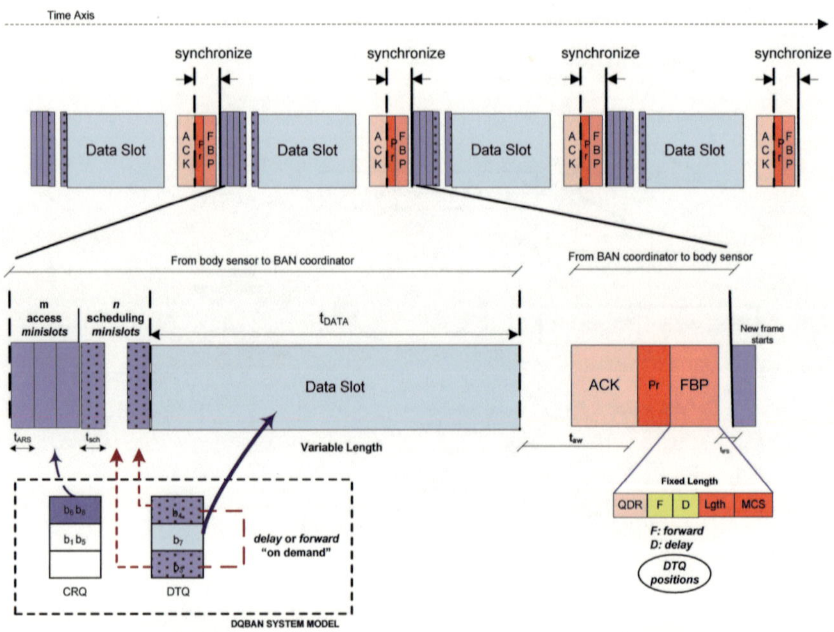

Fig. 7. DQBAN superframe structure

Following the illustration in Fig. 7, DQBAN superframe structure ends with an inter-frame-space, as also defined in 802.15.4. Thanks to the PRE, each body sensor in the BSN uses energy-aware radio activation policies in order to maximize its battery lifetime and minimize its overall energy consumption. Thereafter, it receives all related information of the state of the queues CRQ and DTQ via the FBP. As aforementioned, the FBP is of fixed duration and includes the MCS and the packet length (Lgth) of the following data packet to be transmitted, to allow body sensors to autonomously regulate their own power management activity. Note that, apart from the PRE, the scheduling *minislots* and the strategic FBP subfields F (Forward) and D (Delay) are all brand-new fields especially designed to fulfill the specific BSN requirements in healthcare systems. A detailed description follows.

DQBAN scheduling minislots

Those sensors occupying the *n* first positions in DTQ – with the exemption of the one transmitting in the "data slot" of the current superframe – may send a warning in the assigned scheduling *minislot* to demand or refuse the next "data slot" in case of danger (see Fig. 7). This situation can happen (a) if a non-transmitting body sensor requires urgently to send its packet sooner as indicated in its current position in DTQ (for example due to excessive packet system delay or not enough residual battery lifetime), or (b) whenever a body sensor occupying the second position in DTQ does not find it convenient to transmit in the next frame (for example due to interferences). Since all active body sensors in the BAN are constantly aware of the state of the queues via the FBP, the number of scheduling *minislots* (*n*) might be configurable from DQBAN superframe to superframe, though always equal or smaller than the total number of occupied positions in DTQ.

Thus, now DQBAN behaves as an intelligent MAC protocol adapting itself to traffic load, channel link quality (i.e. interferences) and QoS requirements. That is, DQBAN operates as

i) a slotted ALOHA protocol for light traffic load,

ii) a reservation protocol for high traffic load,

iii) a "polling" protocol to guarantee – "on demand" – a collision-free "data slot".

Notice that to for iii), apart from the new "scheduling minislots" the strategic subfields in FBP (F and D) are essentially required.

DQBAN F and D subfields in FBP

The FBP contains the new strategic fields F (Forward) and D (Delay), which are used by the BAN coordinator to inform body sensors about the overall result of their own decisions (i.e. after their having applied the fuzzy-logic algorithm). That is,

i) the F field refers to "the position occupied by the body sensor in DTQ", which requires to be forwarded to transmit in the next collision-free "data slot". Should more than one body sensor demand simultaneously to be forwarded, the BAN coordinator selects the one occupying the first relative position in DTQ. That is fair, since that body sensor has been waiting longer in the DQBAN system (i.e. fairness).

ii) the D field is active if "the body sensor occupying the current first position in DTQ" indicated its refusal to transmit in the next "data slot". In the case that the F field was empty, the body sensor in the second position in DTQ transmits.

Note that both fields are implementation dependant. The F field is an integer counter and the D field might be a flag (e.g. 1 byte for both fields).

6. Cross-layer fuzzy-logic highly-reliable scheduling mechanism

The new cross-layer fuzzy-rule based scheduling algorithm pursues the idea of playing a determining role between the different physical layer states and the particular body sensors applications. Its main goal is to optimize MAC layer performance in terms of QoS and energy consumption by applying fuzzy-logic decision techniques into the DQBAN logic system model (see Fig. 5). Relying upon each body sensor application and environmental conditions (i.e. multiple input variables of diverse nature, x_1, x_2, to x_k in Fig. 5), the cross-layer fuzzy-rule based scheduler defers or prioritizes transmissions in order to guarantee high reliability at acceptable message latencies, and maximize body sensor battery lifetime. Hence, it is assumed that all body sensors are likely to achieve the required channel quality at a certain time, given the time-varying nature of the wireless link. Nevertheless, a body sensor that might have been waiting for too long in the system or suffer from critical residual battery lifetime will be prioritized so that its data is not compromised. Our scheduling algorithm employs three input continuous variables derived from each body sensor setting and the interaction with its changeable environmental conditions (i.e. wireless channel, system load) in order to decide the new order in DTQ. Bearing in mind the continuous, but dynamic and unpredictable constraints of our system, we found appropriate the use of fuzzy-logic theory for the scheduling algorithm implementation. The advantage of a fuzzy-logic approach is its simplicity of implementation and scalability when dealing with non-linear systems with multiple inputs of diverse nature (Srinoi et al., 2006).

6.1 Fuzzy-logic overview

Fuzzy logic was introduced by Lofti Zadeh (1965), who claimed that many *sets* in the world that surrounds us are defined by a non-distinct boundary. Zadeh decided to extend two-valued logic, defined by the binary pair {0,1} to the whole continuous interval [0,1] thereby introducing a gradual transition from falsehood to truth. Fuzzy logic is a control and decision system approach that mimics human control logic, in the same way a human would make decisions. Fuzzy logic provides a simple way to arrive at a definite conclusion based upon vague, ambiguous or imprecise input information.

Fuzzy-logic theory has been mainly applied to industrial problems including production systems. There has been significant attention given to modeling scheduling problems within a fuzzy framework. Several fuzzy logic based scheduling systems have been developed, although direct comparisons between them are difficult due to their different implementations and objectives (Srinoi et al., 2006). In general, a Fuzzy Logic System (FLS) is a nonlinear mapping of an input data vector into a scalar output. Fuzzy set theory establishes the specifics of the nonlinear mapping (Mendel, 1995). Fig. 8 depicts a FLS that is widely used in fuzzy logic controllers. A FLS maps crisp inputs into crisp outputs, and this mapping can be expressed quantitatively as $y = f(x)$. It contains four components: *fuzzifier*, *fuzzzy rules*, *inference engine*, and *defuzzifier*.

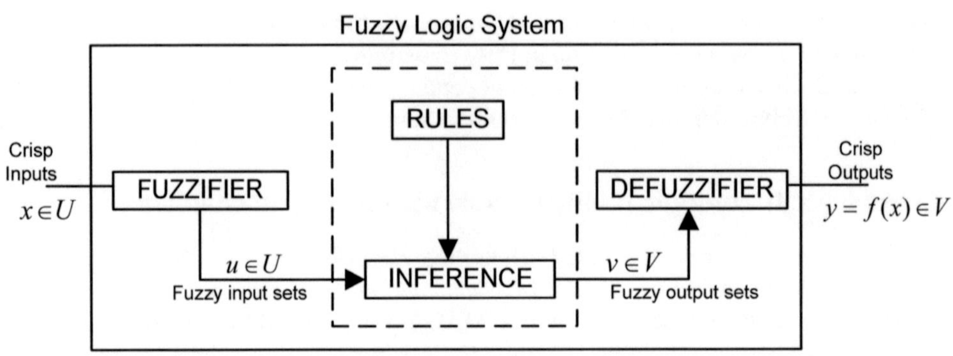

Fig. 8. Fuzzy logic system (FLS)

6.2 Fuzzy-logic scheduling algorithm

In our current implementation design, the fuzzy-logic system integrated in each body sensor employs three cross-layer specific sensor-dependant (i) time-variant (t_i) input variables to satisfy the above-mentioned requirements. These are; (a) the Signal-to-Noise Ratio in dB – $SNR_i(t_i)$ – derived at the reception of the FBP (see Fig. 7), assuming symmetry within uplink and downlink – to and from the BAN coordinator – given a certain coherence time; (b) the Waiting Time in the system in seconds – $WT_i(t_i)$ – calculated from an inherent clock; and, (c) the residual Battery Life in mAh – $BL_i(t_i)$ – derived from an inner hardware indicator. In general, a fuzzy-logic system is a nonlinear mapping of an input data vector into a scalar output and is widely used in fuzzy-logic controllers (Mendel, 1995). Fuzzy set theory establishes the specifics of the nonlinear mapping. A fuzzy logic controller contains four components: *fuzzifier, fuzzzy rules, fuzzy inference process,* and *defuzzifier.* The *fuzzifier* turns the input real values (also called crisp values) into linguistic variables. The *fuzzzy rules* are the linguistic rules, which make up the fuzzy logic controller decision behavior. The *fuzzy inference process* matches the linguistic input variables with the linguistic rules. The result of the *fuzzy inference process* is that the linguistic values are assigned to a set of linguistic output variables. Note that in our fuzzy-logic system implementation, the use of the *defuzzifier* is not required, since body sensors make use of a unique *output linguistic variable* (**Decision**), whose linguistic values remain invariable independently of the number of input real variables.

Fuzzifier

To facilitate the implementation design at the entrance of the fuzzy-logic system, we use normalized values with respect to each body sensor specific constraints: SNR_i^{min}, derived from its particular Bit-Error-Rate (BER_i); WT_i^{max} and BL_i^{min}, application-related maximal message latency and body sensor minimal battery lifetime to send a packet of a specified length. Thus, at the entrance of the *fuzzifier,* there are the following normalized input crisp variables: (a) $SNR_i^*(t_i) = SNR_i(t_i) - SNR_i^{min}$ [dB]; (b) $WT_i^*(t_i) = WT_i(t_i) - WT_i^{max}$ [s]; and (c) $BL_i^*(t_i) = BL_i(t_i) - BL_i^{min}$ [mAh]. These input normalized crisp variables in the *fuzzifier* are associated to the fuzzy sets with the following linguistic terms:

$$\begin{aligned} &\text{SNR} \subset \{dangerous, poor, superior\}; \\ &\text{WT} \subset \{acceptable, boundary, excessive\}; \\ &\text{BL} \subset \{critical, balanced, substancial\}. \end{aligned} \tag{4}$$

The input linguistic values {*dangerous, poor, superior*} constitute the antecedents of the linguistic rules for the associated input fuzzy variable SNR. The set of linguistic values {*acceptable, boundary, excessive*} and {*critical, balanced, substantial*} are associated to the input fuzzy variables WT and BL, respectively. Fig. 9 portrays an illustrative example of the membership functions used in our fuzzy-logic system for all the same sort of antecedents and consequents. The representation of *linguistic2* is an isosceles triangle and the corresponding $\{X_1, X_2, X_3\}$ figures are implementation dependant for each input fuzzy variable and adjusted as a function of the known values SNR_i^{min}, WT_i^{max} and BL_i^{min}. We choose the triangular membership function for its simple expression (i.e. low implementation cost and processing power), as explained in (Srinoi et al., 2006).

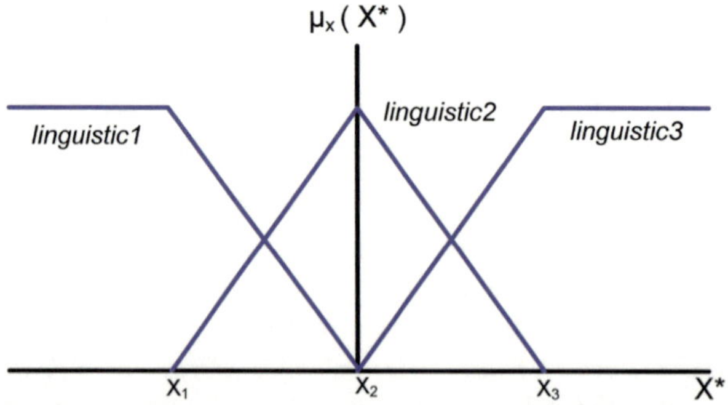

Fig. 9. Membership function example for antecedents and consequents

Fuzzy-logic rules and fuzzy-inference process

Since the linguistic input variables SNR, WT, and BL have each three different states, the total number of possible ordered triplets of these states is 27 (3×3×3). For each of these ordered triplets of states, we have to determine an appropriate state of the *output linguistic variable* **Decision**. That is,

$$\textbf{Decision} \subset \{delay, onschedule, forward\}. \tag{5}$$

The *output linguistic variable* **Decision** is associated to the fuzzy set {*delay, onschedule, forward*}, which forms the consequents of our fuzzy rules. A body sensor **Decision** can be to *delay* its transmission to a future DQBAN superframe, to keep its current position in DTQ by indicating *onschedule,* or to demand the next frame "data slot" by indicating *forward.* Body sensors are allowed to send the value of its output linguistic variable **Decision** in the corresponding scheduling *minislot.* A convenient way of defining all required *fuzzy-logic rules,* that play a role in the *fuzzy inference process* to determine the *output linguistic values* of **Decision**, is with a decision table as the one shown in Table 1.

WT	*SNR*			*BL*
	dangerous	*poor*	*superior*	
acceptable	***delay***	***delay***	***onschedule***	*substantial*
acceptable	***delay***	***delay***	***onschedule***	*balanced*
acceptable	***delay***	***delay***	***delay***	*critical*
boundary	***delay***	***onschedule***	***onschedule***	*substantial*
boundary	***delay***	***onschedule***	***onschedule***	*balanced*
boundary	***forward***	***forward***	***forward***	*critical*
excessive	***forward***	***forward***	***forward***	*substantial*
excessive	***forward***	***forward***	***forward***	*balanced*
excessive	***forward***	***forward***	***forward***	*critical*

Table 1. Output linguistic values of **Decision** (fuzzy inference process)

Next, we provide seven high level *fuzzy-logic rules* for the *output linguistic variable* (**Decision**) with their antecedents and consequent as a result of the combination of the states in Table 1. The first three rules indicate when data transmission requires to be delayed. $R_i^{(1)}$ is used to detect a bad link channel before transmitting. If there is still enough time and battery lifetime left, the aim is to defer data transmission; otherwise it may not be possible to guarantee a particular BER_i for the lowest power transmission state. $R_i^{(2)}$ claims to wait until batteries have been replaced, so that enough battery lifetime can be guaranteed during a packet transmission interval. In the same line, $R_i^{(3)}$ delays a transmission waiting for a better channel quality link following Table 1 solution.

$R_i^{(1)}$: IF SNR is *dangerous* and WT is not *excessive* and
BL is not *critical* THEN **Decision** is *delay*.
$R_i^{(2)}$: IF BL is *critical* and WT is *acceptable* THEN **Decision** is *delay*. (6)
$R_i^{(3)}$: IF SNR is not *superior* and WT is *acceptable*
THEN **Decision** is *delay*.

Both $R_i^{(4)}$ and $R_i^{(5)}$ show when a body sensor can remain in the same position in DTQ since its situation is not critical.

$R_i^{(4)}$: IF SNR is *superior* and WT is *acceptable* and
BL is not *critical* THEN **Decision** is *onschedule*. (7)
$R_i^{(5)}$: IF SNR is not *dangerous* and WT is *boundary* and
BL is not *critical* THEN **Decision** is *onschedule*.

On the contrary, the last two rules warn body sensors about a critical situation to demand the next possible collision-free "data slot" to guarantee QoS. $R_i^{(6)}$ is used when a packet system waiting time is too close to its maximum latency. Note that if SNR were *dangerous*, a body sensor in that situation could even increase its power transmission to compensate the bad quality link, assuming the implementation design allows that. $R_i^{(7)}$ warns each body sensor about its critical residual battery life. The idea is to let the sensor send its packet in the next frame before batteries are replaced due to time constraints.

$R_i^{(6)}$: IF WT is *excessive* THEN **Decision** is *forward*.
$R_i^{(7)}$: IF BL is *critical* and WT is not *acceptable* (8)
THEN **Decision** is *forward*.

7. Case study

In this section, we describe how to analytically model the three sensor-dependant time-variant input variables, $SNR_i(t_i)$, $WT_i(t_i)$ and $BL_i(t_i)$ in the fuzzy-logic system integrated in each body sensor. Further, a new way of implementing the output variable **Decision** is introduced in order to have a comparable relative reference for the evaluation results in the next section. Thereafter, we describe how to evaluate the performance of the overall proposed techniques.

7.1 The cross-layer input variables model

Signal-to-Noise Ratio

Every active body sensor (*i*) obtains its current $SNR_i(t_i)$, in dB, of the link to the BAN coordinator – separated at a random distance (d_i) – upon reception of the FBP at the instant (t_i) (see Fig. 7). Like the authors in (Howitt & Wang, 2004), we define here the received signal as $P_i^R(t_i, d_i) = \overline{P}_i^R(d_i) + X_{\sigma_s}(t_i)$, in dBm, where $X_{\sigma_s}(t_i)$ is a zero mean log-normal distributed random variable with a particular standard deviation 12 dB (i.e. to model interference scenarios). The time-variant received signal model $P_i^R(t_i, d_i)$ includes Additive White Gaussian Noise (AWGN) and the effect of log-normal shadowing assuming the channel is coherent within the transmission of a DQBAN superframe in indoor environments. The calculations are based on the path loss model from the (802.15.4, 2003), where the average received power $\overline{P}_i^R(d_i)$ is expressed as a function of an arbitrary T-R separation distance $d_i < 8$ meters (i.e. within a hospital setting). Here, we compute $SNR_i(t_i)$ by generalizing the formula in (Howitt & Wang, 2004) as,

$$SNR_i(t_i) = SNR_i^{\min} + (P_i^R(t_i, d_i) - P_i^{sens}), \tag{9}$$

where the power sensitivity P_i^{sens} and the current received power $P_i^R(t_i, d_i)$ are sensor-dependant and expressed in dBm. Further, as indicated in the previous section, $SNR_i^{\min}$ depends on a predefined BER_i.

System Waiting Time

An active body sensor calculates its current system Waiting Time $WT_i(t_i)$, in seconds, at the end of each DQBAN superframe at instant (t_i), every time it has a packet to transmit in the queuing system (i.e. CRQ or DTQ). Analytically, $WT_i(t_i)$ is computed, as the sum of all different time superframes $T_{FRAME}(t_i)$ (see Fig. 7), counting from the body sensor first access request at instant ($t = 0$) until the current time ($t = t_i$) for a particular packet in the DQBAN system. That is,

$$WT_i(t_i) = WT_i(t_{i-1}) + T_{FRAME}(t_i) = \sum_{t=0}^{t_i} T_{FRAME}(t) \tag{10}$$

where $T_{FRAME} = m \cdot t_{ARS} + n(t) \cdot t_{sch} + t_{DATA} + t_{aw} + t_{PRE} + t_{FBP} + t_{IFS}$. Please refer to Section 4.1 for the specific time definitions and bear in mind that the number of scheduling *minislots* $n(t)$ might be configurable from DQBAN superframe to DQBAN superframe.

Residual Battery Life

Body sensor *residual* Battery Lifetime $BL_i(t_i)$, in mAh, is obtained as the difference from its *initial* charged battery B_i^{ini} at the time the sensor sends its first access request ($t = 0$) and the *consumed* battery B_i^{cons} at the end of each time frame ($t = t_i$) for a particular packet in the DQBAN queuing system. That is,

$$BL_i(t_i) = B_i^{ini} - B_i^{cons}(t_i) = B_i^{ini} - \sum_{t=0}^{t_i}(B_i^{tx}(t) + B_i^{rx} + B_i^{idle}(t)), \tag{11}$$

where $B_i^{cons}(t_i)$ has been calculated following the power management scenario described in Section 4 for a sensor waiting in DTQ. Further,

$$\begin{aligned} B_i^{tx}(t) &= (t_{ARS}(t) + t_{sch}(t)) \cdot I_{tx}, \\ B_i^{rx} &= (t_{pre} + t_{FBP}) \cdot I_{rx}, \\ B_i^{idle}(t) &= (m \cdot t_{ARS} + n(t) \cdot t_{sch} + T_{DATA}(t) + t_{aw} + t_{IFS}) \cdot I_{idle}, \end{aligned} \tag{12}$$

where I_{tx}, I_{rx} and I_{idle} are the minimum consumption values in *transmit, receive* and *idle* modes corresponding to Chipcon specification data sheet for CC2420 transceiver (Chipcon) in mAh. Note that all other time values have been defined in Section 4.1.

7.2 Performance evaluation metrics

The performance of the proposed techniques is evaluated in a star-based topology BSN where different body sensors with their specific medical requirements communicate with the BAN coordinator in a hospital care scenario through a shared wireless indoor radio channel (see Fig. 1). For scalability reasons, the proposed techniques have been assessed in two specific scenarios,

i) a *homogenous* scenario characterized by a BSN with only wireless ECG body sensors.

ii) a *heterogeneous* scenario characterized by a BSN with a number of ECG body sensors and other different medical sensors with their own specific QoS demands.

BODY SENSORS	ECG	Doctor PDA	Blood Pressure	Respiratory Rate	Endoscope Imaging
BER	10^{-6}	10^{-6}	10^{-8}	10^{-7}	10^{-4}
Latency	0.3 s	1 s	0.75 s	0.6 s	0.5 s
Traffic distribution	Constant	Poisson	Constant	Constant	Poisson
Message generation rate	500 byte/s	1000 byte/s	512 byte/s	1024 byte/s	1538,46 bytes/s
Inter-arrival packet time	0.20 s	0.10 s	0.195 s	0.097 s	0.065 s

Table 2. Medical body sensors specifications

Without losing generality, the PHY layer follows the 802.15.4 standard (802.15.4, 2003) and the hereby introduced DQBAN system is used to model the MAC layer. The performance generation evaluation metrics are defined as follows;

Delivery Ratio

The authors in (Bourgard et al., 2005) performed an energy-saving study about WSNs and estimated the bit error probability on a testbench composed of a CC2420 transmitter wired to a second CC2420 in receiving mode, through a set of calibrated attenuators. Let's consider here their estimated bit error probability – for a body sensor at a random distance (d_i) from the BAN coordinator and at instant (t_i) –, as the exponential regression equation $\rho_i^{bit}(t_i) = 2.35 \cdot 10^{-30} \cdot e^{-0.659 \cdot P_i^R(t_i,d_i)}$. Thereby, we define the probability of success as $\rho_i^{success}(t_i) = (1-\rho_i^{bit}(t_i))^{L_i}$, where L_i corresponds to the total amount of payload data in the DQBAN MAC superframe expressed in bits (see Fig 7.). From the previous $P_i^R(t_i,d_i)$ and $SNR_i(t_i)$ expressions in (9), we defined numerically the probability of success $\rho_i^{success}$, as a function of $SNR_i(t_i)$ values (see Table 3). Further, $\rho_i^{success}$ is grouped in several interval values to ease the fuzzy-logic representation of the SNR membership function, which is used in our simulation scenario. Thus, the "Delivery Ratio" for each particular body sensor is here computed as the percentage of packets that is transmitted successfully, considering:

i) the probability of success $\rho_i^{success}$ in the wireless channel, as defined in Table 3;

ii) the packet timeout due to latency limits and specified for every body sensor in Table 2;

iii) the battery lifetime limitations for each body sensor, as defined in the next section.

$\Delta = SNR_i^*(t_i) = SNR_i(t_i) - SNR_i^{min}$	$\rho = \rho_i^{success}(t_i)$
$\Delta > 12.8$ dB	$0.9824 < \rho < 1$
6.8 dB $< \Delta <$ 12.8 dB	$0.9359 < \rho < 0.9824$
4.8 dB $< \Delta <$ 6.8 dB	$0.7881 < \rho < 0.9359$
2.8 dB $< \Delta <$ 4.8 dB	$0.6199 < \rho < 0.7881$
1.8 dB $< \Delta <$ 2.8 dB	$0.3967 < \rho < 0.6199$
0.8 dB $< \Delta <$ 1.8 dB	$0.0314 < \rho < 0.3967$
$\Delta <$ 0.8 dB	$0 < \rho < 0.0314$

Table 3. Probability of success

Mean Packet Delay and Average Energy Consumption per Utile Bit

The "Mean Packet Delay" is computed for every packet in the system based on (10). On the one hand, the purpose is to prove that the fact of using the fuzzy-logic scheduling algorithm does not affect the overall delay system performance. On the other hand, each body sensor shall satisfy its own latency limits as previously defined in Table 2. Similarly, to obtain the "Average Energy Consumption per Utile Bit", we compute the average time each body sensor is in *transmit*, *receive* and *idle* modes (see Section 4) and multiply these calculated times by the corresponding reference power consumption, following Chipcon specification data sheet for CC2420 transceiver (Chipcon). Note that this computation derives from formulas (11) and (12). To eventually attain the energy consumption per utile bit, we divide per the total average number of information (*utile*) bits per frame.

8. DQBAN performance evaluation results

By means of MATLAB computer simulations, we evaluate the aforementioned metrics – "Delivery Ratio", "Mean Packet Delay" and "Average Energy Consumption per Utile Bit" –, to assess the scalability of the DQBAN system performance as the number of body sensors – in a star-based BSN with a single BAN coordinator – increases until saturation conditions,

i) from 5 to 35 in a *homogenous* scenario with 1-lead ECG body sensors with different initial amount of battery; and,

ii) from 10 to 35 in a *heterogeneous* scenario characterized by 4 different medical sensors as defined in Table 2 (i.e. Clinical PDA, Blood Pressure, Respiratory Rate, Endoscope Imaging) and a growing number of 1-lead ECG sensors.

Be aware that all body sensors are randomly placed at 1-meter to 8-meter distance away from the BAN coordinator in order to symbolize different channel link qualities, as previously detailed in Section 7. In order to define the particular characteristics of the medical sensors, we have considered a similar approach as authors in (Golmie et al., 2005); (Chevrollier & Golmie, 2005). Medical sensors specifications in Table 2 typify each body sensor requirements in terms of BER, latency, traffic generation distribution and message generation rate or inter-arrival packet time at 250 Kb/s as in 802.15.4 (802.15.4, 2003). The selected medical sensors are just a mere example of possible applications in hospital settings. For the sake of simplicity, all body sensors in the *heterogeneous* scenario are initially charged with the same amount of battery, i.e. 5500 mAh in our simulations. Whenever a body sensor runs out of battery, its replacement is supposed to be automatically, since the number of body sensors just increases from iteration to iteration and, it never decreases.

8.1 System parameters

Following DQBAN superframe structure (see Fig 7.), the chosen reference scenario is defined by the set of system parameters provided in Table 4, whose fields correspond to 802.15.4 MAC default values in the upper frequency band at 2.4 GHz and at the unique standardized data rate 250 Kb/s (802.15.4, 2003).

PHY header	6 bytes	**ACK**	11 bytes
MAC header	9 bytes	**Preamble**	4 bytes
Data Payload	100 bytes	**FBP**	11 bytes
T_{aw}	864 µs	T_{IFS}	192 µs

Table 4. DQBAN parameters based on 802.15.4 MAC values

We use one of the longest possible data packet payload lengths – 100 bytes – in order to minimize PHY and MAC overhead per utile (information) bit. Observe that DQBAN preamble and FBP lengths have been based on the 802.15.4 PHY preamble and MAC beacon frame, respectively. For each of the four FBP subfields shown in Fig. 7 though, just 1 byte is required (i.e. 4 bytes). Here the DQBAN *m* access *minislots* occupy each the equivalent of 1 byte. That is a conservative estimate, since theoretically a single bit could do the job, and practically speaking, each body sensor access request could be a separate modulated signal transmission (Xu & Campbell, 1992). Similarly, for the DQBAN novel *n* scheduling *minislots*, the same length of 1 byte is reserved to indicate either *forward* or *delay* (i.e. **Decision** *output linguistic values*). In our current DQBAN simulations, there are $m = 3$ access *minislots* (as in the original (Xu & Campbell, 1992); and $n = 5$ scheduling *minislots*, even though *n* could be configurable from DQBAN superframe to DQBAN superframe, depending on the number of body sensors in DTQ. To simulate the fuzzy-logic system integrated each body sensor, we utilize a MATLAB fuzz-logic toolbox. The aforementioned (X_1, X_3) values for each membership function (see Fig 8) are derived by computer simulations as: (a) $(X_1, X_3) = (1.8, 12.8)$ dB for SNR (following Table 3); (b) $(X_1, X_3) = (-0.108, 0.012)$ seconds for WT, and (c) $(X_1, X_3) = (1000, 2000)$ mAh for BL.

8.2 Simulation results

For the overall evaluation of the DQBAN MAC system performance, we carried out the following models and comparisons among them in both *homogenous* and *heterogeneous* depicted hospital care scenarios,

A. DQBAN model (i.e. with the fuzzy-logic system scheduler and energy-aware radio activation policies),

B. DQ model with a general cost function scheduler as in (Chen et al., 2006) and energy-aware radio activation policies,

C. DQ without any scheduler implementation as in Section 4 (i.e. though with the energy-aware radio activation policies),

D. DQ with neither any energy-aware radio activation policy nor any scheduling algorithm implementation, that is as in (Lin & Campbell, 1993); (Xu & Campbell, 1992).

The results of the "Delivery Ratio", "Mean Packet Delay" and "Average Energy Consumption per Utile Bit" metrics are portrayed in Fig. 9 and Fig. 10 after long iterating and achieving the permanent regime of the DQBAN scheme.

Homogenous Scenario

Fig. 10 depicts the DQBAN MAC performance in a *homogenous* BSN with an increasing number of 1-lead ECG body sensors, whose characteristics are specified in Table 2. Note that 20% of the ECG sensors involved in each simulation are initially charged with much less amount of battery. The idea is to evaluate the energy-saving behavior of the DQBAN system as the traffic load rises until saturation conditions. The "Average Energy Consumption per Utile Bit" in graphic Fig. 10(a) illustrates the requirement of an energy-aware activation policy. In a typical DQ MAC protocol (Lin & Campbell, 1993); (Xu & Campbell, 1992), no energy-saving techniques are utilized. Therefore, as the traffic load increases in the BSN, body sensors remaining longer in the system may run out of battery. As a result, the average energy-consumption per delivered information bit increases. Fig. 10(c) emphasizes that by using energy-aware radio activation policies plus a scheduling algorithm, the MAC layer improves in terms of average energy consumption per utile bit. DQBAN outperforms the aforementioned B. and C. implementations. Notice that it was already proved in Section 4 that the energy-consumption of the DQ MAC (implementation C.) outperforms 802.15.4 in all possible scenarios. The "Delivery Ratio" graphic Fig. 10(b) proves that the fact of scheduling data packets taking cross-layer constraints into account outperforms the first come first served discipline of the original DQ protocol by guaranteeing the QoS requirements of high reliability, right message latency and enough battery lifetime to all body sensors transmissions in the BSN (as described in Section 7.2). The use of DQBAN with the proposed cross-layer fuzzy-rule base scheduling algorithm reaches more than 95% of transmission successes, even though 20% of the ECG sensors have critical battery constraints. Close to saturation limits, DQBAN achievement is specifically 42.75% superior to the original DQ protocol without any energy-aware policy (i.e. implementation D.) and 11.78% superior compared to implementation C. The slight raise in the "Delivery Ratio", in implementations A. and B., results from the growing number of body sensors in DTQ. That is, it is easier to find a body sensor with the appropriate environmental conditions to be scheduled in the first place, while others are reluctant to transmit. Further, Fig. 10(d) confirms that the use DQBAN is also appropriate in terms of "Mean Packet Delay" and still outperforms implementation B., as in all previous studied scenarios.

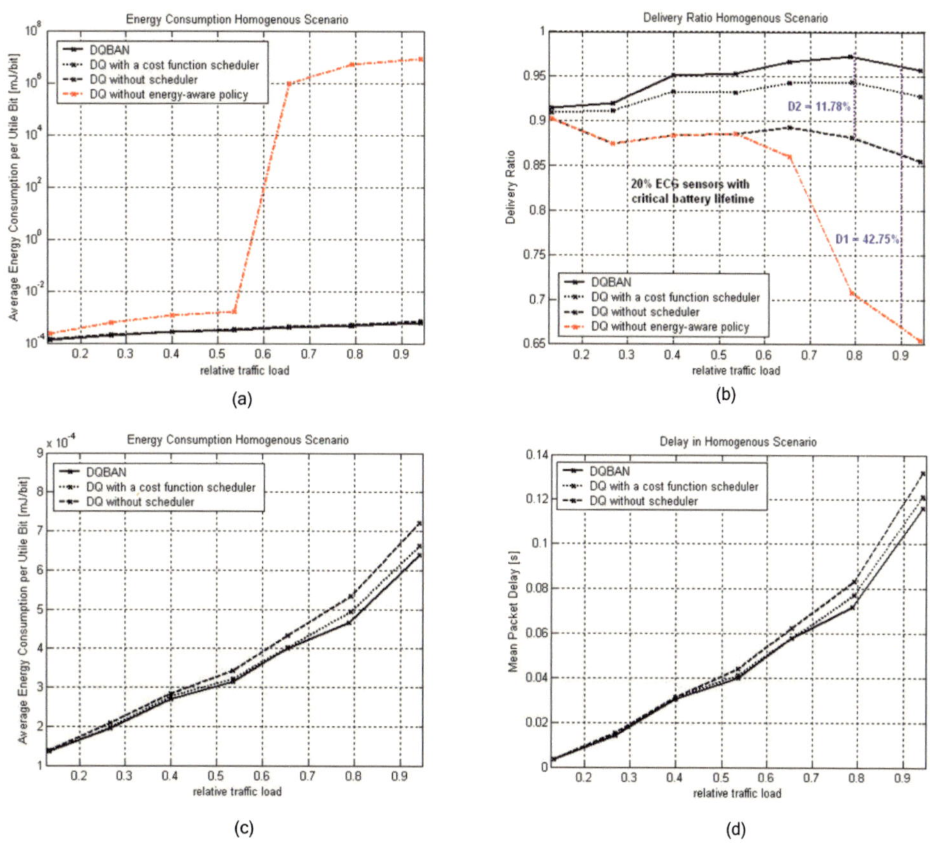

Fig. 10. "Average energy consumption per utile bit" (a) - (c), "Delivery Ratio" (b) and "Mean Packet Delay" (d) in the *homogenous* Scenario

Heterogeneous Scenario

Fig. 11 illustrates the DQBAN MAC performance in a hospital scenario with *heterogeneous* traffic. The *heterogeneous* BSN is characterized by four specific medical body/portable sensors defined in Table 2; a blood pressure body sensor, a respiratory rate body sensor, a real-time endoscope camera and a portable clinical PDA, while the number of ECG body sensors increases from simulated iteration to iteration, as previously explained. In order to facilitate the evaluation of the "Delivery Ratio" metric of the implementations A., B. and C., Fig. 11(a) portrays the performance of the Blood Pressure body sensor and the average performance of the total number of ECG sensors in the *heterogeneous* BSN, separately. When it comes to evaluate the "Delivery Ratio" of the Blood Pressure body sensor, DQBAN is specifically 3.44% and 10% higher than that of implementations B. and C., respectively. In the average ECG case, DQBAN is 3.38% and 10.83% better than B. and C., respectively, while reaching more than 96% of transmission successes. Similarly, Fig. 11(b) depicts the DQBAN achievements for the Respiratory Rate body sensor (17.10%) and the Endoscope Imaging (13.18%) with respect to implementation C. As aforementioned, the slight raise in the "Delivery Ratio", in implementations A. and B., results from the growing number of body sensors in DTQ.

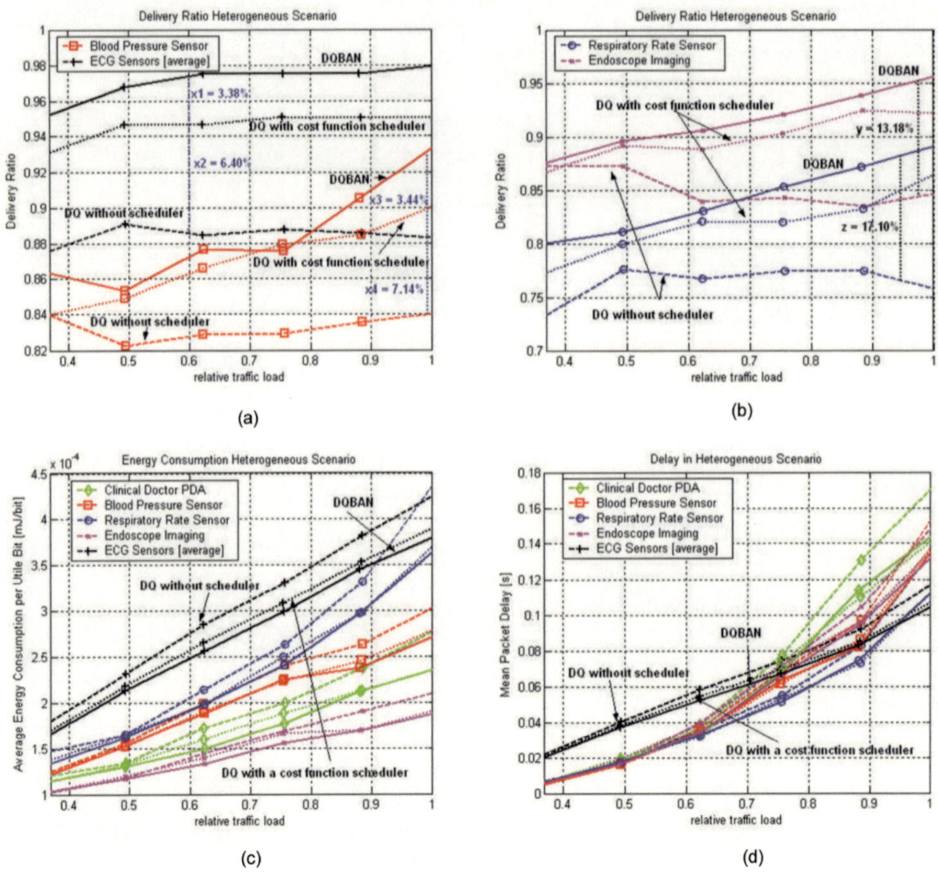

Fig. 11. DQBAN "Delivery Ratio" (a) - (b), "Average Energy Consumption per Utile Bit" (c) and "Mean Packet Delay" (d) in the *heterogeneous* Scenario

In saturation conditions, DQBAN reaches nearly 90% (Respiratory Rate sensor) and 95% (Endoscope Imaging) of transmission successes. Like in the previous studied *homogenous* scenario, Fig. 11 (c) and (d) show the "Average Energy Consumption per Utile Bit" and the "Mean Packet Delay" of all medical body sensors involved therein, confirming again the good inherent performance of the DQBAN model. In general, DQBAN outperforms the B. and C. implementations in all analyzed scenarios, while being more appropriate than B. in terms of scalability for healthcare applications.

9. Conclusions

In this chapter, a new energy-efficiency theoretical analysis for an enhanced DQ MAC protocol has been introduced, as a potential candidate for future BSNs. For that purpose, energy-aware radio activation policies are first introduced in order to allow power management regulation to minimize the energy consumption per information bit. The analytical study has been validated by simulation results, which have shown that the proposed mechanism outperforms IEEE 802.15.4 MAC energy-efficiency for all traffic loads in a generalized BSN scenario. Further, the proposed MAC protocol commitment is to also guarantee that all packet transmissions are served with their particular application-dependant QoS requirements (i.e. reliability and message latency), without endangering body sensors battery lifetime in BSNs. For that purpose, a cross-layer fuzzy-rule scheduling algorithm has been introduced. This scheduling mechanism permits a body sensor, though not occupying the first position in the new MAC queuing model, to send its packet in the next frame in order to achieve a far more reliable system performance. The new DQBAN MAC model has been evaluated in a star-based BSNs under two different realistic hospital scenarios with diverse medical body sensor characterizations. The evaluation metric results are in terms of "delivery ratio", "average energy consumption per utile bit" and "mean packet delay", as the traffic load in the BSN rises to saturation limits. By means of computer simulations, the DQBAN MAC model has shown to achieve higher reliabilities than other possible MAC implementations, while fulfilling body sensor specific latency demands and battery limits. Thus, the use of DQBAN MAC reaches high transmission successes even in saturation conditions, while keeping the good inherent energy-saving protocol behaviour. This proves to scale for future BSN in healthcare scenarios.

10. References

Alonso, L.; Ferrús, R. & Agustí, R. (2005). WLAN Throughput Improvement via Distributed Queuing MAC, *IEEE Communication Letters*, pp. 310–12, Vol. 9, No. 4, April 2005.

Bourgard, B.; Catthoor, F.; Daly, D.C.; Chandrakasam A. & Dehaene, W. (2005). Energy Efficiency of the IEEE 802.15.4 Standard in Dense Wireless Microsensor Networks: Modeling and Improvement Perspectives, *Proceedings of IEEE Design Automation and Test in Europe Conference and Exhibition*, pp. 196-201, Calgary, Canada, March 2005.

Chen, J-L.; Chang, Y-C. & Chen, M-C. (2006). Enhancing WLAN/UMTS Dual-Mode Services Using a Novel Distributed Multi-Agent Scheduling Scheme, *Proceedings of the 11th IEEE Symposium on Computers and Communications* (ISCC'06), Sardinia, Italy, June 2006.

Chevrollier, N. & Golmie, N. (2005). On the Use of Wireless Network Technologies in Healthcare Environments, *Proceedings of 5th Workshop on Applications and Services n Wireless Networks (ASWN'05)*, pp. 147-152, Paris, France, June 2005.

Chipcon, *SmartRF CC2420: 2.4 GHz IEEE802.15.4/Zigbee RF Transceiver*, Data Sheet.

Golmie, N.; Cypher, D. & Rebala, O. (2005). Performance Analysis of Low-Rate Wireless Technologies for Medical Applications, *Elsevier Computer Communications*, pp. 1266–1275, Vol. 28, No. 10, June 2005.

Howitt, I. & Wang, J. (2004). Energy Efficient Power Control Policies for the Low Rate WPAN, *Proceedings IEEE Sensor and Ad Hoc Communications and Networks (SECON 2004)*, pp. 527–536, Santa Clara, California, US, October 2004.

IEEE Std. 802.15.4-2003, *IEEE Standards for Information Technology Part 15.4: Wireless Medium Access Control (MAC) and Physical Layer (PHY) Specifications for Low-Rate Wireless Personal Area Networks (LR-WPANs)*, 1st October 2003.

Kumar, P.; Günes, M.; Almamou, A.B. & Schiller, J. (2008). Real-time, Bandwidth, and Energy Efficient IEEE 802.15.4 for Medical Applications, *Proceedings of 7th GI/ITG KuVS Fachgespräch Drahtlose Sensornetze,* FU Berlin, Germany, September 2008.

Lin, H.J. & Campbell, G. (1993). Using DQRAP (Distributed Queuing Random Access Protocol) for local wireless communications, *Proceedings of Wireless'93*, pp. 625-635, Calgary, Canada, July 1993.

Mendel, J.M. (1995). Fuzzy Logic Systems for Engineering: A Tutorial, *Proceedings of the IEEE*, pp. 345-377, Vol. 83, No. 3, March 1995.

Otal, B.; Alonso, L. & Verikoukis, C. (2009). Highly Reliable Energy-Saving MAC for Wireless Body Sensor Networks in Healthcare Systems, *IEEE Journal on Selected Areas in Communications (JSAC) - Wireless and Pervasive Communications for Healthcare*, June 2009.

Park, T-R.; Kim, T.H.; Choi, J.Y.; Choi, S. & Kwon, W.H. (2005). Throughput and Energy Consumption Analysis of IEEE 802.15.4 slotted CSMA/CA, *Electronic Letters*, Vol. 41, No.18, September 2005.

Pollin S. et al. (2005). Performance Analysis of Slotted IEEE 802.15.4 Medium Access Layer, *Technical Report DAWN Project*, September 2005.

Srinoi, P.; Shayan, E. & Ghotb, F. (2006). Scheduling of Flexible Manufacturing Systems Using Fuzzy Logic, *International Journal of Production Research*, pp. 1-21. Vol. 44, No. 11 2006.

Xu, X. & Campbell, G. (1992). A Near Perfect Stable Random Access Protocol for a Broadcast Channel, *Proceedings of IEEE Communications, Discovering a New World of Communications (SUPERCOMM/ICC'92)*, pp. 370–374, Vol. 1, Chicago, USA, June 1992.

Yang, G-Z. (Ed.) (2006), *Body Sensor Networks*, Springer-Verlag London Limited 2006, ISBN-10: 1-84628-272-1.

Zhang & Campbell, G. (1993). Performance Analysis of Distributed Queuing Random Access Protocol - DQRAP, *DQRAP Research Group Report 93-1*, Computer Science Dept. IIT, August 1993.

Zhen, B.; Li, H-B. & Kohno, R. (2007), IEEE Body Area Networks for Medical Applications, *Proceedings of IEEE 4th International Symposium on Wireless Communication Systems (ISWCS 2007)*, pp. 327-331, Trondheim, Norway, October 2007.

7

Throughput Analysis of Wireless Sensor Networks via Evaluation of Connectivity and MAC performance

Flavio Fabbri and Chiara Buratti
WiLAB, IEIIT-BO/CNR, DEIS University of Bologna
ITALY

1. Introduction

The data throughput that a wireless sensor network (WSN) can guarantee is influenced by a plethora of concurrent causes. Among those, limited connectivity and medium access control (MAC) failures are major issues that should be carefully considered. The aim of this chapter is to provide the reader with a neat and general mathematical framework for the analytical computation of key performance metrics of WSNs. The focus is on connectivity and MAC issues. Quantitative answers to such questions as the following will be given: how well is the network -or a subset of it- connected? What is the rate at which sensors are able to transmit their data to sink(s)? What is the overall throughput of a sensor network deployed on a specific domain?

We consider a multi-sink WSN where sensor and sink nodes are both randomly deployed on a finite or infinite domain. Sensors are in charge of sampling the surrounding environment and send their data to one of the sinks, possibly the one providing the best signal strength. The computation requires some basic assumptions that hold throughout the chapter: two nodes are considered connected if the path loss (including both a deterministic distance-dependent component and a random fluctuation) is above a fixed threshold; all nodes employ the same transmission power; sinks have an ideal connection to an infrastructured processing center.

We first address connectivity issues by considering single-hop networks with nodes deployed on the infinite plane, then, after discussing the role of border effects and providing a mathematical means to deal with them, we consider networks on finite regions of square shape. The probabilities that a randomly chosen sensor is connected to one of the sinks, that all sensors -or some percentage of them- are connected, are computed. The connectivity model is then generalized to handle the case of rectangular deployment regions as well as inhomogeneous nodes densities. However, signal strength based connectivity is not exhaustive for real-life applications where failures may occur due to packet collisions, even in perfect channel conditions. For this reason, we also present a rigorous approach for modeling the MAC layer under a carrier-sense multiple access with collision avoidance (CSMA/CA) protocol when several sensor nodes compete for accessing the same channel at the same time. In particular, the analysis is carried out in the specific case of IEEE 802.15.4 MAC algorithm under both Beacon- and Non Beacon-Enabled operation modes. By looking at a single sink scenario with a number of

sensors, the practical outcome is the probability of successful packet reception by the sink, used to derive the throughput from sensors to sink.
Finally, going back to a multi-sink scenario, we now have the means for computing the probabilities that a sensor is connected to an arbitrary sink and that it succeeds in transmitting its packet. Therefore, by integrating the two building blocks mentioned before, we end up with an analytical tool for studying the performance of multi-sink WSNs, where MAC and connectivity issues are taken into account. Network performance is synthesized by introducing the concept of Area Throughput, that is, the number of samples per unit of time successfully delivered by the sensors to the infrastructure. Numerical results are given for the case of IEEE 802.15.4 MAC protocol. The model is also applicable to WSNs employing any MAC protocol.
The chapter is organized as follows. In Section 2 the application scenario is described and some related works are presented. Section 3 introduces the link and connectivity models used. In Sections 4 and 5 connectivity results are derived for the case of unbounded and bounded networks, respectively. Section 6 is devoted to the MAC model and finally Section 7 reports throughput results.

2. Application Scenario

A multi-sink WSN is considered where data collection from the environment is performed by sampling some physical entities and sending them to some external user. The reference application is spatial/temporal process estimation Verdone et al. (2008) and the environment is observed through queries/response mechanisms: queries are periodically generated by the sinks, and sensor nodes respond by sampling and sending data. Through a simple polling model, sinks periodically issue queries, causing all sensors perform sensing and communicating their measurement results back to the sinks they are associated with. The user, by collecting samples taken from different locations, and observing their temporal variations, can estimate the realisation of the observed process. Good estimates require sufficient data taken from the environment. Often, the data must be sampled from a specific portion of space, even if the sensor nodes are distributed over a larger area. Therefore, only a location-driven subset of sensor nodes must respond to queries. The aim of the query/response mechanism is then to acquire the largest possible number of samples from the area. Since the acquisition of samples from the target area is the main issue for the application scenario considered, a new metric for studying the behavior of the WSN, namely the *Area Throughput*, denoting the amount of samples per unit of time successfully transmitted to the final user originating from the target area, is defined. As expected, area throughput is larger if the density of sensor nodes is larger; on the other hand, if a contention-based MAC protocol is used, the density of nodes significantly affects the ability of the protocol to avoid packet collisions (i.e., simultaneous transmissions from separate sensors toward the same sink). In fact, if the number of sensor nodes per cluster is very large, collisions and backoff procedures can make data transmission impossible under time-constrained conditions, and samples taken from sensors do not reach the sinks and, consequently, the final user. Therefore, the optimization of the area throughput requires proper dimensioning of the density of sensors, in a framework model where both MAC and connectivity issues are considered. Although our model could be applied to any MAC protocol, we particularly refer to CSMA-based protocols, and specifically to IEEE 802.15.4 air interface. In this case, sinks act as PAN coordinators periodically transmitting queries to sensors and waiting for replies. According to the standard, the different personal area network (PAN) coordinators, and therefore the PANs, use different frequency channels. Therefore no collisions may occur between nodes belonging to different PANss; however, nodes belonging to the same PANs compete when trying to transmit their packets to the sink. An infinite area where sensors and sinks are uniformly distributed at random, is considered. Then, a specific portion of space, of finite size and given shape (without loss of generality, we consider a square or a rectangle), is considered as target area (see Figure 1).

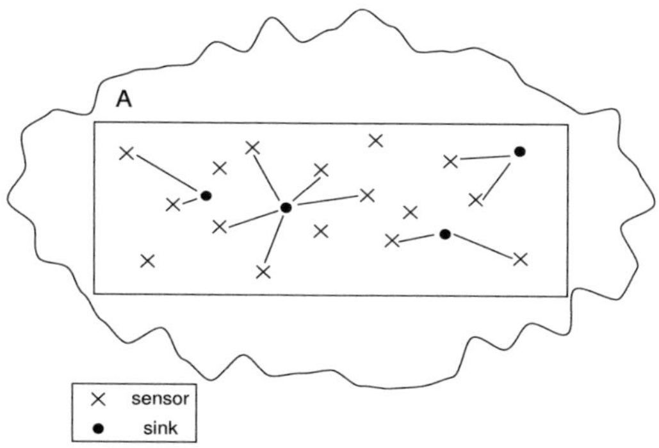

Fig. 1. The Reference Scenario considered.

We assume that sensors and sinks are distributed over the bi-dimensional plane with densities ρ_s and ρ_0, respectively, with the latter much smaller than the former. Denoting with A the area of the target domain and by k the number of sensor nodes in A, k is Poisson distributed with mean $\bar{k} = \rho_s \cdot A$ and p.d.f.

$$g_k = \frac{\bar{k}^k e^{-\bar{k}}}{k!}. \tag{1}$$

We also let $I = \rho_0 \cdot A$ be the average number of sinks in A.
The frequency of the queries transmitted by the sinks is denoted as $f_q = 1/T_q$. Each sensor takes, upon reception of a query, one sample of a given phenomenon and forwards it through a direct link to the sink. Once transmission is performed, it switches to an idle state until reception of the next query. We denote the interval between two successive queries as *round*. The amount of samples available from the sensors deployed in the area, per unit of time, is denoted as *Available Area Throughput*. In this Chapter we determine how the area throughput depends on the available area throughput for different scenarios and system parameters.

2.1 Related Works

Many works in the literature devoted their attention to connectivity in WSNs or to the analytical study of carrier-sense multiple access (CSMA)-based MAC protocols. However, very few papers jointly consider the two issues under a mathematical approach. Some analysis of the two aspects are performed through simulations: as examples, Studi et al. (2005) related to ad hoc networks, and Buratti & Verdone (2006), to WSN. Many papers based on random graph theory, continuum percolation and geometric probability Bollobàs (2001); Meester & Roy (1996); Penrose (1993; 1999); Penrose & Pistztora (1996) addressed connectivity issues of networks. In particular, wireless ad hoc and sensor networks have recently attracted a growing attention Bettstetter (2002); Bettstetter & Zangl (2002); Pishro-Nik et al. (2004); Salbaroli & Zanella (2006); Santi & Blough (2003); Vincze et al. (2007). A great insight on connectivity of ad hoc wireless networks is provided in Bettstetter (2002); Bettstetter & Zangl (2002); Santi & Blough (2003). Nonetheless, the authors do not account for random channel fluctuations and do not explicitly discuss the presence of one or more fusion centers (sinks) in the given region. Connectivity-related issues of WSNs are addressed in Salbaroli & Zanella (2006); Vincze et al. (2007). In Salbaroli & Zanella (2006), while considering channel randomness, the authors restrict the analysis to a single-sink scenario. Although single-sink scenarios have attracted more attention so far, multi-sink networks have been increasingly considered in the very recent time. As an example, Vincze et al. (2007) addresses the problem of deploying multiple sinks in a multi-hop limited WSN. However, the work presents a deterministic approach to distribute the sinks on a given region, rather than considering a more general uniform random deployment. Furthermore, since the finiteness of deployment region plays a not secondary role on connectivity, those models based on bounded domains turn out to be of more practical use.

Concerning the analytical study of CSMA-based MAC protocols, in Takagi & Kleinrock (1985) the throughput for a finite population when a persistent CSMA protocol is used, is evaluated. An analytical model of the IEEE 802.11 CSMA-based MAC protocol, is presented by Bianchi in Bianchi (2000). In these works no physical layer or channel model characteristics are accounted for. Capture effects with CSMA in Rayleigh channels are considered in Zdunek et al. (1989), whereas Kim & Lee (1999) addresses CSMA/CA protocols. However, no connectivity issues are considered in these papers: the transmitting terminals are assumed to be connected to the destination node. In Siripongwutikorn (2006) the per-node saturated throughput of an IEEE 802.11b multi-hop ad hoc network with a uniform transmission range, is evaluated under simplified conditions from the viewpoint of channel fluctuations and number of nodes. Also, some studies have tried to describe analytically the behavior of the 802.15.4 MAC protocol. Few works devoted their attention to non beacon-enabled mode (see, e.g. Kim et al. (2006)); most of the analytical models are related to beacon-enabled networks Misic et al. (2004; 2005; 2006); Park et al. (2005); Pollin et al. (2008). Some of these fail to match simulation results (see, e.g. Pollin et al. (2008)), whereas slightly more accurate models are proposed in Park et al. (2005) and Chen et al. (2007), where, however, the sensing states are not correctly captured by the Markov chain. In conclusion, the most relevant difference between the previously cited models and the one developed in Buratti & Verdone (2009) and Buratti (2009) and used here, is that the latter precisely captures the algorithm defined by the standard, while considering a typical WSN scenario. In our scenario nodes only have one packet to transmit to the sink (i.e., when they receive the query and have to transmit data before the reception of the subsequent query). Therefore, the number of nodes competing for channel at a given time is unknown and not constant (as it is in the above cited works) but it decreases with time, since successful nodes go to sleep till next query.

Finally, to the best of the Authors knowledge, no one has so far introduced any connectivity/MAC model for WSNs while jointly considering the following aspects: presence of both sensors and multiple sinks, random deployment of nodes, bounded scenarios, channel fluctuations, realistic MAC protocol in non-saturation condition.

3. Link and Connectivity Models

Many works in the WSN scientific literature assume deterministic distance- dependent and threshold-based packet capture models. This means that all nodes within a circle centered at the transmitter can receive a packet sent by the transmitting one Bettstetter (2002); Bettstetter & Zangl (2002); Santi & Blough (2003). While the threshold-based capture model, which assumes that a packet is captured if the signal-to-noise ratio (in the absence of interference) is above a given threshold, is a good approximation of real capture effects, the deterministic

channel model does not represent realistic situations in most cases. The use of realistic channel models is therefore of primary importance in wireless systems.
In this chapter, a narrow-band channel, accounting for the power loss due to propagation effects including a distance-dependent path loss and random channel fluctuations, is considered.
Specifically, the power loss in decibel scale at distance d is expressed in the following form

$$L(d) = k_0 + k_1 \ln d + s, \tag{2}$$

where k_0 and k_1 are constants, s is a Gaussian r.v. with zero mean, variance σ^2, which represents the channel fluctuations. This channel model was also adopted by Orriss and Barton Orriss & Barton (2003) and other Authors Miorandi & Altman (2005). In Verdone et al. (2008) experimental measurement results, performed with 802.15.4 devices at 2.4 [GHz] Industrial Scientific Medical (ISM) band, deployed in different environments (grass, asphalt, indoor, etc), are shown. It is found for the received power in logarithmic scale that in general a Gaussian model can approximate the measurement variation fairly well, with different values of the standard deviation. By suitably setting k_1, it is possible to accommodate an inverse square law relationship between power and distance ($k_1 = 8.69$), or an inverse fourth-power law ($k_1 = 17.37$), as examples.
For what concerns the link model, a radio link between two nodes is said to exist, which means that the two nodes are *connected* or *audible* to each other [1], if $L < L_{th}$, where L_{th} represents the maximum loss tolerable by the communication system. The threshold L_{th} depends on the transmit power and the receiver sensitivity.
By solving (2) for the distance d with $L = L_{\text{th}}$, we can define the transmission range

$$TR = e^{\frac{L_{\text{th}} - k_0 - s}{k_1}}, \tag{3}$$

as the maximum distance between two nodes at which communication can still take place. Such range defines the connectivity region of the sensor. Note that by adopting independent r.v.'s s for separate links, we have different values of TR for different sinks, given a generic sensor. In other words, unlike many papers dealing with connectivity issues in the literature Bettstetter (2002); Bettstetter & Zangl (2002); Santi & Blough (2003), we do not use circles to predict sensor connectivity. However, by setting $\sigma = 0$, we neglect the channel fluctuations and may still define an ideal transmission range, as a reference, as

$$TR_{\text{i}} = e^{\frac{L_{\text{th}} - k_0}{k_1}}. \tag{4}$$

Finally, we can define a connection function between any node pair whose distance is d as

$$g(d) = \text{Prob}\{L(d) < L_{\text{th}}\} = 1 - \frac{1}{2}\text{erfc}\left(\frac{L_{\text{th}} - k_0 - k_1 \ln d}{\sqrt{2}\sigma}\right). \tag{5}$$

3.1 Connectivity properties in Poisson fields

Connectivity theory studies networks formed by large numbers of nodes distributed according to some statistics over a limited or unlimited region of $\mathbb{R}^d$, with d=1,2,3, and aims at describing the potential set of links that can connect nodes to each other, subject to some constraints from the physical viewpoint (power budget, or radio resource limitations).

[1] link's reciprocity is assumed.

It is widely accepted that, a WSN is *fully-connected* in case any sensor node is able to reach at least one sink node, either directly or through other sensor nodes Verdone et al. (2008) (not necessarily requiring any node to be reached by any other node).
Let us consider a stationary Poisson Point Process (PPP) $\Phi = \{\mathbf{x_1}, \mathbf{x_2}, \ldots\}$ having intensity ρ, with $\mathbf{x_i} = (x_i, y_i)$, $i = 1, 2, \ldots$ being a random point in $\mathbb{R}^2$. Φ may also be regarded as a random measure on the Borel sets in $\mathbb{R}^2$: taken any $\Omega \subset \mathbb{R}^2$ having area W_Ω, $\Phi(\Omega)$ is a Poisson r.v. which counts the number of points of Φ that lie in the set Ω, whose first order moment is

$$\mathbf{E}(\Phi(\Omega)) = \rho \nu_d(\Omega) = \rho \int_\Omega d\mathbf{x} = \rho W_\Omega, \tag{6}$$

where $\nu_d(\Omega)$ is the Lebesgue measure of Ω. Now suppose we want to count only those points in Ω which are connected to an arbitrary node $\mathbf{x_0}$: this implies a thinning procedure on Φ such that each point is retained with probability $C(||\mathbf{x_0} - \mathbf{x_i}||)$ and discarded with probability $1 - C(||\mathbf{x_0} - \mathbf{x_i}||)$, $i = 1, 2, \ldots$, where $C(x)$ is a non-negative measurable function such that $0 \leq C(x) \leq 1$. By so doing, the new inhomogeneous process Φ' is obtained.
By recalling the *Campbell Theorem* for point processes Gardner (1989) that we report for later use

$$\mathbf{E}\left(\sum_{\mathbf{x} \in \Omega} f(\mathbf{x})\right) = \rho \int_\Omega f(\mathbf{x}) d\mathbf{x}, \tag{7}$$

for any non-negative measurable function f, we have for Φ'

$$\mu = \mathbf{E}(\Phi'(\Omega)) = \mathbf{E}\left(\sum_{\mathbf{x} \in \Omega} C(||\mathbf{x_0} - \mathbf{x}||)\right) = \rho \int_\Omega C(||\mathbf{x_0} - \mathbf{x}||) d\mathbf{x}. \tag{8}$$

In particular, when the channel model of eq. (2) is used (i.e., $C(x) \equiv g(x)$), the mean number of nodes audible within a range of distances r_1 and r, to a generic node ($r \geq r_1$), is denoted as $\mu_{r_1,r}$ and can be written as Orriss & Barton (2003); Orriss et al. (1999)

$$\mu_{r_1,r} = \pi\rho[\Psi(a_1, b_1; r) - \Psi(a_1, b_1; r_1)], \tag{9}$$

where ρ is the initial nodes' density and

$$\begin{aligned} \Psi(a_1, b_1; r) &= r^2 \Phi(a_1 - b_1 \ln r) \\ &- e^{\frac{2a_1}{b_1} + \frac{2}{b_1^2}} \Phi(a_1 - b_1 \ln r + 2/b_1), \end{aligned} \tag{10}$$

and $a_1 = (L_{\text{th}} - k_0)/\sigma$, $b_1 = k_1/\sigma$ and $\Phi(x) = \int_{-\infty}^{x} (1/\sqrt{2\pi}) e^{-u^2/2} du$.

4. Connectivity in Unbounded Networks

Since the channel model described by eq. (2) is used, the number of audible sinks within a range of distances r_1 and r from a generic sensor node ($r \geq r_1$), $n_{r_1,r}$, is Poisson distributed with mean $\mu_{r_1,r}$, given by eq. (9) by simply substituting ρ with ρ_0. Then by letting $r_1 = 0$ and $r \to \infty$, we obtain

$$\mu_{0,\infty} = \pi\rho_0 \exp[(2(L_{\text{th}} - k_0)/k_1) + (2\sigma^2/k_1^2)]\,. \tag{11}$$

Equation (11) represents the mean value of the total number, $n_{0,\infty}$, of audible sinks for a generic sensor, obtained considering an infinite plane Orriss & Barton (2003).
Its non-isolation probability is simply the probability that the number of audible sinks is greater than zero

$$q_\infty = 1 - e^{-\mu_{0,\infty}} . \tag{12}$$

5. Connectivity in Bounded Networks

When moving to networks of nodes located in bounded domains, two important changes happen. First, even with ρ_0 unchanged, the number of sinks that are audible from a generic sensor will be lower due to geometric constraints (a finite area contains (on average) a lower number of audible sinks than an infinite plane). Second, the mean number of audible sinks will depend on the position (x, y) in which the sensor node is located in the region that we consider. The reason for this is that sensors which are at a distance d from the border, with $d \sim TR_i$, have smaller connectivity regions and thus the average number of audible sinks is smaller. These effects, known in literature as *border effects* Bettstetter & Zangl (2002), are accounted for in our model.

The result (9) can be easily adjusted to show that the number of audible sinks within a sector of an annulus having radii r_1 and r and subtending an angle 2θ, is once again Poisson distributed with mean

$$\mu_{r_1,r;\theta} = \theta\rho_0[\Psi(a_1, b_1; r) - \Psi(a_1, b_1; r_1)], \tag{13}$$

$0 \le \theta \le \pi$. If the annulus extends from r to $r + \delta r$, and $\theta = \theta(r)$, this mean value becomes

$$\mu_{r,r+\delta r;\theta} = \theta(r)\rho_0 \frac{\delta\Psi(a_1, b_1; r)}{\delta r}\delta r, \ 0 \le \theta \le \pi. \tag{14}$$

Consider now a polar coordinate system whose origin coincides with a sensor node. As a consequence of (14), if a region is located within the two radii r_1 and r_2 and its points at a distance r from the origin are defined by a $\theta(r)$ law (see Fabbri & Verdone (2008), Fig. 1), then the number of audible sinks in such a region is again Poisson distributed with mean $\mu_{r_1,r_2;\theta(r)} = \int_{r_1}^{r_2} \theta(r)\rho_0 \frac{d\Psi(a_1,b_1;r)}{dr} dr$, that is, from (10) and after some algebra,

$$\mu_{r_1,r_2;\theta(r)} = \int_{r_1}^{r_2} 2\theta(r)\rho_0 r \Phi(a_1 - b_1 \ln r) dr. \tag{15}$$

5.1 Square Regions

Now consider a square SA of side L meters and area $A = L^2$, sensors and sinks uniformly distributed on it with densities ρ_s and ρ_0, respectively. Equation (15) is suitable for expressing the mean number of audible sinks from an arbitrary point (x, y) of SA, provided that such point is considered as a new origin and that the boundary of SA is expressed with respect to the new origin as a function of r_1, r_2 and $\theta(r)$. In order to apply equation (15) to this scenario and obtain the mean number, $\mu(x, y)$, of audible sinks from the point (x, y), it is needed to set the origin of a reference system in (x, y), partition SA in eight subregions $(S_{r,1} \dots S_{r,8})$ by means of circles whose centers lie in (x, y) (see Fabbri & Verdone (2008), Fig. 2). Thank to the properties of Poisson r.v.'s, the contribution of each region can be summed and we obtain an exact expression for

$$\mu(x, y) = \sum_{i=1}^{8} \int_{r_{1,i}}^{r_{2,i}} 2\theta_i(r) \cdot \rho_0 \cdot r \cdot \Phi(a_1 - b_1 \ln r) dr, \tag{16}$$

which is the mean number of sinks in SA that are audible from (x, y), where $r_{1,i}$, $r_{2,i}$, $\theta_i(r)$ are reported in Fabbri & Verdone (2008), Tables 1-2.

If we assume a single-hop network, a sensor potentially located in (x, y) is isolated (i.e., there are no audible sinks from its position) with probability $p(x, y) = e^{-\mu(x,y)}$ and it is non isolated with probability

$$q(x, y) = 1 - e^{-\mu(x,y)}. \tag{17}$$

Owing to the assumption that sensor nodes are uniformly and randomly distributed in *SA*, if we now want to compute the probability that a randomly chosen sensor node is not isolated, we need to take the average $q(x, y)$ on *SA*. In fact, the probability that a randomly chosen sensor node is not isolated (which is an ensemble measure) and the average non-isolation probability over a single realization coincides due to the ergodicity of stationary Poisson processes (see Stoyan et al. (1995), page 104). This was also verified by simulation.
Recalling that we have considered the lower half of the first quadrant, which is one eighth of the totality, we have

$$\overline{q} = \frac{8}{A} \int_0^{L/2} \int_0^x q(x, y) dy dx. \tag{18}$$

5.2 Rectangular Regions

We now consider a rectangular domain C of sides S_1 and S_2, $S_1 > S_2$, area $W = S_1 \cdot S_2$, with sensors and sinks uniformly distributed on it with densities ρ_s and ρ_0, respectively. We aim at computing the mean number of audible sinks from a fixed position (x, y) which are contained in C. Since we are dealing with a rectangular domain whose points have to be expressed in polar coordinates in order to apply (15), such a domain has to be properly partitioned into a set of subregions, to be defined in terms of r_1, r_2, and θ. Moreover, unlike the case of square domain, the nature of the partition depends on the position (x, y) considered. In particular, if we restrict the analysis to the upper-right quart, we can identify 4 different cases depending on whether (x, y) belongs to A_1, A_2, A_3 or A_4 (see Figure 2). Let us denote as *case i* the event $(x, y) \in A_i$, for $i = 1, 2, 3, 4$. In each of the latter cases, the domain is differently partitioned into 8 subregions that are sectors of annuli. What changes from one case to another is the definition of each subregion. As an example, the subregion having r in the range $[0, S_1/2 - y[$ lies completely in C only when $(x, y) \in A_2$; otherwise it partially exceeds the borders of C. Thus, the corresponding angle $\theta(r)$ is π in case 2 and some function of r in the other cases. The following tables define A_1-A_4 and the values of r and θ in each subregion for case $i = 1, 2, 3, 4$, respectively. In the following, we denote by $[r_{1,j}^{(A_i)}, r_{2,j}^{(A_i)}[$ the range of r of the jth subregion when in case i, and by $\theta_j^{(A_i)}(r)$ the corresponding angle.

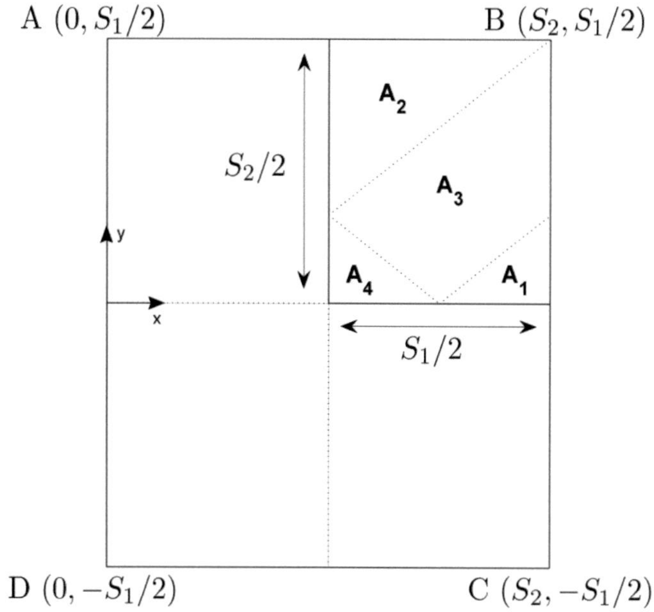

Fig. 2. Geometric partitioning of the rectangular region.

Case	Definition
A_1	$(x,y) \mid \{S_1/2 \le x \le S_2,\ \ 0 \le y \le x - S_1/2\}$
A_2	$(x,y) \mid \{S_2/2 \le x \le S_2,\ \ x + S_1/2 - S_2 \le y \le S_1/2\}$
A_3	$(x,y) \mid \{S_2/2 \le x \le S_2,\ \ \max(S_1/2 - x, x - S_1/2) \le y \le S_1/2 - S_2 + x\}$
A_4	$(x,y) \mid \{S_2/2 \le x \le S_1/2,\ \ 0 \le y \le S_1/2 - x\}$

Region	Range: $r_1^{(A_1)} \le r < r_2^{(A_1)}$	$\theta^{(A_1)}(r)$
1	$0 \le r < S_2 - x$	π
2	$S_2 - x \le r < S_1/2 - y$	$\frac{\pi}{2} + \arcsin \frac{S_2 - x}{r}$
3	$S_1/2 - y \le r < \sqrt{(S_2 - x)^2 + (S_1/2 - y)^2}$	$\frac{\pi}{2} + \arcsin \frac{S_1/2 - y}{r} - \arccos \frac{S_2 - x}{r}$
4	$\sqrt{(S_2 - x)^2 + (S_1/2 - y)^2} \le r < S_1/2 + y$	$\frac{\pi}{2} + \frac{1}{2}\left(\arcsin \frac{S_2 - x}{r} - \arccos \frac{S_1/2 - y}{r}\right)$
5	$S_1/2 + y \le r < \sqrt{(S_2 - x)^2 + (S_1/2 + y)^2}$	$\frac{\pi}{2} - \arccos \frac{S_1/2 + y}{r} + \frac{1}{2}\left(\arcsin \frac{S_2 - x}{r} - \arccos \frac{S_1/2 - y}{r}\right)$
6	$\sqrt{(S_2 - x)^2 + (S_1/2 + y)^2} \le r < x$	$\frac{\pi}{2} - \frac{1}{2}\left(\arccos \frac{S_1/2 + y}{r} + \arccos \frac{S_1/2 - y}{r}\right)$
7	$x \le r < \sqrt{x^2 + (S_1/2 - y)^2}$	$\frac{1}{2}\left(\arcsin \frac{S_1/2 - y}{r} + \arcsin \frac{S_1/2 + y}{r}\right) - \arccos \frac{x}{r}$
8	$\sqrt{x^2 + (S_1/2 - y)^2} \le r < \sqrt{x^2 + (S_1/2 + y)^2}$	$\frac{1}{2}\left(\arcsin \frac{S_1/2 + y}{r} - \arccos \frac{x}{r}\right)$

Region	Range: $r_1^{(A_2)} \le r < r_2^{(A_2)}$	$\theta^{(A_2)}(r)$
1	$0 \le r < S_1/2 - y$	π
2	$S_1/2 - y \le r < S_2 - x$	$\frac{\pi}{2} + \arcsin \frac{S_1/2 - y}{r}$
3	$S_2 - x \le r < \sqrt{(S_2 - x)^2 + (S_1/2 - y)^2}$	$\frac{\pi}{2} + \arcsin \frac{S_1/2 - y}{r} - \arccos \frac{S_2 - x}{r}$
4	$\sqrt{(S_2 - x)^2 + (S_1/2 - y)^2} \le r < x$	$\frac{\pi}{2} + \frac{1}{2}\left(\frac{S_1/2 - y}{r} - \arccos \frac{S_2 - x}{r}\right)$
5	$x \le r < \sqrt{x^2 + (S_1/2 - y)^2}$	$\frac{\pi}{2} - \arccos \frac{S_1/2 + y}{r} + \frac{1}{2}\left(\arcsin \frac{S_1/2 + y}{r} - \arccos \frac{S_2 - x}{r}\right)$
6	$\sqrt{x^2 + (S_1/2 - y)^2} \le r < S_1/2 + y$	$\frac{1}{2}\left(\arcsin \frac{S_2 + x}{r} + \arcsin \frac{x}{r}\right)$
7	$S_1/2 + y \le r < \sqrt{(S_2 - x)^2 + (S_1/2 + y)^2}$	$\frac{1}{2}\left(\arcsin \frac{x}{r} + \arcsin \frac{S_2 - x}{r}\right) - \arccos \frac{S_1/2 + y}{r}$
8	$\sqrt{(S_2 - x)^2 + (S_1/2 + y)^2} \le r < \sqrt{x^2 + (S_1/2 + y)^2}$	$\frac{1}{2}\left(\arcsin \frac{x}{r} - \arccos \frac{S_1/2 + y}{r}\right)$

Region	Range: $r_1^{(A_3)} \leq r < r_2^{(A_3)}$	$\theta^{(A_3)}(r)$
1	$0 \leq r < S_2 - x$	π
2	$S_2 - x \leq r < S_1/2 - y$	$\frac{\pi}{2} + \arcsin \frac{S_2-x}{r}$
3	$S_1/2 - y \leq r < \sqrt{(S_2-x)^2 + (S_1/2-y)^2}$	$\frac{\pi}{2} + \arcsin \frac{S_1/2-y}{r} - \arccos \frac{S_2-x}{r}$
4	$\sqrt{(S_2-x)^2 + (S_1/2-y)^2} \leq r < x$	$\frac{\pi}{2} + \frac{1}{2}\left(\arcsin \frac{S_1/2-y}{r} - \arccos \frac{S_2-x}{r}\right)$
5	$x \leq r < \sqrt{x^2 + (S_1/2-y)^2}$	$\frac{\pi}{2} - \arccos \frac{S_1/2+y}{r} + \frac{1}{2}\left(\arcsin \frac{S_1/2-y}{r} - \arccos \frac{S_2-x}{r}\right)$
6	$\sqrt{x^2 + (S_1/2-y)^2} \leq r < S_1/2 + y$	$\frac{\pi}{2} - \frac{1}{2}\left(\arccos \frac{x}{r} + \arccos \frac{S_2-x}{r}\right)$
7	$S_1/2 + y \leq r < \sqrt{(S_2-x)^2 + (S_1/2+y)^2}$	$\arcsin \frac{S_1/2+y}{r} - \frac{1}{2}\left(\arccos \frac{S_2-x}{r} + \arccos \frac{x}{r}\right)$
8	$\sqrt{(S_2-x)^2 + (S_1/2+y)^2} \leq r < \sqrt{x^2 + (S_1/2+y)^2}$	$\frac{1}{2}\left(\arcsin \frac{x}{r} - \arccos \frac{S_1/2+y}{r}\right)$

Region	Range: $r_1^{(A_4)} \leq r < r_2^{(A_4)}$	$\theta^{(A_4)}(r)$
1	$0 \leq r < S_2 - x$	π
2	$S_2 - x \leq r < x$	$\frac{\pi}{2} + \arcsin \frac{S_2-x}{r}$
3	$x \leq r < S_1/2 - y$	$\frac{\pi}{2} + \arcsin \frac{S_2-x}{r} - \arccos \frac{x}{r}$
4	$S_1/2 - y \leq r < \sqrt{(S_2-x)^2 + (S_1/2-y)^2}$	$\frac{\pi}{2} + \arcsin \frac{S_1/2-y}{r} - \arccos \frac{x}{r} - \arccos \frac{S_2-x}{r}$
5	$\sqrt{(S_2-x)^2 + (S_1/2-y)^2} \leq r < \sqrt{x^2 + (S_1/2-y)^2}$	$\frac{\pi}{2} - \arccos \frac{S_1/2+y}{r} + \frac{1}{2}\left(\arcsin \frac{S_1/2-y}{r} - \arccos \frac{S_2-x}{r}\right)$
6	$\sqrt{x^2 + (S_1/2-y)^2} \leq r < S_1/2 + y$	$\frac{\pi}{2} - \frac{1}{2}\left(\arccos \frac{S_2-x}{r} + \arccos \frac{x}{r}\right)$
7	$S_1/2 + y \leq r < \sqrt{(S_2-x)^2 + (S_1/2+y)^2}$	$\frac{\pi}{2} - \arccos \frac{S_1/2+y}{r} - \frac{1}{2}\left(\arccos \frac{x}{r} + \arccos \frac{S_2-x}{r}\right)$
8	$\sqrt{(S_2-x)^2 + (S_1/2+y)^2} \leq r < \sqrt{x^2 + (S_1/2+y)^2}$	$\frac{1}{2}\left(\arcsin \frac{S_1+y}{r} - \arccos \frac{x}{r}\right)$

Note that when $S_1 = S_2$ the partitioning scheme degenerates to the one for square regions. Now, starting from (15) and owing to the linearity of Poisson independent r.v.'s, the mean number of sinks that are audible from (x, y), with $(x, y) \in A_i$, may be computed as

$$\mu^{(A_i)}(x,y) = \sum_{j=1}^{8} \int_{r_{1,j}^{(A_i)}}^{r_{2,j}^{(A_i)}} 2\theta_j^{(A_i)}(r) \cdot \rho_0 \cdot r \cdot \Phi(a_1 - b_1 \ln r) dr, \tag{19}$$

for $i = 1, 2, 3, 4$ and with $a_1 = (L_{\text{th}} - k_0)/\sigma$, $b_1 = k_1/\sigma$ and $\Phi(x) = \int_{-\infty}^{x} (1/\sqrt{2\pi}) e^{-u^2/2} du$. Owing to the Poisson distribution of the number of audible sinks, the probability that the position (x, y), with $(x, y) \in A_i$, is isolated (i.e., no sink is heard) is simply

$$p^{(A_i)}(x,y) = e^{-\mu^{(A_i)}(x,y)}, \tag{20}$$

while the probability that the position (x, y), with $(x, y) \in A_i$, is not isolated is

$$q^{(A_i)}(x,y) = 1 - p^{(A_i)}(x,y) = 1 - e^{-\mu^{(A_i)}(x,y)}. \tag{21}$$

Now, the mean number of sinks that are audible from (x, y), with $(x, y) \in \{A_1 \cup A_2 \cup A_3 \cup A_4\}$, is

$$\mu(x,y) = \begin{cases} \mu^{(A_1)}(x,y) & ,(x,y) \in A_1 \\ \mu^{(A_2)}(x,y) & ,(x,y) \in A_2 \\ \mu^{(A_3)}(x,y) & ,(x,y) \in A_3 \\ \mu^{(A_4)}(x,y) & ,(x,y) \in A_4 \end{cases} \tag{22}$$

Equally, the isolation and non-isolation probabilities may be computed as

$$p(x,y) = \begin{cases} p^{(A_1)}(x,y) = e^{-\mu^{(A_1)}(x,y)} & ,(x,y) \in A_1 \\ p^{(A_2)}(x,y) = e^{-\mu^{(A_2)}(x,y)} & ,(x,y) \in A_2 \\ p^{(A_3)}(x,y) = e^{-\mu^{(A_3)}(x,y)} & ,(x,y) \in A_3 \\ p^{(A_4)}(x,y) = e^{-\mu^{(A_4)}(x,y)} & ,(x,y) \in A_4 \end{cases} \tag{23}$$

and

$$q(x,y) = \begin{cases} q^{(A_1)}(x,y) = 1 - e^{-\mu^{(A_1)}(x,y)} & ,(x,y) \in A_1 \\ q^{(A_2)}(x,y) = 1 - e^{-\mu^{(A_2)}(x,y)} & ,(x,y) \in A_2 \\ q^{(A_3)}(x,y) = 1 - e^{-\mu^{(A_3)}(x,y)} & ,(x,y) \in A_3 \\ q^{(A_4)}(x,y) = 1 - e^{-\mu^{(A_4)}(x,y)} & ,(x,y) \in A_4, \end{cases} \tag{24}$$

respectively. Hence, the average probability of non-isolation over $\mathcal{C}$ is

$$\begin{aligned} \overline{q} &= \mathbb{E}_{x,y}[q(x,y)] = \frac{4}{W} \int_{S_2/2}^{S_2} \int_0^{S_1/2} q(x,y)dydx \\ &= \frac{4}{W} \left(\int_{S_1/2}^{S_2} \int_0^{x-S_1/2} q^{(A_1)}(x,y)dydx + \int_{S_2/2}^{S_2} \int_{x+S_1/2-S_2}^{S_1/2} q^{(A_2)}(x,y)dydx \right. \\ &+ \left. \int_{S_2/2}^{S_2} \int_{\max(S_1/2-x,x-S_1/2)}^{S_1/2-S_2+x} q^{(A_3)}(x,y)dydx + \int_{S_2/2}^{S_1/2} \int_0^{S_1/2-x} q^{(A_4)}(x,y)dydx \right) \end{aligned} \tag{25}$$

5.3 Composite Domains

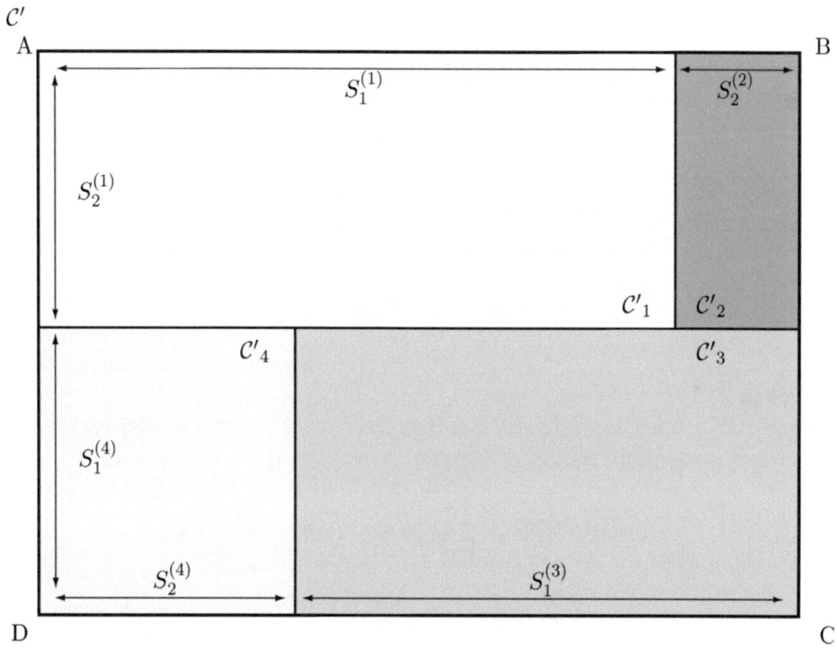

Fig. 3. Reference scenario for the analysis of composite domains.

The scenario that we now want to analyze is of the kind of the one depicted in Figure 3. Consider a rectangular domain $\mathcal{C}'$ of area W' which is composed of n rectangular sub-domains $\mathcal{C}'_i$ of sides $S_1^{(i)}$ and $S_2^{(i)}$ (note that $S_1^{(i)} \geq S_2^{(i)}$ holds), area $W^{(i)}$, $i = 1,2,\ldots,n$. We assume the sinks are uniformly and randomly distributed in $\mathcal{C}'_i$ with density $\rho_{0,i}$, $i = 1,2,\ldots,n$. Instead, sensors are uniformly and randomly distributed over the whole domain (i.e., in $\mathcal{C}'$) with density ρ_S. As a consequence, sinks are distributed according to a inhomogeneous PPP over $\mathcal{C}'$, while sensors are distributed according to a homogeneous PPP over $\mathcal{C}'$.

Our final goal is to compute the probability that a randomly chosen sensor in $\mathcal{C}'$ is not isolated. Now suppose there is a sensor node, S, located in $(S_x, S_y) \in \mathcal{C}'_k$ and we want to find the probability that it is not isolated. It is clear that the number of sinks that S can hear is not limited to the number of sinks contained in $\mathcal{C}'_k$. Rather, the more its transmission range is large compared to the sides of $\mathcal{C}'_k$, the more it can benefit from the connectivity offered by the sinks located in the other sub-domains (e.g., the adjacent ones). On the contrary, when S is not close to one of the borders of $\mathcal{C}'_k$ and its transmission range is small (i.e., the connectivity area of S lies entirely within $\mathcal{C}'_k$), what happens in $\mathcal{C}'_j$, $\forall j \neq k$ is totally negligible. We can intuitively state that the same happens when $\rho_{0,k} \gg \rho_{0,j}$, $\forall j \neq k$, since the other sub-domains present too few sinks to provide connectivity to a sensor in $\mathcal{C}'_k$.
Thus, when we are allowed to neglect the interaction between different sub-domains, we can simply treat each of them in a separate way. In this way we end up with the n-tuple $\bar{\mathbf{q}} = (\bar{q}_1, \bar{q}_2, \ldots, \bar{q}_n)$. The overall approximated non-isolation probability over $\mathcal{C}'$ is obtained as the weighted average of $\bar{\mathbf{q}}$. This case is detailed in Subsection 5.3.1.
As an alternative, a direct application of (8) with a careful choice of Ω (i.e., without partitioning) would lead to an exact result. However, the complexity of carrying out the integration can sometimes make this approach unfeasible. The details can be found in Subsection 5.3.2.

5.3.1 Approach 1

We have $\bar{\mathbf{q}} = (\bar{q}_1, \bar{q}_2, \ldots, \bar{q}_n)$, with (from (25))

$$\bar{q}_i = \mathbb{E}_{x,y}[q_i(x,y)] = \frac{4}{W^{(i)}} \int_{S_2^{(i)}/2}^{S_2^{(i)}} \int_0^{S_1^{(i)}/2} q_i(x,y)dydx, \tag{26}$$

where $q_i(x,y)$ is computed on $\mathcal{C}'_i$, which has sides $S_1^{(i)}$ and $S_2^{(i)}$ with $S_1^{(i)} \geq S_2^{(i)}, i = 1,2,\ldots,n$.
Now, the probability, $\bar{q}_P$, that a randomly chosen sensor in $\mathcal{C}'$ is not isolated is simply

$$\bar{q}_P = \frac{1}{W'} \sum_{i=1}^{n} W^{(i)} \bar{q}_i. \tag{27}$$

5.3.2 Approach 2

From (8) and owing once again to the fact that the sum of Poisson independent r.v.'s having mean $\lambda_i, i = 1,2,\ldots$, is still Poisson with mean $\Lambda = \lambda_1 + \lambda_2 + \ldots$, we have

$$\mu_M(x_0,y_0) = \sum_{k=1}^{n} \rho_{0,k} \int_{\mathcal{C}'_k} C(||\mathbf{x} - \mathbf{x}_0||)d\mathbf{x}, \tag{28}$$

i.e., the average number of audible sinks from (x_0, y_0).
Equation (28) is very general and takes the interaction between sub-domains into account. Now, in order to obtain a result which is analogous to (25), we let

$$p_M(x_0,y_0) = e^{-\mu_M(x_0,y_0)} \tag{29}$$

and

$$q_M(x_0,y_0) = 1 - p_M(x_0,y_0) = 1 - e^{-\mu_M(x_0,y_0)} \tag{30}$$

to end up with the isolation and non-isolation probabilities of the location (x_0, y_0), respectively. Then, we simply take the average over the points (x_0, y_0) such that $(x_0, y_0) \in \mathcal{C}'$ and get

$$\bar{q}_M = \frac{1}{W'} \int\int_{\mathcal{C}'} q_M(x_0,y_0)dx_0dy_0. \tag{31}$$

5.4 Practical Cases With Numerical Results

5.4.1 Single Rectangle

Equation (25) can be evaluated numerically once S_1, S_2, ρ_0, L_{th}, k_0, k_1, σ are known. As an example, in Fig. 4 we plot $\bar{q}$ as a function of the ratio $\gamma = S_2/S_1$.

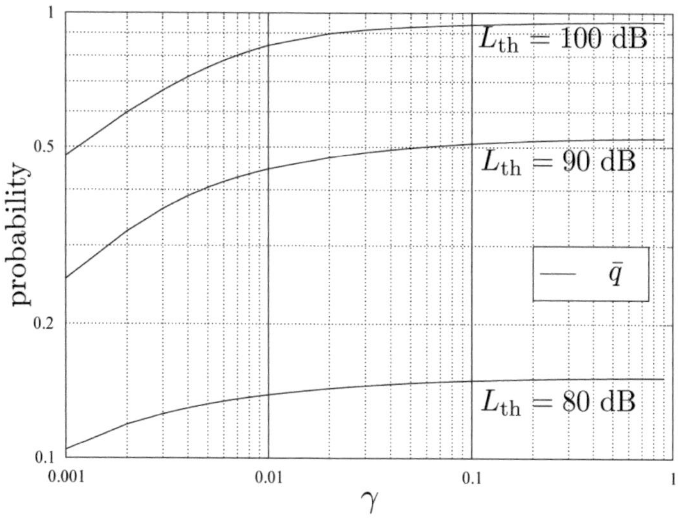

Fig. 4. $\bar{q}$ as a function of γ for different values of L_{th}, with $W = 1$ Km^2, $\rho_0 = 100/W$, $k_0 = 40$, $k_1 = 13.03$, $\sigma = 3.5$.

As γ varies from 1 to 0, the area W remains constant while the domain C gets increasingly squeezed. The general trend suggests that the smaller is γ, the smaller is the level of connectivity. This is due to border effects: when S_2 becomes comparable with the transmission range, the connectivity area of the sinks is very likely to overstep the domain area, thus resulting in a decrement in the average number of connected sensors per sink. In particular, we expect this to be more appreciable for greater transmission ranges. In fact, from Fig. 4 we can observe that for $L_{\text{th}} = 80$ dB ($TR_i \approx 21.54$ m), when γ ranges from 1 to 0.001 (S_2 ranging from 1000 m to 31.62 m) the loss in connectivity is only $\bar{q}(L_{\text{th}} = 80\text{ dB}; \gamma = 1) - \bar{q}(L_{\text{th}} = 80\text{ dB}; \gamma = 0.001) \approx 0.04$. Instead, for $L_{\text{th}} = 100$ dB ($TR_i \approx 99.96$ m) and γ ranging as above, the loss in connectivity is no less than $\bar{q}(L_{\text{th}} = 100\text{ dB}; \gamma = 1) - \bar{q}(L_{\text{th}} = 100\text{ dB}; \gamma = 0.001) \approx 0.51$.

5.4.2 Composite Domain

Consider now the non-isolation probability for the composite domain of Figure 3. Assume $S_1^{(1)} = 850$ m, $S_2^{(1)} = 400$ m, $S_2^{(2)} = 150$ m, $S_1^{(3)} = 700$ m, $S_1^{(4)} = 400$ m, $S_2^{(4)} = 300$ m and the densities $\rho_{0,1} = 4.E\text{-}4$, $\rho_{0,2} = 3.E\text{-}3$, $\rho_{0,3} = 1.E\text{-}3$, $\rho_{0,4} = 6.E\text{-}4$.
From (27), the computation of $\bar{q}_{\text{p}}$ is straightforward. In Figure 6 we report $\bar{q}_{\text{p}}$, $\bar{q}_1$, $\bar{q}_2$, $\bar{q}_3$, $\bar{q}_4$.

As for $\bar{q}_{\mathrm{M}}$, set the origin in D and let (x_0, y_0) be a generic point in C'. Accounting for the 4 different zones, the mean number of audible sinks from (x_0, y_0) is

$$\mu_{\mathrm{M}}(x_0, y_0) = \sum_{k=1}^{4} \rho_{0,k} \int_{C'_k} C(||\mathbf{x} - \mathbf{x}_0||)d\mathbf{x} \tag{32}$$

$$\begin{aligned} &= \rho_{0,1} \int_{-x_0}^{S_1^{(1)}-x_0} \int_{S_1^{(4)}-y_0}^{S_1^{(4)}+S_2^{(1)}-y_0} C(\sqrt{(x-x_0)^2+(y-y_0)^2})dydx \\ &+ \rho_{0,2} \int_{S_1^{(1)}-x_0}^{S_1^{(1)}+S_2^{(2)}-x_0} \int_{S_1^{(4)}-y_0}^{S_1^{(4)}+S_2^{(1)}-y_0} C(\sqrt{(x-x_0)^2+(y-y_0)^2})dydx \\ &+ \rho_{0,3} \int_{S_2^{(4)}-x_0}^{S_2^{(4)}+S_1^{(3)}-x_0} \int_{-y_0}^{S_1^{(4)}-y_0} C(\sqrt{(x-x_0)^2+(y-y_0)^2})dydx \\ &+ \rho_{0,4} \int_{-x_0}^{S_2^{(4)}-x_0} \int_{-y_0}^{S_1^{(4)}-y_0} C(\sqrt{(x-x_0)^2+(y-y_0)^2})dydx, \end{aligned} \tag{33}$$

while the probabilities of non-isolation of the position (x_0, y_0) is obtained as

$$q_{\mathrm{M}}(x_0, y_0) = 1 - e^{-\mu_{\mathrm{M}}(x_0, y_0)}. \tag{34}$$

In Figure 5 $q_{\mathrm{M}}(x_0, y_0)$ is reported. Note that we have $q_{\mathrm{M}}(x_0, y_0) \neq 0$ on the boundaries, a fact that confirms that we are not introducing factitious border effects between different sub-domains. Note also that equations (32), (33) contain a double integral: this implies a greater computational complexity with respect to (19) employed in the Approach 1. On the other hand, (32) and (33) are exact (i.e., interactions among sub-domains C'_i are not neglected).
Now, accordingly to (25), the average probability $\bar{q}_{\mathrm{M}}$ that a sensor randomly chosen in C' is not isolated is

$$\bar{q}_{\mathrm{M}} = \mathbb{E}_{x_0, y_0}[q_{\mathrm{M}}(x_0, y_0)] = \int_0^{S_2^{(4)}+S_1^{(3)}} \int_0^{S_1^{(4)}+S_2^{(1)}} q_{\mathrm{M}}(x_0, y_0)dy_0 dx_0. \tag{35}$$

In Figure 6 we also plot $\bar{q}_{\mathrm{M}}$ as a function of L_{th} [dB]. It is possible to compare the non-isolation probabilities obtained through the two different approaches (bold curves): Approach 2, as said, accounts for interactions between sub-domains and thus does not introduce border effects that would be fake. This is the reason why we observe $\bar{q}_{\mathrm{M}} \geq \bar{q}_{\mathrm{P}}$ (i.e., the WSN performs better). Thus $\bar{q}_{\mathrm{P}}$ is a lower bound.

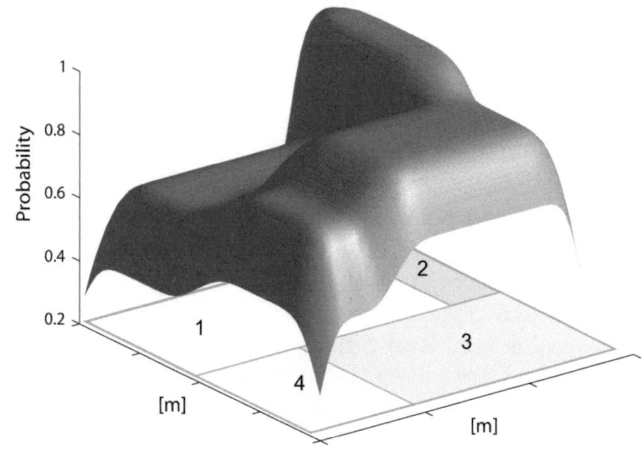

Fig. 5. $\bar{q}_M(x_0, y_0)$ on the domain of Figure 3 obtained with $L_{th} = 90$ [dB], $k_0 = 40$, $k_1 = 13.03$, $\sigma = 3.5$.

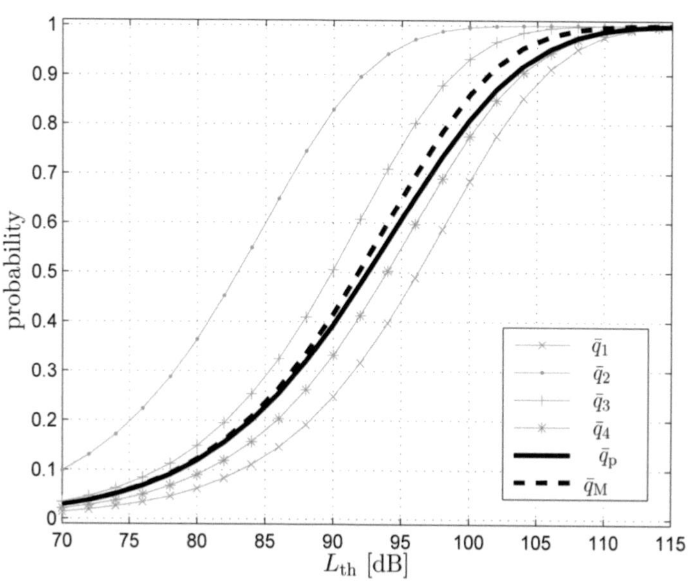

Fig. 6. Non-isolation probabilities referred to the scenario of Figure 3 obtained with $k_0 = 40$, $k_1 = 13.03$, $\sigma = 3.5$.

6. The IEEE 802.15.4 MAC protocol

When dealing with contention-based MAC protocols, there exists a certain probability that a node does not succeed in accessing the channel or in transmitting its packet correctly (i.e.,

without collisions). A single-sink scenario, where n 802.15.4 sensors transmit data to the sink through a direct link is accounted for, in this Section. We assume all sensor nodes are audible to the sink.
Both, Beacon- and Non Beacon-Enabled modes are considered. We assume that nodes transmit packets having a size, denoted as z, equal to $D \cdot 10$ bytes, where D is an integer parameter. We also assume that the size of the query packet is equal to 60 bytes.We denote as T the time needed for transmitting 10 bytes. Since a bit rate of 250 kbit/sec is used, $T = 320\mu sec$.
The Non Beacon-Enabled mode is based on CSMA/CA protocol to access the channel, whereas in the Beacon-Enabled case both contention-based and contention-free protocols, are implemented. In the latter case a superframe is defined, which starts with a packet denoted as Beacon (it coincides with the query packet in our scenario), and divided into two parts: inactive and active part. The active part is composed of the Contention Access Period (CAP), where a CSMA/CA protocol is used, and the Contention Free Period (CFP), where a maximum number of 7 Guaranteed Time Slots (GTSs) could be allocated to specific nodes (see Figure 7, below). The use if GTSs is optional.
The duration of the whole superframe and of its active part depends on the value of two integer parameters ranging from 0 to 14, called superframe order, denoted as SO, and beacon order, denoted as BO, with $BO \geq SO$. In particular, the interval of time between two successive Beacons, that is the query interval T_q in our scenario, is given by: $T_q = 16 \cdot 60 \cdot 2^{BO} \cdot T_s$, where $T_s = 16$ μsec is the symbol time. Instead, the duration of the active part, denoted as T_A, is given by: $T_A = 16 \cdot 60 \cdot 2^{SO} \cdot T_s$, where $60 \cdot 2^{SO} T_s$ is the slot size.
The inactive part of the superframe is generally used when tree-based or mesh topologies are applied; here, since we are dealing with star topologies, we set $SO = BO$ and $T_A = T_q$.
Each GTS must contain the packet to be transmitted and an inter-frame space equal to 40 T_s. This is, in fact, the minimum interval of time that must be guaranteed between the reception of two subsequent packets. The sink (PAN coordinator, in 802.15.4 jargon) may allocate up to seven GTSs; however, a sufficient portion of the CAP must remain for contention-based access. The minimum CAP size is 440 T_s. By varying packet size D and SO (i.e., the slot duration), the number of slots occupied by each GTS and the maximum number of GTSs that could be allocated to ensure a CAP larger than 440 T_s, will vary as well. As an example, if $D = 2$ and $SO = 0$, two slots are needed for a GTS, to contain the packet and the inter-frame space and a maximum number of 4 GTSs could be allocated. In case $SO = 2$, instead, each GTS will occupy one slot and seven Guaranteed Time Slots (GTSs) could be allocated. We denote as N_{GTS} the number of GTSs allocated.
We assume that in case a node does not succeed in accessing the channel by the end of the superframe (in the Beacon-Enabled case) or till reception of the subsequent query (in the Non Beacon-Enabled case), the packet will be lost.This implies that by increasing the superframe duration the success probability for a node will increase since the node will have more time to try to access the channel. Note that in the Beacon-Enabled case, T_q may assume only a finite set of values (depending on the values of BO); instead, in the Non Beacon-Enabled case T_q may assume any value. Note that, being $(120 + D) \cdot T$ the maximum delay with which a packet can be received by the sink Buratti & Verdone (2009) and having set the query size equal to 60 bytes, the sink should set $T_q \geq (126 + D) \cdot T$ to make sure all nodes have completed the CSMA/CA algorithm. In case lower values of T_q are set, a node may receive a new query while still trying to access the channel, this resulting in the loss of the old packet.
We parametrized the behavior of 802.15.4 MAC protocol by means of a function, $P_{MAC}(n)$, which returns the probability that a sensor node is successful in transmitting its packet when

$(n-1)$ more sensors are trying to do the same. We refer to Buratti & Verdone (2008; 2009) and Buratti (2009), Buratti (2010) for derivation and expression of $P_{MAC}(n)$ in Non Beacon- and Beacon-Enabled cases, respectively. A finite state transition diagram has been used to model sensor nodes states, in both cases Beacon- and Non Beacon-Enabled mode. Here we do not report equations for the sake of brevity. In these papers details on formulae are given and also a validation of the model against simulation is provided for $n \leq 50$ and different values of D.

6.1 Numerical results

Some examples of results obtained through the mathematical model developed are shown, with the aim of comparing those achieved with the two operation modes (i.e., Beacon- and Non Beacon-Enabled).

In Figures 8(a) $P_{MAC}(n)$ as functions of n for the Beacon-Enabled case, for different values of SO, with $D = 2$, is shown. The cases of no GTSs allocated and N_{GTS} equal to the maximum number of GTSs allocable, are considered. As explained above, this maximum number depends on the values of D and SO. As we can see, P_{MAC} decreases monotonically (for $n > 1$ when $N_{GTS} = 0$ and for $n > N_{GTS}$ when $N_{GTS} > 0$), by increasing n, since the number of sensors competing for the channel increases. Once we fix SO, by increasing N_{GTS}, P_{MAC} also increases, since less nodes have to compete for the channel. Moreover, once N_{GTS} is fixed, by increasing SO, P_{MAC} also grows, since the CAP size is greater and nodes have a larger amount of time to try to access the channel.

In Figure 8(b) $P_{MAC}(n)$ for different values of D and T_q, considering a Non Beacon-Enabled network, is shown. As we can see, a decrease of T_q, results in a decrement of P_{MAC}, since nodes have a smaller amount of time to access the channel.

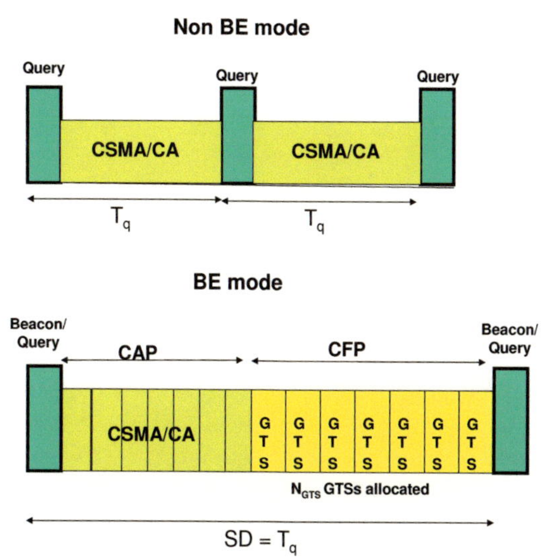

Fig. 7. Above part: The IEEE 802.15.4 Non Beacon-Enabled mode. Below part: The IEEE 802.15.4 Beacon-Enabled mode.

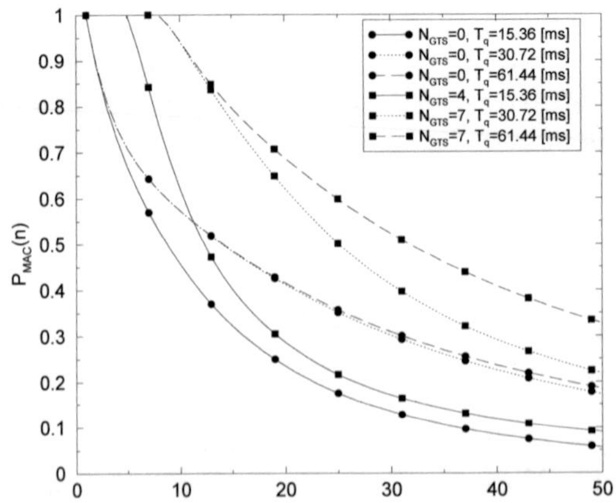

(a)

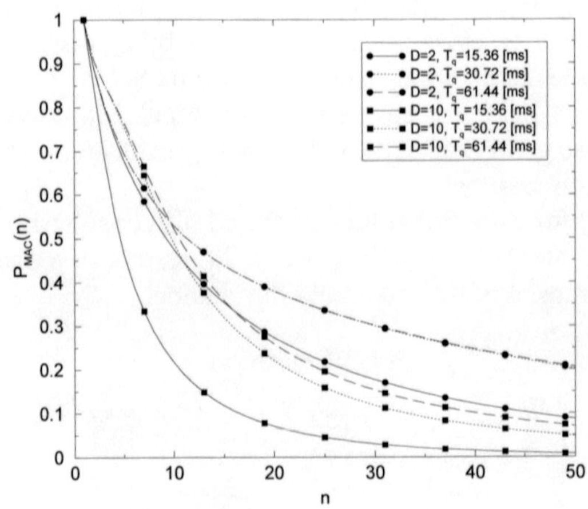

(b)

Fig. 8. (a): $P_{MAC}(n)$ as a function of n, in the Beacon-Enabled case, for different values of SO and N_{GTS}, having fixed $D = 2$. (b): $P_{MAC}(n)$ as a function of n, in the Non Beacon-Enabled case, for different values of T_q and D.

If we compare the above Figures, we notice that once the superframe duration is fixed, results are approximatively the same if no GTSs are allocated, whereas, there is a considerable increment of $P_{MAC}(n)$ in the Beacon-Enabled case when GTSs are allocated. Note that the cases $T_q = 15.36$ [ms], $T_q = 30.72$ [ms] and $T_q = 61.44$ [ms] correspond to $SO = 0, 1$ and 2, respectively.

7. Evaluation of the Area Throughput

The area throughput is mathematically derived through an intermediate step: first the probability of successful data transmission by an arbitrary sensor node, when k nodes are present in the monitored area, is considered. Then, the overall area throughput is evaluated based on this result.

7.1 Joint MAC/Connectivity Probability of Success

Let us consider an arbitrary sensor node that is located in the observed area A at a certain time instant. The aim is computing the probability that it can connect to one of the sinks deployed in A and successfully transmit its data sample to the infrastructure. Such an event is clearly related to connectivity issues (i.e., the sensor must employ an adequate transmitting power in order to reach the sink and not be isolated) and to MAC problems (i.e., the number of sensors which attempt at connecting to the same sink strongly affects the probability of successful transmission). For this reason, we define $P_{s|k}(x,y)$ as the probability of successful transmission conditioned on the overall number, k, of sensors present in the monitored area, which also depends on the position (x,y) of the sensor relative to a reference system with origin centered in A. This dependence is due to the well-known border effects in connectivity Bettstetter (2002).

In particular,

$$\begin{aligned} P_{s|k}(x,y) &= E_n[P_{MAC}(n) \cdot P_{CON}(x,y)] \\ &= E_n[P_{MAC}(n)] \cdot P_{CON}(x,y). \end{aligned} \tag{36}$$

where the impact of connectivity and MAC on the transmission of samples are separated. A packet will be successfully received by a sink if the sensor node is connected to at least one sink and if no MAC failures occur. The two terms that appear in (36) are now analysed.

$P_{CON}(x,y)$ represents the probability that the sensor is not isolated (i.e., it receives a sufficiently strong signal from at least one sink). This probability decreases as the sensor approaches the borders (border effects). P_{CON} for multi-sink single-hop WSNs, in bounded and unbounded regions, has been computed in the previous Sections. In particular, for unbounded regions, $P_{CON}(x,y) \simeq P_{CON}$, that is equal to q_∞, given by eq. (12). Whereas, when bounded regions are considered, $P_{CON}(x,y)$ is equal to $q(x,y)$ given by eq. (17).

Specifically, since the position of the sensor is in general unknown, $P_{s|k}(x,y)$ of (36) can be deconditioned as follows:

$$\begin{aligned} P_{s|k} &= E_{x,y}[P_{s|k}(x,y)] \\ &= E_{x,y}[P_{CON}(x,y)] \cdot E_n[P_{MAC}(n)]. \end{aligned} \tag{37}$$

$E_{x,y}[P_{CON}(x,y)]$ is equal to $\overline{q}$ given by, e.g., eq. (25) when a rectangular region is accounted for. When, instead border effects are negligible, $E_{x,y}[P_{CON}(x,y)] = E_{x,y}[P_{CON}] = P_{CON}$, given by eq. (12).

Given the channel model described in (2) (and following), the average connectivity area of the sensor, that is the average area in which the sinks audible to the given sensor are contained, can be defined as

$$A_{\sigma_s} = \pi e^{\frac{2(L_{th}-k_0)}{k1}} e^{\frac{2\sigma_s^2}{k_1^2}}. \tag{38}$$

In Fabbri & Verdone (2008) it is also shown that border effects are negligible when $A_{\sigma_s} < 0.1A$. In the following only this case will be accounted for. Thus we have

$$P_{CON}(x,y) \simeq P_{CON} = 1 - e^{-\mu_0}, \tag{39}$$

where $\mu_0 = \rho_0 A_{\sigma_s} = I A_{\sigma_s}/A$ is the mean number of audible sinks on an infinite plane from any position Orriss & Barton (2003), being $I = \rho_0 \cdot A$ the average number of sinks in A.

$P_{MAC}(n)$, $n \geq 1$, is the probability of successful transmission when $n-1$ interfering sensors are present introduced in Section 6 for the 802.15.4 MAC case.

In general, when CSMA-based MAC protocols are considered, $P_{MAC}(n)$ is a monotonic decreasing function of the number, n, of sensors which attempt to connect to the same serving sink. This number is in general a random variable in the range $[0, k]$. In fact, note that in (36) there is no explicit dependence on k, except for the fact that $n \le k$ must hold. Moreover in our case we assume $1 \le n \le k$, as there is at least one sensor competing for access with probability P_{CON} (39).

Orriss et al. (2002) showed that the number of sensors uniformly distributed on an infinite plane that hear one particular sink as the one with the strongest signal power (i.e., the number of sensors competing for access to such sink), is Poisson distributed with mean

$$\bar{n} = \mu_s \frac{1 - e^{-\mu_0}}{\mu_0}, \tag{40}$$

with $\mu_s = \rho_s A_{\sigma_s}$ being the mean number of sensors that are audible by a given sink. Such a result is relevant toward our goal even though it was derived on the infinite plane. In fact, when border effects are negligible (i.e., $A_{\sigma_s} < 0.1A$) and k is large, n can still be considered Poisson distributed. The only two things that change are:

- n is upper bounded by k (i.e., the pdf is truncated)
- the density ρ_s is to be computed as the ratio k/A $[m^{-2}]$, thus yielding $\mu_s = k\frac{A_{\sigma_s}}{A}$.

Therefore, we assume $n \sim \text{Poisson}(\bar{n})$, with

$$\bar{n} = \bar{n}(k) = k\frac{A_{\sigma_s}}{A}\frac{1 - e^{-\mu_{sink}}}{\mu_{sink}} = k\frac{1 - e^{-IA_{\sigma_s}/A}}{I}. \tag{41}$$

Finally, by taking the average in (37) explicit and neglecting border effects (see (39)), we get

$$P_{s|k} = (1 - e^{-IA_{\sigma_s}/A}) \cdot \frac{1}{M} \sum_{n=1}^{k} P_{MAC}(n) \frac{\bar{n}^n e^{-\bar{n}}}{n!}, \tag{42}$$

where

$$M = \sum_{n=1}^{k} \frac{\bar{n}^n e^{-\bar{n}}}{n!} \tag{43}$$

is a normalizing factor.

7.2 Area Throughput

The amount of samples generated by the network as response to a given query is equal to the number of sensors, k, that are present and active when the query is received. As a consequence, the average number of data samples-per-query generated by the network is the mean number of sensors, $\bar{k}$, in the observed area.

Now denote by G the available area throughput, that is the average number of samples generated per unit of time, given by

$$G = \bar{k} \cdot f_q = \rho_s \cdot A \cdot \frac{1}{T_q} \text{ [samples/sec]}. \tag{44}$$

From (44) we have $\bar{k} = GT_q$.

The average amount of samples received by the infrastructure per unit of time (area throughput), S, is given by:

$$S = \sum_{k=0}^{+\infty} S(k) \cdot g_k \text{ [samples/sec]}, \tag{45}$$

where

$$S(k) = \frac{k}{T_q} P_{s|k}, \tag{46}$$

g_k as in (1) and $P_{s|k}$ as in (42).
Finally, by means of (42), (43) and (44), equation (45) may be rewritten as

$$S = \frac{1 - e^{-IA_{\sigma_s}/A}}{T_q} \cdot \sum_{k=1}^{+\infty} \frac{\sum_{n=1}^{k} P_{MAC}(n) \frac{\bar{n}^n e^{-\bar{n}}}{n!}}{\sum_{n=1}^{k} \frac{\bar{n}^n e^{-\bar{n}}}{n!}} \cdot \frac{(GT_q)^k e^{-GT_q}}{(k-1)!}. \tag{47}$$

7.3 Numerical Results

In this section the area throughput obtained with the two modalities Beacon- and Non Beacon-Enabled, considering different values of D, SO, N_{GTS}, T_q and different connectivity levels, is shown.

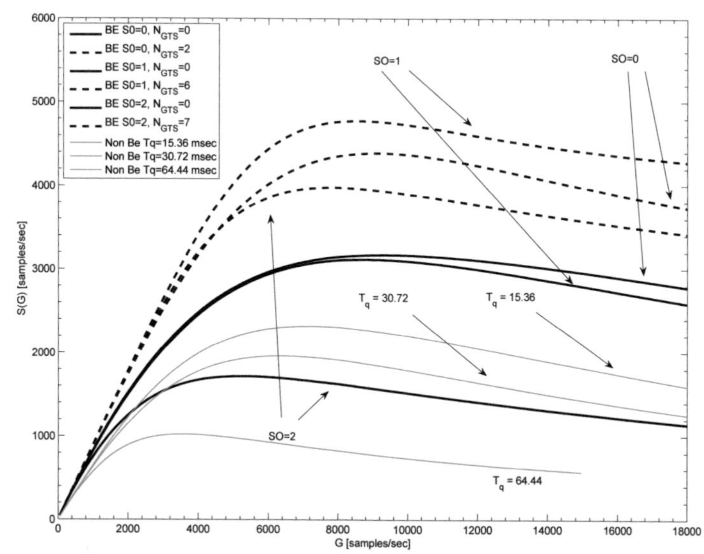

Fig. 9. S as a function of G, for the Beacon- and Non Beacon-Enabled cases, by varying SO, N_{GTS} and T_q, having fixed $D = 10$.

In Figure 9, S as a function of G, when varying SO, N_{GTS} and T_q for $D = 10$, is shown. The input parameters that we entered give a connection probability $P_{CON} = 0.89$. It can be noted

that, once SO is fixed (Beacon-Enabled case), an increase of N_{GTS} results in an increment of S, since P_{MAC} increases. Moreover, once N_{GTS} is fixed, there exists a value of SO maximising S. We can note that, a part for the case, Beacon-Enabled with GTSs allocated, an increase of SO results in a decrement of S. In fact, even though P_{MAC} gets greater the query interval increases and the number of samples per second received by the sink decreases. On the other hand, when the Beacon-Enabled mode is used and GTSs are allocated, the optimum value of SO is 1. This is due to the fact that, having large packets, when $SO = 0$ too many packets are lost, owing to the short duration of the superframe.
Concerning the Non Beacon-Enabled case, in both Figures it can be noted that, by decreasing T_q, S gets larger even though P_{MAC} decreases, since, once again, the MAC losses are balanced by larger values of f_q.

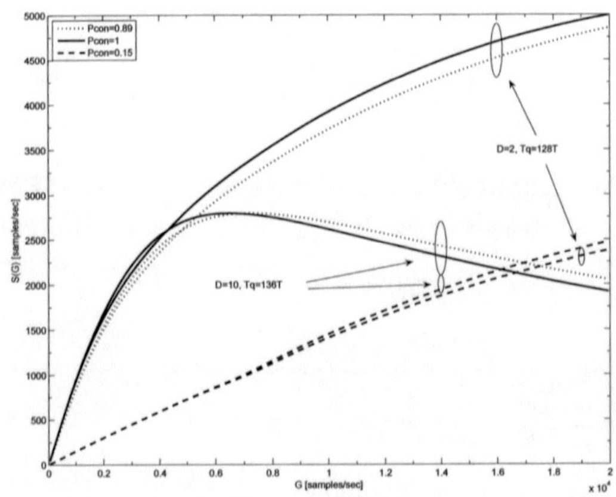

Fig. 10. S as a function of G, in the non beacon-enabled case, for different values of D and P_{CON}, having fixed T_q to the maximum delay.

Finally, we show the effects of connectivity on the area throughput. When P_{CON} is less than 1, only a fraction of the deployed nodes has a sink in its vicinity. In particular, an average number, $\bar{k} = P_{CON}GT_q/I$, of sensors compete for access at each sink. In Figure 10 we consider the non beacon-enabled case with $D = 2$, $T_q = 128\,T$ and $D = 10$, $T_q = 136\,T$. When $D = 10$, $T_q = 136\,T$, for high G the area throughput tends to decay, since packet collisions dominate. Hence, by moving from $P_{CON} = 1$ to $P_{CON} = 0.89$, we observe a slight improvement due to the fact that a smaller average number of sensors tries to connect to the same sink. Conversely, when $D = 2$, $T_q = 128\,T$, S is still increasing with G, then by moving from $P_{CON} = 1$ to $P_{CON} = 0.89$, we just reduce the useful traffic. Furthermore, when $P_{CON} = 0.15$, the available area throughput is very light, so that we are working in the region where $P_{MAC}(D = 2, T_q = 128T) < P_{MAC}(D = 10, T_q = 136\,T)$, resulting in a slightly better performance of the case with $D = 2$. Thus we conclude that the effect of lowering P_{CON} results in a stretch of the curves reported in the previous plots.

8. Acknowledgments

This work was supported by the European Commission in the framework of the FP7 Network of Excellence in Wireless Communications NEWCOM++ (contract n. 216715). Authors would like to thank Roberto Verdone for the fruitful discussions about the model.

9. List of acronyms

r.v. random variable

PAN Personal Area Network

CAP Contention Access Period

CFP Contention Free Period

CSMA carrier-sense multiple access

CSMA/CA carrier-sense multiple access with collision avoidance

GTS Guaranteed Time Slot

ISM industrial scientific medical

MAC medium access control

p.d.f. probability distribution function

PPP Poisson Point Process

PAN personal area network

WSN wireless sensor network

10. References

Bettstetter, C. (2002). On the minimum node degree and connectivity of a wireless multihop network, *Mobile Ad Hoc Networks and Comp.(Mobihoc), Proc. ACM Symp. on*.

Bettstetter, C. & Zangl, J. (2002). How to achieve a connected ad hoc network with homogeneous range assignment: an analytical study with consideration of border effects, *Mobile and Wireless Communications Network, 2002 4th International Workshop on*, pp. 125–129.

Bianchi, G. (2000). Performance analysis of the ieee 802.11 distributed coordination function, *IEEE Journal on Selected Areas of Communication (JSAC)* **18**: 535–547.

Bollobàs, B. (2001). *Random Graphs, Cambridge University Press, second ed.*

Buratti, C. (2009). A mathematical model for performance of ieee 802.15.4 beacon-enabled mode, *ACM IWCMC 2009*, Leipzig, Germany, June 21-24.

Buratti, C. (2010). Performance analysis of ieee 802.15.4 beacon-enabled mode., *Accepted for publication on IEEE Transactions on Vehicular Technology.*

Buratti, C. & Verdone, R. (2006). On the number of cluster heads minimizing the error rate for a wireless sensor network using a hierarchical topology over ieee 802.15.4, *Proc. of IEEE Int. Symp. on Personal, Indoor and MoRadio Communications, PIMRC 2006*, pp. 1–6.

Buratti, C. & Verdone, R. (2008). A mathematical model for performance analysis of ieee 802.15.4 non-beacon enabled mode, *Proc. IEEE European Wireless, EW2008*, Prague, Czech Republic.

Buratti, C. & Verdone, R. (2009). Performance analysis of ieee 802.15.4 non-beacon enabled mode.

Chen, Z., Lin, C., Wen, H. & Yin, H. (2007). An analytical model for evaluating ieee 802.15.4 csma/ca protocol in low rate wireless application, *Proc. IEEE AINAW 2007*.

Fabbri, F. & Verdone, R. (2008). Throughput analysis of an ieee 802.1lb multihop ad hoc network, *Proc. IEEE European Wireless, EW2008*, Prague, Czech.

Gardner, W. (1989). *Introduction to random processes: with applications to signals and systems*, second edn, McGraw Hill.

Kim, J. H. & Lee, J. K. (1999). Capture effects of wireless csma/ca protocols rayleigh and shadow fading channels, *IEEE Electronics Letters* **48**(4): 1277–1286.

Kim, T. O., Kim, H., Lee, J., Park, J. S. & Choi, B. D. (2006). Performance analysis of the ieee 802.15.4 with non beacon-enabled csma/ca in non-saturated contition, *International Conference on Embedded And Ubiquitous Computing, 2006. EUC 2006*, pp. 884–893.

Meester, R. & Roy, R. (1996). *Cambridge University Press, Cambridge UK.*

Miorandi, D. & Altman, E. (2005). Coverage and connectivity of ad hoc networks in presence of channel randomness, *Proc. of 24th Annual Joint Conference of the IEEE Computer and Communications Societies, INFOCOM 2005.*, Vol. 1, pp. 491–502.

Misic, J., Misic, V. B. & Shafi, S. (2004). Performance of ieee 802.15.4 beacon-enabled pan with uplink transmissions in non-saturation mode - access delay for finite buffers, *Proc. First International Conference on Broadband Networks, 2004. BroadNets 2004*, pp. 416–425.

Misic, J., Shafi, S. & Misic, V. B. (2005). The impact of mac parameters on the performance of 802.15.4 pan, *Elsevier Ad hoc Networks Journal* **3**: 509–528.

Misic, J., Shafi, S. & Misic, V. B. (2006). Maintaining reliability through activity management in an 802.15.4 sensor cluster, **3**: 779–788.

Orriss, J. & Barton, S. K. (2003). Probability distributions for the number of radio transceivers which can communicate with one another, **51**(4): 676–681.

Orriss, J., Phillips, A. & Barton, S. (1999). A statistical model for the spatial distribution of mobiles and base stations, *Proc. of IEEE Vehicular Technol. Conference, VTC 1999*, Vol. 1, pp. 19–22.

Orriss, J., Zanella, A., Verdone, R. & Barton, S. (2002). Probability distributions for the number of radio transceivers in a hot spot with an application to the evaluation of blocking probabilities, *IEEE Proc. of Personal, Indoor and Mobile Radio Communications, 2002*, Vol. 2.

Park, T., Kim, T., Choi, J., Choi, S. & Kwon, W. (2005). Throughput and energy consumption analysis of ieee 802.15.4 slotted csma/ca, *IEEE Electronics Letters* **41**: 1017–1019.

Penrose, M. D. (1993). On the spread-out limit for bond and continuum percolation, *Annals of Applied Probability* **3**: 253–276.

Penrose, M. D. (1999). On k-connectivity for a geometric random graph, *Random Structures and Algorithms* **15**: 145–164.

Penrose, M. D. & Pistztora, A. (1996). Large deviations for discrete and continous percolation, *Advances in Applied Probability* **28**: 29–52.

Pishro-Nik, Chan, K. & Fekri, F. (2004). On connectivity properties of large-scale sensor networks, *Sensor and Ad Hoc Communications and Networks, 2004. IEEE SECON04. First Annual IEEE Communications Society Conference on*, pp. 498–507.

Pollin, S., Ergen, M., Ergen, S., Bougard, B., der Pierre, L. V., Catthoor, F., Moerman, I., Bahai, A. & Varaiya, P. (2008). Performance analysis of slotted carrier sense ieee 802.15.4 medium access layer, **7**: 3359–3371.

Salbaroli, E. & Zanella, A. (2006). A statistical model for the evaluation of the distribution of the received power in ad hoc and wireless sensor networks, *Sensor and Ad Hoc Communications and Networks, SECON '06, 3rd Annual IEEE Communications Society on*, Vol. 3, pp. 756–760.

Santi, P. & Blough, D. M. (2003). The critical transmitting range for connectivity in sparse wireless ad hoc networks, **2**(1): 25–39.

Siripongwutikorn, P. (2006). Throughput analysis of an ieee 802.11b multihop ad hoc network, *Proc. IEEE TENCON 2006*, pp. 1–4.

Stoyan, D., Kendall, W. S. & Mecke, J. (1995). *Stochastic Geometry and its Applications*.

Stuedi, P., Chinellato, O. & Alonso, G. (2005). Connectivity in the presence of shadowing in 802.11 ad hoc networks, *Proc. IEEE WCNC, 2005*.

Takagi, H. & Kleinrock, L. (1985). Throughput analysis for persistent csma systems, **33**(7): 627–638.

Verdone, R., Dardari, D., Mazzini, G. & Conti, A. (2008). *Wireless sensor and actuator networks*, Elsevier.

Vincze, Z., Vida, R. & Vidacs, A. (2007). Deploying multiple sinks in multi-hop wireless sensor networks, *Pervasive Services, IEEE International Conference on*, pp. 55–63.

Zdunek, K., Ucci, D. & Locicero, J. (1989). Throughput of nonpersistent inhibit sense multiple access with capture, *IEEE Electronics Letters* **25**(1): 30–31.

8

Energy-aware Selective Communications in Sensor Networks

Rocio Arroyo-Valles[(1)], Antonio G. Marques[(2)], Jesus Cid-Sueiro[(1)]
[(1)]*Universidad Carlos III de Madrid,* [(2)]*Universidad Rey Juan Carlos de Madrid*
Madrid, Spain

1. Introduction

During the last years, Wireless Sensor Networks (WSN) have attracted the attention of researchers from electronics, signal processing, communications, and networking communities due to their potential for providing new capabilities. Among the many design challenges that have been identified, the ability of sensors to behave in an autonomous and self-organized manner using limited energy and computation resources has emerged as a fundamental factor to take into account when WSN are deployed. In fact, the limitation of resources at the network nodes is often a critical factor that conditions the design of applications for sensor networks. Among the multiple limitations to consider, energy consumption emerges as a primary concern. This is because in many practical scenarios, sensor node batteries cannot be (easily) refilled, thus nodes have a finite lifetime. Since every task carried out by the WSN has an impact in terms of energy consumption, an enormous variety of solutions, both software and hardware, have been proposed in the literature to optimize energy management; see, e.g., (Shih et al., 2001; Akyildiz et al., 2002).

Communication processes are typically among the most energy-expensive of such tasks. Many works have focused on the minimization of the energy cost taking into account the physical behavior of the WSN; see, e.g., (Shih et al., 2001; Marques et al., 2008; Wang et al., 2008). However, energy savings can also be obtained by taking a higher level approach and considering the different nature of the information that nodes have to transmit. This way, in order to enlarge the network lifetime and optimize the overall network performance, sensor nodes should weigh up: (a) the potential benefits of transmitting information and (b) the cost of the subsequent communication process. A first step to address such optimum design is to properly quantify or estimate both costs and benefits. This is possible in many practical cases because the energy consumed during the different communications tasks (cost) is typically well-characterized and because applications where messages are graded according to an importance indicator (benefit) are frequent in WSN. The message importance can be, for instance, a priority value established by the routing protocol, or an information value specified by the application supported by the sensor network. Relevant examples in the context of Sensor Networks can be found in the fields of: security (attack reports (Wood & Stankovic, 2002)), medical care (critical alerts (Shnayder et al., 2005)), or data fusion (DAIDA algorithm in (Qiu et al., 2005)), to name a few.

In such scenarios, energy in WSN can be saved by making intelligent importance-driven decisions about message transmission, in an autonomous and self-organized manner, adapting forwarding decisions to the traffic importance. This way, a *selective forwarding scheme* allows nodes to keep the capacity for managing their own resources at the same time that optimizes communication expenses by *only transmitting the most relevant messages*.

That is precisely the objective pursued in this work: to develop optimum selective message forwarding schemes for energy-limited sensor networks where sensors (re-) transmit messages of different importance (priority). In order to decide whether to transmit or discard a message, sensors will take into account factors such as the energy consumed during the different tasks that a sensor has to carry out (transmission, reception, etc.), the available battery, the importance of the received message, the statistical model of such importances, or their neighbors' behavior.

Related ideas have recently been explored in literature. The IDEALS algorithm (Merrett et al., 2005), built under the concept of message and power priorities, tries to extend network lifetime for important messages, discarding all messages except those of high importance when battery resources are scarce. The PGR (Prioritized Geographical Routing) algorithm (Mujumdar, 2004) selects the appropriated routing technique depending on the priority of the message (low, medium or high). Moreover, a fuzzy logic approach to deal with message transfer priority arbitration that considers fifteen different priority levels has been presented in (Rivera et al., 2007). Rather than using a heuristic approach, the aim here is to obtain analytical results that building on a mathematical formulation, provide basic guidelines to design such energy-efficient schemes. This will be done by following a probabilistic and statistical approach that will open the door to a long-term optimization of the network. The optimal forwarding schemes will be obtained then as the optimal solution of the formulated problem.[1]

The initial step will be to carefully select the model for the WSN. On the one hand the model has to be rich enough so that different real scenarios can be fit into, on the other hand it has to be simple enough so that the mathematical formulation is tractable and closed-form solutions can be derived. This way, basic principles to guide the design of energy-efficient importance-driven schemes can be identified. Once the mathematical model is set, we will derive optimum schemes for three different scenarios.

First we will consider the case when the forwarding schemes are designed so that sensors maximize the importance of their own transmitted messages. Second, we enrich the model by also considering the behavior of neighboring nodes. Third, we develop a forwarding scheme for nodes optimizing the importance of the messages that successfully arrive to the sink. Clearly, from an overall network efficiency perspective the first scenario will perform worse than its counterparts, but it will require less signaling overhead. On the contrary, the last scheme will optimize the overall network performance, but it will require full coordination among the nodes of the WSN. Differences among the proposed schemes will be quantified both from a theoretical and numerical perspective. Together with those optimal schemes, suboptimal schemes that operate under less demanding conditions than those for the optimal ones are also developed. [2]

[1] Noticeably, the statistical model presented in this chapter exhibits similarities to other problems in Operations Research and Stochastic Dynamic Programming (see, e.g., (Sennott, 1999)), and the equations describing the energy evolution at the sensor node and the importance sum can be restated as a particular type of Markov decision process. Nonetheless, our treatment of the problem and the theoretical derivations are self-contained.

[2] To facilitate exposition, most of the chapter will be devoted to the first (and simplest) scenario. Nevertheless it should be noted that the specific results presented only for that scenario can be easily extended to the other two scenarios. Under the same philosophy, no mathematical proofs have been included in the chapter. Readers who are interested can always check our original work in (Arroyo-Valles et al., 2009;

It will be shown that in most cases, the optimal forwarding scheme is fairly simple. More specifically, it will turn out that the optimal decision is made comparing the importance of the received message with a threshold whose optimum value varies along time. We will show that our schemes improve the global performance in terms of quantity and quality of the messages that really arrive at the destination node. Finally, it will be also shown that the gain of the selective forwarding schemes (compared to a non-selective ones) will critically depend on factors such as the relationship among the energy consumed during each of the tasks that nodes have to implement, the frequency of idle times, or the statistical distribution of the importances, to name a few.
The theoretical results will be complemented with numerical simulations that not only will corroborate the theoretical claims but also will help us to quantify the gains of implementing the selective scheme for a broader range of practical scenarios.
It is worth stressing that besides the theoretical value of this work: (i) the developed schemes can eventually be incorporated into many existing routing protocols; and (ii) our approach can also be easily integrated with a variety of existing data collection approaches, including schemes that support in network data aggregation.

2. Sensor model

For the purpose of the analysis that follows, we consider a sensor network as a collection of nodes $\mathcal{N} = \{n|n = 0,\ldots,N-1\}$. For the time being, we will focus on the behavior of each node, which receives a sequence of requests to transmit messages (no matter how the network topology is). The node dynamics will be characterized by two variables

- e_k : available energy at a given node at time k. It reflects the "internal state" of the node; and
- x_k : importance of the message to be sent at time k. It reflects the "external input" to the node.

For mathematical reasons, we assume that if the node does not receive any request to transmit at time k, then $x_k = 0$, while true messages will have $x_k > 0$.
At time k, the sensor node must make a decision, d_k, about sending or not the current message, so that $d_k = 1$ if the message is sent, and $d_k = 0$ if the node decides to discard it.
Nodes consume energy at each time slot, by an amount that depends on the message reception and the taken actions. In the literature, up to three different energy expenses are typically considered:

- E_I: energy spent at a silent time, when there is no message reception, and the node may stay at "idle" mode;
- E_R: energy spent when receiving a message; and
- E_T: energy spent when transmitting a message.

The value of these parameters will depend on the system specifications and the specific application (among the factors that will determine the energy costs we find mobility, sensed magnitude, or behavior of the batteries, to name a few). For example, for static dense networks, E_T and E_R values may be very similar, while for mobile networks operating over fading channels, $E_T >> E_R$ is expected.

2008).

Energy at time k can be expressed recursively as

$$e_{k+1} = e_k - d_k E_1(x_k) - (1 - d_k) E_0(x_k), \tag{1}$$

where $E_1(x_k)$ is the energy consumed when the node decides to transmit the message, and $E_0(x_k)$ is the energy consumed when the message is discarded. For positive values of importance, energy consumption is independent of the message importance, and we have

$$E_1(x_k) = E_T + E_R, \qquad x_k > 0 \tag{2}$$

$$E_0(x_k) = E_R, \qquad x_k > 0. \tag{3}$$

Recalling that $x_k = 0$ means that no messages are received, we also have

$$E_1(0) = E_0(0) = E_I. \tag{4}$$

When the sensor node is the source of the message, E_R comprises the energy expense of the message generation process (possibly by a sensing device). When the sensor node acts as a forwarder, E_R comprises the energy expense of receiving the message from other node. Thus, we assume that E_R is the same no matter if the node is the source of the message or it has been requested to forward a message from other node. Even though this assumption is not critical and could be bypassed by splitting E_R between receiving and sensing costs, we adopt it for two reasons: (i) it leads to a simpler mathematical formulation and (ii) nodes are prevented from acting selfishly (note that if the energy cost of sensing were smaller than the cost of receiving, nodes would promote their own messages instead of forwarding others' messages).

Remark 1 *It is important to mention that although this chapter focuses on the case where the energy consumption is given by (2)-(4), we will formulate and solve the general case in (1) by assuming that both consumption profiles, $E_1(x)$ and $E_0(x)$, may arbitrarily depend on x. As a first approach, the model could even be applied to situations where E_T and E_R are random or time-variant (e.g., in sensors operating over fast fading channels where transmissions are adapted based on the channel state information) by substituting E_T and E_R by their respective mathematical expectations. In any case, we assume that both energy functions are perfectly known.*

3. Optimal selective transmission

To derive an optimal transmission policy we will consider that node decisions do not depend on the state and the actions of neighboring nodes, but only on the available information at each node. Therefore, at each time, k, the node decision depends on the internal state and the external input

$$d_k = g(e_k, x_k), \tag{5}$$

with the constraint

$$g(e_k, x_k) = 0, \text{ if } e_k < E_1(x_k) \tag{6}$$

reflecting that, if the sensor node does not have enough energy to receive and transmit the message, it cannot decide $d_k = 1$.

Decisions at each node will be made with *infinite horizon*, i.e., by maximizing (on average) the importance sum of *all* transmitted messages

$$s_\infty = \sum_{k=0}^{\infty} d_k x_k. \tag{7}$$

Since nodes have limited energy resources, this sum only contains a finite number of nonzero values (eventually, for some k, $e_k < \min_k E_1(x_k)$, and $\forall k' \geq k$, we have $d_{k'} = 0$).
The following result provides an optimal selective transmitter.

Theorem 1 Let $\{x_k, k \geq 0\}$ be a statistically independent sequence of importance values, and e_k the energy process driven by (1). Consider the sequence of decision rules

$$d_k = u(x_k - \mu_k(e_k, x_k))u(e_k - E_1(x_k)), \tag{8}$$

where $u(x)$ stands for the Heaviside step function (with the convention $u(0) = 1$), and μ_k is defined recursively through the pair of equations

$$\mu_k(e, x) = \lambda_{k+1}(e - E_0(x)) - \lambda_{k+1}(e - E_1(x)) \tag{9}$$

$$\lambda_k(e) = \left(\mathbb{E}\{\lambda_{k+1}(e - E_0(x_k))\} + \mathbb{E}\{(x_k - \mu_k(e, x_k))^+ u(e - E_1(x_k))\}\right) u(e), \tag{10}$$

where $(z)^+ = zu(z)$, for any z.
The sequence $\{d_k\}$ is optimal in the sense of maximizing $\mathbb{E}\{s_\infty\}$ (with s_∞ given by (7)), among all sequences in the form $d_k = g(e_k, x_k)$ (with $g(e_k, x_k) = 0$ for $e_k < E_1(x_k)$).
The auxiliary function $\lambda_k(e)$ represents the expected increment of the total importance (*expected reward*) at time k , i.e.,

$$\lambda_k(e) = \sum_{i=k}^{\infty} \mathbb{E}\{d_i x_i | e_k = e\}. \tag{11}$$

The proof can be found in (Arroyo-Valles et al., 2009). Although Theorem 1 holds for any energy cost and importance value, it does not provide a clear intuition about the impact of $E_0(x)$ and $E_1(x)$ and the distribution of x_k on the design of the optimal transmission scheme. Moreover, the direct application of this theorem is difficult, because (9) and (10) state a time-reversed recursive relation: in order to make optimal decisions, the node should know the future importance distributions in advance. For these reasons, in the reminder of this chapter we will focus special attention on several particular cases that will lead us to tractable closed-form solutions.

3.1 Stationarity

If all variables $x_1, \ldots, x_k$ have the same distribution, then μ_k does not depend on k [c.f. (9) and (10)]. In this case, the following result can be shown (see (Arroyo-Valles et al., 2009)):

Theorem 2 *Under the conditions of Th. 1, if the importance values* $\{x_k, k \geq 0\}$ *are identically distributed and* $\inf_x\{E_i(x)\} > 0$, *for* $i = 0, 1$, *the sequence of decision rules given by*

$$d_k = u(x_k - \mu(e_k, x_k))u(e - E_1(x_k)), \tag{12}$$

where

$$\mu(e, x) = \lambda(e - E_0(x)) - \lambda(e - E_1(x)) \tag{13}$$

$$\lambda(e) = \left(\mathbb{E}\{\lambda(e - E_0(x))\} + \mathbb{E}\{(x - \mu(e, x))^+ u(e - E_1(x))\}\right) u(e), \tag{14}$$

is optimal in the sense of maximizing $\mathbb{E}\{s_\infty\}$ among all sequences of decision rules in the form $d_k = g(e_k, x_k)$ (with $g(e_k, x_k) = 0$ for $e_k < E_1(x_k)$).
It is important to stress that in most scenarios involving multiple sensors, the stationarity assumption, strictly speaking, is not true. For example, the distribution of messages arriving to a node depends on the transmission policy used by forwarding nodes. Since the optimal policy presented here is energy-dependent [c.f. either (9) or (13)] and the available energy clearly changes along time for all nodes, the importance distribution of the received messages will also change along time. However, it will be shown in the next sections that the simplification obtained in (13) is not only useful from a theoretical perspective, but also valid from a practical point of view for large networks. This (almost) stationary behavior can be justified based on different reasons. First, although the optimal forwarding policy varies along time, this variation turns out to be negligible during most of the time (i.e., it is almost-stationary). The underlying reason is that for medium-high values of available energy the optimal forwarding scheme is not very sensitive to energy changes. Only when nodes are close to run out of batteries, the decision threshold varies significantly as a function of the remaining energy. Second, even if the behavior of a single node is not stationary, the aggregate effect of the entire network may be stationary. In other words, the approximation given by (13) will be accurate during most of the time, and the discrepancy will only arise when the network is close to expire. Theoretical analysis and numerical results will corroborate this intuition.

3.2 Constant energy profiles

Under the constant profile model given by (2)-(4), the optimal threshold can be written as

$$\mu_k(e,x) = \mu_k(e) I_{x>0}, \tag{15}$$

where $I_{x>0}$ is an indicator function (equal to unity if the condition holds and zero otherwise), and using (9) we have

$$\mu_k(e) = \lambda_{k+1}(e - E_R) - \lambda_{k+1}(e - E_T - E_R). \tag{16}$$

Also, (10) becomes

$$\begin{aligned}
\lambda_k(e) &= P_I \lambda_{k+1}(e - E_I) + (1 - P_I)\lambda_{k+1}(e - E_R) - P_I \mu_k(e,0) u(-\mu_k(e,0)) u(e - E_I) \\
&\quad + (1 - P_I)\mathbb{E}\{(x_k - \mu_k(e,x_k))^+ | x_k > 0\} \cdot u(e - E_T - E_R) \\
&= P_I \lambda_{k+1}(e - E_I) + (1 - P_I)\lambda_{k+1}(e - E_R) \\
&\quad + (1 - P_I)\mathbb{E}\{(x_k - \mu_k(e,x_k))^+ | x_k > 0\} \cdot u(e - E_T - E_R)
\end{aligned} \tag{17}$$

where $P_I = \Pr\{x = 0\}$. Defining

$$H_k(\mu) = \mathbb{E}\{(x_k - \mu)^+ | x_k > 0\}, \tag{18}$$

we can write

$$\begin{aligned}
\lambda_k(e) = \quad & P_I \lambda_{k+1}(e - E_I) + (1 - P_I)\lambda_{k+1}(e - E_R) \\
& +(1 - P_I) H(\mu_k(e)) u(e - E_T - E_R).
\end{aligned} \tag{19}$$

Thus, the optimal transmission policy for a sensor with a constant energy profile is described by (16) and (19). In order to analyze the influence of idle times and the relation between transmission and reception energy expenses separately, in the following examples we consider the case of $P_I = 0$ and/or $E_I = 0$. Note that if any of these conditions holds, the expected importance sum in (19) can be rewritten as

$$\lambda_k(e) = \lambda_{k+1}(e - E_R) + H(\mu_k(e))u(e - E_T - E_R). \tag{20}$$

3.3 Examples

As we have already mentioned, there is no general explicit solution to the pair of equations (9) and (10), not even for the stationary case in (16) and (19). For this reason, in this section we focus on systems satisfying the operating conditions that gave rise to (20) (constant energy profiles, stationarity and zero idle energy) and solve the recursive relations for several importance distributions[3]. This simplification will lead to tractable expressions, providing insight into the behavior of the optimal forwarding scheme.

- **Uniform Distribution**: Let $U(0,2)$ denote the uniform distribution between 0 and 2 whose probability density function (PDF) is

  $$p(x) = \frac{1}{2}(u(x) - u(x-2)). \tag{21}$$

  Substituting (21) into (18), we have

  $$H(\mu) = E\{(x-\mu)^+\} = \frac{1}{4}(2-\mu)^2, \tag{22}$$

  and therefore, the expected reward is given by

  $$\lambda(e) = \lambda(e - E_R) + \frac{1}{4}(2 - \mu(e))^2 u(e - E_T - E_R). \tag{23}$$

  Figure 1(a) plots the threshold for *extremely small* values of available energy, e. $E_1(x) = 1$ and different values of the ratio E_T/E_R are considered. Note that, for values of e lower than 1, in spite of the threshold value is 0, there is no actual transmission because $u(e - E_T - E_R) = 0$. For $1 < e < E_1 + E_R$ there is only one opportunity to send the message, so the threshold is also 0, which means that the message will be transmitted whatever its importance value is. For larger energy values, the threshold increases, meaning that the transmission can be made more selective. Note, also, that $\mu(e)$ evolves in a staircase manner, because any energy amount in excess of a multiple of E_R is useless.

  Figure 1(b) represents the expected reward ($\lambda(e)$). Note that the case $E_T = 0$ is equivalent to a non-selective transmitter (because, according to (16), the optimal threshold is 0 in that case, which means that no messages are discarded). Despite that, for e close to 2, there is not energy for a second transmission, the selective transmitter provides a significant expected income with respect to the non-selective one.

  Figure 2(a) shows the optimal threshold for $E_T = 4$, $E_R = 1$ and *high* values of available energy. Note the sawtooth shape of the forwarding threshold: as the available energy is reduced to a value close to a multiple of the energy required to transmit, the forwarding threshold decreases, because if there is not any transmissions, the total number of possible messages to be sent is reduced by a unity.

  Figure 2(b) represents the expected reward of the selective transmitter (continuous line) and the non-selective one (dotted line), which transmits all messages regardless of their importance value, until energy is used up.

[3] In the following, free parameters will be set so that all importance distributions have a mean value equal to one.

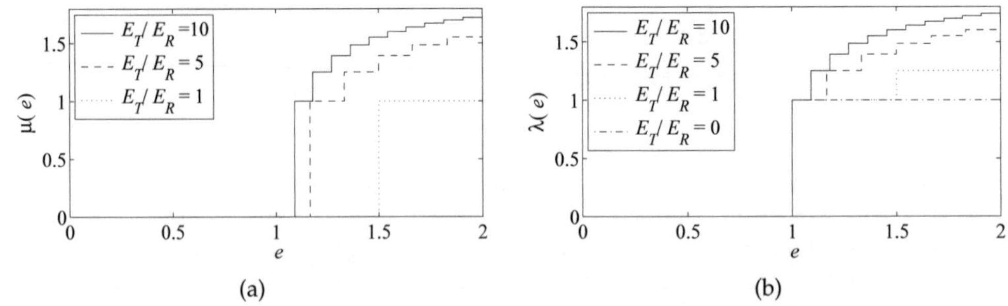

Fig. 1. Variation of the decision threshold (a) and the expected importance sum (b) with respect to the available energy, e. A uniform importance distribution $U(0,2)$ with $E_1(x) = E_R + E_T = 1$ is assumed. Different plots correspond to different values of E_T/E_R.

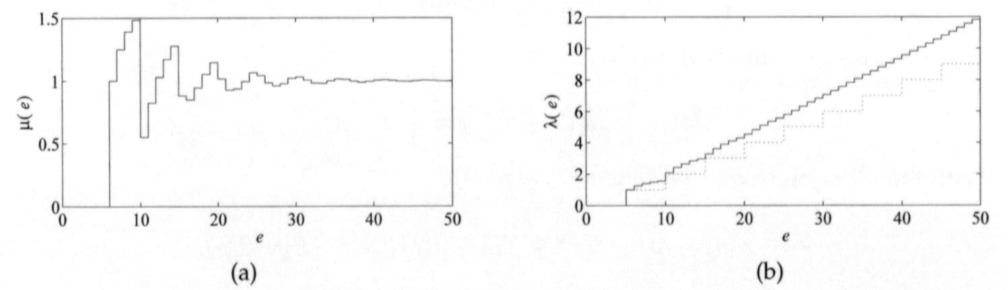

Fig. 2. The decision threshold (a) and the expected importance sum (b) (continuous line) as a function of the available energy. A uniform importance distribution $U(0,2)$ with $E_T = 4$ and $E_R = 1$ is assumed. The stepwise function (dotted line) reflects the behavior of a non-selective transmitter, which transmits any message whatever its importance value is.

- **Exponential**: For an exponential distribution of free parameter a, we have

$$p(x) = \frac{1}{a} \exp\left(-\frac{x}{a}\right) u(x), \tag{24}$$

and

$$H(\mu) = a \exp\left(-\frac{\mu}{a}\right), \tag{25}$$

so that

$$\lambda(e) = \lambda(e - E_R) + a \exp\left(-\frac{\mu(e)}{a}\right) u(e - E_T - E_R). \tag{26}$$

The variation of μ for an exponential distribution with $a = 1$, $E_T = 4$ and $E_R = 1$ is illustrated in Figure 3. The more restrictive threshold, compared to that one shown in Figure 2(a) for the uniform distribution, gives rise to a higher increase in the expected reward with regard to the non-selective forwarder.

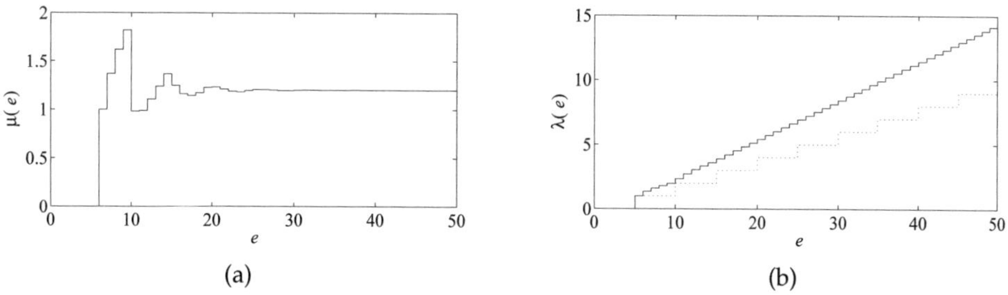

Fig. 3. Variation of the decision threshold (a) and the expected importance sum (b) (continous line) with respect to the available energy. An exponential importance distribution with $a = 1$, $E_T = 4$ and $E_R = 1$ is assumed. The dotted line represents the expected importance sum of the non-selective transmitter.

4. Asymptotic analysis

4.1 Large energy threshold

The above examples show that for large energy values e, the threshold converges to a constant value, and the expected reward tends to grow linearly. Both behaviors are closely related because, as (9) shows, the optimal threshold is the difference between two expected rewards. In this section, we discuss the asymptotic behavior of any selective transmitter in the stationary case. To do so, we first define the *income rate* of a selective transmitter.

Definition 1 The income rate of a selective transmitter with expected reward $\lambda(e)$ is defined as

$$r = \lim_{e \to \infty} \frac{\lambda(e)}{e}. \tag{27}$$

The following theorem (Arroyo-Valles et al., 2009) provides a way to compute the income rate of the optimal selective transmission policy.

Theorem 3 The only threshold function $\mu(e,x)$ which is a solution of (13) and (14) and is constant with e is given by

$$\mu(e,x) = \mu(x) = (E_1(x) - E_0(x))r, \tag{28}$$

where r is a solution of

$$\mathbb{E}\{E_0(x)\}r = \mathbb{E}\{(x - (E_1(x) - E_0(x))r)^+\}. \tag{29}$$

Moreover, if $E_1(x) \geq E_0(x)$, for all x, this solution is unique.

An important consequence of Theorem 3 is that, if $\lim_{e\to\infty} \mu(e,x)$ exists, it must be equal to (28). Even though we will not show any theoretical convergence result, we have found a systematic empirical convergence, and we guess that this could be a general result for any importance distribution, provided it is stationary.

For the constant profile case, the asymptotic threshold (28) becomes

$$\mu(x) = E_T r I_{x>0}. \tag{30}$$

The recursive expression in (29) can be written as a function of $\mu^* = E_T r$ as

$$(P_I E_I + (1 - P_I)E_R)\mu^* = (1 - P_I)E_T H(\mu^*) \tag{31}$$

where $H(\mu^*)$ is given by (18). Defining

$$\rho = \frac{(1 - P_I)E_T}{P_I E_I + (1 - P_I)E_R} \tag{32}$$

we get

$$\mu^* = \rho H(\mu^*). \tag{33}$$

As a reference for comparison, we will consider the income rate of the non-selective transmitter (i.e., the node transmitting any message requested to be sent, provided that the battery is not depleted), which can be shown (Arroyo-Valles et al., 2009) to be equal to

$$r_0 = \frac{\mathbb{E}\{x\}}{\mathbb{E}\{E_1(x)\}}. \tag{34}$$

4.2 Gain of a selective forwarding scheme

In this section we analyze asymptotically the advantages of the optimal selective scheme with regard to the non-selective one. To do so, we define the *gain* of a selective transmitter as the ratio of its income rate, r, and that of the non-selective transmitter, r_0,

$$G = \frac{r}{r_0}. \tag{35}$$

For the optimal selective transmitter in the constant profile case, combining (29) and (34), we get

$$\begin{aligned} G =& \frac{\mu^* \mathbb{E}\{E_1(x)\}}{E_T \mathbb{E}\{x\}} = \frac{\mu^*(P_I E_I + (1 - P_I)(E_T + E_R))}{E_T \mathbb{E}\{x\}} \\ =& (1 - P_I)(1 + \rho^{-1})\frac{\mu^*}{\mathbb{E}\{x\}} = \frac{1+\rho}{\rho}\frac{\mu^*}{\mathbb{E}\{x|x > 0\}}. \end{aligned} \tag{36}$$

In the following, we compute the gain for several importance distributions.

4.3 Examples

Let us illustrate some examples taken from the constant profile case,

- **Uniform Distribution**: Substituting (22) into (33), we get

$$\mu^* = \frac{1}{4}\rho(2 - \mu^*)^2, \tag{37}$$

which can be solved for μ^* as

$$\mu^* = 2\left(\frac{1+\rho}{\rho} - \sqrt{\left(\frac{1+\rho}{\rho}\right)^2 - 1}\right) \tag{38}$$

(the second root is higher than 2, which is not an admissible solution). Note that, for $\rho = 4$, we get $\mu^* = 1$, which agrees with the observation in Fig.2(a).

Therefore, the gain is given by

$$G = 2\frac{1+\rho}{\rho}\left(\frac{1+\rho}{\rho} - \sqrt{\left(\frac{1+\rho}{\rho}\right)^2 - 1}\right). \tag{39}$$

- **Exponential**: Using (25) we find that μ^* is the solution of

$$\mu^* = aW(\rho), \tag{40}$$

where $W(x) = y$ is the real-valued Lambert's W function which solves the equation $ye^y = x$ for $-1 \leq y \leq 0$ and $-1/e \leq x \leq 0$ (Corless et al., 1996). Thus,

$$G = (1+\rho^{-1})W(\rho). \tag{41}$$

Figure 4 compares the gain of the uniform and the exponential distributions as a function of ρ. The graphic remarks that, under exponential distributions, the difference between the selective and the non-selective forwarding scheme is much more significant. The better performance of the exponential distribution compared to the uniform may be attributed to the tailed shape. We may think that, for a long-tailed distribution, the selective transmitter may be highly selective, saving energy for rare but *extremely important* messages. This intuition is corroborated by the Pareto distribution (see (Arroyo-Valles et al., 2009) for further details).

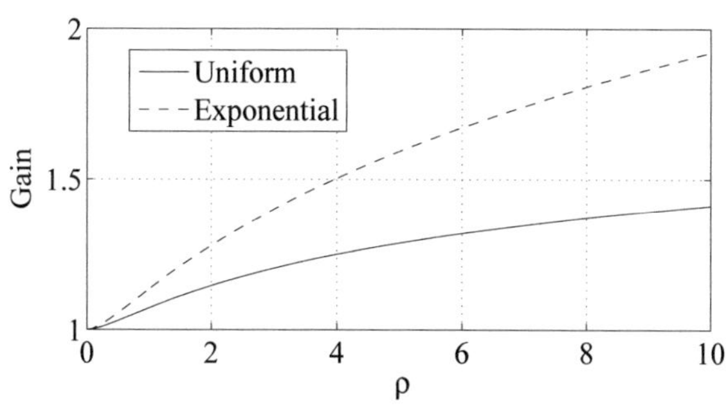

Fig. 4. Gain of the uniform and exponential distributions, as a function of ρ.

4.4 Influence of idle times

The above examples show that the gain of the optimal selective transmitter increases with ρ. By noting that ρ in (32) is a decreasing function of P_I and E_I, the influence of idle times becomes clear: as soon as the frequency of idle times or the idle energy expenses increases, the gain of the selective transmission scheme reduces.

5. Network Optimization

5.1 Optimal selective forwarding

Since each message must travel through several nodes before arriving to destination, the message transmission is completely successful if the message arrives to the sink node. In general, an intermediate node in the path has no way to know if the message arrives to the sink (unless

the sink returns a confirmation message), but it can possibly listen if the neighboring node in the path propagated the message it was requested to forward. If d_k denotes the decision at node i, and q_k denotes the decision at the neighboring node j, the transmission is said to be locally successful through j if $d_k = 1$ and $q_k = 1$.
In this case, we can re-define the cumulative sum of the importance values in (7) by omitting all messages that are not forwarded by the receiver node, as

$$s_\infty = \sum_{i=0}^{\infty} d_i q_i x_i, \tag{42}$$

and, as we did in Section 3, the goal at each node is to maximize its expected value of s_∞. Note that (42) reduces to (7) by taking $q_i = 1$ for all i.
The following result provides the optimal selective forwarder.

Theorem 4 Let $\{x_k, k \geq 0\}$ be a statistically independent sequence of importance values, and e_k the energy process given by (1). Consider the sequence of decision rules

$$d_k = u(Q_k(e_k, x_k)x_k - \mu_k(e_k, x_k))u(e - E_1(x_k)), \tag{43}$$

where $u(x)$ stands for the Heaviside step function (with the convention $u(0) = 1$),

$$Q_k(x_k, e_k) = \mathbb{E}\{q_k | e_k, x_k\} = P\{q_k = 1 | e_k, x_k\} \tag{44}$$

and thresholds μ_k are defined recursively through the pair of equations

$$\mu_k(e, x) = \lambda_{k+1}(e - E_0(x)) - \lambda_{k+1}(e - E_1(x)) \tag{45}$$

$$\lambda_k(e) = \left(\mathbb{E}\{\lambda_{k+1}(e - E_0(x_k))\} + \mathbb{E}\{(Q_k(e_k, x_k)x_k - \mu_k(e, x_k))^+ u(e - E_1(x_k))\}\right) u(e). \tag{46}$$

Sequence $\{d_k\}$ is optimal in the sense of maximizing $\mathbb{E}\{s_\infty\}$ (with s_∞ given by (42)) among all sequences in the form $d_k = g(e_k, x_k)$ (with $g(e_k, x_k) = 0$ for $e_k < E_1(x_k)$).
The auxiliary function $\lambda_k(e)$ represents the increment of the total importance that can be expected at time k, i.e.,

$$\lambda_k(e) = \sum_{i=k}^{\infty} \mathbb{E}\{d_i q_i x_i | e_k = e\}. \tag{47}$$

The proof can be found in (Arroyo-Valles et al., 2009). It is interesting to re-write (43) as

$$d_k = u\left(Q_k(x_k, e_k) - \frac{\mu_k(e)}{x_k}\right) u(e_k - E_1(x_k)) \tag{48}$$

which expresses the node decision as a comparison of Q_k with a threshold inversely proportional to the importance value, x_k. This result is in agreement with our previous models in (Arroyo-Valles et al., 2006), (Arroyo-Valles, Alaiz-Rodriguez, Guerrero-Curieses & Cid-Sueiro, 2007).

5.2 Global network optimization applying a selective transmission policy

In order to complete the theoretical study, the network optimization at a global level is analyzed. In general, and as we mentioned in Sec. 5.1, an intermediate node in the path has no way to know if the message arrives to the sink unless the sink sends a confirmation message. Let's denote a_k as the arrival of a message to the sink node and let's define A_k as $A_k(x_k,e_k) = \mathbb{E}\{a_k|e_k,x_k\} = P\{a_k = 1|e_k,x_k\}$, similar to Q_k definition from Theorem 4. The optimal selective policy when optimizing the global performance can be obtained from Theorem 4 just replacing q_k and Q_k by a_k and A_k. The difference among both theorems will stay in the interpretation of variables a_k and q_k. While q_k indicates the action of a forwarding node, a_k refers to the success of the whole routing process.

6. Algorithmic design

In practice, to compute the optimal forwarding threshold in a sensor network, $Q_k(x_k,e_k)$, $A_k(x_k,e_k)$ and the importance distribution of messages, $p_k(x_k)$, are required. As they are unknown, they can be estimated on-the-fly with data available at time k.

6.1 Estimating Q_k and A_k

A simple estimate of the forwarding policy $Q_k = E\{q_k|x_k,e_k\}$ can be derived by assuming that (1) it does not depend on e_k (i.e., the subsequent forward/discard decision of the receiver node is independent of the energy state at the transmitting node), and (2) each node is able to listen to the retransmission of a message that has been previously sent (i.e. each node can observe q_k when $d_k = 1$). Following an approach previously proposed in (Arroyo-Valles et al., 2006) and (Arroyo-Valles, Marques & Cid-Sueiro, 2007), in (Arroyo-Valles et al., 2008) we propose to estimate Q_k by means of the parametric model

$$Q_k(x_k,w,b) = P\{q_k = 1|x_k,w,b\} = \frac{1}{1+\exp(-wx_k - b)} \tag{49}$$

Note that, for positive values of w, Q_k increases monotonically with x_k, as expected from the node behavior. We estimate parameters w and b via ML (maximum likelihood) using the observed sequence of neighbor decisions $\{q_k\}$ and importance values $\{x_k\}$, by means of stochastic gradient learning rules

$$\begin{aligned} w_{k+1} &= w_k + \eta(q_k - Q_k(x_k,w_k,b_k))x_k \\ b_{k+1} &= b_k + \eta(q_k - Q_k(x_k,w_k,b_k)) \end{aligned} \tag{50}$$

where η is the learning step.

Similarly, the estimation algorithm given by (49) and (50) can be adapted to estimate A_k in a straightforward manner, but it requires the sink node to acknowledge the reception of messages back through the routing path, so as to provide the nodes with a set of observations a_k for the estimation algorithm.

6.2 Estimating asymptotic thresholds

The optimal threshold depends on the distribution of message importances, which in practice may be unknown. Another alternative, apart from estimating it (see (Arroyo-Valles et al., 2009)), consists of estimating parameter r in (29) and replace the optimal threshold function by its asymptotic limit. Parameter r can be estimated in real time based on the available data $\{x_\ell, \ell = 0,\ldots,k\}$ at time k.

However, first of all we should update (29) to incorporate to the formula the information obtained from neighboring nodes and thus, define a formula as general as possible. Comparing (8) and (43), we realize that x in the optimal transmitter is replaced by $xQ(x)$ in the optimal forwarder and so, (29) should be replaced by

$$\mathbb{E}\{E_0(x)\}r = \mathbb{E}\{(xQ(x) - (E_1(x) - E_0(x))r)^+\}. \tag{51}$$

Defining $\Delta(x) = E_1(x) - E_0(x)$, we can estimate the expected value on the right-hand side of (51) as

$$\mathbb{E}\{(xQ(x) - \Delta(x)r)^+\} \approx m_k \tag{52}$$

where

$$m_k = \frac{1}{k}\sum_{i=1}^{k}(x_iQ(x_i) - \Delta(x_i)r)^+ = \left(1 - \frac{1}{k}\right)m_{k-1} + \frac{1}{k}(x_kQ(x_k) - \Delta(x_k)r)^+ \tag{53}$$

According to (51), we can then estimate r at time k as $r_k = m_k/\epsilon_0$, where $\epsilon_0 = \mathbb{E}\{E_0(x)\}$. Using (53) we get

$$r_k = \left(1 - \frac{1}{k}\right)r_{k-1} + \frac{(x_kQ(x_k) - \Delta(x_k)r)^+}{k\epsilon_0} \tag{54}$$

Unfortunately, the above estimate is not feasible, because the left-hand side depends on r. But we can replace it by r_{k-1}, so that

$$r_k = \left(1 - \frac{1}{k}\right)r_{k-1} + \frac{(x_kQ(x_k) - \Delta(x_k)r_{k-1})^+}{k\epsilon_0}. \tag{55}$$

For the constant profile case, the optimal forwarding threshold is computed as

$$\mu_k = \left(1 - \frac{1}{k}\right)\mu_{k-1} + \frac{\rho}{k}\cdot(x_kQ(x_k) - \mu_{k-1})^+ \tag{56}$$

where ρ is given by (32).

7. Experimental work and results

In this section we test the selective message forwarding schemes in different scenarios. All simulations have been conducted using Matlab.

7.1 Sensor network

The scenario of an isolated energy-limited selective transmitter node can be found in (Arroyo-Valles et al., 2009). Although it provides useful insights, from a practical perspective a test case with a single isolated node is too simple. For this reason, we simulate a more realistic scenario consisting of a network of nodes. Experiments have been conducted considering both optimal selective transmitters and optimal selective forwarders (with both local and global optimization). Results focused on the optimal selective transmitters are presented in Section 7.1.1 while results for both selective transmitters and forwarders are presented in Section 7.1.2. Before starting the analysis of those results, we first describe part of the simulation set-up that is common for all the numerical tests run in this Section.

1. All nodes deployed in the sensor network are identical and have the same initial resources except for the sink, that has rechargeable batteries (thus it does not have energy limitations). This static unique sink is always positioned at the right extreme of the field. We will consider that $P_I = 0$, $E_T = 4$, $E_R = 1$ and $E_I = 0$. Sources are selected at random and keep transmitting messages of importances x to the sink until network lifetime expires. Network lifetime is defined as the number of time slots achieved before the sink is isolated from its neighboring nodes. In order to simulate a more realistic set up, the parameters of the two distributions considered (uniform and exponential) will be adjusted so that $x_k \in [0, 10]$ (with $x_k = 0$ representing a silent time).
2. Nodes are considered as neighbors if they are placed within the transmission radius, which for simplicity reasons and due to power limitations is assumed to be the same for all nodes (i.e., a Unit Disk Graph model is assumed). Since nodes can only transmit messages inside their coverage area, they have geographical information about their own position, the location of their neighbors and the sink coordinates. It is naturally assumed that coverage areas are reciprocal, which is common when having a single omnidirectional antenna. Under this assumption nodes can listen to the channel and detect retransmissions of neighboring nodes before retransmitting the message again, in case a loss is detected, or discard it.
3. Performance is assessed in terms of the importance sum of all messages received by the sink, the mean value of these received importances, the number of transmissions made by origin nodes and the network lifetime (measured in time slots).
4. Experimental results are averaged over 50 different topologies which contain different samples of the two previous importance distributions.

7.1.1 Sensor network composed of selective transmitters

In this scenario, the sensor network is considered as a square area of 10×10, where 100 nodes have been uniformly randomly deployed. The initial energy of the nodes is set to $E = 200$ units. Regarding to the transmitting schemes implemented, four different types of sensors are compared.

- *Type NS* (Non-Selective): Non-selective node. The threshold is set to $\mu = 0$, so that it forwards all messages.
- *Type OT* (Optimal Transmitter): Optimal selective node. Threshold μ is computed according to (16) and (19), where nodes know the source importance distribution $p(x)$.
- *Type CT* (Constant Threshold): Asymptotically optimal selective node. The sensor node establishes a constant threshold which is set to the asymptotic value of the optimal threshold given by (33).
- *Type AT* (Adaptive Transmitter): Adaptive selective node. The threshold is also computed following (16) and (19). Nevertheless, the node is unaware of $p(x)$ and it uses the Gamma distribution estimation strategy, proposed in (Arroyo-Valles et al., 2009).

The routing algorithm implemented by the network follows a greedy forwarding scheme (Karp & Kung, 2000). Although the disadvantages of the greedy forwarding algorithm are well-known (e.g., when the number of nodes close to the sink is small or there is a void), we choose this algorithm due to its simplicity, which will contribute to minimize its influence on the final results. This way, we can gauge better the effect of implementing our optimal selective schemes in a network, which indeed is the main objective of the simulations. It is worth re-stressing that we are not proposing a new routing algorithm but a forwarding scheme with a selective mechanism and therefore, this scheme can also be integrated into other more efficient routing algorithms. Periodical "keep alive" beacons are sent to keep nodes updated. Link losses have also been included and so, the algorithm is made more robust by establishing a maximum number of retransmissions before discarding the message, which has been set to 5 in our simulations.

	Total Import. Received Sink	Importance mean value	Number of Transmissions	Network Lifetime
Type NS	1021.92	5.06	688.56	7896.00
Type OT	1388.40	7.49	677.38	8467.90
Type CT	1384.26	7.49	656.92	8441.08
Type AT	1377.22	7.80	720.78	8812.74

Table 1. Averaged performance when the importance values are generated according to a uniform distribution - routing scenario

Simulation results for the scenario composed of selective transmitters are summarized in Tables 1 and 2. The numerical results validate our theoretical claims. As expected, the main conclusion is that the selective transmission scheme outperforms the non-selective one.

	Total Import. Received Sink	Importance mean value	Number of Transmissions	Network Lifetime
Type NS	331.72	1.76	672.84	7798.02
Type OT	610.96	3.84	613.30	8758.00
Type CT	609.45	3.86	596.82	8713.88
Type AT	594.92	4.18	685.98	9309.56

Table 2. Averaged performance when the importance values are generated according to an exponential distribution - routing scenario

Regardless of the distribution tested, both the mean value of the importance of messages received by the sink and the network lifetime are higher when the selective transmission scheme is implemented.

Among the selective policies, OT nodes exhibit the best performance. Nevertheless, performance differences among OT, CT and AT are not extremely high. The underlying reason is that decisions made at neighboring nodes and path losses may alter the shape of the original importance distribution. Since AT nodes estimate the importance distribution $p(x)$ based on real received data, they are able to correct this alteration. This is not the case of OT and CT nodes, which calculate μ based on the original distribution, without accounting for the alterations introduced by the network. The existence of a transitory phase through the calculation of the adaptive threshold in the AT scheme may also justify small differences with respect to the other non-adaptive selective schemes.

7.1.2 Performance comparison among selective nodes

In this subsection, we compare the performance of different networks each of them comprising a different type of selective nodes, namely:

- *Type NS* (Non-Selective) : Non-selective sensor node, it forwards all the received messages, no matter which its importance value is.
- *Type AT* (Adaptive Transmitter): Adaptive Selective transmitter sensor node. This sensor corresponds to the particular case of (42) taking $q_k = 1$, which is equivalent to assume that the node does not take into account the neighbors' behavior, i.e. it maximizes the importance sum of all messages transmitted by the node, no matter if they are forwarded by the neighboring node or not.
- *Type LAF* (Local Adaptive Forwarder): Local Adaptive Selective forwarder sensor node. This sensor type computes the forwarding threshold according to (45) and (46). It bears in mind the influence of neighboring nodes decisions.
- *Type GAF* (Global Adaptive Forwarder): Global Adaptive Selective forwarder sensor node. The forwarding threshold is set according to (45) and (46); however a_k and A_k are used instead of q_k and Q_k in order to achieve a global network optimization.

Since the transmission policies implemented by each node can (and will) alter the importance distribution originally generated by the sources, all selective types of nodes considered here are adaptive and the forwarding threshold is computed using the asymptotic threshold estimate given by (56).

For illustrative purposes, we simplify the simulation set-up by considering 30 nodes that are equally-spaced placed in a row, so that each sensor can only communicate with the adjoining sensors. This configuration is a simple but illustrative manner of emulating the traffic arriving to a sink, as nodes located close to the sink have to route more messages (both those generated by themselves and the ones arriving from others far-away located). The energy values of the different energy states are the same as the ones used in previous sections. Nodes have the same initial amount of battery, set to 5000. The channel is ideal (loss free path). Parameter η in (50) is set to .005. All nodes generate messages according to the same importance distribution, which is equivalent to say that the source importance distribution is the same for all nodes. Again, results averaged over 50 runs for different importance distributions are listed in Tables 3 and 4. Simulations are stopped when the sink is isolated.

	Total Import. Received	Importance mean value	Number of Receptions	Network Lifetime
Type NS	4989.26	4.99	999.02	1000
Type AT	8158.45	8.28	985.52	2963.42
Type LAF	8210.73	8.33	985.38	3056.90
Type GAF	8209.80	8.33	985.36	3056.64

Table 3. Averaged performance when the importance values are generated according to a uniform distribution

According to the analytical formulation, the non-selective sensor nodes perform worse (regardless of the metrics) than any type of the selective nodes. It is worth mentioning that the

mean value of the messages received by the sink is slightly higher in this scenario than in the precedent which corresponds to an arbitrary topology.
If we look closely among the selective nodes, the selective forwarding (local or global) yields a better performance than the selective transmission for all the proposed importance distribution types. Nevertheless, looking at the averaged values of the importance sum, the goal metric to be maximized, it is revealed that the improvement, although substantial, is not extreme. The reason stems from the fact that all nodes have an identical source importance distribution. More noticeable differences will appear whenever the nodes generate messages of different importance distributions.

	Total Import. Received	Importance mean value	Number of Receptions	Network Lifetime
Type NS	1755.40	1.76	999.02	1000
Type AT	5526.04	5.99	923.12	11580.70
Type LAF	5612.34	6.11	919.18	12459.76
Type GAF	5612.22	6.11	919.08	12468.58

Table 4. Averaged performance when the importance values are generated according to an exponential distribution

Additionally, the difference is almost unnoticeable when comparing the LAF and GAF nodes (the actual difference depends on the distribution tested). This extremely low difference is due to the effect that nodes tend to propagate their current thresholds to adjoining nodes and, therefore, the local and global optimization are almost coincident.
Figure 5 shows the threshold evolution for Adaptive Transmitters (a) and Local Adaptive Forwarders (b). Going into detail, results in Figure 5(a) point out that each node behaves independently and sets its threshold according to its own available information. The furthest node from the sink sets the lowest threshold, which clearly corresponds to the isolated node scenario given that it only has its own generated traffic. Nevertheless, the subsequent nodes in the network increase their thresholds as a consequence of receiving messages with clipped importances from their previous nodes. Thus, the closer a node is placed to the sink, the larger the threshold value is. On the other hand, LAF nodes in Figure 5(b) follow a similar trend. Again, after a transitory phase, nodes tend to converge to the threshold value established by the nearest node from the sink. This is a reasonable behavior because it would not make sense to transmit a message up to the last but one node and then, discard it for not being important enough. Nodes tend to learn the threshold that the neighbor closer to the sink node is using to ensure that the message to transmit is forwarded, so that in the end, nodes learn the threshold estimated by the nearest node to the sink. Learning the probability of retransmission (Q_k or A_k in case of global optimization) is equivalent to the effect of backward propagating the threshold value to the whole sensor network.
Once the last but one node is isolated, two effects can be observed. The first is related to that node, which is now free to fix its own threshold value according to the messages generated by itself. And the second is related to the remaining nodes in the network. From the moment the network is broken down and there is no manner to reach the sink, nodes located on the isolated side of the breakdown will tend to set a lower threshold since the lack of collaboration is then propagated backwards (the estimation of the probability that a neighbor will re-transmit

the messages decreases). Moreover, since this effect is produced in cascade, nodes will end up adjusting their thresholds to the threshold of the node located next to the breakdown.

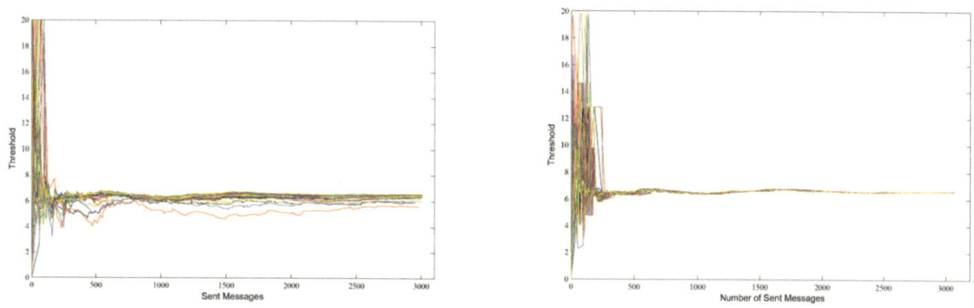

(a) (b)

Fig. 5. The decision threshold evolution for Adaptive Transmitters (a) and Local Adaptive Forwarders (b) as a function of the number of sent messages in a simulation run. A network topology of 30 equally-spaced nodes located in a row is considered. A uniform importance distribution $U(0,10)$ is assumed.

In order to enhance the advantages of using selective forwarding schemes, a new scenario is proposed. In this case, nodes generate messages according to an exponential distribution, but the source importance distribution is different in every node so that parameter a follows an exponential trend, too. Remark that the manner of selecting parameter a implies that message importance $x_k \notin [0,10]$ any more. For concision, Table 5 lists results only for the AT and LAF cases.

	Total Import. Received	Importance mean value	Number of Receptions	Network Lifetime
Type AT	11229.32	13.92	811.60	27014.90
Type LAF	11763.35	14.37	825.48	28583.16

Table 5. Averaged performance when the importance values are generated according to an heterogeneous exponential distribution

In summary, numerical results corroborate that selective forwarding sensor nodes are more energy-efficient than their non-selective counterparts. On the one hand, the selective forwarding schemes significantly increase the network lifetime. On the other hand, they also allow high importance messages to reach the sink when batteries are scarce.

8. Conclusions

This chapter has introduced an optimum selective forwarding policy in WSN as an energy-efficient scheme for data transmission. Messages, which were assumed to be graded with an importance value and which could be eventually discarded, were transmitted by sensor nodes according to a forwarding policy, which considered consumption patterns, available energy resources in nodes, the importance of the current message and the statistical description of such importances.

Forwarding schemes were designed for three different scenarios (a) when sensors maximize the importance of their own transmitted messages (selective transmitter); (b) when sensors maximize the importance of messages that have been successfully retransmitted by at least one of its neighbors (selective forwarder with local optimization); and (c) when sensors maximize the importance of the messages that successfully arrive to the sink (selective forwarder with global optimization). Interestingly, the structure of the optimal scheme was the same in all three cases and consisted of comparing the received importance and the forwarding threshold. The expression to find the optimum threshold varies with time and is slightly different for each scenario. It is worth remarking that the developed schemes were optimal from an importance perspective, efficiently exploited the energy resources, entailed very low computational complexity and were amenable to distributed implementation, all desirable characteristics in WSN.

The three schemes have been compared under different criteria. From an overall network efficiency perspective, the first scheme performed worse that its counterparts, but it required less signaling overhead. On the contrary, the last scheme was the best in terms of network performance, but it required the implementation of feedback messages from the sink to the nodes of the WSN. Numerical results showed that for the tested cases the differences among the three schemes were small. This suggests that the second scheme, which is just slightly more complex than the first one and performs evenly with the third one, can be the best candidate in most practical scenarios.

Finally, suboptimal schemes that operate under less demanding conditions than those for the optimal ones were also explored. Under certain simplifying operating conditions, a constant forwarding threshold which did not change along time and entailed asymptotic optimality, was also developed and closed-form expressions were obtained. The gain of the selective forwarding policy compared to a non-selective one was quantified and it was proved to have a strong dependence on energy expenses (transmission, reception and idle), the frequency of idle times and the statistical distribution of importances. Going further, as nodes are integrated in a sensor network, information coming from the neighborhood was incorporated into the statistical model and thus, an expression for the optimal forwarding threshold was obtained, which turned into a general expression of the optimal selective transmitter. Finally, for cases were the importance distribution of messages was unknown (or it varied with time), a blind algorithm, which is based on the received messages, caught this distribution on-the-fly and required less computational complexity, was proposed.

9. Acknowledgments

This work was partially funded by the Spanish Ministry of Science and Innovation Grant No. TEC2008-01348 and by the Gov. of C.A. Madrid Grant No. P-TIC-000223-0505. We also want to thank Harold Molina for the technical support given to the elaboration of this manuscript.

10. References

Akyildiz, I. F., Su, W., Sankarasubramaniam, Y. & Cayirci, E. (2002). A Survey on Sensor Networks, *IEEE Comm. Magazine* **40**(8): 102–114.

Arroyo-Valles, R., Alaiz-Rodriguez, R., Guerrero-Curieses, A. & Cid-Sueiro, J. (2007). Q-Probabilistic Routing in Wireless Sensor Network, *Proc. 3th Int'l Conf. Intelligent Sensor, Sensor Networks and Information Processing (ISSNIP '07).*

Arroyo-Valles, R., Marques, A. G. & Cid-Sueiro, J. (2007). Energy-aware Geographic Forwarding of Prioritized Messages in Wireless Sensor Networks, *Proc. 4th IEEE Int'l Conf. on Mobile Ad-hoc and Sensor Systems (MASS '07).*

Arroyo-Valles, R., Marques, A. G. & Cid-Sueiro, J. (2008). Energy-efficient Selective Forwarding for Sensor Networks, *Proc. Workshop on Energy in Wireless Sensor Networks (WEWSN'08), in conjunction with DCOSS'08.*

Arroyo-Valles, R., Marques, A. G. & Cid-Sueiro, J. (2009). Optimal Selective Transmission under Energy Constraints in Sensor Networks, *IEEE Transactions on Mobile Computing* .

Arroyo-Valles, R., Marques, A. G., Vinagre-Díaz, J. & Cid-Sueiro, J. (2006). A Bayesian Decision Model for Intelligent Routing in Sensor Networks, *Proc. 3rd IEEE Int'l Symp. on Wireless Comm. Systems (ISWCS '06).*

Corless, R. M., Gonnet, G. H., Hare, D. E. G., Jeffrey, D. J. & Knuth, D. E. (1996). On the Lambert W function, *Advances in Computational Mathematics* **5**: 329–359.

Karp, B. & Kung, H. (2000). Greedy Perimeter Stateless Routing for Wireless Networks, *Proc. 6th Annual ACM/IEEE Int'l Conf. on Mobile Computing and Networking (MobiCom 2000)*, pp. 243–254.

Marques, A. G., Wang, X. & Giannakis, G. B. (2008). Minimizing Transmit-Power for Coherent Communications in Wireless Sensor Networks with Finite-Rate Feedback, *IEEE Transac. on Signal Processing* **56**(8): 4446–4457.

Merrett, G., Al-Hashimi, B., White, N. & Harris, N. (2005). Information Managed Wireless Sensor Networks with Energy Aware Nodes, *Proc. NSTI Nanotechnology Conf. and Trade Show (NanoTech '05)*, pp. 367–370.

Mujumdar, S. J. (2004). *Prioritized Geographical Routing in Sensor Networks*, Master's thesis, Vanderbilt University, Tennessee.

Qiu, J., Tao, Y. & Lu, S. (2005). *Grid and Cooperative Computing*, Vol. 3795/2005, Springer Berlin / Heidelberg, chapter Differentiated Application Independent Data Aggregation in Wireless Sensor Networks, pp. 529–534.

Rivera, J., Bojorquez, G., Chacon, M., Herrera, G. & Carrillo, M. (2007). A Fuzzy Message Priority Arbitration Approach for Sensor Networks, *Proc. North American Fuzzy Information Processing Society (NAFIPS '07)*, pp. 586–591.

Sennott, L. I. (1999). *Stochastic Dynamic Programming and the Control of Queueing Systems*, Wiley-Interscience.

Shih, E., Cho, S.-H., Ickes, N., Min, R., Sinha, A., Wang, A. & Chandrakasan, A. (2001). Physical layer driven protocol and algorithm design for energy-efficient wireless sensor networks, *of the 7th Annual ACM/IEEE International Conference on Mobile Computing and Networking (Mobicom 01).*

Shnayder, V., Chen, B., Lorincz, K., Fulford-Jones, T. & Welsh, M. (2005). Sensor Networks for Medical Care, *Proc. 3rd Int'l Conf. on Embedded networked sensor systems.*

Wang, X., Marques, A. G. & Giannakis, G. B. (2008). Power-Efficient Resource Allocation and Quantization for TDMA Using Adaptive Transmission and Limited-Rate Feedback, *IEEE Transac. on Signal Processing* **56**(8): 4470–4485.

Wood, A. D. & Stankovic, J. A. (2002). Denial of Service in Sensor Networks, *IEEE Computer* **35**(10): 54–62.

9

Machine Learning Across the WSN Layers

Anna Förster[1,2] and Amy L. Murphy[3]
[1]*University of Lugano*, [2]*Networking Laboratory SUPSI*, [3]*FBK-IRST*
[1,2]*Switzerland*, [3]*Italy*

Wireless sensor networks (WSNs) have seen rapid research and industrial development in recent years. Both the costs and size of individual nodes have been constantly decreasing, opening new opportunities for a wide range of applications. Nevertheless, designing software to achieve energy-efficient, robust and flexible data dissemination remains an open problem with many competing solutions.

In parallel, researchers have effectively exploited machine learning techniques to achieve efficient solutions in environments with distribution and rapidly fluctuating properties, analogous to WSN domains. Applying machine learning techniques to WSNs inherently has the potential to improve the robustness and flexibility of communications and data processing, while simultaneously optimizing energy expenditure.

This chapter concentrates on applications of machine learning at all layers in the WSN network stack. First, it provides a brief background and summary of three of the most commonly used machine learning techniques: reinforcement learning, neural networks and decision trees. Then, it uses example research from the literature to describe current efforts at each level of the stack, and outlines future opportunities.

1. Wireless Sensor Networks

Extensive research effort has been invested in recent years to optimize communications in wireless sensor networks (WSNs). Researchers and application developers typically use a communication stack model such as that depicted in Figure 1 to structure the communications of WSNs and to better manage its challenges. In particular, the following properties of WSNs should be considered while designing innovative and efficient solutions (Akyildiz et al., 2002; Römer & Mattern, 2004).

- *Wireless ad-hoc nature.* No fixed communication infrastructure exists. The shared wireless medium places restrictions on the communication between nodes and poses new problems such as asymmetric links. However, it offers the broadcast advantage: a transmitted packet, even if sent in unicast to another node, can be overhead and thus received by all neighbors of the transmitter.
- *Mobility and topology changes.* WSNs may support dynamic application scenarios. New nodes may be added to the network, and existing nodes may move either within or out of the network. Nodes may cease to function, and connectivity among surviving nodes changes over time. WSN applications must be robust against such topology dynamics.
- *Energy limitations.* The basic WSN scenario includes a large number of sensor nodes, and a limited number of more powerful base stations. As such, most WSN nodes have

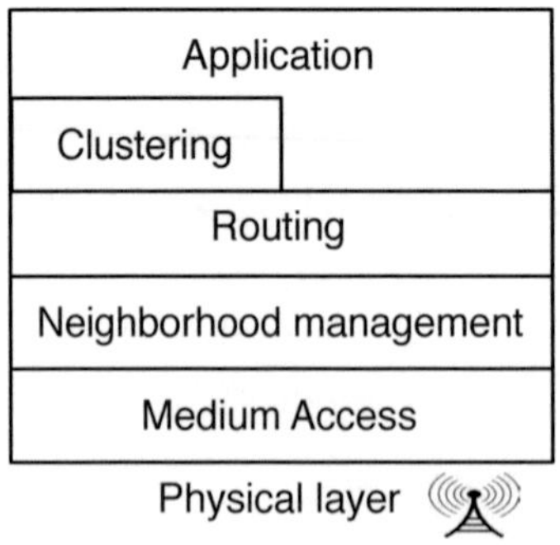

Fig. 1. The WSN communication stack

limited energy supplies and maintenance or battery recharging is often impossible after deployment. Communication tasks consume a large proportion of the energy available on the nodes, and thus to ensure sustained long-term operation, radio communication must be frugally managed.

- *Physical distribution.* Each node in a WSN is an autonomous computational unit that communicates with its neighbors via messages. Data is collected throughout the network and can be gathered at a central station only with high communication costs. Consequently, algorithms that require global information from the entire network become very expensive. Thus, distributed algorithms are highly desirable.

The next section proceeds with a brief introduction to machine learning approaches that have been successfully applied to one or more layers of the communication stack. We then provide concrete examples of how machine learning has been exploited to minimize communication overhead at all layers from neighborhood management up to the application.

2. Machine Learning Techniques

Machine learning (ML) is a sub-field of artificial intelligence that *"is concerned with the question of how to construct computer programs that automatically improve from experience"* (Mitchell, 1997). Precisely this property makes the family of ML algorithms and techniques appealing for efficient communications in WSNs. This section presents some widely applied ML approaches that form the basis for the exemplary applications in the following sections. Alternate ML techniques include, among many others, genetic algorithms (Mitchell, 1997) and swarm intelligence algorithms such as ant colony optimization (Dorigo & Stuetzle, 2004). While these are powerful machine learning techniques for solving various challenging problems, they are less suitable for communications in wireless sensor networks (Kulkarni et al., 2009) because of their high communication overhead.

2.1 Decision Tree Learning

In many classification problems the items to be classified exhibit a number of clearly defined features, represented as attribute-value pairs. For example, if we want to classify all possible fruits, we can use features such as size, shape, color, taste, etc. with corresponding attribute-value pairs such as *color = orange*. We could define the possible classification clusters by their features and attribute-value pairs. Then, for some unclassified object, we check all of its features to match it with one of the clusters. However, a so called classification tree is more efficient, since it offers structure the classification approach and usually classifies a sample based only on a few features. In such a tree the leaves represent classification clusters and the branches represent conjunctions of features. Continuing with our fruit example, a classification tree will ask at the very first branch what is the color of the sample. If there is only one cluster with the color blue (e.g., blueberry), then the branch leads directly to the classification leaf of blueberries without asking for any other features. It is clear from this example that the most important question when constructing such trees is *"which attribute to check at the root of the tree, which next?"*

Decision tree learning is a machine learning technique that uses a set of already classified training samples for constructing the optimal tree. Optimal in this case refers to the number of feature checks before classification. Of course, the classification problem might exhibit noise samples, which also need to be accommodated. For example, strawberries are usually red, but sometimes we observe also green ones. Thus, the decision tree will either wrongly classify the green strawberry as something else or it needs to use all of the other features (size, shape, etc.) and ignore the color. The final decision depends on the samples in the training set and on the importance of different features. As we have seen above, some of the features may become irrelevant, while others become highly important.

There are two main algorithms for constructing decision trees: ID3 and the its successor C4.5 (Mitchell, 1997). Each sample s_i from the training set S consists of a vector of feature values f_i and is already classified as belonging to cluster c_j. C4.5 computes for each feature the information gain when splitting on this feature. In other words, which feature separates the clusters best? In our fruit example from above, checking for the shape in the root of the tree is probably a bad decision, since many if not all fruits are round. However, checking for the size might separate watermelons and melons from all the rest very well. Thus, the information gain of the feature *size* is higher than for any other feature. C4.5 takes the feature with the highest information gain and puts it in the root of the tree. Then it recursively computes the information gain for the resulting subclasses until all or nearly all samples from the training set are classified. Clearly, not all of the samples will be classified successfully, as exemplified in the discussion above. However, this is not possible even with the brute-force method of checking all possible features and their values, because the training set also includes noisy data. A formal description of decision tree learning can be found in (Mitchell, 1997).

In the context of wireless sensor networks, classification problems like this arise when classifying links as good or bad based on data such as signal strength or delivery rate, or classifying sensory data as important or not. We show an application of decision trees to link quality estimation in Section 3. Decision tree learning is suited for such classification problems since it is fast to both train and execute. Additionally, implementing a decision tree on a resource-restricted sensor node is simple. On the other hand, training should be performed offline to save node energy, requiring the classification problem to be relatively stable.

2.2 Neural Networks

An artificial neural network (or simply neural network, NN) is a mathematical models of a function $F : X \rightarrow Y$. The initial inspiration comes from biological networks of neurons. NNs consist of simple nodes or neurons, interconnected as in Figure 2. Simple functions are usually associated with each node (e.g., addition) and weights are assigned to the connections between the nodes. Data flows from the input (left column of neurons in Figure 2) through the whole network, using the connections between the nodes and arriving at the output neurons (right column of neurons). The most important property of neural networks is their ability to

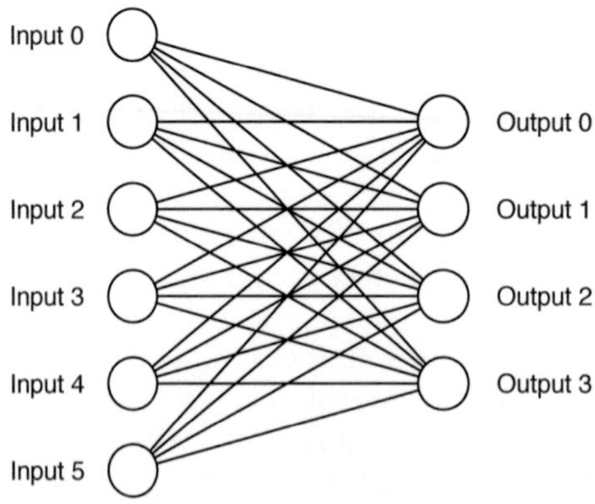

Fig. 2. A generic architecture of an artificial neural network with input and output layers.

learn — to adjust the weights between the input and the output to exactly reflect the learned function.

For learning or *training* a neural network, a set of training data is needed, where possible inputs have already been mapped to the needed output. For example, for classification of hand-written numbers, different pictures (input) are classified as numbers (output). However, in contrast to decision trees, the input cannot be described with features and attribute-value pairs. Instead, it is represented as a point in an N-dimensional space. For example, a hand written picture of the size 32×32 pixels is represented as a point in the $32 \times 32 = 1024$ dimensional space. There will also be 1024 input neurons in the neural network and exactly 10 output neurons, one for each digit. The weights connecting the input neurons with the output ones need to be set such that the correct output neuron "fires" — only the output neuron has a value of 1 and all others a value of 0. This is done by presenting the network with examples, consisting of input and output. With every sample, the weights are corrected such that the correct neuron fires. Thus, in our 1024-dimensional space, the hand-written samples will cluster around some points in this space, representing the different digits from 0 to 9. Incoming input samples can be then classified according to their distance to the clusters and the closest cluster is taken.

The above described neural network is a so called supervised offline learning algorithm. *Supervised* refers to the training set, which has already been classified. *Offline* refers to the necessary training of the network before using it for classification. However, there also exist *unsupervised* and *online* learning neural networks. An example of such a network is used for learning the data model for incoming sensor readings in Section 6. More information about neural networks and how to train them can be found in (Mitchell, 1997).

Neural networks are well suited for complex classification problems where features or attribute-values pairs are not available. However, they have larger memory and processing requirements than, for example, decision tree learning. On the other hand, as we will show in Section 6, these techniques are applicable in WSNs for static classification problems such as data models or link quality estimation. In addition, they can be efficiently implemented even on standard sensor nodes because of their relatively low memory requirements.

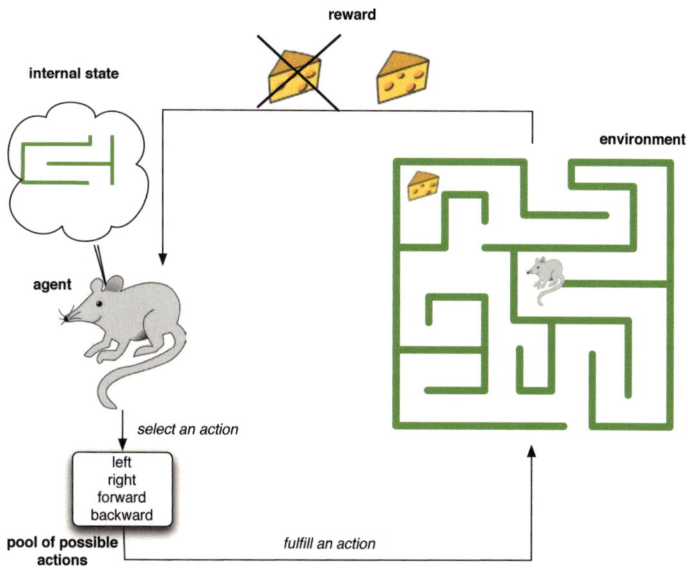

Fig. 3. General reinforcement learning model. The agent selects one action according to its current internal state (current view of the environment and previous knowledge), fulfills this action and observes a reward.

2.3 Reinforcement Learning

Reinforcement learning (RL) (Mitchell, 1997; Sutton & Barto, 1998) is a biologically inspired machine learning technique, where the learning agent acquires its knowledge from direct interaction with its environment. A simple example is a mouse in a maze, trying to find the path to a piece of cheese (see Figure 3). At any moment, it must select a direction to move. The result of each action is either finding cheese or not. This maps to the reinforcement learning technique in which agents (e.g., the mouse) select actions (e.g., direction to move) and receive rewards (e.g., cheese) from the environment for each action. A well-known and widely used RL algorithm is Q-Learning, which model consists of:

Agent states. The learning agent has a finite set of possible states S and s_t represents the agent's state at time step t. In our example from Figure 3, the state of the mouse is its current position in the maze.

Actions. Q-Learning associates a different set of actions A_S to each of the states in S. In our maze environment, the actions are represented by the movement steps of the mouse — forward, backward, left, right.

Immediate rewards. There is an associated immediate reward $r(s_t, a_t)$ with each of the state transitions. In our example, all of the state transitions that do not lead to the goal state have immediate rewards of 0 (no cheese) and the ones leading to the goal state have an immediate reward of 1 (cheese reached). The agent can see only the actions with their associated rewards from its current state. It does not have any global knowledge about the environment, its states and their rewards.

Action costs. In addition to rewards, there is also a cost $c(s_t, a_t)$ associated with each action in each state. This is again a scalar value, representing how costly this action is. In our example, it costs one unit of energy (one bite of cheese) for the mouse to make any movement. Costs are often considered negative rewards, thus they are subtracted directly from the immediate reward.

Value function. In contrast to immediate rewards, which are associated to each action in each state and are easily observable, the value function represents the *expected total accumulated reward*. The goal of the agent is to learn a sequence of actions with a maximum value function, that is, the reward on the taken path is maximized.

Q-Values. To represent the currently expected total future reward at any state, a Q-Value is associated to each action and state $Q(s_t, a_t)$. The Q-Value represents the memory of the learning agent in terms of the quality of the action in this particular state. In the beginning Q-Values are usually initialized with zeros, representing the fact that the agent knows nothing. Through trial and experience the agent learns how good some action was. The Q-Values of the actions change through learning and finally represent the absolute value function. After convergence, taking the actions with the greatest Q-Values in each state guarantees taking the optimal decision (path).

Updating a Q-Value. A simple rule exists to update a Q-Value after each step of the agent:

$$Q(s_{t+1}, a_t) = Q(s_t, a_t) + \gamma(R(s_t, a_t) - Q(s_t, a_t)) \quad (1)$$

The new Q-Value of the pair $\{s_{t+1}, a_t\}$ in state s_{t+1} after taking action a_t in state s_t is computed as the sum of the old Q-Value and a correction term. This term consists of the received reward and the old Q-Value. γ is the learning constant. It prevents the Q-Values from changing too fast and thus oscillating. The total received reward is computed as:

$$R(s_t, a_t) = r(s_t, a_t) + c(s_t, a_t) \quad (2)$$

Where $r(s_t, a_t)$ is the immediate reward as defined above and $c(s_t, a_t)$ is the cost of taking the action a_t in state s_t.

Exploration strategy (action selection policy). Learning is performed in episodes, e.g., the mouse takes actions in its environment and updates the associated Q-Values until reaching the cheese. After completion, a new episode begins, repeating until the Q-Values no longer change. The question is how to select the next action. Always taking the actions with maximum Q-Value (greedy policy) will result in finding locally minimal solutions. On the other hand, selecting always random (random policy) will mean ignoring prior experience and spending too much energy to learn the complete environment.
These two extreme strategies are called *exploitation* and *exploration* of routes. The problem of combining and weigthing both so that optimal results are achieved as fast as possible has been extensively studied in machine learning (Sutton & Barto, 1998). The most commonly used strategy is called *ϵ-greedy*: with probability ϵ the agent takes a random action and with probability $(1 - \epsilon)$ it takes the best available action.
RL is well suited for distributed problems such as routing. It has medium requirements for memory and rather low computation needs at the individual nodes. This arises from the need to keep many different possible actions and their values. It needs some time to converge, but it is easy to implement, highly flexible to topology changes and learns the optimal solution (e.g., shortest paths).

3. Neighborhood Management Layer

One major problem of communications in wireless sensor networks is the unreliability of the links. At any time, a previously reliable link may disappear, while others might become more reliable than before. This is influenced by the environmental conditions (weather, moving people, etc.) and cannot be controlled or predicted. Unreliable links are a great challenge for routing protocols, since selecting reliable routes is crucial for saving energy in the network as a whole. Thus, a special layer is needed between the medium access and the routing layers to provide the routing layer with up-to-date information of the reliability of connections to neighbors. The resulting protocols are called link or neighborhood management protocols. The most important properties of a good neighborhood management protocol are (Karl & Willig, 2005):

- **Precision.** The links should be precisely evaluated in their quality and reliability.
- **Agility.** The link manager should react quickly to changes.
- **Stability.** The link manager should not be influenced by short aberrations.
- **Energy efficiency.** The link manager should spend as little communication and processing power for its operation as possible.

Many researchers have put extensive effort in searching for good link estimators. Two main classes exist: passive and active estimators. Passive estimators use readily available information on the nodes for their estimations, such as RSSI of received packets, number of received packets, etc. Active estimators pro-actively send probe packets to discover the link quality to their neighbors. Of course combinations of passive and active estimators also exist that use readily available information as much as possible and send additional probe packets when needed.

Traditional approaches use rules of thumb to estimate the quality of links given some local information on the nodes. Typically they use rules such as "if $RSSI > 80$ then $quality = good$", implement them on a hardware testbed, test it and fine-tune the parameters of the approach. However, this design phase is long and inefficient, based mainly on experience and intuition. Nevertheless, some of these approaches have been extensively evaluated and widely used for real applications, e.g., through integration with existing routing protocols such as MintRoute (Woo et al., 2003) or Arbutus (Puccinelli & Haenggi, 2008).

3.1 MetricMap: Supervised Learning for Link Quality Estimation.

A more sophisticated approach is to try to automatically gather relevant features and properties readily available at the nodes, and to learn to estimate the quality of the links from them. A simple, yet powerful algorithm is MetricMap (Wang et al., 2006), developed at Princeton University in 2006. MetricMap uses decision tree learning to offline learn to estimate link quality based on previously gathered link samples. The decision trees uses locally available data and learns to classify links as good or bad. The acquired rules are integrated with a routing protocol (in this case MintRoute (Woo et al., 2003)) and are used online to predict link quality based only on locally available information such as delivery rate or RSSI levels of incoming packets. The authors of MetricMap designed their algorithm in two main steps: sample collection and offline training. First, they used the MistLab [1] sensor network testbed at MIT to gather link samples together with all available features, shown in Table 1. Each link sample was labeled "good" or "bad", according to its Link Quality Indication (LQI) value.

[1] http://mistlab.csail.mit.edu

Table 1. Link sample features used in MetricMap.

Feature	Description	Locality
RSSI	received signal strength indication	local
sendBuf	send buffer size	local
fwdBuf	forward buffer size	local
depth	node depth from base station	non-local
CLA	channel load assessment	local
pSend	forward probability	local
pRecv	backward probability	local

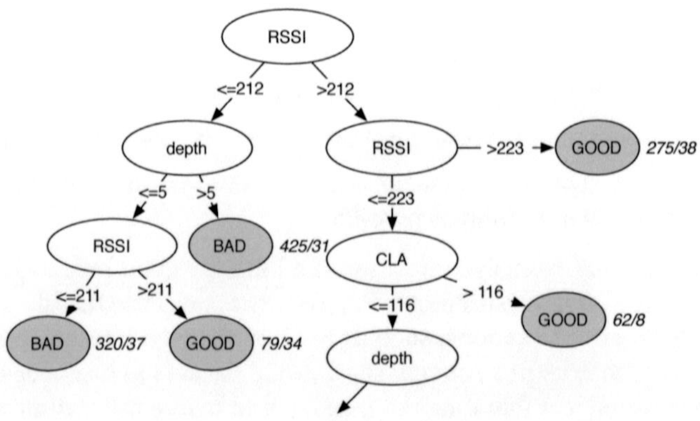

Fig. 4. Part of the decision tree for estimating link quality, computed by MetricMap.

LQI is an indicator of the strength and quality of a received packet, introduced in the 802.15.4 standard and provided by the CC2420 radios of the MicaZ nodes in MistLab. Measurement studies with LQI have shown it is a reliable metric when estimating link quality. However, LQI is available only after sending the packet. It is not available for estimating the future quality of some link before any packets are sent.

The training set, consisting of labeled link samples, was used to compute offline a decision tree, which classifies the links as good or bad, based on the features from Table 1. The output of the decision tree learner is presented in Figure 4 (a), together with classification results from the training phase in the format: (total samples in category / false positive classifications). The authors used the Weka workbench (Witten & Frank, 2005), which contains many different implementations of machine learning techniques, including the C4.5 algorithm for decision tree learning (see Section 2.1).

The acquired rules are used to instrument the original implementation of MintRoute. In a comparative experimental evaluation on a testbed the authors showed that MetricMap outperforms MintRoute significantly in terms of delivery rate and fairness, see Figure 4 (b) and (c). MetricMap also does not incur any additional processing overhead, since the evaluation of the decision tree is straightforward.

3.2 Discussion of MetricMap

The authors of MetricMap have clearly shown that supervised learning approaches are easy to implement and use in a wireless sensor network environment and significantly improve the routing performance of a real system. Similar approaches can be applied to other testbeds and real deployments. The only requirement is that the general communication properties of the network do not change over time. This could be particularly challenging in outdoor environments, where weather, temperature, sunlight, etc., influence the wireless communications. Detailed and long-running experiments under changing climate conditions are necessary to demonstrate the applicability of MetricMap-like routing optimizations. However, the expectation is that the offline learning procedure needs to be re-run in order to adapt to the changing environment, which could be very costly. In case this hypothesis proves to be true, distributed methods for automatic link quality estimation need to be developed. On the other hand, implementing decision tree or rule-based learning on sensor nodes seems to be practical, since these techniques do not have high memory or processing requirements.

4. Routing Layer

The *routing* challenge refers to the general problem of transferring a data packet from one node in the network to another one, where direct communication between the nodes is impossible. The problem is also known as multi-hop routing, referring to the fact that typically multiple intermediate nodes are used to relay the data packet to its destination. A routing protocol identifies the sequence of intermediate nodes to ensure delivery of the packet. A differentiation between unicast and multicast routing protocols exists in which unicast protocols route the data packet from a single source to a single destination, while multicast routing protocols route the data packet to multiple destinations simultaneously.

There is a huge body of research on routing for WSNs and in general for wireless ad hoc networks. The main challenges are managing unreliable communication links, node failures and node mobility, and, most importantly, using energy efficiently. Well-known unicast routing paradigms for WSNs are for example Directed Diffusion (Silva et al., 2003) and MintRoute (Woo et al., 2003), which select shortest paths based on hop counts, latency and link reliability. Geographic routing protocols such as GPSR (Karp & Kung, 2000) use geographic progress to the destination as a cost metric to greedily select the next hop.

Next we present an effort to achieve good routing performance and long network lifetimes with Q-Learning, a reinforcement learning algorithm presented in Section 2.3. It uses a latency-based cost metric to minimize delay to the destination and is one of the fundamental works on applying machine learning to communication problems.

4.1 Q-Routing: Applying Q-Learning to Packet Routing

Q-Routing (Boyan & Littman, 1994) is one of the first applications of Q-Learning, as outlined in Section 2.3 and (Watkins, 1989), to communications in dynamically changing networks. Originally it was developed for wired packet-switched networks, but it is also easily adaptable to the wireless domain.

The learning agents are the nodes in the network, which learn independently from one another the minimum-delay route to the sink. At each node, the available actions are the node's neighbors. A value $Q_{x,t}(d,y)$ is associated with each neighbor, reflecting the delay estimate d at time t of node x to reach the sink through neighbor y. The update rule for the Q-Values is:

$$Q_{x,t+1}(d,y) = Q_{x,t}(d,y) + \gamma\,(q + s + R - Q_{x,t}(d,y)) \tag{3}$$

where γ is the learning rate, fixed to 0.5 in the original Q-Routing paper (Boyan & Littman, 1994), q is the time the last packet spent in the queue of the node, s is the transmission time to reach neighbor y and R is the reward received from neighbor y, calculated as:

$$R_y = \min_{z \in (neighbors\ of\ y)} Q_{y,t}(d, z) \tag{4}$$

The authors applied their algorithm to three different fixed topologies with varying numbers of nodes. They measured the network performance of Q-Routing against a shortest-path routing algorithm under multiple network loads. Under high network loads (the paper does not specify the exact load) Q-Routing performs significantly better than shortest-path because it takes into account the waiting time in the queue. Thus, it spreads the traffic more uniformly, achieves lower end-to-end delivery rates and avoids queue overflows. Importantly, the network load can change during its lifetime and Q-Routing quickly and non intrusively re-learns the optimal paths.

4.2 Discussion of Q-Routing

While the original paper contains no explanation for the selected learning rate, nor details about initialization and action selection policy, and the reward delivery implementation is not given, the experience of other researchers offer answers to these questions. They show that a simple ϵ-greedy action policy is energy-efficient and easy to implement. Initialization of Q-Values can be random, zero or with some a priori available routing information on the nodes, such as estimation of the delay to the sinks. The main goal of the learning rate is to avoid initial oscillations of the Q-Values. We have shown in our analysis of the multicast routing protocol FROMS (Förster & Murphy, 2007) that it can be fixed to 1 if the Q-Values are initialized with good estimates of the real costs. In such a case, a learning rate of 1 speeds up the learning process significantly without the risk of oscillating values. We have also shown an efficiently mechanism to implement the reward mechanism in WSNs, specifically by piggybacking rewards on usual data packets. Due to the inherent broadcast nature of the wireless communication,all the neighboring nodes hear the data packets together with the rewards. Additionally, not only will the preceding node update its Q-Values, but all overhearing nodes can as well, further speeding up the learning process.

The authors of Q-Routing have clearly shown how to efficiently apply reinforcement learning techniques to challenging communication problems and to significantly improve network performance. Although the work is rather preliminary as the experiments are limited to only a few topologies and evaluation metrics, Q-Routing has inspired a number of other routing protocols, especially in WSNs.

5. Clustering and Aggregation Layer

Clustering and data aggregation are powerful techniques that inherently reduce energy expenditure in wireless sensor networks while at the same time maintaining sufficient quality of the delivered data. Clustering is defined as the process of dividing the sensor network into groups. Often a single cluster head is then identified within each group and made responsible for collecting and processing data from all group members, then sending it to one or more base stations.

While this approach is seemingly simple and straightforward, efficiently achieving it involves solving four challenging problems. First, the clusters themselves must be identified. Second, cluster heads must be chosen. Third, routes from all nodes to their cluster head must be discovered. And finally, the cluster heads must efficiently route data to the sink(s).

Traditional clustering schemes can be coarsely divided into two main classes: random- and agreement-based approaches. The first class are mostly variations or modifications of

LEACH (Rabiner-Heinzelman et al., 2000), in which nodes choose to be cluster heads with an a-priori probability. Subsequently, cluster heads flood a cluster head role assignment message to their neighbors, which in turn identify the nearest cluster head as their own. In contrast, agreement-based protocols first gather information about their k-hop neighborhood and then decide on the cluster heads (Bandyopadhyay & Coyle, 2003; Demirbas et al., 2004; Younis & Fahmy, 2004). Again, the cluster heads announce themselves to the network. The main difference between these two classes are the properties of the resulting clusters: their shape, size, number of nodes per cluster, and spreading of remaining energy among the nodes in a cluster. Random-based protocols produce non-uniformly sized clusters with varying remaining energies on the nodes. However, they do not require a lot of communication overhead for selecting the cluster heads. On the other hand, agreement-based protocols produce well-balanced clusters, but require extensive communication overhead for gathering the neighborhood information and for agreeing on the cluster head role.

5.1 CLIQUE: Role-Free Clustering Protocol with Q-Learning

One of the challenges facing state of the art clustering is handling node and cluster head failures without losing a substantial part of the data during the recovery process. Here we present a protocol that explicitly addresses recovery after such failures, while at same time avoiding completely the cluster head agreement process. CLIQUE (Förster & Murphy, 2009) is our own role-free clustering protocol based on Q-Learning (Section 2.3). First, it assumes that cluster membership is known a priori, for example based on a geographic grid or room location information on the sensor nodes. It further assumes that the possibly multiple sinks in the network announce themselves through network-wide data requests. During the propagation of these requests all network nodes are able to gather 1-hop neighborhood information including the remaining energy, hops to individual sinks and cluster membership. When data to transmit becomes available, nodes start routing it directly to the sinks. At each intermediate node they take localized decisions whether to route it further to some neighbor or to act as a cluster head and aggregate data from multiple sources.
The learning agents are the nodes in the network. The available actions are $a_{n_i} = (n_i, D)$ with $n_i \in \{N, self\}$, in other words either routing to some neighbor in the same cluster or serving as cluster head and aggregating data arriving from other nodes. After aggregation, CLIQUE hands over the control of the data packet to the routing protocol, which sends it directly and without further aggregation to the sinks. In contrast to the original Q-Learning, we initialize the Q-Values not randomly or with zeros, but with a initial estimation of the real costs of the corresponding routes, based on the hop counts to all sinks and the remaining batteries on the next hops.
The update rule for the Q-Values is:

$$Q_{new}(a_{n_i}) = Q_{old}(a_{n_i}) + \alpha(R(a_{n_i}) - Q_{old}(a_{n_i})) \tag{5}$$

where $R(a_{n_i})$ is the reward value and α is the learning rate of the algorithm. We use $\alpha = 1$ to speed up learning and because we initialize the Q-values with non-random values. Therefore, with $\alpha = 1$, the formula becomes $Q_{new}(a_{n_i}) = R(a_{n_i})$, directly updating the Q-value with the reward. The reward is calculated as:

$$R(n_{self}) = c_{n_i} + \min_{n_i \in N} Q(a_{n_i}) \tag{6}$$

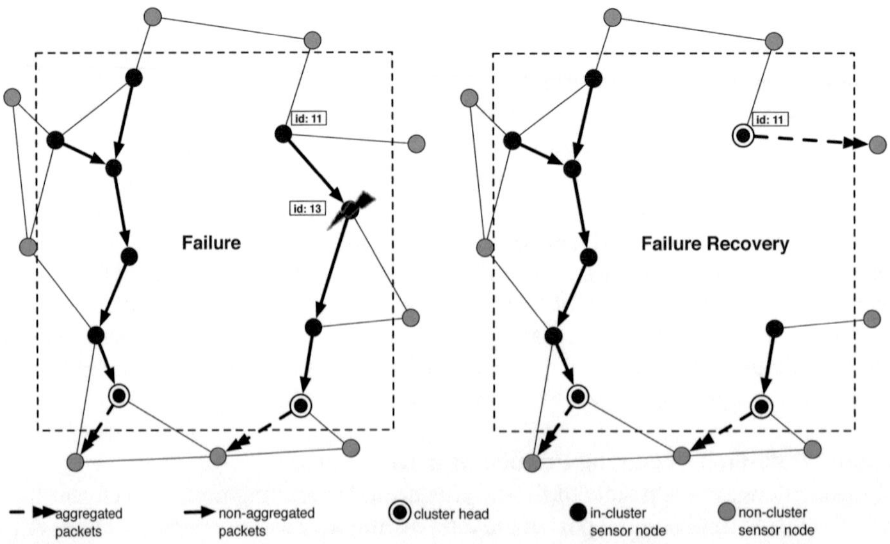

Fig. 5. Learned cluster head in a disconnected scenario (a), recovery after node failure (c) and some experimental results with CLIQUE for delivery rate and network lifetime.

where c_{n_i} is the cost of reaching node n_i and is always 1 (hop) in our model. This propagation of Q-values upstream is piggybacked on usual DATA packets and allows all nodes to eventually learn the actual costs. We use traditional ϵ-greedy action selection policy with low ϵ for exploring the routes and learning the optimal cluster head.

5.2 Discussion of CLIQUE

The most important property of CLIQUE is its role-free nature. In contrast to most cluster head selection algorithms, it does not try to find the optimal cluster head (in terms of cost), but incrementally *learns* the best without knowing either where or who the real cluster heads are. As a result, at the beginning of the protocol, multiple nodes in the cluster may act as cluster heads. While this temporarily increases the overhead, it is a short-term tradeoff in comparison to the overhead required to agree on a single cluster head. Later in the protocol operation, after the real costs have been learned, multiple cluster heads occur only in disconnected clusters, where a single cluster head cannot serve all cluster members.

A particularly interesting cluster head learning scenario is presented in Figure 5 (left), where the cluster is disconnected. Such a scenario is challenging for traditional clustering approaches as they need a complicated recovery mechanism, typically with large control overhead. On the contrary, CLIQUE automatically identifies two cluster heads, as shown in the figure. Figure 5 (right) shows a recovery scenario in which node 13 fails. Node 11 is no longer able to send its data to the cluster head and needs to find a new solution. Instead of searching for a new route to the cluster head it simply becomes a cluster head itself. Because of its learning properties and network status awareness, this requires no control overhead.

We believe that CLIQUE represents the beginning of a new family of role-free clustering protocols, with low communication overhead and very robust against node failures. Various cost metrics can be easily incorporated. Nevertheless, one drawback is the use of the geographic grid for cluster membership, which requires location information on the nodes. Further research in this area is desirable to improve the protocol.

6. Data Integrity

One of the major problems of in-network processing and aggregation in WSNs is the recognition and filtering of faulty data readings before they are sent to the base stations. This is often referred to as the data integrity problem. A typical example is a large climate monitoring sensor network, delivering information about temperature, humidity or light conditions. Multiple sensors are usually deployed to monitor the same area for redundancy. While in the previous sections we have broadly discussed how to manage communication failures, data integrity refers to the problem of sensing failures. For example, some light sensing nodes could be covered by debris and deliver faulty readings. It is desirable to recognize these readings as fast as possible in a distributed way before they are sent to the base station to minimize communication.

6.1 CLNN-Integrity: Using Neural Networks to Recognize Faulty Sensor Data

Neural networks are very often used to learn to classify data readings. Here we present a semi-distributed approach to learn the data characteristics of incoming sensory data and to classify it as valid or faulty. The learning neural network is implemented on cluster heads, where they use the data coming from their cluster members. The application uses competitive learning neural networks (CLNN), therefore we refer to it here as CLNN-Integrity (Bokareva et al., 2006). Their NN consists of eight input and eight output neurons, which are connected with weights, represented as the weight matrix W. Each row of it w_i represents a connection between all input neurons $x_0, ..., x_7$ and the one output neuron y_i. Every time an input is presented to the network, the Euclidean distances between the input and each of the outputs is calculated and the *winning* output neuron is the one with the smallest distance. The corresponding weights row w_i of the winning neuron is updated according to the following rule:

$$w_i(t+1) = w_i(t) + \lambda \times (x(t) - w_i(t)) \tag{7}$$

where λ is a constant learning rate and $w_i(t+1)$ is the updated weight vector of the winning neuron. Thus, when the network is next presented with a similar input, the probability that the same output neuron will win is higher. After the network has been trained with many input samples, it learns to differentiate between valid and false data. Of course, one of the main requirements is that during training most samples are valid. A further requirement is the intelligent initialization of the weights of the neural network. It is important that in the beginning the output neurons are spread throughout the whole possible output space. For example, the authors use light measurements, which are between 0 and 1200 units. Thus, the output neurons need to classify data into 8 different classes spread from 0 to 1200 units.
The neural network of CLNN-Integrity is deployed at dedicated cluster heads in the network. They gather data from all cluster members, use it for training the network first and then to classify data readings and to filter faulty ones. The authors have implemented the approach on a real hardware testbed consisting of 30 MicaZ motes and have tested the neural network with light measurements. The authors have simulated faulty data readings by placing paper cups on top of the light sensors of some of the nodes.

WSN Comm. Layer / ML approach	Application	Clustering	Routing	Neighborhood Management	MAC
Neural Networks	***CLNN (Bokareva et al, 2006)***			**SIR (Barbancho et al, 2006)** Link quality estimation	**NN-TDMA (Shen & Wang, 2008)** Centralized optimal TDMA scheduling
Decision Trees				***MetricMap (Wang et al, 2006)***	
Reinforcement Learning		***Clique (Förster & Murphy, 2009)***	***Q-Routing (Boyan & Littman, 1994)*** **FROMS (*Förster & Murphy, 2007*)** A multicast routing protocol with flexible cost function **Q-PR (Arroyo-Valles et al, 2007)** A geographic-based unicast routing protocol		**Actor-Critic-Links (Pandana & Liu, 2005)** Point-to-point communications **RL-MAC (Liu & Elahanami, 2006)** TDMA-based MAC protocol

not suited | less suited | moderately suited | well suited

Fig. 6. Summary of machine learning applications to various layers of the WSN communication stack. The protocols used in this chapter as examples are emphasized.

6.2 Discussion of CLNN-Integrity

The authors of CLNN-Integrity have shown that implementing neural networks for WSNs is possible, even with online learning and on typical sensor nodes (the cluster heads, on which the CLNN was implemented, are normal sensor nodes, not special, dedicated hardware). Neural networks are very well suited for solving complex classification problems, such as recognizing faulty data readings or detecting various events based on sensor readings.

7. Conclusions and Further Reading

As demonstrated with several examples in this chapter, machine learning is a powerful tool for optimizing the performance of wireless sensor networks at all layers of the communication stack. Additional protocols and algorithms are summarized in Figure 6, where we also address the general applicability of various ML approaches to networking concerns (Kulkarni et al., 2009).

Neural networks have been successfully applied to data model learning, as in the CLNN-Integrity example described in Section 6. They are also relatively well suited for link quality estimation, since for many networks and environments the training of the neural network can be performed offline. However, neural networks are not suited for problems in distributed and fast changing environments such as at the medium access control layer. For example, (Shen & Wang, 2008) uses a NN to centrally compute the optimal TDMA schedule for a WSN. The optimality of the schedule, however, depends on the current network traffic and is thus a

distributed problem, making a distributed technique such as reinforcement learning a better option. Further applications of neural networks in WSNs and their high-level descriptions can be found in (Di & Joo, 2007; Kulkarni et al., 2009).
Section 3 showed MetricMap, an application of decision tree learning to neighborhood management. This approach is well suited for nearly all layers of the communication stack due to its low memory and processing requirements and easy applicability. However, the decision tree is usually formed offline and only the rules are applied online. On the other side, this is not an issue with many classification problems, where learning samples can be easily gathered and future samples for classification are not expected to change their features. These and other benefits strongly support the investment of additional research in this direction.
Based on our survey, reinforcement learning seems to be the most widely used technique, due to its distributed nature and flexible behavior in quickly changing environments. As discussed in Section 4, Q-Routing has inspired multiple WSN routing protocols. Q-Probabilistic Routing (Arroyo-Valles et al., 2007) uses geographic progress and ETX as a cost metric for optimizing unicast routing. FROMS (Förster & Murphy, 2007) is our own multicast routing protocol, able to accommodate various cost functions, including number of hops, remaining energy at nodes, latency, etc. Additional routing protocols based on reinforcement learning, together with their properties are discussed in (Di & Joo, 2007; Kulkarni et al., 2009; Predd et al., 2006). Examples of applying reinforcement learning to medium access are available in (Liu & Elahanany, 2006; Pandana & Liu, 2005).
Another candidate for improving routing performance in WSNs is swarm intelligence. This technique, especially Ant Colony Optimization (Dorigo & Stuetzle, 2004), has been successfully applied to routing in Mobile Ad Hoc Networks (MANETs), as in AntHocNet (Di Caro et al., 2005). However, all attempts to apply it to the highly energy-restricted domain of WSNs (Kulkarni et al., 2009) have been rather unsatisfying, achieving good routes with low delay, but introducing a large amount of communication overhead for the traveling ants. One possibility to counter this communication overhead is to attach the ants to standard data packets. This will lengthen the paths taken by data packets and will increase the overall delivery delay, but at the same time will decrease total communication overhead. Further research is required to test this hypothesis.
In contrast to the widely held belief that machine learning techniques are too heavy for the resource constraints of WSN nodes, this chapter clearly demonstrates the opposite, namely that the domains of machine learning and WSNs can be effectively combined to achieve low cost solutions throughout the communication stack on wireless sensing nodes. This has been successfully shown through multiple examples, evaluated in both simulation to show scalability and in real testbeds, to concretely demonstrate feasibility.

8. References

Akyildiz, I., Su, W., Sankarasubramaniam, Y. & Cayirci, E. (2002). A survey on sensor networks, *IEEE Communications Magazine* **40**(8): 102–114.

Arroyo-Valles, R., Alaiz-Rodrigues, R., Guerrero-Curieses, A. & Cid-Suiero, J. (2007). Q-probabilistic routing in wireless sensor networks, *Proceedings of the 3rd International Conference on Intelligent Sensors, Sensor Networks and Information Processing (ISSNIP)*, Melbourne, Australia, pp. 1–6.

Bandyopadhyay, S. & Coyle, E. (2003). An energy efficient hierarchical clustering algorithm for wireless sensor networks, *Proceedings of the Annual Joint Conference of the IEEE*

Computer and Communications Societies (INFOCOM), Vol. 3, San Francisco, CA, USA, pp. 1713 – 1723.

Barbancho, J., León, C., Molina, J. & Barbancho, A. (2006). Giving neurons to sensors: QoS management in wireless sensors networks., *in* C. Leon (ed.), *Proceedings of the IEEE Conference on Emerging Technologies and Factory Automation (ETFA)*, Prague, Czech Republic, pp. 594–597.

Bokareva, T., Bulusu, N. & Jha, S. (2006). Learning sensor data characteristics in unknown environments., *Procedings of the 1st International Workshop on Advances in Sensor Networks (IWASN)*, San Jose, California, USA, p. 8pp.

Boyan, J. A. & Littman, M. L. (1994). Packet routing in dynamically changing networks: A reinforcement learning approach, *Advances in Neural Information Processing Systems* **6**: 671–678.

Demirbas, M., Arora, A., Mittal, V. & Kulathumani, V. (2004). Design and analysis of a fast local clustering service for wireless sensor networks, *Proceedings of the 1st International Conference on Broadband Wireless Networking (BroadNets)*, San Jose, CA, USA, pp. 700–709.

Di Caro, G., Ducatelle, F. & Gambardella, L. (2005). AntHocNet: an adaptive nature-inspired algorithm for routing in mobile ad hoc networks, *European Transactions on Telecommunications* **16**: 443–455.

Di, M. & Joo, E. (2007). A survey of machine learning in wireless sensor networks, *Proceedings of the 6th International Conference on Information, Communications and Signal Processing (ICICS)*, Singapore, pp. 1–5.

Dorigo, M. & Stuetzle, T. (2004). *Ant Colony Optimization*, MIT Press.

Förster, A. & Murphy, A. L. (2007). FROMS: Feedback routing for optimizing multiple sinks in WSN with reinforcement learning, *Proceedings 3rd International Conference on Intelligent Sensors, Sensor Networks and Information Processing (ISSNIP)*, Melbourne, Australia, pp. 371–376.

Förster, A. & Murphy, A. L. (2009). CLIQUE: Role-Free Clustering with Q-Learning for Wireless Sensor Networks, *Proceedings of the 29th International Conference on Distributed Computing Systems (ICDCS)*, Montreal, Canada.

Karl, H. & Willig, A. (2005). *Protocols and Architectures for Wireless Sensor Networks*, John Wiley & Sons.

Karp, B. & Kung, H. T. (2000). GPSR: greedy perimeter stateless routing for wireless networks, *Proceedings of the 6th annual international conference on Mobile computing and networking (MobiCom)*, Boston, MA, USA, pp. 243–254.

Kulkarni, S., Förster, A. & Venayagamoorthy, G. (2009). A survey on applications of computational intelligence for wireless sensor networks, *under review* .

Liu, Z. & Elahanany, I. (2006). RL-MAC: A reinforcement learning based MAC protocol for wireless sensor networks, *International Journal on Sensor Networks* **1**(3/4): 117–124.

Mitchell, T. (1997). *Machine Learning*, McGraw-Hill.

Pandana, C. & Liu, K. J. R. (2005). Near-optimal reinforcement learning framework for energy-aware sensor communications, *IEEE Journal on Selected Areas in Communications* **23**(4): 788–797.

Predd, J., Kulkarni, S. & Poor, H. (2006). Distributed learning in wireless sensor networks, *IEEE Signal Processing Magazine* **23**(4): 56–69.

Puccinelli, D. & Haenggi, M. (2008). Arbutus: Network-layer load balancing for wireless sensor networks, *Proceedings of the IEEE International Conference on WWireless Communications and Networking Conference (WCNC)*, pp. 2063–2068.
Rabiner-Heinzelman, W., Chandrakasan, A. & Balakrishnan, H. (2000). Energy-efficient communication protocol for wireless microsensor networks, *Proceedings of the 33rd Hawaii International Conference on System Sciences (HICSS)*, Hawaii, USA, p. 10pp.
Römer, K. & Mattern, F. (2004). The design space of wireless sensor networks, *IEEE Transactions on wireless communications* **11**(6): 54–61.
Shen, Y. J. & Wang, M. S. (2008). Broadcast scheduling in wireless sensor networks using fuzzy hopfield neural network, *Expert Systems with Applications* **34**(2): 900–907.
Silva, F., Heidemann, J., Govindan, R. & Estrin, D. (2003). *Frontiers in Distributed Sensor Networks*, CRC Press, Inc., chapter Directed Diffusion, p. 25pp.
Sutton, R. S. & Barto, A. G. (1998). *Reinforcement Learning: An Introduction*, The MIT Press.
Wang, Y., Martonosi, M. & Peh, L.-S. (2006). A supervised learning approach for routing optimizations in wireless sensor networks, *Proceedings of the 2nd International Workshop on Multi-hop ad hoc networks: from theory to reality (REALMAN)*, Florence, Italy, pp. 79–86.
Watkins, C. (1989). *Learning from Delayed Rewards*, PhD thesis, Cambridge University, Cambridge, England.
Witten, I. & Frank, E. (2005). *Data Mining: Practical machine learning tools and techniques*, 2nd. edn, Morgan Kaufmann.
Woo, A., Tong, T. & Culler, D. (2003). Taming the underlying challenges of reliable multihop routing in sensor networks, *Proceedings of the 1st international conference on Embedded networked sensor systems (SenSys)*, Los Angeles, CA, USA, pp. 14–27.
Wu, Q., Rao, N., Barhen, J., Iyengar, S., Vaishnavi, V., Qi, H. & Chakrabarty, K. (2004). On computing mobile agent routes for data fusion in distributed sensor networks, *IEEE Transactions of Knowledge Data Engineering* **16**(6): 740–753.
Younis, O. & Fahmy, S. (2004). HEED: a hybrid, energy-efficient, distributed clustering approach for ad hoc sensor networks, *IEEE Transactions on Mobile Computing* **3**(4): 366–379.

10

Secure Data Aggregation in Wireless Sensor Networks

Hani Alzaid
Queensland University of Technology
Australia
King Abdulaziz City for Science and Technology
Saudi Arabia

Ernest Foo and Juan Gonzalez Neito
Queensland University of Technology
Australia

DongGook Park
Sunchon University
Korea

Abstract

Recent advances in wireless sensor networks (WSNs) have led to several new promising applications including habitat monitoring and target tracking. However, data communication between nodes consumes a large portion of the entire energy consumption of the WSNs. Consequently, data aggregation techniques can significantly help to reduce the energy consumption by eliminating redundant data travelling back to the base station. The security issues such as data integrity, confidentiality, and freshness in data aggregation become crucial when the WSN is deployed in a remote or hostile environment where sensors are prone to node failures and compromises. There is currently research potential in securing data aggregation in WSNs. With this in mind, the security issues in data aggregation for the WSN will be discussed in this paper. Then, the adversarial model that can exist in any aggregation protocol will be explained. After that, the "state-of-the-art" in secure data aggregation schemes will be surveyed and then classified into two categories based on the number of aggregator nodes and the existence of the verification phase. Finally, a conceptual framework will be proposed to provide new designs with the minimum security requirements against a certain type of adversary. This framework gives a better understanding of those schemes and facilitates the evaluation process.

Keywords: Secure aggregation, wireless sensor networks, performance analysis, security analysis, survey.

1. Introduction

A WSN is a highly distributed network of small wireless nodes deployed in large numbers to monitor the environment or other systems by the measurement of physical parameters such as temperature, pressure, or relative humidity (Murthy & Manoj, 2004, p 647). Sensor nodes collaborate to form an ad hoc network capable of reporting network activities to a data collection sink. Recently, WSNs have been used in many promising applications including habitat monitoring (Mainwaring et al., 2002) and target tracking (He et al., 2006). However, WSNs are resource constrained with limited energy lifetime, slow computation, small memory, and limited communication capabilities (Yick et al., 2008). The current version of sensors such as mica2 uses a 16 bit, 8MHz Texas Instruments MSP430 micro-controller with only 10 KB RAM, 48 KB program space, 1024 KB external flash, and is powered by two AA batteries (Crossbow Technology Inc., 2006). Therefore, the energy impact of adding security features should be considered. For example, data authentication in TinyOS increases the consumed energy by almost 3% while data authentication and encryption by 14% (Guimarães et al., 2005). Furthermore, the processing capabilities in sensor nodes are generally not as powerful as those in the nodes of a wired network. Complex cryptographic algorithms are consequently impractical for WSNs.

Not only do the resource limitations affect the WSN performance, but also the deployment nature. Most WSNs are deployed in remote or hostile environments where nodes are exposed to physical attacks since anyone can access the deployment area. Moreover, since the WSNs are deployed in a remote environment, the only way to manage and control the network is via wireless communication, which makes any physical operation such as battery replacement difficult. Another factor that affects the performance of WSNs is communication instability due to the nature of the unreliable wireless communication. For example, if two sensors that have the same aggregator node start sending packets at the same time, conflicts will occur near the aggregator node and the transfer process will fail. In addition, packets might be dropped at highly congested nodes, since the packet based routing of the WSN is connectionless, which is inherently unreliable. As a result, any proposed protocol might also lose critical security packets such as keys, if it does not maintain a reasonable channel error rate. Finally, network congestion, multi-hop routing, node processing, and data aggregation introduce delays in the network and might lead to greater latency. Achieving synchronization between sensor nodes will, therefore, be difficult once latency is getting bigger. The synchronization issue can also be critical for data aggregation security since a part of the security scheme, such as key distribution, cannot work efficiently without achieving a low latency rate.

Due to these limitations, devising security protocols for WSNs is complicated and may not be successfully accomplished by the simple adaptation of security solutions designed for wired networks. Studies by Wagner (2004) and Krishnamachari et al. (2002) showed that data transmission consumes much more energy than computation. Data transmission accounts for 70% of the energy cost of computation and communication for the SNEP protocol (Perrig et al., 2002). Data aggregation can significantly help to reduce this consumption by eliminating redundant data. However, the aggregators are vulnerable to attack, especially if they are not equipped with tamper-resistant hardware. When an aggregator node is compromised, it is easy for the adversary to change the aggregation result and inject false data into WSNs. Unfortunately, the security mechanisms used in other

network environments are not appropriate for WSN domains, since they are typically based on public key cryptography which is too expensive for sensor nodes.
Secure data aggregation schemes are classified, in this chapter, based on how many times the data is aggregated during its travel to the base station. Our contributions in this chapter include the following:

- The secure data aggregation is defined informally and then the security issues in data aggregation for WSNs are discussed.
- An adversarial model, which can be expected in any secure data aggregation scheme, is proposed. This model covers different types of adversaries where the computational strength, the network access level, and node's secret-access level may vary.
- A survey of the "state-of-the-art" in secure data aggregation schemes is presented and these schemes are then classified into two groups according to the number of aggregator nodes, and whether the verification phase of the aggregated result is considered or not.
- Finally, the security and performance analysis of current secure data aggregation protocols are given and then a conceptual framework is proposed in order to establish common ground (or test-bed) to compare different secure data aggregation schemes. This framework also helps to draw the road map for the future design of attack resistant secure data aggregation.

The rest of the chapter is organized as follows: Section 2 gives introductory information about secure data aggregation in WSNs and discusses the security requirements for secure data aggregation protocols. Section 3 discusses different types of the expected adversarial model that threaten secure data aggregation protocols in WSNs. Section 4 surveys, in detail, some of the current secure data aggregation protocols and classifies them into two models. A security analysis of these protocols is discussed in Section 5. Section 6 discusses the performance analysis of these protocols. Finally, the chapter is concluded.

2. Secure Data Aggregation in Wireless Sensor Networks

In many applications, the physical phenomenon is sensed by sensor nodes and then reported to the base station. To reduce the energy consumption of the sensor nodes, these applications may employ in-network aggregation before the data reaches the base station. Compromised nodes can thus perform malicious activities which affect the aggregation results. Before these malicious activities are discussed, the motivation behind secure data aggregation in WSNs is explained, followed by the security requirements of WSNs required to strengthen attack-resistant data aggregation protocols.

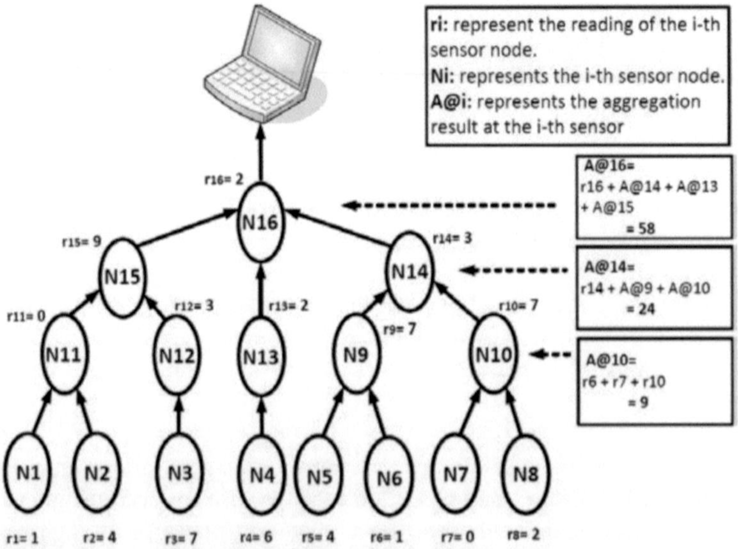

Fig. 1. An aggregation scenario using the SUM aggregation function.

2.1 Data Aggregation in Wireless Sensor Networks

Typically, there are three types of nodes in WSNs that perform in-network processing activities: normal sensor nodes, aggregators, and a querier. The aggregators collect data from a subset of the network, aggregate the data using a suitable aggregation function, and then transmit the aggregated result to an upper aggregator or to the querier who generated the query. The querier is entrusted with the task of processing the received sensor data and derives meaningful information reflecting the events in the target field. It can be the base station or sometimes an external user who has permission to interact with the network depending on the network architecture. Data communication between sensors, aggregators and the querier consumes a large portion of the total energy consumption of the WSN. For example, the WSN in Figure 1 contains 16 sensor nodes and performs SUM as the aggregation function in order to minimize the number of packets that are reported back to the base station, thus reducing the energy consumption. Node 1, node 2, ..., and node 8 are normal nodes that collect data and report them back to the upper nodes, whereas node 9, node 10, ..., and node 16 are aggregators that perform both sensing and aggregating activities.

In our example in Figure 1, every node will respond to a query and report its sensed information individually, and the total number of packets, reported back to the base station, would therefore be 50 packets if there was no in-network processing (or aggregation) capability. However, the number of packets drops to 16 if the in-network processing (aggregation) capability is enabled.

Most existing proposals for data aggregation are subject to attack (Wagner, 2004). Once a single node is compromised, it is easy for an adversary to inject false data into the network and mislead the aggregator to accept false readings. Because of this, the need for secure data aggregation is raised and its importance needs to be highlighted. However, the design principles for secure data aggregation schemes are poorly understood. There is no clear definition of what secure data aggregation should mean, what requirements they should have, and what type of adversary they have to defend. Existing protocols might have one or more of the security requirements discussed in section 2.2 depending on what the secure aggregation looks like to the authors. Unfortunately, following this method to address the security in data aggregation is impractical. For example, Przydatek et al. addressed secure data aggregation in their protocol from the point of view of detecting forged data aggregation values (2003). This does not cover security issues such as how to elect aggregators or how to set up trust between aggregators and sensor nodes. Some protocols provide more security requirements than others, or send more bits than others as seen in Sections 5 and 6. There is no common ground that allows for comparison between different aggregation protocols.

Przydatek et al. defined secure data aggregation as "*the efficient delivery of the summary of sensor readings that are reported to an off-site user in such a way that ensures these reported readings have not been altered*" (2003). They considered an aggregation application where the querier is located outside the WSN and the base station acts as an aggregator. A detailed definition of secure data aggregation is needed for the sake of better understanding. Shi and Perrig highlighted the error sources that affect the aggregated data, and defined secure data aggregation as "*the process of obtaining a relative estimate of the sensor readings with the ability to detect and reject reported data that is significantly distorted by corrupted nodes or injected by malicious nodes*" (2004). However, rejecting reported data injected by malicious nodes consumes the network resources, specifically the nodes' batteries, since the malicious packet will be processed each time at the aggregator point. The damage caused by malicious nodes or compromised nodes should be reduced by adding a self-healing property to the network. This property helps the network in learning how to handle new threats through extensive monitoring of network activities, machine learning, and modelling of the network behaviour. Therefore, we take a step further and stipulate the main components of a robust secure data aggregation protocol as follows:

- Ability to provide fair approximations of the sensor readings although a limited number of nodes are compromised.
- Dynamic response to attack activities by the execution of a self-healing mechanism.

These properties should work together to provide accurate aggregation results securely without exhausting the network.

2.2 Requirements for Data Aggregation Security

Since WSNs share some properties with the traditional wireless networks, the data security requirements in the WSNs are similar to those in traditional networks (Perrig et al., 2002; Shi & Perrig, 2004). However, there are some unique specifications that can only be found in WSNs, as discussed in Section 1, which require more attention during the design process. This section discusses the security requirements for strengthening attack-resistant data aggregation protocols.

- **Data Confidentiality:** ensures that information content is never revealed to anyone unauthorized to receive it. It can be divided (in secure data aggregation schemes) into a hop-by-hop basis and an end-to-end basis. In the hop-by-hop basis, any aggregator point needs to decrypt the received encrypted data, apply some sort of aggregation function, encrypt the aggregated data, and send it to the upper aggregator point. This kind of confidentiality implementation is not practical for the WSN since it requires extra computation, which leads to more delays in the network and increases the energy consumption. This kind of confidentiality also facilitates the adversary's mission. For example, the secrecy of sensed data is disclosed once any hop (or any sensor node included in the route) is compromised. On the other basis, the aggregator does not need to decrypt and encrypt the received data, and instead needs to apply the aggregation functions directly on the encrypted data by using homomorphic encryption (Westhoff et al., 2006). End-to-end confidentiality greatly reduces the energy consumption since there is no need for decryption and encryption at intermediate nodes. To the best of our knowledge, only SUM and AVE aggregation functions are implemented in the current literature.

- **Data Integrity:** ensures that the content of a message has not been altered, either maliciously or accidentally, during the transmission process. Confidentiality itself is not enough since an adversary is still able to change the data although it knows nothing about it. Suppose a secure data aggregation protocol provides only data confidentiality in order to defeat an adversary that is capable to compromise sensor nodes near aggregator points. The adversary can alter the sensed information to affect the overall aggregation results. Moreover, even without the existence of an adversary, data might be damaged or lost due to the nature of the wireless environment.

- **Data Freshness:** ensures that the data are recent and no old messages have been replayed, thereby protecting data aggregation protocols against replay attacks. In this kind of attack, it is not enough that these protocols provide only data confidentiality and data integrity because a passive adversary is able to listen to even encrypted messages, which is transmitted between sensor nodes, and can replay them later on to disrupt the data aggregation results. More importantly, the adversary can replay the distributed shared key and mislead the sensor about the current key used to secure sensing information and aggregated results.

- **Data Availability:** ensures that the network is alive and data are accessible. In the presence of malicious nodes, it is highly recommended that the network react to these bad (compromised) nodes and eliminate them. Once an attacker gets into the WSN by compromising a node, the attack can affect the network services and data availability, especially in those parts of the network where the attack has been launched. Moreover, the data aggregation security requirements should be carefully implemented to avoid extra energy consumption. If no more energy is left, the data will no longer be available. When the network size and the adversary capability are increased, it is preferable that a secure data aggregation protocol contains some of the following mechanisms to ensure a reasonable level of data availability in the network:

   - **Self-healing** which can diagnose and react to the adversary's activities especially when it gets into the network, and then start corrective actions based on defined policies to recover the network or a node.
   - **Aggregator rotation** that rotates the aggregation duties between honest nodes, to balance the energy consumption in the WSN.

- **Authentication:** allows the receiver to verify whether the message is sent by the claimed sender or not. The adversary will, therefore, not be able to participate and inject data into the network unless it has valid authentication keys. If the authentication is not implemented, the adversary can impersonate other nodes and get access to some sensitive data. In the aggregation context, without authentication, the adversary can masquerade the aggregator and report an aggregation result x′ instead of x to the querier.

One major outcome of any secure data aggregation protocol is to provide the aggregated data as accurately as possible with a minimum number of bits transmitted within the network. A trade-off between data accuracy and the size of the aggregated data should be considered at the design stage. Before surveying secure data aggregation protocols, we discuss the security environments and the adversarial model considered in these protocols.

3. Adversarial Model

In this section, we describe the different capabilities that an adversary may have against the secure data aggregation protocols designed for WSNs. We further classify existing protocols according to the type of adversary the protocol designers considered.

3.1 Types of Attacks on Data Aggregation in Wireless Sensor Networks

WSNs are vulnerable to different types of attacks due to the nature of the transmission medium (broadcast), remote and hostile deployment location, and the lack of physical security in each node (Roosta et al., 2006). However, the damage caused by these attacks varies from one protocol to another, according to the adversarial model assumed by the protocol designers, which will be discussed in Section 5.3. The attacks that affect aggregation in WSNs are as follows:

- **Denial of Service Attack (DoS)** is a standard attack on WSNs that can be launched at any layer. One format of DoS attack can be radio signal transmission that interferes with the radio frequencies used by the WSN, which is sometimes called jamming. As the adversary capability increases, it can affect larger portions of the network. Another DoS format can include changing the node status from active to silent, thereby disabling the node. In the aggregation context, the DoS can be launched at the aggregator point in order to refuse executing aggregation functions and prevent data from travelling into the higher levels (or the base station).

- **Node Compromise Attack (NC)** is where the adversary is able to reach any deployed sensor node and extract the information stored on it. This attack is referred to as the supervision attack and sometimes the physical attack.

Considering the data aggregation scenario, once a node has been taken over, all the secret information stored on it can be extracted and the adversary can then participate in the aggregation activities.

- **Sybil Attack (SY)** is a type of attack where the attacker is able to present more than one identity within the network. It affects aggregation schemes in different ways. Firstly, an adversary may create multiple identities to generate additional votes in the aggregator election phase to make a malicious node the aggregator. Secondly, the aggregated result may be affected if the adversary is able to generate multiple entries with different readings. Thirdly, some protocols use witness-based mechanisms where witnesses are used to validate the aggregated data and the data is only valid if n out of m witnesses agreed on the aggregation results (Du et al., 2003). The adversary, however, can launch a Sybil attack and generate n or more witness identities to mislead the base station to accept incorrect aggregation results.

- **Selective Forwarding Attack (SF)** With no consideration about security, it is assumed in WSNs that each node will accurately forward received messages. A compromised node may refuse to do so since it is up to the adversary controlling the compromised node whether to forward the received messages or not. In the aggregation context, any intermediate nodes under the adversary supervision have the ability to launch the selective forwarding attack, and this subsequently affects the aggregation results.

- **Replay Attack (RE)** is a type of attack where the adversary is able to listen to the network and record some transmitted messages without even understanding their content and replays them later on. The adversary aims from launching this attack to mislead the aggregator with those old messages in order to affect the aggregation results.

Generally speaking, the adversary aims to inject false data into the network without revealing its existence. This happens when the adversary has the capability to launch any type of attack discussed above, or a mixture of them without revealing its existence. For example, the adversary can compromise a sensor node (NC attack) and subsequently generate more than one identity (SY attack) in order to affect the overall aggregation result. In a data aggregation scenario, the injected false value leads to a false aggregation result. A compromised node can report significantly biased or fictitious values, and perform a Sybil attack to affect the aggregation result.

3.2 Adversary Characteristics

Secure data aggregation protocols are threatened by two types of adversaries: passive and active adversaries. Differences between these two types are as follows:

- **Passive Adversary** is the adversary that takes advantage of the wireless communication nature (broadcasting) and eavesdrops on the traffic to obtain any important information about the sensed data. For example, if the adversary is able to hear the traffic near the aggregator point, it can gain some knowledge about the aggregated result especially if the secure data aggregation scheme does not ensure data confidentiality service.

- **Active Adversary** is the adversary that interacts with the WSN by injecting packets, destroying nodes, compromising nodes, extracting sensitive data, and stopping/delaying packets from being delivered to the querier, etc. To put it another way, an active adversary can launch any type of attack listed in Section 3.1. The adversary has total access to the node's secrets, is able to extract *all* sensitive information stored in the sensor's memory and then harm the aggregation results.

As discussed in Section 2.1, there are three types of nodes in WSNs: sensor nodes, aggregators, and the base station with different functionalities and capabilities. The adversary's ability to compromise these three elements is discussed as follows:

- **Total Access:** The adversary that has total access to the network is powerful and has access to the whole WSN. Passive adversary can listen to all communications between. On the other hand, active adversary can interact maliciously with all types of components in the WSN (nodes, aggregators, base stations) by launching any type of attack listed in Section 3.1.

- **Partial Access:** This adversary has less power compared to the previous one. Its goal is to listen to communications between a subset of nodes in the network, if the adversary is passive. On the other hand, if the adversary is active, this means that it can only interact with a subset of nodes in the WSN.

3.3 Adversary Type

Adversaries in secure data aggregation protocols have two aspects: behavioural and network access. The adversary type can, therefore, be divided into four types:

- **Type 0:** refers to a passive adversary with limited access to the network. It eavesdrops on the communication in some parts of the network to which it has access. To the best of our knowledge, this type of adversary has never been considered in any secure data aggregation protocol.

- **Type I:** refers to a passive adversary that eavesdrops on the communication and is interested in revealing the encrypted data. The difference between type 0 and type I is the network access capability. Type I has total access to the network while type 0 has partial access.

- **Type II:** refers to an active adversary with limited access to the network (or it is able to compromise limited number of nodes) to launch attacks against secure data aggregation protocols and then mislead the base station about the aggregation results. Within its network limits, the adversary can launch any type of attacks listed in Section 3.1.

- **Type III:** refers to an active adversary that has total access to the network. It is interested in affecting the data aggregation results by launching any attack listed in Section 3.1 against any network component (nodes, aggregators, base stations).

We believe that this adversary classification can help to make better evaluation of the proposed schemes and facilitate making decisions on which protocol is more suitable for specific conditions as discussed in Section 5. In the following section, current secure data aggregation protocols are discussed in detail.

4. Current Secure Data Aggregation Protocols

To the best of our knowledge, there are four surveys in which current secure data aggregation protocols are compared. Setia et al. discussed the security vulnerabilities of data aggregation protocols and presented a survey of robust and secure data aggregation protocols that are resilient to false data injection attacks (2008). However, this survey covered only a few protocols. Sang et al. classified secure aggregation protocols into: hop-by-hop encrypted data aggregation and end-to-end encrypted data aggregation (2006). However, this classification does not detail the security analysis or the performance analysis of these protocols. Alzaid et al. classified these protocols based on how many times the data is aggregated during its travel to the base station, and whether these protocols have a verification phase or not (2008b). Their survey provided details on the security services offered by each protocol, security primitives used to defeat an adversary considered by the protocol designers. Ozdemir and Xiao surveyed the current work in the area of secure data aggregation and provided some details on the security services provided in each protocol (2009). We found that their security analysis is similar to Alzaid et al.'s work (Alzaid et al., 2008b).

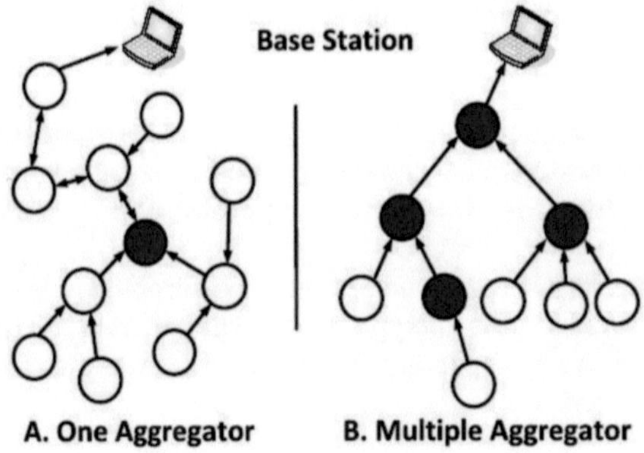

Fig. 2. Sketch of single and multiple aggregator models.

This section extends the work in (Alzaid et al., 2008b) and analyzes more secure data aggregation protocols, and then classifies them into two models: the one aggregator model and the multiple aggregator model (see Figure 2). Under each model, each secure data aggregation protocol either has a verification phase or does not, depending on security primitives used to strengthen the accuracy of the aggregation results although the protocol is threatened by some malicious activities. To put in another way, this verification phase is used to validate the aggregation results (or the aggregator behaviour) by using methods such as interactive protocols between the base station (or the querier) and normal sensor nodes. We provide insights into the aggregation phase, verification phase, security primitives used to defeat the considered adversary, security services offered, and weaknesses of each protocol. Due to lack of space we discuss eight representative protocols in detail (four for each model) and summarize other protocols in subsections 4.1.5 and 4.2.5.

4.1 Single Aggregator Model

The aggregation process, in this model, takes place once between the sensing nodes and the base station or the querier. All individual collected physical phenomena (PP) in WSNs, therefore, travel to only one aggregator point in the network before reaching the querier. This aggregator node should be powerful enough to perform the expected high computation and communication. The main role of the data aggregation might not be fully satisfied since redundant data still travel in the network for a while until they reach the aggregator node, as shown in Figure 2-A. This model is useful when the network is small or when the querier is not in the same network. However, large networks are unsuitable places for implementing this model especially when data redundancy at the lower levels is high. Examples of secure data aggregation protocols that follow the one aggregator model are: Du et al.'s protocol (2003), Przydatek et al.'s protocol (2003), Mahimkar and Rappaport's protocol (2004), and Sanli et al.'s protocol (2004). These protocols are discussed in the following subsections.

4.1.1 Witness-based Approach for Data Fusion Assurance in WSNs (Du et al.)

4.1.1.1 Description

Du et al. proposed a witness-based approach for data fusion assurance in WSNs (2003). The protocol enhances the assurance of aggregation results reported to the base station. The protocol designers argued that selecting some nodes around the aggregator (as witnesses) to monitor the data aggregation results can help to assure the validity of the aggregation results.

The leaf nodes report their sensing information to aggregator nodes. The aggregator then needs to perform the aggregation function and forward the aggregation results to the base station. In order to prove the validity of the aggregation results, the aggregator node has to provide proofs from several witnesses. A witness is a node around the aggregator and also performs data aggregation like the aggregator node, but without forwarding its aggregation result to the base station. Instead, each witness computes the message authentication code (*MAC*) of the aggregation result and then sends it to the aggregator node. The aggregator subsequently must forward the proofs with its aggregation result to the base station.

4.1.1.2 Verification Phase

This protocol does not have a verification phase since the base station can verify the correctness of the aggregation results without the need to interact with the network. Instead, the protocol designers rely on the proofs that are computed by the witnesses and coupled with the aggregation results. Upon receiving the aggregation result with its proofs, the base station uses the n out of $m+1$ voting strategy to determine the correctness of the aggregation results. In the n out of m+1 strategy, m denotes the number of witnesses nodes for each aggregator node while n denotes the minimum number of witnesses that should agree with the aggregation result provided by the aggregator. If less than n proofs agreed with aggregation result, the base station discards the result. Otherwise, the base station accepts the aggregation result.

4.1.1.3 Adversarial Model and Attack Resistance

The protocol designers considered an adversary that can compromise some aggregator nodes and witnesses as well. The designers, however, limited the adversary capability to compromising less than n witnesses for a single aggregator node. This type of adversary falls into the type II adversary, according to our discussion in Section 3.

From the discussion above, the NC attack is visible in this protocol. Once the adversary succeeds in NC attack against an aggregator node, it can then decide whether to forward the aggregation result and the proofs or not (SF attack). If the adversary keeps launching the SF attack, then one form of DoS attack is visible, too. The adversary, once it compromises an aggregator node, is able to replay an old aggregation result with its valid proofs instead of the current result to mislead the base station (RE attack). Finally, the adversary can launch NC attack against leaf nodes and then present multiple identities to affect the aggregation results (SY attack). The SY attack is visible in this protocol because the sensed PPs are not authenticated by the aggregator.

4.1.1.4 Security Primitives

The protocol designers used the n out of m +1 voting strategy to determine the correctness of aggregation results. This strategy is discussed in the verification phase for this protocol.

4.1.1.5 Security Services

The data aggregation security is provided by coupling the aggregation result with proofs from the witnesses around the aggregator node. These proofs, as discussed above, are *MACs* computed on the aggregation result to ensure its integrity and authenticate the witnesses to the base station. Other security services are not considered by the protocol designers.

4.1.1.6 Discussion

The security primitives used in this protocol to defend type II adversary is the n out of $m + 1$ voting strategy. This strategy authenticates witnesses and aggregators to the base station but not leaf nodes. The leaf nodes, therefore, are appropriate targets for the adversary to launch NC attack and then report invalid readings to aggregators. Moreover, the resource utilization in this protocol is poor for three reasons:

- The aggregator needs to receive m more proofs from the witnesses and the aggregator then needs to forward these extra proofs with its aggregation result.
- The number of times the aggregation takes place in the network is increased by m times, because every single aggregation function is repeated m times by the witnesses.

- Finally, the aggregation result with the proofs are travelled unchecked all the way to the base station, because the verification process is done at the base station.

4.1.2 Secure Information Aggregation in WSNs (Przydatek et al.)

4.1.2.1 Description

Przydatek et al. proposed a secure information aggregation protocol for WSNs which provides efficient sub-protocols for securely computing the median and the average of the measurements, estimating the network size and finding the minimum and the maximum sensor readings (2003). It consists of three types of network components: an off-site home server (or user), a base station (or aggregator), and a large number of sensors. The protocol designers claimed that their protocol provides resistance against stealthy attacks where the attacker's goal is to make the user accept false aggregation results without revealing its presence. We believe that stealthy attack can be accomplished by using any type of attack discussed in Section 3.1. The protocol employed, to achieve its goal, an aggregate-commit-prove approach where the aggregator performs aggregation activities and then proves to the user that it has computed the aggregation correctly. In this approach, the aggregator helps with computing the aggregation results and then forwards them to the home server together with a commitment to the collected data. The home server and the aggregator then use interactive proofs, where the home server will be able to verify the correctness of the results. Due to lack of space, we limit our discussion to the MIN aggregation function. The designers proposed a secure MIN discovery sub-protocol that enables the home server (or the user) to find the minimum of the reported value. They, however, restricted the adversary capability: it can report only greater values than real values, not smaller. The sub-protocol works by first constructing a spanning tree such that the root of the tree holds the minimum element as illustrated in Algorithm 1.

The tree construction proceeds in iterations. Throughout the protocol, each sensor node S_i maintains a tuple of state variable (p_i, v_i, id_i), where p_i denotes the ID of the current parent of S_i in the tree being constructed, v_i denotes the smallest value seen so far, and id_i denotes the ID of the node whose value is equal to v_i. Each S_i initializes its state variables with its information as in steps 1, 2, and 3 in Algorithm 1. In each iteration, S_i broadcasts (v_i, id_i) to its neighbours. Let (v_i', id_i') denote a message sent by S' with a smaller value picked by S_i. Then, S_i updates its state by setting $p_i = S'$, $v_i = v_i'$, $id_i = id_i'$. The tree construction terminates after d iteration where d is an upper bound on the diameter of the network.

Algorithm 1 Finding the minimum value from nodes' sensed data

/* code for sensor node i */
/* Initialization phase */
1 $p_i = S_i$; // current parent.
2 $v_i = v_i$; // current sensed physical phenomenon.
3 $id_i = S_i$; // owner of the current minimum value.
4 **for** $i = 1 \dots d$ **do**
5 send (v_i, id_i) to all neighbours.

```
    receive (v_j , id_j) from neighbors.
    if (v_j < v_i) for sensor j then
        p_i = S_j ;
        v_i = v_j ;
        id_i = id_j ;
    end if;
end loop;
return < p_i , v_i , id_i > ;
```

Upon constructing the tree, each node S_i authenticates its final state (p_i , v_i , id_i) using the key shared with the home server and then forwards it to the aggregator. The aggregator checks the consistency of the constructed tree with the values committed. If the check is successful, the aggregator commits to the list of all nodes and their states, finds the root of the constructed tree, and reports the root node to the home server. Otherwise, the aggregator reports the inconsistency. The commitment to the collected data is done using the Merkle hash tree (Merkle, 1980) to ensure that the aggregator used the data provided by sensors.

4.1.2.2 Verification Phase

The home server, upon receiving the aggregation results and the commitment of the collected data from the aggregator, needs to verify the correctness of the reported data. The home server checks whether or not the committed data is a good representative of the true values in the sensors network. This is done using interactive proofs, which is discussed in the security primitives' subsection a little later, where the home server checks if the aggregator is trying to provide an invalid aggregation result or not.

4.1.2.3 Adversarial Model and Attack Resistance

The protocol designers considered an adversary which can corrupt, at most, a small fraction of all the sensor nodes and then misbehave in any arbitrary way. However, more restrictions are put in their sub-protocols. They assumed that the adversary, in the secure MIN sub-protocol, cannot lie about its value or is uninterested in reporting a smaller value. This adversary falls in type II according to our discussion in Section 3.

According to the protocol designers, this type II adversary can launch NC attack but it is still unable to affect the secure MIN aggregation function, because the adversary is not allowed to report values smaller than the real values. We argue that this restriction should be relaxed because the adversary, with the ability to launch NC attack, can report whatever data it likes or selectively drop messages. We, thus, found that this protocol is non-resistant to SF attack. Once the adversary decides to keep silent and stop reporting aggregation results, then one form of the DoS attack will be visible. Moreover, the protocol is protected against the RE attack due to the single usage of each temporary key shared with the base station. Finally, the protocol is protected against SY attack because the adversary cannot mislead the base station to accept new hash chains for the faked identities in order to let them participate in the network.

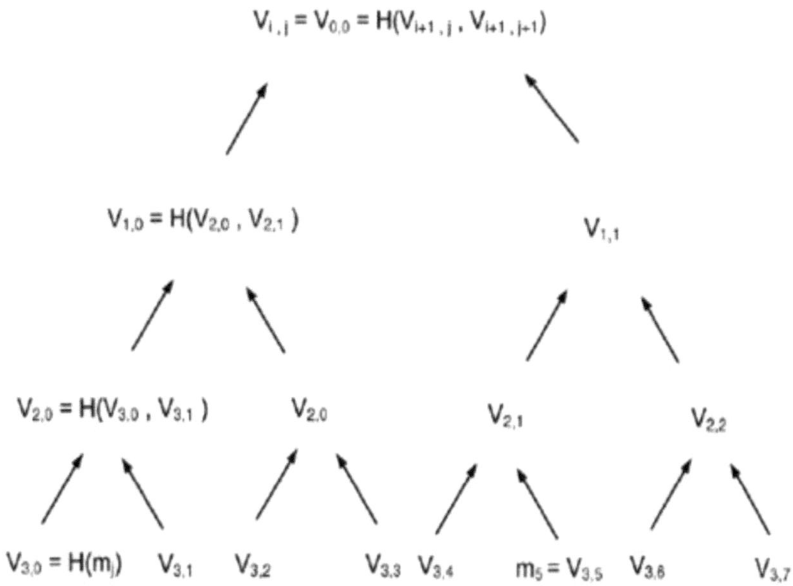

Fig. 3. An example of Merkle hash tree.

4.1.2.4 Security Primitives

The data aggregation security, in this protocol, is achieved by using the Merkle hash tree together with µTESLA (Perrig et al., 2002) and *MAC* security primitives. The aggregator constructs the Merkle hash tree over the sensor measurements $m_0, m_1, m_2, \dots, m_7$ as in Figure 3, and then sends the root of the tree (called a commitment) to the home server. The home server can check whether the aggregator is cheating or not by using an interactive proof with the aggregator. It randomly picks a node in the committed list, say m_5 , and then traverses the path from the picked node to the root using the information provided by the aggregator. During the traversal, the home server checks the consistency of the constructed tree. If the checks are successful, then the home server accepts the aggregation result; otherwise, it rejects it. In other words, the aggregator sends the values of $v_{1,0}$, $v_{3,4}$, $v_{2,2}$ to the base station, and then the base station checks whether the following equality holds:

$$v_{0,0} = H(v_{1,0} \,||\, H(H(v_{3,4} \,||\, H(m_5)) \,||\, v_{2,2}))$$

4.1.2.5 Security Services

The protocol designers employed the Merkle hash tree together with µTESLA and *MAC* to defeat type II adversary. The usage of µTESLA and *MAC* provides authentication and data freshness to the network while the Merkle hash tree provides data integrity. Authentication is offered because only legitimate sensor nodes, with synchronized hash chains with the base station, are able to participate and contribute to the aggregation function. Data freshness is offered because of the single usage of the temporary key provided by µTESLA.

Unfortunately, data availability is not considered by the protocol designers due to the number of bits that travelled within the network in order to accomplish the aggregation task as discussed in Section 6.

4.1.2.6 Discussion

As discussed above, the protocol is able to check the validity of the aggregation result but with no further action to remove or isolate the node which caused inconsistency in the aggregation results. The authors also restricted the adversary capability: it can compromise the node but with no ability to report a value smaller than the real value when calculating the MIN aggregation function. We believe that this assumption should be relaxed because the adversary able to compromise nodes is able to perform whatever activities it likes. Once the assumption is relaxed, then the secure MIN sub-protocol should be revisited.

4.1.3 Secure Data Aggregation and Verification Protocol for WSNs (Mahimkar & Rappaport)

4.1.3.1 Description

A secure data aggregation and verification protocol is proposed by Mahimkar and Rappaport (2004). The protocol is similar to Przydatek et al.'s protocol, discussed in Section 4.1.2, except that it provides one more security service, which is data confidentiality. It uses digital signatures to provide data integrity service by signing the aggregation results.

This protocol is composed of two components: the key establishment phase and the secure data aggregation and verification phase. The key establishment phase generates a secret key for each cluster, and each node belonging to the cluster has a share of the secret key. The node uses this share to generate partial signatures on its reading. The second phase ensures that the base station does not accept invalid aggregation results from the cluster head (or the aggregator).

Each sensor node senses the required physical phenomenon (PP) and then encrypts it using its share of the cluster's private key. It then computes the *MAC* on its PP using the key shared between itself and the base station. The node after that sends these data (the encryption result and the *MAC*) to the cluster head which aggregates the nodes PPs and computes its average. The cluster head then broadcasts the average to all cluster members in order to let them compare their PPs with the average. If the difference is less than a threshold, the node (a cluster member) creates a partial signature on the average using its share of the cluster's private key and then sends it to the cluster head. The cluster head combines these signatures into a full signature and sends it along with the average value to the base station.

4.1.3.2 Verification Phase

The base station, upon receiving the average value and the full signature, verifies the validity of the signature using the cluster's public key. A valid signature is generated by a collusion of t or more nodes within the cluster. The base station accepts the aggregation result, which is the average value, once the signature validity is accepted. Otherwise, the base station rejects the aggregation result and uses the Merkle hash tree to ensure the integrity of the PPs. This is done in the same way suggested by Przydatek et al. and discussed in Section 4.1.2.

4.1.3.3 Adversarial Model and Attack Resistance

The protocol designers aimed to defeat an adversary that is able to compromise up to $t - 1$ nodes in each cluster, where t should be less than half of the total number of sensors in the cluster. This adversary falls into type II according to our discussion in Section 3. Type II adversary is able to launch NC attack as assumed by the designers of the protocol. Once the adversary compromised a sensor node, it can forward messages selectively to upper nodes or drop them (SF attack). Moreover, launching SF attack continuously makes one form of DoS attack visible in the network. The adversary can further replay an old message with its own valid signature, instead of the current message, to affect the aggregation results. Finally, the protocol is SY attack resistant since each node should have a legitimate share of the cluster's private key that cannot be generated by the adversary.

4.1.3.4 Security Primitives

To defeat the adversary considered in this protocol, the designers used Merkle hash tree together with encryption and digital signature. They used elliptic curve cryptography to encrypt PPs reported to the cluster head, digital signature concept to sign aggregation results, and the Merkle hash tree to verify the integrity of the reported aggregation results once the signature verification failed. The encryption and digital signature are common concepts in the security domain and thus discussion about them is out of the chapter's scope. The Merkle hash tree, however, is within the scope of this chapter and already discussed in Section 4.1.2.

4.1.3.5 Security Services

The protocol, through the key establishment component, provides authentication service because only the cluster members with legitimate shares are able to participate in the aggregation processing. Data confidentiality and integrity are offered through the aggregation and verification component. Elliptic curve encryption provides data confidentiality while digital signatures and the Merkle hash tree enhance data integrity of the aggregation results. Data freshness, however, is not considered by the protocol designers.

4.1.3.6 Discussion

If the adversary compromised any sensor node except the aggregator, it is able to affect the aggregation result by reporting invalid PPs. Wagner proved that the average function, which is implemented in this protocol as the aggregation function, is insecure in the existence of only one compromised sensor node (Wagner, 2004). Even worse; when the adversary succeeds in compromising the cluster head (or the aggregator), the adversary can then replay old but valid signed aggregation results to mislead the base station.

Moreover, the protocol designers considered only the average function and, replacing this function with other functions is impossible given the same protocol run. In the current scenario, each sensor node is able to check the aggregation result by dividing its PP by the number of sensor nodes in its cluster, and then comparing the result with the average value broadcasted by the cluster head. The sum function, for example, cannot be implemented because each sensor node encrypts its PP using a different share of the cluster private key.

4.1.4 Secure Reference-based Data Aggregation Protocol for WSNs (Sanli et al.)

4.1.4.1 Description

Sanli et al. proposed a secure reference-based data aggregation protocol that encrypts the aggregation results and applies variable security strength at different levels of the cluster heads (or aggregators) hierarchy (2004). The differential data, which is the difference between the reference value and the sensed data, is reported to aggregator points instead of the sensed data itself in order to reduce the number of transmitted bits.

The protocol designers argued that intercepting messages transmitted at higher levels of clustering hierarchy provides a summary of a large number of transmissions at lower levels. The designers, therefore, believed that the security level of the network should be gradually increased as messages are transmitted through higher levels. Based on this observation, they chose a cryptographic algorithm that allows adjustment of its parameter and the number of encryption rounds to change its security strength as required.

Instead of sending the raw data to the aggregator, a sensor node compares its sensed data with the reference data and then sends the encryption of the difference data. The reference data is taken as the average value of a number of previous sensor readings, *N*, where $N \geq 1$. The aggregator, upon receiving these differential data, performs the following activities:

- Decrypts the data and then determines the distance to the base station in the number of hops (h).
- Encrypts the aggregation result using RC6 with the number of rounds calculated as:

$$number\ of\ rounds = \frac{1}{h} * 100 \quad (1)$$

Forwards the encrypted aggregated data to the base station.

4.1.4.2 Verification Phase

This protocol does not contain a verification phase to check the validity of the aggregation results. The protocol designers, instead, relied on the security primitives, RC6, to enhance the security for the aggregation results. The protocol is designed to encrypt the aggregation results with different numbers of encryption rounds, depending on how far the aggregator node is from the base station. Once the base station has received the encrypted aggregation results, it decrypts them with the corresponding keys.

4.1.4.3 Adversarial Model and Attack Resistance

The protocol designers did not discuss the adversary capability that was considered in their protocol. We believe, from their discussion in the paper, that the adversary type falls into the category of type I adversary for the following reasons:

- They relied only on encryption to provide accurate data aggregation.
- A single node compromise can breach the security of the protocol. For example, once the adversary compromised an aggregator node, the privacy and accuracy of the aggregation results can be manipulated and then affect the overall aggregation activities of the system.

4.1.4.4 Security Primitives
To defeat type I adversary, the designers of the protocol used the block cipher RC6. They adjust the number of rounds, which RC6 performs to accomplish an encryption operation, depending on how far the aggregator point is from the base station. The closer the aggregator is, the larger the number of rounds should be used.

4.1.4.5 Security Services
The data aggregation security is achieved by encrypting travelled data using the block cipher RC6. This provides a data confidentiality service to the network. Data freshness is also provided due to the key update component adhered to the aggregation component. Other security services are not considered because of the type of adversary considered by the protocol designers.

4.1.4.6 Discussion
The security primitives, used to defeat the type I adversary, is impractical for use in constrained devices such as sensor nodes. Law et al. constructed an evaluation framework in which suitable block cipher candidates for WSNs can be identified (2006). They concluded, based on the evaluation results, that RC6 is lacking in energy efficiency (i.e., a large RAM consumer), and performs poorly on 8/16 bits architectures. They further concluded that RC6 with 20 rounds is secure against a list of attacks such as chosen ciphertext attack. However, the number of rounds for RC6 encryption in Sanli et al.'s protocol can be as low as 10 rounds once the aggregator node is 10 hops away from the base station, according to equation 1.

4.1.5 Other Protocols
Wagner proposed a mathematical framework for evaluating the security of several resilient aggregation techniques/functions (2004). The paper measures how much damage an adversary can cause by compromising a number of nodes and then using them to inject erroneous data. Wagner described a number of better methods for securing the data aggregation such as how the median function is a good way to summarise statistics. However, this work focused only on examining the security of the aggregation functions at the base station without studying how the raw data are aggregated. Furthermore, Wagner claimed that trimming and truncation can be used to strengthen the security of many aggregation primitives by eliminating possible outliers. However, eliminating abnormal data with no further reasoning is impractical in some applications such as monitoring bush-fire.

4.2 Multiple Aggregator Model
In this model, collected data in WSNs are aggregated more than once before reaching the final destination (or the querier). This model achieves greater reduction in the number of bits transmitted within the network, especially in large WSNs, as illustrated in Figure 1. The importance of this model is growing as the network size is getting bigger, especially when data redundancy at the lower levels is high. A sketch of the multiple aggregator model can be found in Figure 2-B. Examples for secure data aggregation protocols that fall under this model are: Hu and Evans's protocol (2003), Jadia and Mathuria's protocol (2004), Westhoff

et al.'s protocol (2006), and Sanli et al.'s protocol (2004). These protocols are discussed in the following subsections.

4.2.1 Secure Data Aggregation for Wireless Networks (Hu & Evans)

4.2.1.1 Description

Hu and Evans proposed a secure aggregation protocol that achieves resilience against node compromise by delaying the aggregation and authentication at the upper levels (2003). The required physical phenomena (PP) are, therefore, forwarded unchanged and then aggregated at the second hop instead of aggregating them at the immediate next hop. Thus, the parents need to buffer the data to authenticate it once the shared key is revealed by the base station. It is the first attempt towards studying the problem of data aggregation in WSNs once a node is compromised.

Each sensor node shares a temporary symmetric key with the base station, which lasts for a single aggregation calculation. The base station periodically broadcasts these authentication keys as soon as it receives the aggregation result. Each leaf node, as a part of the aggregation phase, transmits its PP to its parent. This transmission includes the node ID, the sensed PP, and the message authentication code $MAC_{K_{ID}}(ID, PP)$. It uses the temporary key shared with the base station, but not yet known to the other nodes, to calculate the *MAC*. The parent (or any intermediate node) applies the aggregation function on messages received from its children, then calculates the *MAC* of the aggregation result, and transmits messages and *MACs* received from its direct children along with the *MAC* computed on the aggregation result. The parent, which has grandchildren, is permitted to remove its grandchildren's raw data (or PPs) and confirm the aggregation result done by its children (or parents of its grandchildren). It is important that each parent stores raw data received from its children (and its grandchildren if it available) and the *MAC* computed on the reported data from its children (and its grandchildren if available). The parent will use this information at the end of the aggregation process when the base station reveals the temporary keys, as discussed in the following subsection.

4.2.1.2 Verification Phase

This protocol has a verification phase where the base station interacts with sensor nodes and aggregators in order to verify the aggregation results. The protocol designers used μTESLA protocol, which is discussed in the security primitives' subsection, to achieve the interaction between the base station and sensor nodes. When aggregation results arrive at the base station, the base station reveals the temporary symmetric keys shared with every node. Every parent is now able to verify whether the information (raw data and the *MAC*) stored for its children is matched or not. If the parent detects an inconsistent *MAC* from a child or a grandchild, it sends out an alarm message to the base station along with *MAC* computed using the node's temporary key.

4.2.1.3 Adversarial Model and Attack Resistance

The most serious threat considered by the designers of the protocol is that an adversary that can compromise the network to provide false readings without being detected by the operator. Each intermediate node (parent) can thus modify, forge, discard messages, or transmit false aggregation values. The designers, however, limited the adversary capability

to not launching an NC attack for two consecutive nodes in the hierarchy. This type of adversary falls into type II according to our discussion in Section 3.
SY and RE attacks, in this protocol, are not visible while DoS, NC, and SF are visible. The adversary considered by the designers is able to compromise any sensor node (either a leaf node or an aggregator) - this is the NC attack. Once an intermediate node is compromised, the adversary is easily able to launch the SF attack. Even worse, the adversary can decide to keep silent and stop reporting aggregation results, which is one form of the DoS attack. The protocol, however, is protected against the RE attack due to the single usage of each temporary key shared with the base station. Finally, the protocol is protected against SY attack because the adversary cannot mislead the base station to accept new hash chains for the faked identities.

4.2.1.4 Security Primitives

In this protocol, *MAC* and μTESLA are used to provide authentication, data integrity, and data freshness. *MAC* is a well known technique in the cryptographic domain used to ensure authenticity and to prove the integrity of the data. It is calculated using a key shared between two parties (the sender and the receiver). These keys are updated by using μTESLA protocol that delays the disclosure of symmetric keys to achieve asymmetry (Perrig et al., 2002). The base station generates the one-way key chain of length n. It chooses the last key K_n and generates the remaining values by applying a one-way function F as follows:

$$K_j = F(K_{j+1})$$

Because F is a one-way function, anybody can compute backward, such as compute $K_0, K_1, ..., K_j$ given K_{j+1} , but nobody can compute forward such as compute K_{j+1} given $K_0, K_1, ..., K_j$. In the time interval t, the sender is given the key of the current interval K_t by the base station through a secure channel, and then the sender uses the key to calculate MAC_{K_t} on its PP in that interval. The base station then discloses K_t after a delay and then other nodes will be able to verify the received MAC_{K_t} .

4.2.1.5 Security Services

The protocol designers regarded data confidentiality of messages to be unnecessary for their protocol. They focused only on the integrity of aggregation results by using μTESLA protocol, which also provides authentication and data freshness services. Authentication is offered because only legitimate sensor nodes, with synchronized hash chains with the base station, are able to participate and contribute to the aggregation function while data freshness is offered because of the single usage of the temporary key. Unfortunately, data availability is not considered by the designers because each parent has to store and verify received information from its children and grandchildren. This verification requires each parent to listen to every key revealed by the base station until it hears the keys of its children and grandchildren. Even worse for data availability, the data keeps travelling towards the base station even when it has been corrupted because the keys are revealed when the aggregation results reach the base station. Another factor that affects data availability is, once a compromised node is detected, no practical action is taken to reduce the damage caused by this compromise, and the compromised node can still participate in the aggregation activities.

4.2.1.6 Discussion

The protocol designers considered data integrity and used μTESLA to defeat type II adversary. The protocol is able to detect a single node compromise, but without further action to remove or isolate this compromised node. Much worse, once a grandfather node detects a node compromise, it could not decide whether the cheating node is its child or grandchild. The protocol, moreover, fails to provide data integrity once the adversary compromised two consecutive nodes successfully in the hierarchy such as the parent and the grandparent. The protocol also suffers from extra memory overhead because of the delayed authentication and the need to buffer the data received by parents to be authenticated later. Finally, parents waste some energy listening to some of the revealed keys that are not intended for them.

4.2.2 Efficient Secure Aggregation in Sensor Networks (Jadia & Mathuria)

4.2.2.1 Description

Hu and Evans in their protocol, discussed in Section 4.2.1, did not consider data confidentiality service. Jadia and Mathuria, however, argued that messages relayed in data aggregation hierarchy may need confidentiality. Thus, they proposed a secure data aggregation protocol in WSNs that enhances the security services provided by Hu and Evans's protocol by adding data confidentiality (Jadia & Mathuria, 2004). This protocol uses encryption for confidentiality but without requiring decryption at intermediate nodes. The designers of the protocol adopted an encryption method where the data is added to a sufficiently long random encryption key. Let K_A denote the master key shared between node A and the base station. The encryption of the sensed PP reported by a sensor node A can be calculated as follows:

$$C_{K_A} = (PP_A + K_A)$$

After encrypting the required *PPs*, node *A* computes two *MACs* on these *PPs*. One *MAC* is calculated by using one-hop pairwise key shared with the node's parent while the second *MAC* is calculated using two-hop key shared with the node's grandparent. The aggregation phase is accomplished in the same way as the Hu and Evans's protocol, except for two differences listed below:

- Leaf nodes encrypt the node's *PPs* before sending them.
- Leaf nodes compute two *MACs* on the encrypted data.

The leaf node then forwards its *ID*, encrypted data, and two *MACs* to its parent. The parent node (say node *C*) receives the message and verifies the origin of the data using the one-hop pairwise shared key. It performs the aggregation over the encrypted data but does not transmit this aggregated value. The aggregation calculation is performed on the encrypted data received from its children (node *A* and node *B*) as follows:

$$Encrypted\ Aggregation\ Result\ (EAR) = C_{K_A} + C_{K_B} + C_{K_C} \quad (2)$$

Node *C* then calculates a *MAC* of *EAR* using the two-hop pairwise key shared with its grandparent node, and transmits it along with the encrypted *PPs* and *MACs* received from its children (of course without the *MAC* intended for itself).

4.2.2.2 Verification Phase

This protocol does not have a verification phase. The protocol designers argued that the two *MACs*, which are discussed in Section 4.2.2.1, help to provide the integrity of the data while minimizing the communication required between the base station and sensor nodes. In other words, the verification phase in Hu and Evans's protocol, where the base station reveals temporary shared keys with nodes, is replaced with the pairwise-based *MACs* in order to improve data availability in the network. The designers, however, did not discuss how these pairwise keys are distributed and how much bandwidth and energy consumption are required.

If the base station did not receive alarm messages from parents regarding inconsistency between encrypted data and *MACs* computed on them, the base station decrypts the aggregation result (*EAR*) from equation 2 as follows:

$$Aggregation\ result = EAR - (K_A + K_B + K_C)$$

4.2.2.3 Adversarial Model and Attack Resistance

Since this protocol is an extension to Hu and Evans's protocol discussed in Section 4.2.1, the protocol designers considered a similar adversary type that falls into type II adversary according to our discussion in Section 3.

Moreover, DoS, NC, and SF attacks are visible in this protocol due to the capability of type II adversary and to the same discussion that is given in Section 4.2.1.3. The protocol is SY and RE resistant due to the design assumption that the authentication and encryption keys are changed with every message. However, no details on changing these keys are given.

4.2.2.4 Security Primitives

The protocol designers employed *MAC* together with encryption to defeat type II adversary. They used pairwise keys to calculate the *MAC* and the concept of privacy homomorphic encryption to perform aggregation on the encrypted data, as discussed in Section 4.2.2.1.

4.2.2.5 Security Services

This protocol provides data confidentiality, data integrity, data freshness, and authentication services. The usage of two *MACs*, which are calculated by one-hop and two-hop pairwise keys, provides data integrity and authentication for the aggregation results. Data confidentiality is provided by using the adopted end-to-end encryption that is discussed in Section 4.2.2.1. Finally, data freshness service is visible in the network due to the designers' assumption that the authentication and encryption keys are changed with every message.

4.2.2.6 Discussion

As discussed above, the designers of the protocol added data confidentiality service to security services provided by Hu and Evans's protocol. The protocol, here, suffers from the same weaknesses that Hu and Evans's protocol suffered from, discussed in Section 4.2.1.6. However, the memory overhead weakness is not visible in this protocol because it uses pairwise keys and does not need to keep copies of *MACs* information until the base station reveals temporary keys.

4.2.3 Concealed Data Aggregation for Reverse Multicast Traffic in WSNs (Westhoff et al.)

4.2.3.1 Description

Westhoff et al. solved the problem of aggregating encrypted data in WSNs, and proposed a secure data aggregation protocol that provides aggregator nodes with the possibility to perform aggregation functions directly on ciphertexts (2006). This work is an extension to their initial work in (Girao et al., 2005). It uses an additive and multiplicative Privacy Homomorphic (PH) encryption scheme (Domingo-Ferrer, 2002) in order to provide end-to-end encryption. The aggregator nodes do not need to decrypt encrypted messages when they aggregate them. If the usual encryption algorithms, such as RC5, were used instead of PH to provide data confidentiality, hop-to-hop encryption then should be used instead of end-to-end encryption. This is because usual algorithms do not let aggregator nodes apply aggregation functions directly on ciphertexts. Hop-by-hop encryption means that every intermediate node has to decrypt received encrypted messages, and then aggregate them according to the corresponding aggregation function, encrypt the aggregation results, and finally forward the aggregation results to upper nodes. Westhoff et al.'s protocol employs the Domingo-Ferrer's encryption function that chooses the ciphertext corresponding to given plaintexts (or messages) from a set of possible ciphertexts. The public parameters, for the encryption function, are a positive integer $d \geq 2$, and a large integer g that has many small divisors. There should be, at the same time, many integers $< g$ that can inverted modulo g. The secret key is computed as:

$$k = (r, g')$$

The plaintext $r \in \mathbb{Z}_{g'}$ is chosen such that $r^{-1} \, mod \, g$ exists, where $log_{g'} \, g$ indicates the security level provided by the function. The set of plaintext is $\mathbb{Z}_{g'}$ and the set of ciphertext is $(\mathbb{Z}_g)^d$. The encryption process is executed at leaf nodes as follows:

- Randomly split the plaintext $a \in \mathbb{Z}_{g'}$ into secretes $a_1, a_2, \ldots, a_d$ such that

$$\sum_{j=1}^{d} (a_j \, mod \, g') = a$$

- Compute $E_k(a) = (a_1 r^1 \, mod \, g \, , \; a_2 r^2 \, mod \, g \, , \ldots, a_d r^d \, mod \, g)$

Leaf nodes then forward the encrypted data to aggregator nodes where PH is used to apply aggregation function on these encrypted data with no need to decrypt them. The decryption process is performed at the base station (or the querier) and is discussed when we describe the verification process in the following subsection.

4.2.3.2 Verification Phase

This protocol does not have a verification phase. The designers of the protocol, instead, relied on the security primitive, discussed in Section 4.2.3.4, to defeat the considered type of adversary. The protocol is designed to encrypt the required physical phenomenon in a way that aggregators are able to apply aggregation functions directly on ciphertexts. The aggregators then forward the aggregation results to upper nodes. When these aggregation results reach the querier, the querier decrypts them as follows:

- Compute the jth coordinate by $r^{-j}\ mod\ g$ to retrieve $a_j\ mod\ g$.
- In order to compute a, the querier computes $D_k(E_k(a)) = \sum_{j=1}^{d}(a_j\ mod\ g')$

4.2.3.3 Adversarial Model and Attack Resistance

The designers of the protocol aimed to defeat passive adversaries that eavesdrop on communication between sensor nodes, aggregators, and the base station. However, the designers extended the capability of the adversary to be able to takeover aggregator nodes but not other network components. Thus, we classify this adversary to fall under type II category due to its capability to launch NC attack.

Since the adversary is able to compromise aggregator nodes, it can then launch RE attack by replacing old but valid encrypted messages as long as encryption keys of leaf nodes have not been updated/renewed. Once an aggregator is compromised, the adversary is easily able to launch SF attack. Even worse, the adversary can decide to keep silent and stop reporting aggregation results, which is one form of the DoS attack.

4.2.3.4 Security Primitives

The protocol designers employed Privacy Homomorphism (PH) to defeat the type II adversary. During the last few years, PH encryption schemes have been studied extensively since they proved to be useful in many cryptographic applications such as electronic elections (Grigoriev & Ponomarenko, 2003), sensor networks (Castelluccia et al., 2005; Westhoff et al., 2006) and so on. Homomorphic cryptosystem is a cryptosystem that allows direct computation on encrypted data by using an efficient scheme. It is an important tool that can be used in a secure aggregation scheme to provide end-to-end privacy if needed.

The classical RSA scheme is a good example of a deterministic, multiplicative homomorphic cryptosystem on $M = \frac{\mathbb{Z}}{N\mathbb{Z}}$, where N is the product of two large primes (Rivest et al., 1978). Let K_e, K_d, E, D, m, c denote the private key, public key, encryption function, decryption function, message in plaintext, ciphertext, respectively. Thus, $C = \frac{\mathbb{Z}}{N\mathbb{Z}}$ is the ciphertext space while the key space is:

$$K = \{(k_e, k_d) = ((N, e), d) | N = pq, ed \equiv 1\ mod\ \varphi(N)\}$$

The encryption of any message $m \in M$ is defined as:

$$E_{k_e}(m) = m^e \bmod N$$

while the decryption of any ciphertext $c \in C$ is defined as:

$$D_{k_e, k_d}(c) = c^d \bmod N = m \bmod N$$

Obviously, the encryption of the product of two messages $m_1, m_2 \in M$ can be computed by multiplying the corresponding ciphertexts:

$$\begin{aligned} E_{k_e}(m_1 \odot m_2) &= (m_1\, m_2)^e \bmod N \\ &= (m_1^e \bmod N)(m_2^e \bmod N) \\ &= E_{k_e}(m_1) \odot E_{k_e}(m_2) \end{aligned}$$

4.2.3.5 Security Services

The data aggregation security is provided by encrypting the reported data and thus only data confidentiality is provided. Other security services, discussed in Section 2.2, are not provided due to the focus of the paper.

4.2.3.6 Discussion

The security primitive used to defeat the type II adversary is PH. This primitive is impractical to be used in constraint devices, such as the sensor node, due to its high computational cost (Westhoff et al., 2006). The protocol designers argued that their protocol considered this disadvantage, the high computational cost, by rotating the aggregation duties between aggregators to balance the energy consumption.

Moreover, Wagner proved that PH is insecure against chosen plain text attacks (Wagner, 2003). The protocol designers argued that for data aggregation scenarios in WSNs, the security level is still adequate and they used this encryption transformation as a reference PH.

Unfortunately, this protocol can support only "average" and "movement detection" aggregation functions. Applying PH on the context of WSNs in order to support other aggregation functions is an open area of research.

4.2.4 Secure Reference-based Data Aggregation Protocol for WSNs (Yang et al.)

4.2.4.1 Description

Yang et al. proposed a secure data aggregation for WSNs that can tolerate more than one node compromise (2006). The protocol is composed of two components: divide-and-conquer and commit-and-attest. In the former, the protocol uses a probabilistic grouping technique that partitions nodes in a tree topology into several logical groups. In the latter, a commitment-based hop-by-hop aggregation is performed in each group to generate a group aggregate. The base station then identifies the suspicious groups based on a set of group aggregates. Each group under suspect participates in an attestation process to prove the validity of its group aggregation result.

A leaf node encrypts its *ID*, physical phenomenon (*PP*), count value (*C*), and the query sequence number (*SQ*) using a pairwise key shared with its parent. The count value represents the number of the node's children, and therefore C for any leaf node is always zero. It then forwards to its parent the encryption result, a *MAC* computed on inputs to the encryption function, and one bit aggregation flag. This flag instructs the node's parent upon receiving the transmission whether there is a need for further aggregation (flag=0) or not. When an intermediate node receives a message from its child, it first checks the flag and then follows one of the following scenarios:

- **1st scenario (flag=1):** the intermediate node forwards the packet untouched to the base station via its parent.
- **2nd scenario (flag=0):** the intermediate node decrypts the received message and then checks whether or not the received data is a response to the current query. Once this checking is passed, the intermediate node adds its own *PP* and other aggregation results received from other children (with flag=0) to the received data. The *C* is subsequently updated by adding up count values of all other participants.

To set the aggregation flag to one (no more aggregation) for this intermediate node, the node performs the following check:

$$H(SQ|ID) < F_g(C) \tag{3}$$

where *H* is a secure pseudo random function that uniformly maps the input values into the range of [0,1] and F_g is a grouping function that outputs a real number between [0,1]. This check helps the intermediate node to decide whether it is a leader node or not. Using the pairwise key shared with its parent, non-leader node encrypts its *ID*, new *C*, aggregation result, and *SQ*. It then sets the flag to zero and forwards these data along with a *MAC*, which is computed on inputs to the encryption function, and an XOR result for all *MACs* received from its children and included in this aggregation. The leader node on the other hand performs the same operation as the non-leader node, except that it encrypts the new aggregation using the key shared with the base station and sets the flag to one.

4.2.4.2 Verification Phase

The base station, upon receiving the aggregation result from a leader node, needs to verify whether the received aggregation result is accurate and came from a genuine leader node. It decrypts this aggregation result and then applies equation 3 to check the legitimacy of the node as a leader node. Once the test is passed, the base station needs to check the validity of the received aggregation result. First, the base station uses an adaptive Grubbs test (Grubbs, 1969) to verify the abnormality in the aggregation result before accepting or rejecting the received aggregation result. The base station then attests the group where the abnormal aggregation result is reported. Details on checking the validity of the aggregation result is given in the security primitives' section later.

4.2.4.3 Adversarial Model and Attack Resistance

The protocol designers considered an adversary that can compromise a small fraction of sensor nodes to obtain the keys as well as reprogramming these sensor nodes with attacking code. This type of adversary falls within the type II according to our discussion in Section 3.

Although the protocol designers mentioned that they did not consider any type of behaviour-based attack such as SF and DoS attacks, their protocol is examined against these attacks for the sake of a complete survey. We argue that if the adversary is able to launch NC attack in order to mislead the base station about the aggregation results, the adversary can also perform the activity of the SF attack for the same purpose. Beside the visibility of NC and SF attacks, the DoS attack is visible in the network, too. An example of the visibility of the DoS attack is similar to what was discussed in Section 4.2.1.3. The protocol, however, is RE and SY attack-resistant due to the query sequence number embedded in the reported PPs and to the pairwise key updates, respectively.

4.2.4.4 Security Primitives

The designers of the protocol used an encryption algorithm, μTESLA, adaptive Grubbs test, and attestation mechanism to defeat the type II adversary. Since the designers did not provide details about the encryption algorithm and μTESLA was discussed in Section 4.2.1, the adaptive Grubbs test and the attestation mechanism are discussed here.

The adaptive Grubbs test, as shown in Algorithm 2, first computes the sample statistic for each datum X in the set by $\frac{X-\mu}{s}$, where *m* and *s* are the mean and the standard deviation of the data, respectively. The result represents the datum's absolute deviation from the mean in units of the standard deviation. To decide whether H_0 should be accepted or not, the test compares the *p*-value computed based on the sample statistic with the predefined significance level α (α = 0 typically), where *p*-value is set as the product of the *p*-values of the data aggregation and the count (the number of participants in the aggregation). When the *p*-value is smaller than α, H_0 is rejected and the datum under consideration is an outlier, and then the attestation mechanism is called.

The attestation process is similar to the Merkle hash tree discussed in Section 4.1.2. The base station interacts with the group under suspect to prove the correctness of its group aggregation result.

Algorithm 2 Grubbs test algorithm

Input: a set T of n tuple (x, c_x, Agg_x), where x is group leader ID, c_x is group count value, Agg_x is group aggregation result, and n is the total number of groups;

Output: a set L of leader *IDs* of groups with invalid aggregation results.

Procedure:

```
loop
    compute μ_c and s_c for all counts in set T;
    compute μ_v and s_v for all values in set T;
    find the maximum count value c_x in set T;
    compute statistic Z_c for count c_x as |c_x − μ_c| / s_c ;
    compute p-value P_c based on the statistic Z_c ;
    compute statistic Z_v for corresponding values Agg_x as |Agg_x − μ_v| / s_c ;
    compute p-value P_v based on the statistic Z_v ;
    if (P_c * P_v) < α then
```

```
10        T = T − {(x, c_x, Agg_x)};
11        L = L ∪ {x};
12    else
13        break;
14    end if;
15 end loop
16 return L;
```

4.2.4.5 Security Services

The data aggregation security is achieved by encrypting PPs destined to the base station and then by checking the validity of the aggregation results. This ensures data confidentiality, authentication, and data integrity within the network. Due to the query sequence number, which is embedded in any response, data freshness is offered, too. Data availability, however, is not visible because of the high number of transmission required to accomplish the aggregation activities. More details are given in Section 6.

4.2.4.6 Discussion

As discussed above, the protocol designers used an adaptive test to check the validity of aggregation results. This adaptive test is subject to attack when some nodes are compromised. The test uses reported aggregation results to compute the μ and s (see Algorithm 2). Compromised nodes can collude and report invalid aggregation results to mislead the calculation of the mean of the data (m) and then affect steps 3-16 in Algorithm 2. This will affect the base station's decision and may enforce it to start the attestation process with honest groups instead of malicious groups. Moreover, invalid aggregation results are attested (or verified) through centralized verification that incurs high communication cost.

4.2.5 Other Protocols

Furthermore, an extension to Westhoff et al.'s protocol is proposed by Castelluccia et al. (2005). It uses a modular addition instead of the XOR (Exclusive-OR) operation found in the stream ciphers. Thus, even if an aggregator is compromised, original messages cannot be revealed by an adversary (assuming that the aggregator does not have the encryption key). The authors claimed that the privacy protection provided by this protocol is comparable to the privacy protection provided by a protocol that performs end-to-end encryption with no aggregation. However, they admit that their proposed scheme generates significant overhead if the network is unreliable since sensors' identities of non-responding nodes must be sent together with the aggregated result to the base station. More importantly, this scheme provides only one security property which is data confidentiality.

Chan et al. extended Przydatek et al.'s protocol by applying the aggregate-commit-prove framework in a fully distributed network instead of single aggregator model (2006). The protocol detects the existence of any misbehaviour in the aggregation phase. The protocol designers, however, did not consider data availability because they did not aim either to identify or remove nodes that caused this misbehaviour. In general, their protocol offers the same as Przydatek et al.'s protocol: authenticity, data integrity, and data freshness. Each parent performs an aggregation function whenever it has heard from its child nodes. In addition, it has to create a commitment to the set of the input used to compute the aggregated result by using the Merkle hash tree. It then forwards the aggregated data and the commitment to its parent until it reaches the base station. Once the base station has received the final commitment values, it rebroadcasts them into the rest of the network in an authenticated broadcast. Each node is responsible for checking whether its contribution was added to the aggregated result or not. Once its reading is added, it sends an authentication code to the base station where the authentication code for node R is $MAC_{K_R}(N \,||\, OK)$, where K_R is the key that node R shares with the base station, and N denotes a nonce. For communication efficiency, the authentication codes are aggregated along the way to the base station. However, one missing authentication code for any reason leads the base station to reject the aggregated result. Furthermore, noticeable delay, too much transmission, and computation are added as consequences of adding security to this protocol.

Frikken and Dougherty improved the performance of Chan et al.'s protocol by proposing a new commitment tree structure (2008). Let Δ denote the degree of the aggregation tree and n denote the number of sensor nodes. They claimed that their protocol requires each node to perform $O(\Delta \, log \, n)$ communication while Chan et al.'s protocol requires $(\Delta \, log^2 \, n)$.

Most secure data aggregation, discussed previously, can detect the manipulations of aggregation results and then reject it. They have no further attempts to identify nodes which caused the manipulations, and thus a single node compromise gives the adversary the ability to disturb the network resources by participating maliciously during the aggregation phase. Haghani et al. extended Chan et al.'s protocol and enhanced its data availability (2008). The protocol allows the identification of nodes that caused the inconsistency in the aggregation result (or the aggregation disruption) and then allows the removal of malicious nodes. These nodes can be detected through successive polling of the layers on a commitment tree. Their protocol enhances security services provided by Chan et al.'s protocol (authentication, data integrity, and data freshness), and adds data availability.

Another protocol that considered data availability is proposed by Alzaid et al. (2008a). Their protocol integrated the aggregation functionalities with the advantages provided by a reputation system in order to enhance the network lifetime and the accuracy of the aggregated data without trimming the abnormal (but correct) readings. Eliminating abnormal readings with no further investigation is impractical, especially in applications such as monitoring bush fires or monitoring temperatures within oil refineries. The node behaviour is represented in the form of (α, β) tuple where α and β denote the amount of positive and negative ratings calculated by each node for other nodes in its cell (or cluster) and then stored in the reputation table. If node x has behaved well for a specific function, α_x is incremented by one. Otherwise, β_x is incremented. The nodes' behaviours are examined for three functions: data sensing, data forwarding, and data aggregation (if x is the cell representative for an intermediate cell). To fill the reputation table, each node evaluates the sensing, forwarding, and aggregation (if in an intermediate cell) functionalities and computes α and β for each function.

5. Security Analysis

This section provides the security analysis of current secure data aggregation protocols. This analysis can be difficult for the following reasons:

- Each protocol designers solved the data aggregation security from different angles. For example, some designers solved the problem by considering either single aggregator model or multiple aggregator model. Each model has its own challenges that need to be considered carefully. End-to-end encryption, for example, is easier to implement in the single aggregator model than the multiple aggregator model. However, the energy consumption at the single aggregator model has to be minimized in order to extend the network lifetime and enhance data availability service.

- There is no standard adversarial model where current secure data aggregation protocols compete to provide a higher level of security, or resilience to attacks discussed in Section 3.1. For example, secure data aggregation protocols that defeat type I adversary are secure in the face of SY, SF, and RE attacks. However, this resilience against these attacks is not provided by the protocol itself, but is due to the limited capabilities of type I adversary as discussed in Section 3.

Existing secure data aggregation protocols, consequently, are compared in a number of different ways: the aggregation model they follow, security services they provide, cryptographic primitives they use, and resilience against attacks described in section 3.1.

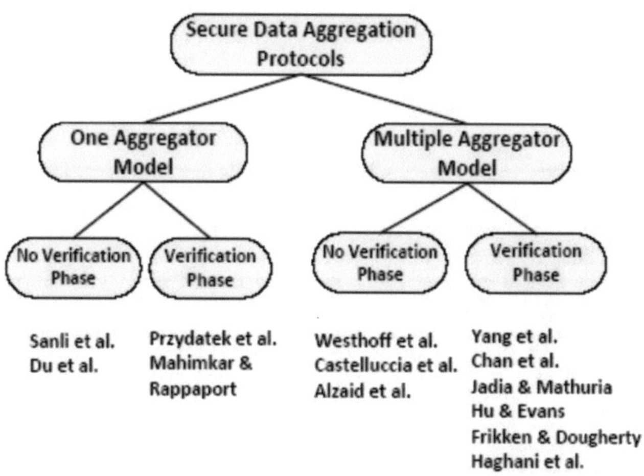

Fig. 4. Classification of current secure data aggregation protocols.

5.1 Aggregation Models

Based on our discussion in Section 4, current secure data aggregation protocols fall under either single aggregator model or multiple aggregator model. A sketch of these two aggregation models can be found in Figure 2. The aggregation process, in the single aggregator model, takes place once between the sensing nodes and the base station or the querier. All collected physical phenomena (PP) in WSNs, therefore, travel to only one aggregator point in the network before reaching the querier. On the other hand, collected data in WSNs are aggregated more than one time before reaching the final destination or the querier. This model achieves greater reduction in the number of bits transmitted within the network, especially in large WSNs. The importance of this model is growing as the network size is getting bigger, especially when data redundancy at the lower levels is high. Figure 4 concludes the discussion in Section 4 and classifies secure aggregation protocols depending on the aggregation model they follow and whether they have a verification phase or not. This verification phase, if it exists, is used to validate the aggregation results (or the aggregator behaviour) by using some methods such as interactive protocols between the base station (or the querier) and normal sensor nodes.

5.2 Security Services

Since the considered adversarial model varies from one secure data aggregation protocol to another, as discussed in Section 3.3, each protocol provides different security services to defeat the expected type of adversary. Table 2 shows security services provided by each secure data aggregation protocol. It is obvious that protocols designed with type I adversary in mind, such as (Castelluccia et al., 2005; Sanli et al., 2004), do not provide authentication service while authentication is a must in protocols that defeat type II or type III adversaries as in (Alzaid et al., 2008a; Chan et al., 2006; Du et al., 2003; Frikken & IV, 2008; Haghani et al., 2008; Hu & Evans, 2003; Jadia & Mathuria, 2004; Mahimkar & Rappaport, 2004; Przydatek et al., 2003; Yang et al., 2006; Westhoff et al., 2006). As discussed in Section 3.3, type II and type III adversaries can launch, for example, SY attack where adversaries are able to present more than one node and then interact with the network. If authentication is not implemented, the adversaries can then successfully affect the overall aggregation results.

Scheme	CO	IN	FR	AV	AU	AT
Westhoff et al. (2006)	√				√	II
Hu & Evans (2003)		√	√		√	II
Przydatek et al. (2003)	√	√	√		√	II
Chan et al. (2006)		√	√		√	III
Du et al. (2003)		√			√	II
Mahimkar & Rappaport (2004)	√	√			√	II
Sani et al. (2004)	√		√			I
Yang et al. (2006)	√	√	√		√	II
Jadia & Mathuria (2004)	√	√	√		√	II
Castelluccia et al. (2005)	√					I
Frikken & Dougherty (2008)		√	√		√	III
Haghani et al. (2008)		√	√	√	√	III
Alzaid et al. (2008)		√	√	√	√	II

CO	Confidentiality	**IN**	Integrity
FR	Freshness	**AV**	Availability
AU	Authentication	**AT**	Adversary Type

Table 2. Security services provided in current secure data aggregation protocols.

Data confidentiality, furthermore, is provided in secure data aggregation protocols where the privacy of the data is important. Some of the protocols designers who considered type I adversary in their protocols (Castelluccia et al., 2005; Sanli et al., 2004) aimed to secure the raw data and the aggregated data from being revealed by the adversary. They focused on providing data confidentiality service only, and this level of security is acceptable where the adversary has no interest in destroying the overall performance but is interested in knowing the content of the reported information as in type I adversary. Other designers who considered type II or type III adversaries in their protocols (Jadia & Mathuria, 2004; Mahimkar & Rappaport, 2004; Przydatek et al., 2003; Yang et al., 2006; Westhoff et al., 2006) provide data confidentiality service in conjunction with other services to protect data privacy and strengthen their protocols' resilience against attacks that can be launched by the considered adversary model (type II or type III adversary).

Data integrity, moreover, is provided in secure data aggregation protocols where the protocols designers considered type II or type III adversaries. These two types, as discussed in Section 3.3, can launch NC attack and are consequently able to alter the content of the data received from downstream nodes, and needs to be forwarded to upper stream nodes. If data integrity service is not offered by the protocol, upper stream nodes therefore have no idea about this alteration. Table 2 shows that most secure data aggregation protocols that have type II or type III adversary in mind, such as (Alzaid et al., 2008a; Chan et al., 2006; Du et al., 2003; Frikken & IV, 2008; Haghani et al., 2008; Hu & Evans, 2003; Jadia & Mathuria, 2004; Mahimkar & Rappaport, 2004; Przydatek et al., 2003; Yang et al., 2006) provide data integrity service. However, Westhoff et al.'s protocol does not offer data integrity although it is built with type II adversary in mind. This is because the protocol designers limited their discussion to data confidentiality only.

Data freshness, furthermore, is considered by some of the protocols designers when they constructed their protocols (Chan et al., 2006; Hu & Evans, 2003; Jadia & Mathuria, 2004; Przydatek et al., 2003; Yang et al., 2006) in order to defeat type II or type III adversary. These types of adversary, as discussed in Section 3.3, can launch different types of attacks such as RE attack. The adversary, in RE attack, can affect the aggregation result by simply replaying old messages into the network if data freshness is not provided. For example, the designers of the witness-based secure data aggregation protocol (Du et al., 2003) did not provide data freshness service as discussed in Section 4.1.1. Although witnesses help the base station (or the querier) to validate the aggregation results, the aggregator - if compromised- can mislead the base station by replaying old messages with valid (but old) proofs from the witnesses.

Finally, data availability gained some attention from the protocols designers (Alzaid et al., 2008a; Haghani et al., 2008). Detecting the inconsistency in the aggregation results with no further action is not enough because the adversary can keep manipulating the aggregation result in order to bring the network down by consuming the energy resources of sensor nodes.

5.3 Cryptographic Primitives

The section lists cryptographic primitives used by the designers of secure data aggregation protocols to defeat the considered type of adversary. As discussed in Section 4, cryptographic primitives vary from one protocol to another depending on the type of adversary the protocols designers considered, and the security services they wanted their protocols to provide. Table 4 summarizes all security primitives used in the secure data aggregation protocols discussed in this chapter.

The message authentication code (*MAC*) is used to exclude unauthorized parties from sending forged aggregated data and to protect the original message from being altered in protocols (Chan et al., 2006; Du et al., 2003; Hu & Evans, 2003; Jadia & Mathuria, 2004; Przydatek et al., 2003; Yang et al., 2006). On the other hand, Mahimkar and Rappaport's protocol used digital signature (Mahimkar & Rappaport, 2004) and Castelluccia et al.'s (Castelluccia et al., 2005) and Westhoff et al.'s (Westhoff et al., 2006) protocols relied on privacy homomorphic encryption to prevent unauthorized parties from participating in the network, and affecting the data integrity of the aggregation result.

Scheme	MA	DS	SK	PK	RS	PH	BA	IP	VS	AT
Westhoff et al. (2006)			√			√				II
Hu & Evans (2003)	√		√				√			II
Przydatek et al. (2003)	√		√				√	√		II
Chan et al. (2006)	√		√				√	√		III
Du et al. (2003)	√		√						√	II
Mahimkar & Rappaport (2004)		√		√						II
Sani et al. (2004)			√							I
Yang et al. (2006)	√		√				√	√		II
Jadia & Mathuria (2004)	√		√							II
Castelluccia et al. (2005)			√			√				I
Frikken & Dougherty (2008)	√		√				√	√		III
Haghani et al. (2008)	√		√				√	√		III
Alzaid et al. (2008)	√				√					II

MA	Message Authentication	**DS**	Digital Signature
SK	Symmetric Key	**PK**	Public Key
RS	Reputation System	**PH**	Privacy Homomorphic
BA	Broadcast Authentication	**IP**	Interactive Protocol
VS	Voting Scheme	**AT**	Adversary Type

Table 4. Cryptographic primitives used in current secure data aggregation protocols

Symmetric and public key cryptography are used to achieve either hop-by-hop or end-to-end encryption whenever data confidentiality is required. Table 4 shows that all secure data aggregation protocols, discussed in this chapter, except Mahimkar and Rappaport's protocol. It used symmetric key cryptography. Mahimkar and Rappaport's protocol used elliptic curve cryptography (public key cryptography) to implement the encryption and the digital signature.
As discussed in Section 4, secure data aggregation protocols may or may not have a verification phase in order to check the validity of the aggregation results. The verification phase was designed using one of the following methods: an authenticated broadcast such as μTESLA (Hu & Evans, 2003), interactive proofs (Chan et al., 2006; Frikken & IV, 2008; Haghani et al., 2008; Yang et al., 2006; Przydatek et al., 2003), or voting systems (Du et al., 2003). The security primitives' subsections in Section 4 provide more details about these verification options.

5.4 Attack Visibility

This section concludes the attack visibility analysis that is discussed in the adversarial model and attack resistance subsections in Section 4. Secure data aggregation protocols, presented in this chapter, are investigated to determine whether or not they are vulnerable to different types of attack listed in Section 3.1.
Due to the communication nature in WSNs, only adversary of types II and III can launch DoS attack by sending radio signals that interfere with the radio frequencies used by WSNs. Another form of DoS attack occurs when the adversary refuses to compute (or forward) aggregation information and starts dropping messages when it succeeds in compromising a sensor node. Table 6 shows that all secure data aggregation protocols are vulnerable to DoS attack, especially its first form.

Scheme	DoS	NC	SY	SF	RE	AT
Westhoff et al. (2006)	√	√		√	√	II
Hu & Evans (2003)	√	√		√		II
Przydatek et al. (2003)	√	√		√		II
Chan et al. (2006)	√	√		√		III
Du et al. (2003)	√	√	√	√	√	II
Mahimkar & Rappaport (2004)	√	√		√	√	II
Sani et al. (2004)						I

Yang et al. (2006)	√	√		√		**II**
Jadia & Mathuria (2004)	√	√		√		**II**
Castelluccia et al. (2005)						**I**
Frikken & Dougherty (2008)	√	√		√		**III**
Haghani et al. (2008)	√	√				**III**
Alzaid et al. (2008)	√	√				**II**

DoS	Denial of Service	**NC**	Node Compromise
SF	Selective Forwarding	**SY**	Sybil
AC	Adversary Type	**RE**	Replay

Table 6. Attacks visibility in current secure data aggregation protocols.

Moreover, NC attack explains whether or not the adversary is able to reach any deployed sensor nodes and extracts its information stored in its memory. The NC attack is visible in all secure data aggregation protocols except for Sanli et al.'s and Castelluccia et al.'s protocols because these two protocols only considered type I adversary. In other words, NC attack is not visible in type I due to its limited capability as discussed in Section 3. It is worth mentioning that we classify the adversary considered in Westhoff et al.'s protocol into type II category although the designers aimed initially to defend passive adversary in their previous protocol (Girao et al., 2005). They then extended the adversary capability to launch NC attack against aggregator nodes.

As the capability of the adversary varies from type I to type III, the damage caused by these attacks also varies. Type I adversary, as discussed in Section 3.3, has not enough power to launch SY, SF, NC attacks. Therefore, SY and SF attacks are not visible in protocols (Castelluccia et al., 2005; Sanli et al., 2004) because of the adversary capability, not because of the security primitives the protocols designers used. SY attack is visible only in Du et al.'s protocol because leaf nodes are not authenticated to the aggregator (Du et al., 2003). An adversary, upon compromising a leaf node, can present more than one identity and then mislead the aggregator about the aggregation results, as discussed in Section 4.1.1.

Once the NC attack is visible in the network, this means the adversary has full control of the compromised node and can then selectively drop messages (SF attack). All secure data aggregation protocols, which considered type II and type III adversaries, are vulnerable to SF attack except for Haghani et al.'s and Alzaid et al.'s protocols. The former protocol has the adversary localizer component that marks nodes that disrupted the acknowledgment collection, and can then detect any SF attack activity (Haghani et al., 2008). The latter protocol computes nodes' reputation values for sensing, forwarding, and aggregating activities. Once the adversary has launched SF attack, the node's reputation value is reduced. If its reputation value falls below a threshold value due to performing malicious activities, the node is then black-listed (Alzaid et al., 2008).

Finally, RE attack occurs when the adversary has the ability to re-inject (or replay) old messages without even understanding its content. Most secure data aggregation protocols are resistant to this type of attack except (Castelluccia et al., 2005; Du et al., 2003; Mahimkar & Rappaport, 2004; Sanli et al., 2004; Westhoff et al., 2006). Surprisingly, RE attack is visible in Du et al.'s, and Mahimkar and Rappaport's protocols (Du et al., 2003; Mahimkar & Rappaport, 2004) although they defeat type II adversary and the visibility of NC attack is considered. For example, once the adversary has compromised the aggregator node in Du et al.'s protocol, it is able to replay an old aggregation result with its valid proofs instead of the current result to mislead the base station. The adversary in Mahimkar and Rappaport's protocol can replay old valid signed aggregation results to mislead the base station when it succeeds in compromising the aggregator. The adversary in Westhoff et al.'s protocol can replay old encrypted messages once the compromise of an aggregator node is succeeded, which affects the aggregation results.

5.4 Framework for Evaluating New Schemes

Based on the analysis provided in the previous sections, a conceptual framework for secure data aggregation protocols is proposed. The framework helps the designers of new secure data aggregation protocols to strengthen their new design in the face of the adversary. To the best of our knowledge, this framework is the first work that establishes a common ground to compare different secure data aggregation protocols and draws the security map for new protocols.

Figure 5 suggests the minimum security requirements that a new protocol should maintain. The designers need to first study the adversary capability and then estimate the network size where the protocol will run.

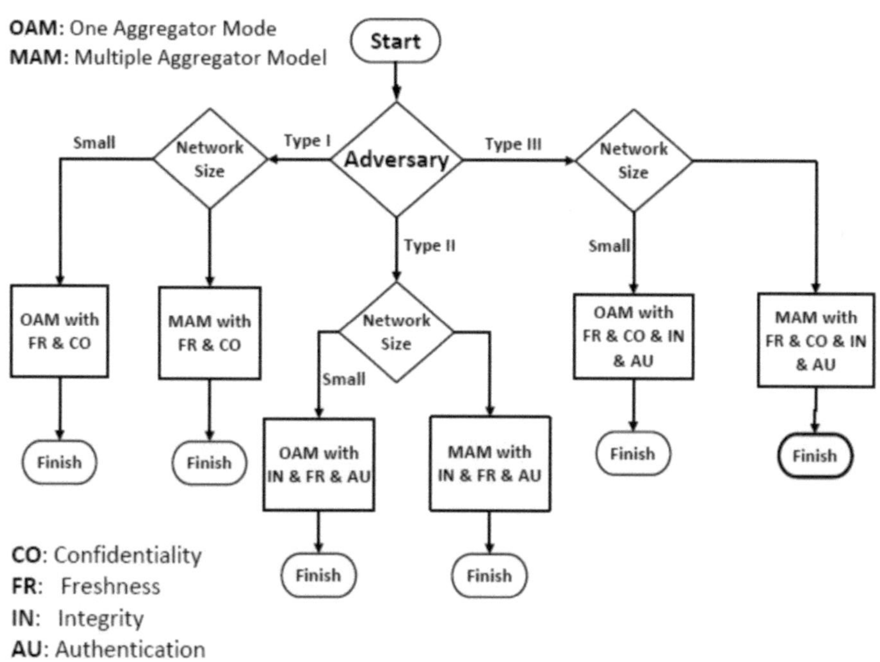

Fig. 5. The proposed framework.

Once the designers decided to defend type I adversary, they need to design a protocol that is at least resistant to passive adversary activities. As discussed in Section 3, type I adversary maybe able to eavesdrop on traffic to obtain some knowledge about aggregated data. Thus, the protocol should at least provide data confidentiality. However, data confidentiality is application-dependent and is offered only when data privacy is needed. Data integrity, data freshness, and authenticity are not included with the minimum security requirement because type I adversary has not enough power to interact with the network and launch NC, SF, RE, DoS, and SY attacks in order to affect the overall performance of secure aggregation protocol.

Moreover, the designers of new protocols may consider type II or type III adversaries that have stronger capabilities than type I adversary. These adversaries can launch any type of attack listed in Section 3.1 in order to mislead the base station about the reported aggregation results. To defeat type II adversary, the framework in Figure 5 suggests that new secure data aggregation protocols should provide data integrity as well as data freshness, and authentication. As the adversary becomes stronger, the minimum security requirement should be enhanced by new services in order to provide resiliency against the adversary's attack. The framework suggests hiding the data (or providing data confidentiality) as well as authentication, data integrity, and data freshness.

The designers of new protocols should then consider the network size to decide whether to follow the one aggregator model or multiple aggregator model. The multiple aggregator model achieves greater reduction in the number of bits transmitted within the network especially in large WSNs, as illustrated in Figure 1. The importance of this model is growing as the network size is getting bigger, especially when data redundancy at the lower levels is high. In the following section, the performance analysis of selected secure data aggregation protocols is discussed.

6. Performance Analysis

This section provides the performance analysis of current secure data aggregation protocols in WSNs. Due to lack of space, we limit our discussion to the communication overhead only.

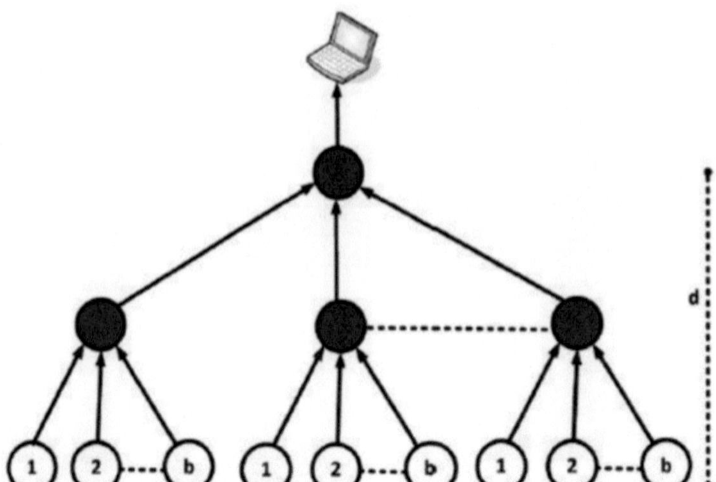

Fig. 6. The tree model used to analyze the performance of current secure data aggregation protocols.

This analysis focuses on calculating the number of bits transmitted within the network in order to show which secure data aggregation protocol is energy hungry and sends more information to accomplish the protocol objectives. We discuss seven scenarios where both aggregation models (single and multiple) are covered. These scenarios are: no aggregation, aggregation but no security, Hu and Evans's protocol (2003), Jadia and Mathuria's protocol (2004), Yang et al.'s protocol (2006), Przydatek et al.'s protocol (2003), and Du et al.'s protocol (2003). Since these scenarios may or may not have a verification phase, we limit our analysis to the aggregation phase only.

For concreteness, we consider an aggregation tree where its depth is d and each node (except leaf nodes) has b children as shown in Figure 6. This means the distance between the base station and leaf nodes are d, where d starts with zero at the first level. The total number of nodes (N) in this type of tree is n bits long and can be computed as:

$$N = \left(\frac{b^{d+1} + 1}{b-1}\right) \tag{4}$$

This kind of tree, therefore, has b^d leaf nodes. If the scenario belongs to the single aggregator model, we consider the root of the tree to be the aggregator. Otherwise, any parent node acts as an aggregator (see Figure 6). In both models, each sensor node in the tree has to participate in the aggregation activity by sensing the environment and then reports its reading to upper nodes.

Let us explain some notations used in this section before we discuss those scenarios. Let x denote the length of the reported information (without the packet's header) where this information can be either raw data (reported from leaf nodes) or aggregated data (reported from the aggregator nodes).

Also, let y denote the length of the sensor node ID in bits, z denote the MAC's length in bits, and qn denote the length of the query nonce in bits. Moreover, TinyOS packet is preconfigured with a maximum size of 35 byte (29 byte payload and 6 byte header) and thus we denote the packet header by h.

6.1 First Scenario (No Aggregation & No Security)

We analyze the number of transmitted bits by considering the situation where no aggregation and no security are used within our example summarized in Figure 6. Leaf sensor nodes sense some physical phenomenon and report them to the upper nodes (their parents). The parents subsequently forward this information to upper nodes until the information is delivered and collected by the base station (or the querier). Each reported information contains the sensor node ID and the sensed physical phenomenon, which required each sensor node at level d to send $x + y + h$ bits long message to its parent. Each parent (intermediate node) needs to forward $(x + y + h)$ bits for each child it has and $(x + y + h)$ bits to report its reading. Thus, the total number of bits forwarded by each parent at level $d - i$ (where $i = d - 1$) is:

$$(b + 1)(x + y + h) \tag{5}$$

The total number of bits travelled in the network can be estimated from equation 5 as follows:

$$\sum_{i=0}^{d}(d - i)\, b^{(d-i)}\, (x + y + h) \tag{6}$$

6.2 Second Scenario (Aggregation but No Security)

We analyze and calculate the length in bits for transmitted information in the case where no security is provided in our example but the aggregation functionality is implemented. This scenario is similar to the example discussed in Section 2. Each parent, in this scenario, combines the reported b messages from its children and reports only one message that represents these b messages. The number of bits forwarded by each parent at any level is estimated as $x + y + h$ and the total number of bits, travelled in the network in order to accomplish the aggregation phase, is calculated as:

$$\left(\frac{b^{(d+1)}-1}{b-1}\right)(x+y+h) \tag{7}$$

6.3 Third Scenario (Hu & Evans)

We analyze the protocol by Hu and Evans (2003). The protocol, as discussed in Section 4, follows the multiple aggregator model with a verification phase. Each leaf node (at level $d - i$ where $i = 0$) needs to send its ID, data, and one message authentication code toward its parent. The length of this message in bits is $x + y + z + h$. The total number of bits that the protocol requires leaf nodes to send to their parents (at level $d - i$ where $i = 0$) is:

$$b^d(x+y+z+h) \tag{8}$$

Each parent (at levels $d - i$ where $i = 1, 2, ..., d$) needs to forward the received data unchanged and add one more *MAC*. Thus, the length of this message in bits can be calculated as $b(x + y + z) + z + h$ and the total number of bits sent by all parents is:

$$\sum_{i=1}^{d} b^{(d-i)}[b(x+y+z)+z+h] \tag{9}$$

Thus, the approximate number of bits transmitted to perform the aggregation phase, in this Protocol, can be calculated by adding equation 8 and equation 9 together as follows:

$$b^d(x+y+z+h)+\sum_{i=1}^{d} b^{(d-i)}[b(x+y+z)+z+h]$$

$$= b^d(x+y+z+h)+\left(\frac{b^{(d+1)}-1}{b-1}-b^d\right)[b(x+y+z)+z+h] \tag{10}$$

6.4 Fourth Scenario (Jadia & Mathuria)

The improvement done by Jadia and Mathuria's protocol (2004), in order to add data confidentiality service to the security services provided by Hu and Evans's protocol, requires each node to add one more message authentication into each message. So, each sensor node (at level $d - i$ where $i = 0$) sends $x + y + 2z + h$ bits instead of sending $x + y + z + h$ bits in Hu and Evans's protocol (Hu & Evans, 2003). Therefore, the total number of bits sent by all leaf nodes is $b^d(x+y+2z+h)$ and the total number of bits sent by the protocol to accomplish the aggregation function is approximately:

$$b^d(x+y+2z+h)+\sum_{i=1}^{d} b^{(d-i)}[b(x+y+z)+z+h]$$

$$= b^d(x+y+2z+h)+\left(\frac{b^{(d+1)}-1}{b-1}-b^d\right)[b(x+y+z)+z+h] \quad (11)$$

6.5 Fifth Scenario (Yang et al.)

Yang et al., as discussed in Section 4, followed the multiple aggregator model and used the divide-and-conquer principle to divide the network tree into multiple logical subtrees, which increases the number of aggregators and reduces the number of nodes in each subtree. For simplicity, we assume that the total number of sensor nodes is N and each subtree has an average size of s sensors. The number of subtrees, therefore, is $\frac{N}{s}+1$ considering the base station as a subtree. Also, the height of a subtree can be approximated by $\frac{d}{2}$ and the distance from each subtree's leader to the base station is $\frac{d}{2}$. Each leaf node needs to send its ID, aggregation flag (one bit), an encrypted sensed data concatenated with a *MAC*, and the query sequence number. This transmission is about $x + y + z + 1 + h$ bits long. Therefore, the total number of bits transmitted in each subtree (or group) can be calculated as:

$$(s-1)(x+y+z+1+h)$$

The distance between the subtree's leader and the base station varies, depending on the position of the subtree. It can be anything between $[0, \frac{d}{2}]$ and for simplicity we assume that the distance between all subtrees' leaders and the base station is $\frac{d}{4}$. Each subtree's leader forwards the aggregation result toward the base station and this increases the number of travelled bits within the network by $\left(\frac{N}{s}\right)\left(\frac{d}{4}\right)(x+y+z+1+h)$ bits. Therefore, the total number of bits sent across the network to accomplish the aggregation function is approximated by:

$$\left(\frac{N}{s}\right)(s-1)(x+y+z+1+h)+\left(\frac{N}{s}\right)\left(\frac{d}{4}\right)(x+y+z+1+h)$$
$$= \left(\frac{N}{s}\right)(x+y+z+1+h)\left[(s-1)+\frac{d}{4}\right] \quad (12)$$

6.6 Sixth Scenario (Przydatek et al.)

We analyze the number of transmitted bits across the network in order to accomplish the aggregation function in Przydatek et al.'s protocol (Przydatek et al., 2003). Their protocol used the aggregate-commit-prove approach discussed in Section 4.1.2. In the aggregate phase, each sensor needs to send its ID, data, query nonce, and two message authentication codes keyed with two shared keys: the first key is shared with the aggregator and the other key is shared with the base station. The length of this message in bits is $x+y+qn+2z+h$ and it travels all the way toward the aggregator. Therefore, the total number of bits travelled within the network until the sensed data reaches the aggregator is:

$$\sum_{i=0}^{d}(d-i)\ b^{(d-i)}(x+y+qn+2z+h) \tag{13}$$

In the commit phase, the aggregator constructs a Merkle hash tree of the received messages and sends the root of this tree as a commitment value, the number of leaves in the hash tree, and aggregated result. Let us assume for simplicity the length of the commitment value is $x+y+qn+2z+h$ bits long and the length of the aggregated result as long as the reported data x. Thus, the total number of bits sent to the home server (or remote user) by the aggregator is:

$$n+2x+y+qn+2z+h \tag{14}$$

Adding the number of bits in equations 13 and 14 gives the total number of travelled bits required to perform the aggregation function in this protocol as follows:

$$n+2x+y+qn+2z+h+\sum_{i=0}^{d}(d-i)\ b^{(d-i)}(x+y+qn+2z+h) \tag{15}$$

6.7 Seventh Scenario (Du et al.)

In Du et al.'s protocol, the designers assumed that leaf nodes are honest and the sensed data reaches the aggregator and witnesses correctly. Let us assume that each sensor needs to send at least its ID and its sensed data. The length of this message in bits is $x+y+h$. Therefore, the total number of bits travelling within the network to reach the aggregator for each event is:

$$\sum_{i=0}^{d}(d-i)\ b^{(d-i)}(x+y+h) \tag{16}$$

Also, the same number of bits goes to each witness (w) and consequently the total number of travelled bits is:

$$w\sum_{i=0}^{d}(d-i)\ b^{(d-i)}(x+y+h) \tag{17}$$

Each witness computes the aggregation result and sends to the aggregator the message authentication code (*MAC*) that contains its ID and aggregation result. Finally, the aggregator forwards its ID, aggregation result (computed by itself), and all *MAC*s received from the witnesses. Therefore, the total number of travelled bits is:

$$\begin{gathered}\sum_{i=0}^{d}(d-i)\ b^{(d-i)}(x+y+h)\ +\ w\sum_{i=0}^{d}(d-i)\ b^{(d-i)}(x+y+h)+\\ w(z+h)+(x+y+wz+h)\\ =\ 2wz+x+y+h(w+1)+\ (w+1)\sum_{i=0}^{d}(d-i)b^{(d-i)}(x+y+h)\end{gathered} \tag{18}$$

6.8 Example

For better understanding the transmission overhead caused by secure data aggregation protocols chosen in the above scenarios, we give an example with numbers. Let us select the length of the reported information without the header (x), the length of the sensor ID in bits (y), the MAC's length in bits (z), the number of witnesses (w), the length in bits for the average number of sensors in any subtree (s), the length of the query number in bits (qn), and the length in bits for the total number of sensor nodes (n) to be 7 bytes, 2 bytes, 6 bytes,

5 witnesses, 1 byte, 3 bytes, and 4 bytes respectively. We compute the number of bytes that each secure aggregation protocol transmits to accomplish the aggregation phase by substituting the values given above into equations 6, 7, 10, 11, 12, 15, and 18. Table 7 investigates our scenarios and substitutes variables with numbers to give a clearer idea.

Scenarios	*b=2*		*b=3*		*b=4*	
	d=3	*d=4*	*d=3*	*d=4*	*d=3*	*d=4*
First Scenario (No Aggregation & No Security)	510	1470	1530	6390	3420	18780
Second Scenario (Aggregation but No Security)	225	465	600	1815	1275	5115
Third Scenario (Hu & Evans, 2003)	462	966	1113	3381	2226	8946
Fourth Scenario (Jadia & Mathuria, 2004)	510	1062	1275	3867	2610	10482
Fifth Scenario (Yang et al., 2006)	317	682	844	2662	1792	7502
Sixth Scenario (Przydatek et al., 2003)	1061	2981	3101	12821	6881	37601
Seventh Scenario (Du et al., 2003)	3165	8925	9285	38445	20625	112785

Table 7. Number of bytes transmitted across the network to accomplish the aggregation phase.

7. Conclusion

This chapter gives a detailed review of secure data aggregation protocols in wireless sensor networks. It first explains the motivation behind secure data aggregation and discusses the security requirements of wireless sensor networks required to strengthen attack-resistant data aggregation protocols. It then describes the adversarial model that can threaten any secure aggregation protocol. The different capabilities an adversary may have against secure data aggregation protocols are discussed. After that, the state-of-the-art in secure data aggregation protocols is surveyed and classified into two categories (one aggregator model and multiple aggregator model) based on the number of aggregator nodes and the existence of the verification phase. To provide the security and performance analysis, current secure data aggregation protocols are compared in a number of different ways: the aggregation model they follow, security services they provide, cryptographic primitives they use, attacks they secure against, and the number of bits they require nodes to send in order to accomplish the aggregation phase. Based on this security and performance analysis, a conceptual framework that leads to better evaluation of secure aggregation schemes is given.

8. References

Alzaid, H., Foo, E. & Nieto, J. G. (2008a). RSDA: Reputation-based secure data aggregation in wireless sensor networks, *Proceedings of the 9th International Conference on Parallel and Distributed Computing, Applications and Technologies, PDCAT'08*, pp. 419-424, Dunedin, New Zealand, December, 2008, IEEE Computer Society.

Alzaid, H., Foo, E. & Nieto, J. G. (2008b). Secure data aggregation in wireless sensor network: a survey, *Proceedings of the 6th Australasian conference on Information security, AISC'08*, pp. 93–105, Wollongong, NSW, Australia, January, 2008, Australian Computer Society.

Castelluccia, C., Mykletun, E. & Tsudik, G. (2005). Efficient aggregation of encrypted data in wireless sensor networks, *Proceedings of the 2nd Annual International Conference on Mobile and Ubiquitous Systems, MobiQuitous'05*, pp. 109-117, San Diego, CA, USA, July, 2005, IEEE Computer Society.

Chan, H., Perrig, A. & Song, D. (2006). Secure hierarchical in network aggregation in sensor networks, *Proceedings of the 13th ACM Conference on Computer and Communications Security, CCS'06*, pp. 278–287, Alexandria, VA, USA, November, 2006, ACM.

Crossbow Technology Inc. (2006). Mica2 datasheet. *Crossbow Technology Inc.* Retrieved October 13, 2009, from: http://www.xbow.com/Products/Product_pdf_files/Wireless_pdf/MICA2_Datasheet.pdf.

Domingo-Ferrer, J. (2002). A provably secure additive and multiplicative privacy homomorphism, *Proceedings of the 5th International Conference on Information Security, ISC'02*, Vol. 2433 of Lecture Notes in Computer Science, pp. 471–483, Sao Paulo, Brazil, October, 2002, Springer .

Du, W., Deng, J., Han, Y. S. & Varshney, P. (2003). A witness-based approach for data fusion assurance in wireless sensor networks, *Proceedings of IEEE Global Communications Conference, GLOBECOM'03*, Vol. 3, pp. 1435–1439, San Francisco, USA, December, 2003, IEEE Computer Society.

Frikken, K. B. & IV, J. A. D. (2008). An efficient integrity-preserving scheme for hierarchical sensor aggregation, *Proceedings of the First ACM Conference on Wireless Network Security, WISEC'08*, pp. 68–76, Alexandria, VA, USA, April, 2008, ACM.

Girao, J. , Westhoff, D., Schneider, S. (2005). CDA: Concealed Data Aggregation for Reverse Multicast Traffic in Wireless Sensor Networks, *Proceedings of IEEE International Conference on Communications, ICC'05*, Vol. 5, pp. 3044–3049, Seoul, Korea, May, 2005, IEEE.

Grigoriev, D. & Ponomarenko, I. V. (2003). Homomorphic public key cryptosystems over groups and rings, *The Computing Research Repository, CoRR*, Vol. cs.CR/0309010, September, 2003, Cornell University.

Grubbs, F. (1969). Procedures for detecting outlying observations in samples, Technometrics Vol. 11, No. 1, pp. 1–21, February, 1969, American Statistical Association.

Guimarães, G., Souto, E., Sadok, D. F. H. & Kelner, J. (2005). Evaluation of security mechanisms in wireless sensor networks, *Proceedings of the 2005 Systems Communications (ICW/ICHSN/ICMCS/SENET)*, pp. 428–433, Montreal, Canada, August, 2005, IEEE Computer Society.

Haghani, P., Papadimitratos, P., Poturalski, M., Aberer, K. & Hubaux, J.-P. (2008). Efficient and robust secure aggregation for sensor networks, *The Computing Research Repository (CoRR)*, Vol. CoRR abs/0808.2676, August, 2008, Cornell University.

He, T., Vicaire, P., Yan, T., Luo, L., Gu, L., Zhou, G., Stoleru, R., Cao, Q., Stankovic, J. A. & Abdelzaher, T. F. (2006). Achieving real-time target tracking using wireless sensor networks, *Symposium of the 12th IEEE Real-Time and Embedded Technology and Applications, RTAS'06*, pp. 37–48, San Jose, California, USA, April, 2006, IEEE Computer Society.

Hu, L. & Evans, D. (2003). Secure aggregation for wireless network, *Symposium on Applications and the Internet Workshops, SAINT'03*, pp. 384-394, Orlando, FL, USA, January, 2003, IEEE Computer Society.

Jadia, P. & Mathuria, A. (2004). Efficient secure aggregation in sensor networks, *Proceedings of the 11th conference on High Performance Computing, HiPC'04*, Vol. 3296 of Lecture Notes in Computer Science, pp. 40-49, Bangalore, India. December, 2004, Springer.

Krishnamachari, B., Estrin, D. & Wicker, S. B. (2002). The impact of data aggregation in wireless sensor networks, *Proceedings of the 22nd International Conference on Distributed Computing Systems, Workshops, ICDCSW'02*, pp. 575-578, Vienna, Austria, July, 2002, IEEE Computer Society.

Law, Y. W., Doumen, J. & Hartel, P. H. (2006). Survey and benchmark of block ciphers for wireless sensor networks, *ACM Transaction on Sensor Networks, TOSN*, Vol. 2, No. 1, pp. 65-93, February, 2006, ACM.

Mahimkar, A. & Rappaport, T. S. (2004). SecureDAV: A secure data aggregation and verification protocol for sensor networks, *Proceedings of IEEE Global Communications Conference, GLOBECOM'04*, Vol. 4, pp. 2175- 2179, Dallas, Texas, USA, December, 2004, IEEE Computer Society.

Mainwaring, A. M., Culler, D. E., Polastre, J., Szewczyk, R. & Anderson, J. (2002). Wireless sensor networks for habitat monitoring, *Proceedings of the First ACM International Workshop on Wireless Sensor Networks and Applications, WSNA'02*, pp. 88-97, Atlanta, Georgia, USA, September, 2002, ACM.

Merkle, R. C. (1980). Protocols for public key cryptosystems, *IEEE Symposium on Security and Privacy*, pp. 122-134, Atlanta, CA, USA, April, 1980, IEEE Computer Society.

Murthy, C. S. R. & Manoj, B. (2004). *Ad Hoc Wireless Sensor Networks Architectures and Protocols*, Prentice Hall PTR, ISBN 978-0-13-147023-1, Upper Saddle River, NJ, USA.

Ozdemir, S. & Xiao, Y. (2009). Secure data aggregation in wireless sensor networks: A comprehensive overview, *Computer Networks*, Vol. 53, No. 12, pp. 2022-2037, August, 2009, Elsevier.

Perrig, A., Szewczyk, R., Tygar, J. D., Wen, V. & Culler, D. E. (2002). SPINS: security protocols for sensor networks, *Wireless Network*, Vol. 8, No. 5, pp. 521-534, September, 2002, Springer.

Przydatek, B., Song, D. X. & Perrig, A. (2003). SIA: secure information aggregation in sensor networks, *Proceedings of the 1st International Conference on Embedded Networked Sensor Systems, SenSys '03*, pp. 255-265, Los Angeles, California, USA, November, 2003, ACM.

Rivest, R. L., Shamir, A. & Adleman, L. M. (1978). A Method for Obtaining Digital Signatures and Public-Key Cryptosystems, *Communication of the ACM*. Vol. 21, No. 2, pp. 120-126, February, 1978, ACM.

Roosta, T., Shieh, S. & Sastry, S. (2006). Taxonomy of security attacks in sensor networks, *The First IEEE International Conference on System Integration and Reliability Improvements, SIRI'06*, pp. 13-22, Hanoi, Vietnam, December, 2006, IEEE Computer Society.

Sang, Y., Shen, H., Inoguchi, Y., Tan, Y. & Xiong, N. (2006). Secure data aggregation in wireless sensor networks: a survey, *Proceedings of the Seventh International Conference on Parallel and Distributed Computing, Applications and Technologies, PDCAT'06*, pp. 315-320, Taipei, Taiwan, December, 2006, IEEE Computer Society.

Sanli, H. O., Ozdemir, S. & Cam, H. (2004). SRDA: secure reference-based data aggregation protocol for wireless sensor networks, *Proceeding of the IEEE 60th Vehicular Technology Conference, VTC'04*, pp. 4650- 4654, Los Angeles, USA, September, 2004, IEEE Computer Society.

Setia, S., Roy, S. & Jajodia, S. (2008). Secure data aggregation in wireless sensor networks, In *Wireless Sensor Network Security*, in J. Lopez & J. Zhou (eds), chapter 8, pp. 204–222, April, 2008, IOS Press, ISBN 978-1586038137, Amsterdam, The Netherlands.

Shi, E. & Perrig, A. (2004). Designing secure sensor networks, *IEEE Wireless Communications*, Vol. 11, No. 6, pp. 38–43, December, 2004, IEEE Computer Society.

Wagner, D. (2003). Cryptanalysis of an algebraic privacy homomorphism., in C. Boyd & W. Mao (eds), *Proceedings of the Sixth International Conference on Information Security, ISC'03*, Vol. 2851 of Lecture Notes in Computer Science, pp. 234- 239, Bristol, UK, October, 2003, Springer.

Wagner, D. (2004). Resilient aggregation in sensor networks, *Proceedings of the 2nd ACM Workshop on Security of ad hoc and Sensor Networks, SASN '04*, pp. 78–87, Washington DC, USA, October, 2004, ACM.

Westhoff, D., Girao, J. & Acharya, M. (2006). Concealed data aggregation for reverse multicast traffic in sensor networks: encryption, key distribution, and routing adaptation, *IEEE Transactions on Mobile Computing*, Vol. 5, No. 10, pp. 1417–1431, October, 2006, IEEE.

Yang, Y., Wang, X., Zhu, S. & Cao, G. (2006). SDAP: a secure hop-by-hop data aggregation protocol for sensor networks, *Proceedings of the 7th ACM International Symposium on Mobile Ad Hoc Networking and Computing, MobiHoc'06*, pp. 356–367, Florence, Italy, May, 2006, ACM.

Yick, J., Mukherjee, B. & Ghosal, D. (2008). Wireless sensor network survey, *Computer Networks*, Vol. 52, No. 12, pp. 2292–2330, August, 2008, Elsevier.

As a result, those bottleneck nodes around the sink deplete their batteries much faster than other nodes and, therefore, their lifetime upper bounds the lifetime of the whole network.

11

Indoor Location Tracking using Received Signal Strength Indicator

Chuan-Chin Pu[1], Chuan-Hsian Pu[2], and Hoon-Jae Lee[3]
[1]*Sunway University College*, [2]*Taylor's University College*, [3]*Dongseo University*
[1] *Malaysia*, [2]*Malaysia*, [3]*South Korea*

1. Introduction

The development pace of location tracking research is highly tied up with the advancement of wireless sensor network (WSN) and wireless technologies. As sensor nodes in WSN became smaller and stronger, the ability of processing information and managing network operation also became more intelligent. This can be observed from the application of tracking from coarse-grained to fine-grained advancement.

In coarse-grained tracking such as (Zhao, et al., 2003), the location of target is just detected by two or more sensor nodes along the movement path of the target. The coordinate of the tracked target is then determined by averaging the location coordinates of those sensor nodes which are able to detect the target. Using this approach, the accuracy and resolution of location estimation is affected by the density of sensor nodes in the area.

In fine-grained tracking such as (Smith, et al., 2004), three or more sensor nodes are responsible to track the target in the area. Instead of just detection, the distances between the target and the sensor nodes are measured. The determination of distance between two entities is called "ranging". Using the measured distances, the exact location coordinate of the target can be computed by angulation or lateration techniques (Hightower, et al., 2001). Therefore, increasing the node density of the area does not really increase the accuracy of location estimation. It rather depends on the accuracy of the ranging method.

This chapter presents the authors' research investigation of developing an indoor tracking and localization system. The experimental system was tested and achieved in the laboratory of Dongseo University for supporting author's PhD studies. The thesis (Pu, 2009) provides further technical details for the design and implementation of the tracking system. For the ease of reading, this chapter was organized as follows: section 1 gives overall fundamentals of location tracking systems, from every aspect of considerations. Section 2 analyzes the nature of wireless ranging using received signal strength indicator, especially for the case of indoor signal propagation and ranging. Section 3 provides the complete flow of designing and implementing indoor location system based on received signal strength. Finally, section 4 concludes the whole work.

1.1 Classification of Location Tracking Systems

Localization of sensor nodes and location tracking applications have been an important study since WSN concept was introduced. Today, various techniques and technologies (Zhao, et al., 2004) are available for the development of off-the-shelf location systems (Hightower, et al., 2001). The selection requirement of location systems can be more specific to suit different needs and environments such as accuracy, indoor/outdoor environment, positioning techniques, ranging methods, security and privacy, device available, WSN deployment restriction, network scale, implementation cost, healthy consideration, and etc. From the technology point of view, classification of location systems can be categorized in a tree as shown in Fig. 1.

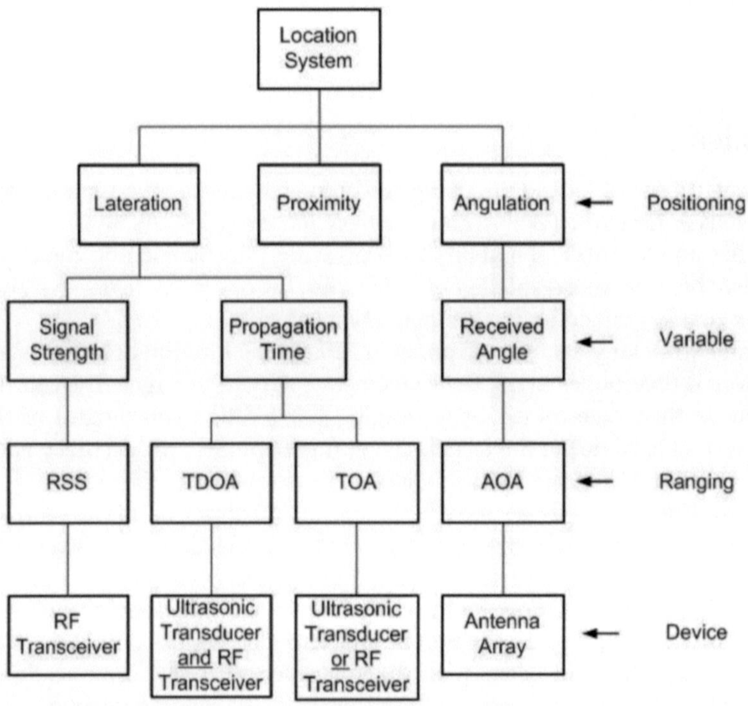

Fig. 1. Classification of Location Tracking Systems (Pu, 2009).

1.1.1 Positioning Aspect

In Fig. 1, classification is first viewed from positioning aspect, followed by variable, ranging, and device aspects. From the positioning aspect, three kinds of location estimation techniques can be used to determine location coordinate including proximity, angulation, and lateration methods (Hightower, et al., 2001).

Proximity estimation is a range-free (He, et al., 2005) or detection (Nakajima, 2007) based technique that does not compute the exact location coordinate of the tracking target. Hence, this kind of location estimation is a "coarse-grained" method. Both angulation and lateration estimations are range based technique which are able to compute the exact location coordinate of the tracking target from measured sensor data. Hence, this kind of location estimation is a "fine-grained" method. The difference between them is the way of estimation. Angulation (Kamath, et al., 2007) computes location coordinate from the angles between target location and reference locations, whereas lateration (Rice, et al., 2005) computes location coordinate from the distances between target location and reference locations.

1.1.2 Variable Aspect

From the variable aspect of location system in Fig. 1, there are three types of variable can be used to find location-related sensor data. These variables are easy to measure from physical world: received angle, propagation time, and signal strength. Received angles between target and reference locations are the main variables measured for angulation estimation.
Propagation time is the time duration taken for a signal to travel from transmitter to receiver. Since the propagation speed of a kind of signal through a medium is constant, it is convenient to find distance between transmitter and receiver from propagation time. Signal strength can be measured at receiver when it receives the signal from transmitter. If distance is further, signal strength becomes weaker by attenuation of path. Using this relationship, it is possible to find distance by evaluating total attenuation. Both propagation time and signal strength are able to provide distance between transmitter and receiver, thus they are used in lateration estimation.

1.1.3 Ranging Aspect

From the ranging aspect of location system in Fig. 1, there are four types of distance measurement techniques. They are angle of arrival (AOA), time of arrival (TOA), time difference of arrival (TDOA), and received signal strength (RSS). AOA (Tian, et al., 2007) is a method to measure the angle of arrival of a received signal. By comparing the direction of signal arrival with a reference orientation, received angle can be measured. The receiver may also know its own orientation for better angle measurement.
TOA (Mak, et al., 2006) is used when centralized communication is possible. This ranging method measures the arrival time between transmitter and receiver. Two approaches can be used to implement this ranging method. First approach uses a transmitter to transmit signal to many receivers. All receivers then forward their signal arrival time to a centralized system for comparison. Another approach uses many transmitters to send signals to a receiver. The receiver measures arrival time of all signals and makes comparison in the receiver system. This approach may have technical problems as all transmitters must be synchronized so that they send signal among certain time segments. In addition, signals may be lost due to multiple signals received at the same time if signal propagation time is exactly equal to the duration of time segment.
TDOA (Najar, et al., 2001) is an improved version of TOA to avoid synchronization difficulty and packet loss problems. To implement TDOA, a transmitter is required to send two different signals with different propagation speeds. When the two signals are received at the receiver, the difference of arrival times between two signals can be measured. Using the difference of arrival times, time of flight (TOF) of a signal can be found, and it is exactly equal to propagation time of a signal.
RSS (Cong, et al., 2008) is a method to find distance from attenuation of propagation path. If the transmission power is known, the total attenuation of signal propagation through the path can be calculated by subtracting the received power from transmitted power.

1.1.4 Device Aspect

From the device aspect of location system in Fig. 1, there are basically three types of distance measurement tools: antenna array, RF transceiver, ultrasonic transducer. Among them, antenna array is used to measure angle of received signal (Abdalla, et al., 2003) by comparing the phase difference of signals from different antennas. The measurement result can be used in AOA ranging.

If only RF transceiver is used, it can measure the received power and provide to RSS ranging method. In most of the RF transceiver, a dedicated register is used to store the received signal strength indicator (RSSI). Therefore, it is a low-cost and convenient way to measure distance.

If either RF transceiver or ultrasonic transducer is used, then they only can measure arrival time of signals. Thus, it can be used in TOA ranging method. If both RF transceiver and ultrasonic transducer are used (Smith, et al., 2004), then two different signals: RF and ultrasound signals are propagating through the path with different speeds. In small range applications, RF propagation time can be ignore and considered zero second whereas ultrasound takes longer time. Therefore, the time difference between two signals can be measured by starting a timer at RF signal arrival and stopping the timer at ultrasonic signal arrival.

1.2 Positioning Techniques

Positioning techniques are the first to consider in the initial state of location system design. This is because positioning techniques determine the ways of computation, and thus the methods used in distance measurement, and finally devices selection. In the previous section, three major positioning methods were mentioned. In this section, the details of location estimation using proximity, angulation, and lateration are given.

1.2.1 Proximity Estimation

Proximity estimation is usually used in localization of the wireless sensor nodes in a network. Because of the nature of information provided, exact location coordinate is not available but locations of surrounding sensor nodes can be obtained. Thus, it is not suitable to be selected for location tracking applications. However, it is good for localizing large scale sensor network (He, et al., 2005).

Many approaches to proximity estimation have been proposed. The typical and authoritative range-free location estimation schemes include centroid algorithm (Bulusu, et al., 2000), DV-hop scheme (Niculescu, et al., 2003), and area-based approximate point-in-triangulation test (APIT) algorithm (He, et al., 2005).

Centroid localization algorithm broadcasts all possible reference node's location information to all other target nodes. The target nodes use the location information (x_i, y_i) from surrounding reference nodes to estimate its location coordinate (x_{target}, y_{target}) as shown in the following expression (Bulusu, et al., 2000):

$$\left(x_{\text{target}}, y_{\text{target}}\right) = \left(\frac{1}{N}\sum_{i=1}^{N} x_i, \frac{1}{N}\sum_{i=1}^{N} y_i\right) \tag{1}$$

where N is the total number of surrounding reference nodes considered in the location estimation iteration.
Centroid algorithm is not considered accurate enough because of the simplicity and incompleteness. The difficulty of centroid algorithm is the number of reference nodes to be considered in the estimation. By default, it is the total number of surrounding reference nodes that the target node can detect and communicate. However, estimation result could be unacceptable if the target node is located near the edge of the whole network.
To avoid the problem of centroid algorithm, it is necessary to take into consideration of the distance between reference node and target node. More precisely, the "distance" is measured in a form of hop counting as range-free approach does not perform distance ranging task. Therefore, the number of surrounding reference nodes can be limited in first or second levels (hops) of message passing.
DV-Hop localization algorithm (Niculescu, et al., 2003) was proposed to consider hop counting for distance estimation. This work uses an approach that is similar to vector routing algorithms. At first, all sensor nodes broadcast their node ID and information to the nearest sensor nodes. These surrounding nodes receive it first-hand, thus a distance vector is stored in these nodes with reference to the source nodes as first hop. These first-hand nodes diffuse distance vector outward with hop-count values incremented at every intermediate hop. If the reference nodes receive distance vector with higher hop-count value as compared to previously received hop-count value, no action is to be taken. As a result, all sensor nodes have a distance vector of all other sensor nodes. An example of a target node A and the stored hop-count for the distance vector in all other nodes is shown in Fig. 2 (He, et al., 2005).

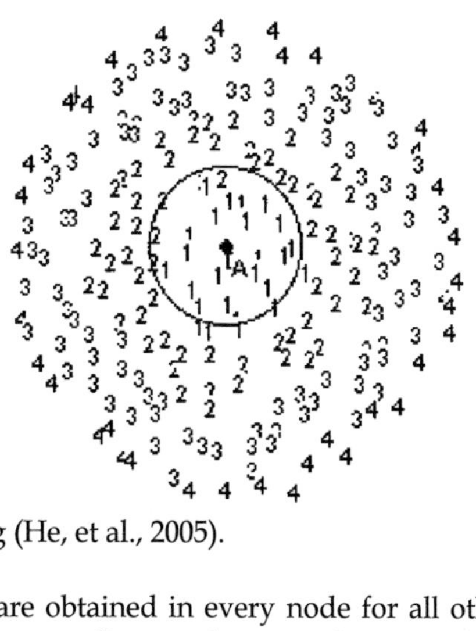

Fig. 2. Hop-count Spreading (He, et al., 2005).

After hop-count distances are obtained in every node for all other nodes, the next step of DV-Hop is to find the average distance between hops using the following expression (Niculescu, et al., 2003):

$$HopSize_i = \frac{\sum \sqrt{(x_i - x_j)^2 + (y_i - y_j)^2}}{\sum h_j} \tag{2}$$

where *HopSize*$_i$ is the average single hop distance for sensor node i. (x_i, y_i) is the location of the node i and (x_j, y_j) is the location for all other nodes. h_j is the hop-count distance from node j to node i. If the target sensor node can hear more than three sensor nodes which are location aware, trilateration or multilateration can be used to estimate the location of target node by combining hop-count distance vector and *HopSize*.

DV-Hop performs well when the deployment of sensor nodes is regular in node density and the distances among sensor nodes. However, the estimation result may not be optimal if the radio pattern is irregular and random node deployment is used in practical. To solve this problem and have better localization result, APIT algorithm (He, et al., 2005) was proposed for area-based range-free localization solution. In APIT approach, all sensor nodes can be localized from just few GPS equipped anchors. Using the location information provided from these anchors, APIT algorithm divides the area occupied by sensor nodes into many triangular regions among beaconing nodes as shown in Fig. 3 (He, et al., 2005).

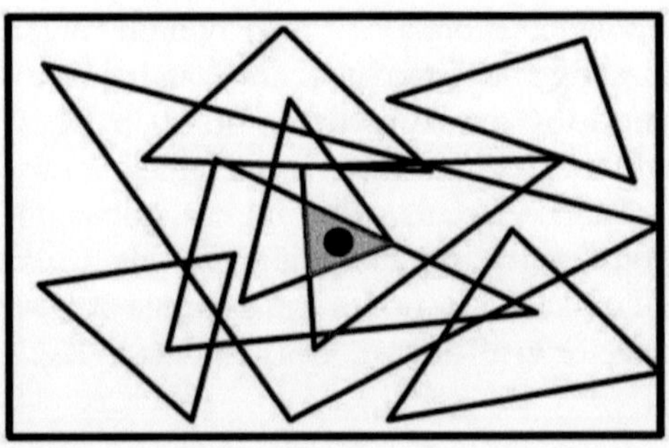

Fig. 3. Localization using APIT (He, et al., 2005).

The process of APIT algorithm first starts from localizing sensor nodes using the three GPS equipped anchors to reduce the possible area that a sensor node may be inside or outside the triangular regions. After the possible region is reduced, some sensor nodes can be anchors to further divide the area into more and smaller triangular regions in next round. This process continues until the possible region of a node can be resided small enough to obtain more accurate location estimation. This approach provide excellent accuracy when irregular radio patterns and random node placement are considered, thus it is sufficient to support location information to various scenarios of applications in sensor networks deployment.

1.2.2 Triangulation Estimation

Triangulation estimation is a trigonometric approach of determining an unknown location based on two angles and a distance between them. In sensor network, two reference nodes are required to be located on a horizontal baseline for x axis, and two sensor nodes are located on a vertical baseline for y axis. The distance d_r between the two reference nodes on the baseline can be measured in preliminary stage and stored in memory. The two angles α_1 and α_2 are measured between the baseline and the line formed by the reference node and target node as shown in Fig. 4.

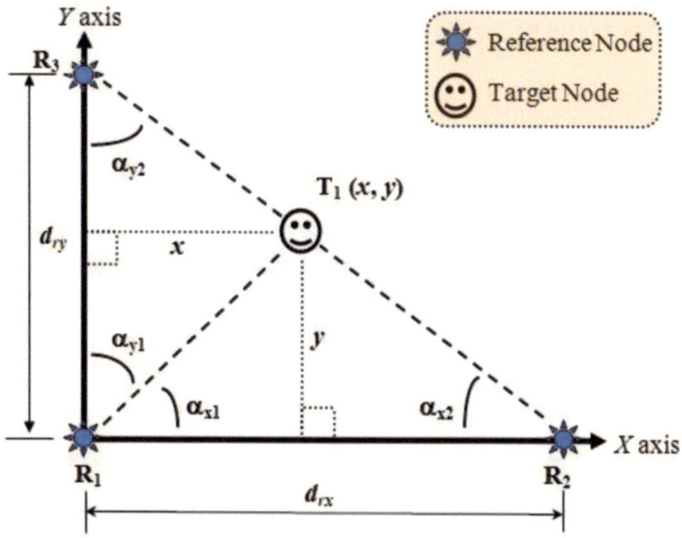

Fig. 4. Triangulation Estimation (Pu, 2009).

In Fig. 4, reference nodes R_1 and R_2 form the baseline of X-axis. Reference node R_1 can be reused to form the baseline of Y-axis together with reference node R_3. A target node T_1 moves freely around in the area. Based on basic triangulation, the location coordinate (x, y) of T_1 can be determined by using the combination of R_1 and R_3 to find x, and the combination of R_1 and R_2 to find y (Pu, 2009):

$$x = \frac{d_{ry} \sin(\alpha_{y1}) \sin(\alpha_{y2})}{\sin(\alpha_{y1} + \alpha_{y2})} \quad (3)$$

$$y = \frac{d_{rx} \sin(\alpha_{x1}) \sin(\alpha_{x2})}{\sin(\alpha_{x1} + \alpha_{x2})}$$

Alternatively, the expressions can be reformed to a simpler way using trigonometric identity (Pu, 2009):

$$x = \frac{d_{ry}}{\tan^{-1}(\alpha_{y1}) + \tan^{-1}(\alpha_{y2})} \quad (4)$$

$$y = \frac{d_{rx}}{\tan^{-1}(\alpha_{x1}) + \tan^{-1}(\alpha_{x2})}$$

Depending on the architecture of location system, the computation of triangulation can be performed either in a centralized system that collects those angle measurements from distributed reference nodes, or in the target node itself. For the first case, the target node broadcasts a signal and the surrounding reference nodes measure the angle of received signal. The reference nodes forward the measured angles to a centralized system as shown in Fig. 5. In this case, the first reference node measures acute angle α and the second node measures obtuse angle β. Thus, the supplementary angle of β or (π - β) is the acute angle for the second node.

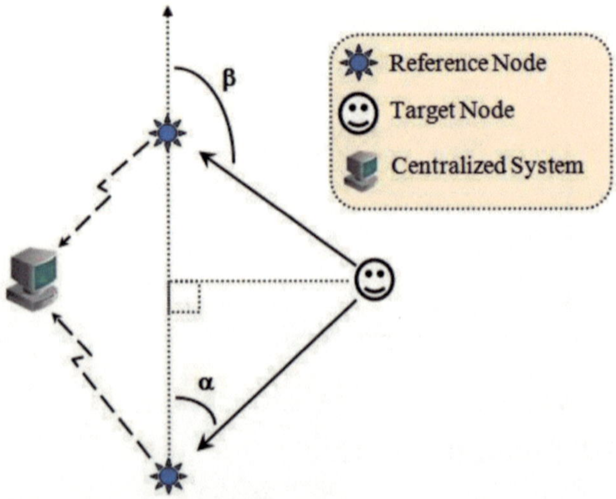

Fig. 5. Estimation in Centralized System (Pu, 2009).

For the second case, computation of triangulation can be performed inside the target node if a magnetic compass is attached to the sensor node. The magnetic compass provides orientation of the sensor node. All reference nodes broadcast signal to the target node. Hence, the target node measures the angles α, β, and γ from the received signals of the three reference nodes as shown in Fig. 6. The target sensor node computes its location coordinate using triangulation and forwards the result to centralized system for data storage or monitoring purpose.

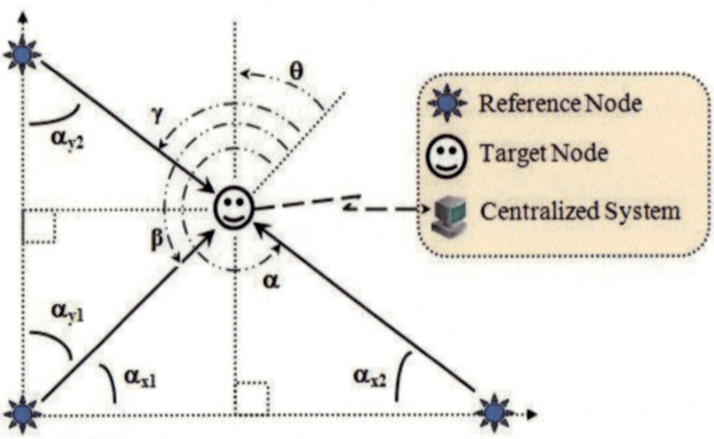

Fig. 6. Estimation in Target Node (Pu, 2009).

Using electronic magnetic compass (EMC) module attached to the sensor node, an offset angle θ can be obtained. This offset angle θ is used to justify all measurements to a reference orientation regardless of the sensor node's orientation. Thus, all acute angles for triangulation using (3) or (4) can be found as follows (Pu, 2009):

$$\begin{aligned} \alpha_{x1} &= (\beta - \theta) - 0.5\pi \\ \alpha_{x2} &= -(\alpha - \theta) + 1.5\pi \\ \alpha_{y1} &= -(\beta - \theta) + \pi \\ \alpha_{y2} &= (\gamma - \theta) \end{aligned} \tag{5}$$

Besides the mentioned basic triangulation solutions, there are more complicated and complete solutions using triangulation for different kinds of implementation and environment such as (Rao, et al., 2007). In addition, the needs of locating objects in three dimensions lead to the development of dynamic triangulation algorithm (Favre-Bulle, et al., 1998).

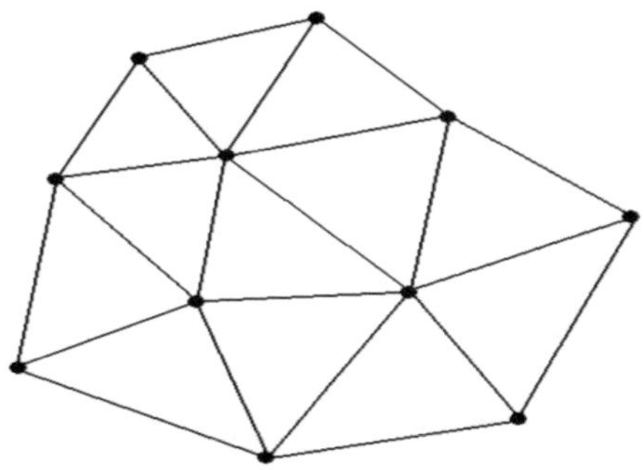

Fig. 7. Delaunay Triangulation (Pu, 2009).

With today's technology, large scale implementation is possible to achieve. Therefore, localization algorithms also must be good enough for such large scale sensor network operation. To realize this scenario as shown in Fig. 7, Delaunay triangulation (Li, et al., 2003, Satyanarayana, et al, 2008) can be used for the localization of multiple points that randomly forms complicated and connected triangles in the field. The formation of meshed triangles shape can be optimized using steepest descent method as in (He, 2008). An objective function was suggested to optimize the shape of triangle elements for the best mesh construction.

1.2.3 Trilateration Estimation

Trilateration estimation is also used to find an unknown location from several reference locations. However, the difference between trilateration and triangulation is the information provided into the process of estimation. Instead of measuring the angles among locations, trilateration uses the distances among the locations to estimate the coordinate of the unknown location. In trilateration, the distances between reference locations and the unknown location can be considered as the radii of many circles with centers at every reference location. Thus, the unknown location is the intersection of all the sphere surfaces as shown in Fig. 8.

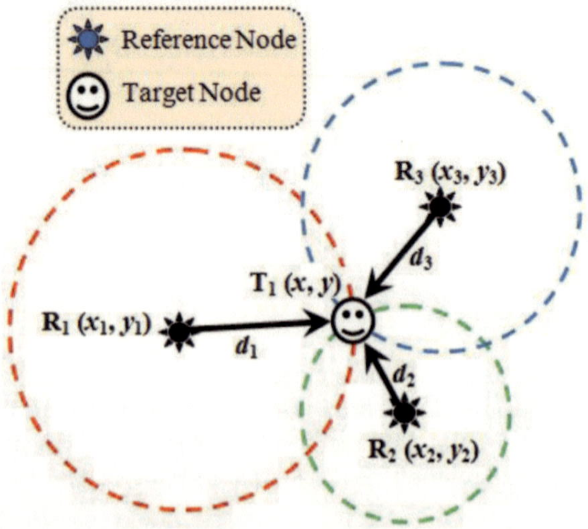

Fig. 8. Trilateration Estimation (Pu, 2009).

In Fig. 8, three reference nodes are randomly allocated. A target node is moving around the reference nodes. The target node (T_1) can be located using the coordinates of the reference nodes (R_1, R_2, and R_3) and the distances (d_1, d_2, d_3) between the reference nodes and the target node. A simple solution can be achieved using Pythagorean theorem as shown in the following expressions (Pu, 2009):

$$\begin{aligned} d_1^{\,2} &= (x_1 - x)^2 + (y_1 - y)^2 \\ d_2^{\,2} &= (x_2 - x)^2 + (y_2 - y)^2 \\ d_3^{\,2} &= (x_3 - x)^2 + (y_3 - y)^2 \end{aligned} \tag{6}$$

Rearrange the equations in (6) and solve for x and y, the location coordinate of the target node can be obtained as shown in the following expressions (Pu, 2009):

$$\begin{aligned} x &= \frac{AY_{32} + BY_{13} + CY_{21}}{2(x_1Y_{32} + x_2Y_{13} + x_3Y_{21})} \\ y &= \frac{AX_{32} + BX_{13} + CX_{21}}{2(y_1X_{32} + y_2X_{13} + y_3X_{21})} \end{aligned} \tag{7}$$

where

$$\begin{aligned} A &= x_1^{\,2} + y_1^{\,2} - d_1^{\,2} \\ B &= x_2^{\,2} + y_2^{\,2} - d_2^{\,2} \\ C &= x_3^{\,2} + y_3^{\,2} - d_3^{\,2} \end{aligned} \tag{8}$$

and

$$\begin{aligned} X_{32} &= (x_3 - x_2) \\ X_{13} &= (x_1 - x_3) \\ X_{21} &= (x_2 - x_1) \end{aligned} \tag{9}$$

$$\begin{aligned} Y_{32} &= (y_3 - y_2) \\ Y_{13} &= (y_1 - y_3) \\ Y_{21} &= (y_2 - y_1) \end{aligned} \tag{10}$$

Localization using (7) is very convenient because the distances (d_1, d_2, d_3) can be obtained from ranging, and the location coordinates of all reference nodes are previously stored in sensor nodes. In large scale sensor network, perhaps there are only several sensor nodes are equipped with GPS module. Thus, all other nodes are required to be located using these GPS equipped sensor nodes.

There are three possible scenarios that localizing a large scale sensor network could meet if only few sensor nodes among them are equipped with GPS:

1. The sensor nodes are able to reach at least three GPS-node
2. The sensor nodes are able to reach one or two GPS-nodes only
3. The sensor nodes are not able to reach any GPS-node

To use lateration techniques, at least three reference nodes are required. The second and third scenarios are not able to fulfill the requirement. For this reason, atomic and iterative multilaterations (Savvides, et al., 2001) were developed for large scale network. Atomic multilateration is used to estimate the location directly from three or more reference nodes as shown in Fig. 9(a). If all sensor nodes are able to reach at least three GPS-nodes, then atomic multilateration is used.

If sensor nodes are too far away from GPS-nodes, it is not able to fulfill the requirement of at least three reference nodes. Therefore, iterative localization may be considered to spread location to other nodes. This approach is called iterative multilateration. In this approach, sensor nodes are converted to reference nodes after localized by GPS-nodes as shown in Fig. 9(b). In next step, these reference nodes can be used to localize other nodes that are not reachable to GPS-nodes. This process continues until all sensor nodes in the network are localized.

In a large scale sensor network, atomic and iterative multilaterations can be used to localize any sensor nodes if the first scenario happens at initial state. However, the random allocation of GPS-nodes could be far to each other. Thus, no sensor node can reach at least three GPS-nodes at initial state. This leads to second and third scenarios at initial state. To solve this problem, collaborative multilateration (Savvides, et al., 2001) was proposed as shown in Fig. 9(c). In this approach, two sensor nodes are close to each other. These two sensor nodes are not able to localize themselves as each of them only can reach two GPS-nodes at initial state. Collaborative multilateration helps to determine their location by exchanging location information between the two sensor nodes.

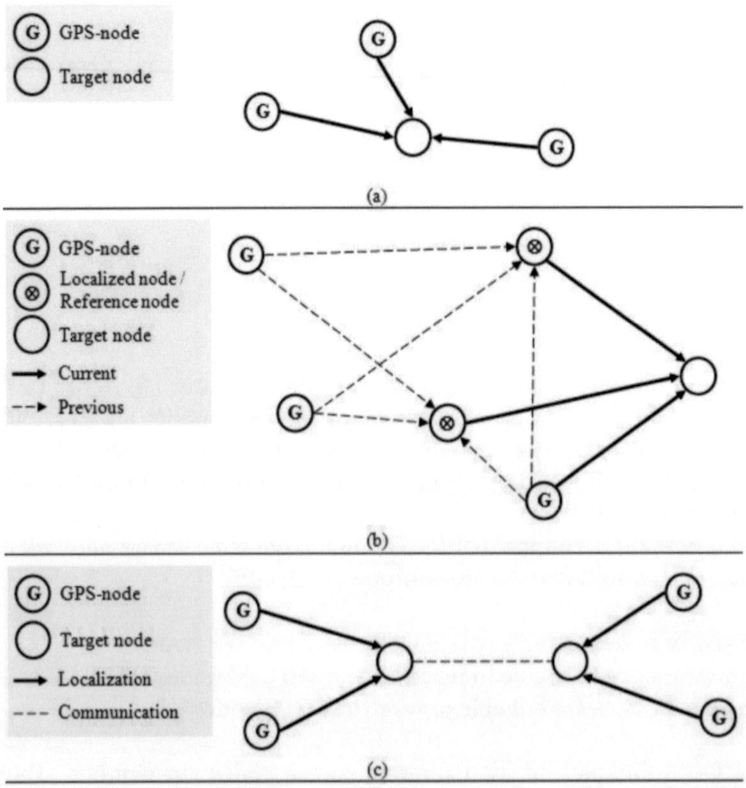

Fig. 9. Atomic, Iterative, and Collaborative Multilateration (Savvides, et al., 2001).

2. RSS Ranging in Indoor Environment

2.1 RSS Ranging

The strength of received power from a signal can be used to estimate distance because all electromagnetic waves have inverse-square relationship between received power and distance (Savvides, et al., 2001) as shown in the following expression:

$$P_r \propto \frac{1}{d^2} \tag{11}$$

where P_r is the received power at a distance d from transmitter. This expression clearly states that the distance of signal travelled can be found by comparing the difference between transmission power and received power, or it is called "path loss".

In practical measurement, the increment of pass loss due to increment of distance may be different when it is in different environments. This leads to environmental characterization using path loss exponent n as shown in the following expression (Pu, 2009):

$$p_r = \frac{P_{(d0)}}{(d/d_0)^n} \tag{12}$$

where $P_{(d0)}$ is the received power measured at distance d_0. Generally, d_0 is fixed as a constant $d_0 = 1$ m. Path loss exponent n in the expression is one of the most important parameters for environmental characterization. If the increment of path loss is more drastic when distance increases, the value of path loss exponent n would be larger as shown in Fig. 10. The solid line on top indicates the attenuation or path loss if $n = 2.0$. The dash line next to the solid line indicates the attenuation if $n = 2.5$, and so forth.

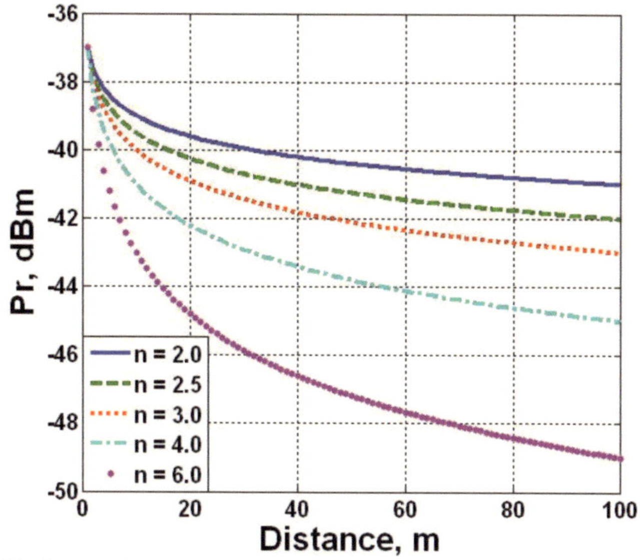

Fig. 10. Effects of Path Loss Exponent (Pu, 2009).

Another important feature that constitutes the rules of path loss in Fig. 10 is the beginning point of each curve. The starting point of all curves is fixed at –37 dBm. If this setting is smaller, then all curves would be shifted lower. In fact $P_{(d0)} = -37$ dBm exactly. Therefore, $P_{(d0)}$ is also one of the important parameters that characterizes environment

In most radio transceiver modules, the measurement of received power is just an auxiliary function. The measured value provided by the module may not be exactly received power in dBm. However, received signal strength indicator (RSSI) is used to represent the condition of received power level. This can be easily converted to a received power by applying offset to calibrate to the correct level.

RSSI is generally implemented in most of the wireless communication standards. The famous standards include IEEE 802.11 and IEEE 802.15.4. RSSI value can be measured in the intermediate frequency stage, which is before the intermediate frequency amplifier, or in the baseband stage of circuits. After obtaining RSSI value, the processor or microcontroller with built-in analog-to-digital converter (ADC) converts it to digital value. This value is then stored in a register of the controller for quick data acquisition.

2.2 RSSI in Indoor Environment

To use RSS ranging method effectively, we have to identify the differences between indoor and outdoor location tracking using RSSI. With RSSI adopted, the performance and implementation methods are totally different between indoor and outdoor. Therefore, if we

just consider indoor location tracking scenario, we are able to simplify system complexity and improve estimation method according to indoor environment.
After going through study and experiments, we considered the differences in design, implementation, and deployment stages. Table 1 illustrates the comparison between indoor and outdoor environment.

	Outdoor	Indoor
Path loss model	Linear	Affected by multi-path and shadowing
Accuracy	Easy to achieve but not necessary (wide space)	Difficult to achieve but important (small space)
Space	Wide and not limited	Small and mostly rectangular
Deployment	Random and ac hoc	Can be planned
Transmission power	Maximum to maintain LQI	Adjusted to avoid interference
Height of reference nodes	Ground	Ceiling
Map	Global	Local

Table 1. Comparison of Indoor and Outdoor Location Tracking (Pu, 2009).

In Table 1, path loss model (Phaiboon, 2002) is a radio signal propagation model, which is used to model the nature of signal attenuation over space. After going through environmental characterization or calibration, we are able to use this model to convert RSSI value to distance value.
In indoor environment, the signal strength is not linear as the distance linearly increased because of multi-path fading (Sklar, 1997) and indoor shadowing (Eltahir, 2007) effects. We have to study a better way to tackle this problem for better estimation accuracy.
From experiments, we knew that non-linear path loss becomes more serious as the size of indoor area (for example, a room) is small, leading to difficult accuracy achievement. However, indoor area is always smaller as compared to outdoor. Thus, the resultant location error becomes obvious as the accuracy is worst.
To calculate the absolute location coordinate, distances among sensor nodes are combined using lateration method. When the number of involved reference nodes is increased, lateration matrix size can be large causing increased computational complexity. Therefore, we can calculate absolute location coordinate by just using three reference nodes in a room (trilateration) (Thomas, et al., 2005). This helps to reduce system complexity and computational power.
In addition, the indoor area is always rectangular shape. During deployment stage, we can carefully plan the location of various reference nodes. Therefore, ac hoc deployment of sensor nodes is not suitable to be used in indoor deployment although many researchers focused on the study of ac hoc sensor network. Through location planning, we can allocate the reference nodes at strategic locations of the squared area (room). Using this kind of deployment, we can further simplify estimation formulas. Hence, in-network processing becomes possible.

Another important difference between indoor and outdoor implementation is the signal transmission power. Our experiments show that radio signal energy spread when it propagates through outdoor free area as shown in Fig. 11. **Error! Reference source not found.** This figure indicates the minimum power required to maintain link quality indicator (LQI) at 100 for various distances. Therefore, transmission power for outdoor environment must be as high as possible to maintain a safety level of LQI, thus ensuring the quality of wireless communication channel.

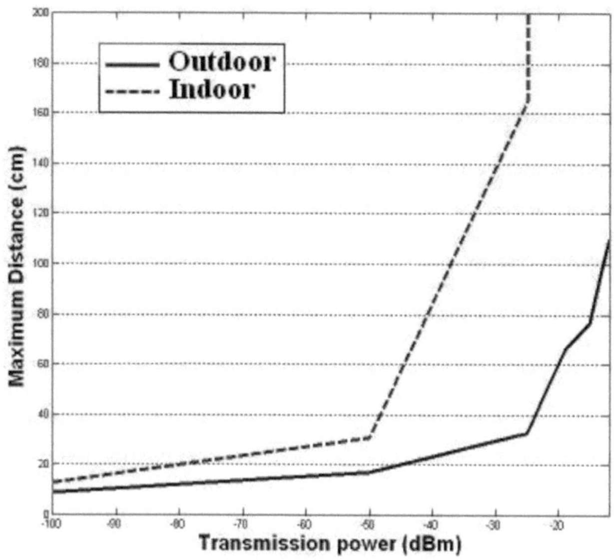

Fig. 11. Minimum Power Required for Communication (Pu, 2009).

On the other hand, signal transmission in indoor environment must be adjusted to suitable level for interference avoidance from neighbor area. It is not encouraged to use the reference sensor nodes located in neighbor area to estimate the location coordinate of the target node in current area. This is because path loss model could be seriously inaccurate and non-linear while radio signal propagates through wall with high signal attenuation. There is no worry about maintaining LQI as difficult as outdoor because the radio signal energy can be conserved within enclosed area.

For outdoor ac hoc deployment, sensor nodes are allocated randomly on ground. However, indoor deployment requires the reference nodes to be fixed beneath ceiling to avoid obstacles and must be the same height among them. This manual installation of reference nodes also needs to be planed for better strategic location. Because of the partitioned area of indoor space, it is more convenient if we display the target node's location using local axis method. In this method, every area has its own axis. To find location in the display map, areas can be differentiated by area ID.

3. Location Tracking System Design and Implementation

The design of a complete location system involves three areas of knowledge including (a) the signal and information processing to compute location information as output, (b) realization of the system by implementing using various technologies available, and (c) acquisition of location data and store, analyze, monitor, and display in a centralized management server. In this chapter, the first two areas are the focus whereas the third area was excluded.

3.1 System Design

In general, the first task to be considered in a location system design work is the core of information handling through signal processing and data mining. This decides how the process goes through from raw signal to valuable information.

3.1.1 System Block Diagram

We need to consider how to find the location coordinate from raw RSSI data. It has to go through several processing steps as shown in Fig. 12.

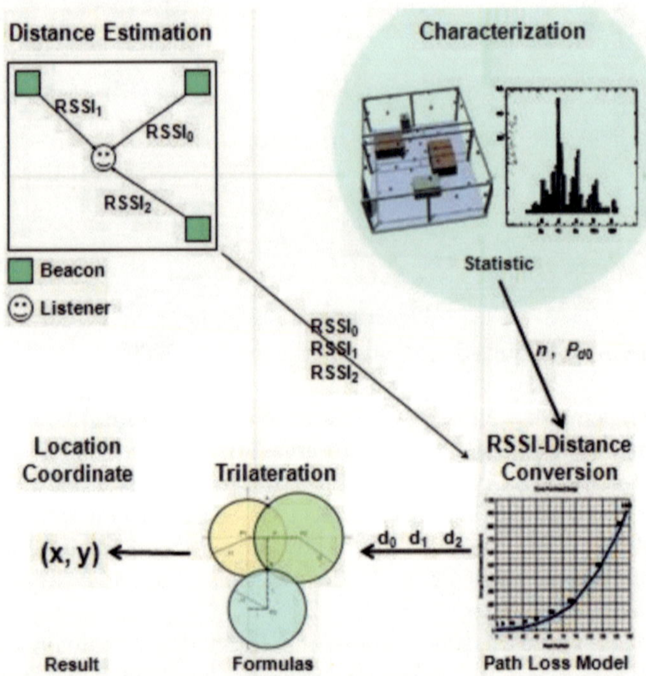

Fig. 12. The Findings of Location from Raw RSSI (Pu, 2009).

In Fig. 12, RSSI values are collected from reference nodes in distance estimation step. Using these RSSI values, we can perform environmental characterization to find suitable parameters for that area. When calibration process is over, the environmental parameters are fixed and will not be change unless large changes happen to the objects within the area.

The next step is to obtain continuous RSSI values from the reference nodes in the online operation. With both RSSI values and environmental parameters ready, we can convert those RSSI values into distance using path loss model.

After RSSI-Distance conversion, we are able to obtain the distances between target sensor node and the reference nodes. By applying trilateration, it combines distances and find the exact location coordinate of the target sensor node within the area. The overall system block diagram is shown in Fig. 13.

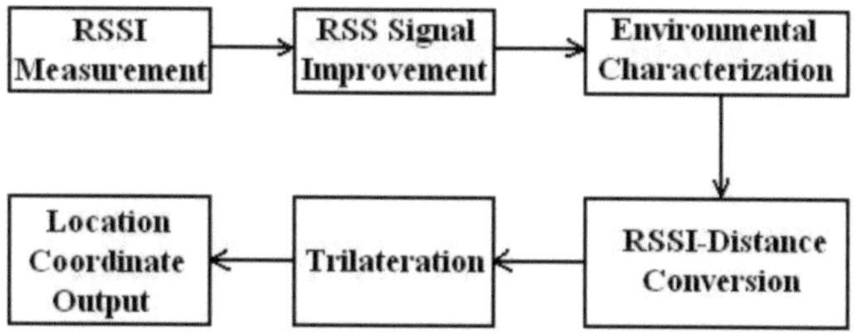

Fig. 13. Overall System Block Diagram (Pu, 2009).

3.1.2 RSSI Measurement Step

In this step, RSSI values are collected from the reference sensor nodes. Practically, RSSI value is not exactly the received power at the RF pins of the radio transceiver. Therefore, it has to be converted to the actual power values in dBm using the following expression (Pu, 2009):

$$P_i = \left(RSSI_i + RSSI_{\text{offset}}\right) \tag{13}$$

where P_i is the actual received power from beacon node i. $RSSI_i$ is the measured RSSI value for reference node i, which is stored in the RSSI register of the radio transceiver. $RSSI_{\text{offset}}$ is the offset found empirically from the front end gain and it is approximately equal to –45 dBm. This is to make sure that the actual received power value has dynamic range from –100 to 0 dBm, where –100 dBm indicates the minimum power that can receive, and 0 dBm indicates the maximum received power.

3.1.3 RSSI Signal Improvement Step

In indoor environment, raw RSSI data is highly uncertain and it is fluctuating over time. The study must go back to the investigation of radio signal propagation in indoor environment. For RSS ranging application, the analysis of the radio propagation manner is slightly different from the well-established theory for just digital communication purpose.

In digital communication, the study of received power is to avoid burst error and ensure high bit-error rate communication. The level change of RSS is not important as long as it is maintained within the safety region. However, when RSS is used in estimating distance, the estimation result is directly based on the level of RSS. Therefore, it is necessary to improve the signal quality of RSS.

From analysis, the reasons of RSSI variation in indoor environment can be well categorized for better understanding as shown in Fig. 14. Based on past research and analysis, we classified the reasons of RSSI variation in terms of both small/large scale and temporal/spatial characteristics. Fig. 14 clearly states all possible reasons of indoor RSSI variation in the two-dimensional classification diagram. In term of scale level, RSSI variation can be fluctuating slowly or quickly if it is in the temporal domain, and fluctuating narrowly or widely if it is in the spatial domain.

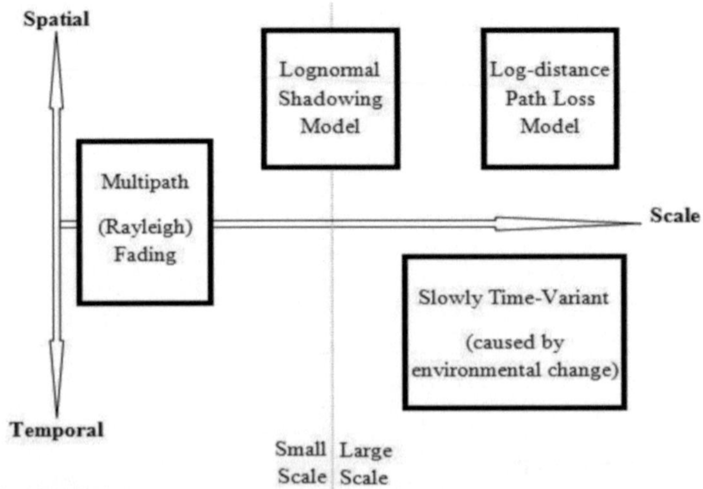

Fig. 14. Types of RSSI Variation in Indoor Environment (Pu, 2009).

Fast fading belongs to small scale variation such as multipath or Rayleigh fading, and environmental changes belongs to large scale variation as it is slowly time-variant. In the spatial domain, RSSI values do not vary in the stationary condition. RSSI values vary only when receiver moves over space or distance. Multipath or Rayleigh fading is also a spatial small scale variation. Log-distance path loss model is a large scale effect in spatial domain. Lognormal shadowing is considered as a medium size variation in the space domain.

To improve RSSI signal from both temporal and spatial variation, we can use a modified version of Kalman filter that estimates the speed of variation and use it to predict the future possible values. Based on past, current and future predicted values, RSSI variation can be reduced. With this, it is also able to cover some parts of small and large scale variation. The update of current RSSI and its variation speed can be found using the following expressions (Pu, 2009):

$$\hat{R}_{est(i)} = \hat{R}_{pred(i)} + a\left(R_{prev(i)} - \hat{R}_{pred(i)}\right) \tag{14}$$

$$\hat{V}_{est(i)} = \hat{V}_{pred(i)} + \frac{b}{T_s}\left(R_{prev(i)} - \hat{R}_{pred(i)}\right) \tag{15}$$

The prediction of the RSSI and its variation speed can be found using the following expressions (Pu, 2009):

$$\hat{R}_{pred(i+1)} = \hat{R}_{est(i)} + \hat{V}_{est(i)} T_s \tag{16}$$

$$\hat{V}_{pred(i+1)} = \hat{V}_{est(i)} \tag{17}$$

where $\hat{R}_{est(i)}$ is the ith estimation value of RSSI, $\hat{R}_{pred(i)}$ is the ith predicted value of RSSI, $R_{prev(i)}$ is the ith previous value of RSSI, $\hat{V}_{est(i)}$ and $\hat{V}_{pred(i)}$ are the ith estimation speed and i^{th} predicted speed. Parameters a and b are the gain constant, T_s is the time duration of samples arrival. After going through this processing, highly fluctuating RSSI values are smoothed and become more stable.

3.1.4 Environmental Characterization Step

In this step, RSSI values are collected with the corresponding location of target node. Using the pair of (RSSI, Location) information to calibrate system parameters to the most appropriate level. After environmental characterization step, the distance estimation of the signal is adjusted to the minimum error state.

The important parameters used to characterize environment include path loss exponent n and the received power $P_{r(d0)}$ measured at distance d_0 to the transmitter. For each enclosed area of indoor environment, a pair of these parameters (n, $P_{r(d0)}$) are used to represent the conditions of the area. To characterize the area for RSS ranging, received power $P_{r(d0)}$ is first measured by allocating a receiver d_0 apart from the transmitter. d_0 is generally fixed at 1 meter. After $P_{r(d0)}$ is obtained, the receiver is moved to other locations to measure path loss exponent n using the following expression (Pu, 2009):

$$n = \frac{P_{r(d0)} - P_{r(d)}}{10 \times \log_{10}(d / d_0)} \tag{18}$$

where $P_{r(d)}$ is the received power of the receiver measured at a distance d to the transmitter, which is expressed in dBm.

Theoretically, every room or area has their environmental parameters. However, the fact is that every location also has their environmental parameters although two locations are in the same room and they are neighbor. The reasons of this problem are from the RSSI variation in indoor environment especially in the medium scale spatial domain variation. Suppose we use inaccurate and uncertain RSSI source for calibration, it is impossible that we are able to obtain accurate environmental parameters from experiments. There will be different environmental parameters obtain at every location. This indeed increases the difficulty of environmental calibration works.

3.1.5 RSSI-Distance Conversion Step

If RSS ranging is used to measure the distances between reference nodes and target node, log-distance path loss model (Phaiboon, 2002) is used to express the relationship between received power and the corresponding distance as shown in the following expression (Pu, 2009):

$$P_{r(d)} = P_{r(d0)} - 10 \times n \times \log_{10}\left(\frac{d}{d_0}\right) \tag{19}$$

After the step of environmental characterization, the two main environmental parameters n and $P_{r(d0)}$ are obtained. Thus, the distance between transmitter and receiver can be estimated using the following expression (Pu, 2009):

$$d = d_0 \exp\left(\frac{P_{r(d0)} - P_{r(d)}}{10n}\right) \tag{20}$$

In this expression, the estimated distance d is in centimeter if the value of d_0 provided is in centimeter such as $d_0 = 100$ cm.

3.1.6 Trilateration Step

In indoor environment, the shapes of target area are in arbitrary shape. The location coordinate of the target node can be estimated using trilateration by applying equation (7). Nevertheless, we are able to implement the reference nodes of location system in a regular way such as in a shape of rectangle or square. This helps to reduce the computation complexity of lateration. Two approaches of strategic reference node allocation can be considered as shown in Fig. 15. **Error! Reference source not found.**

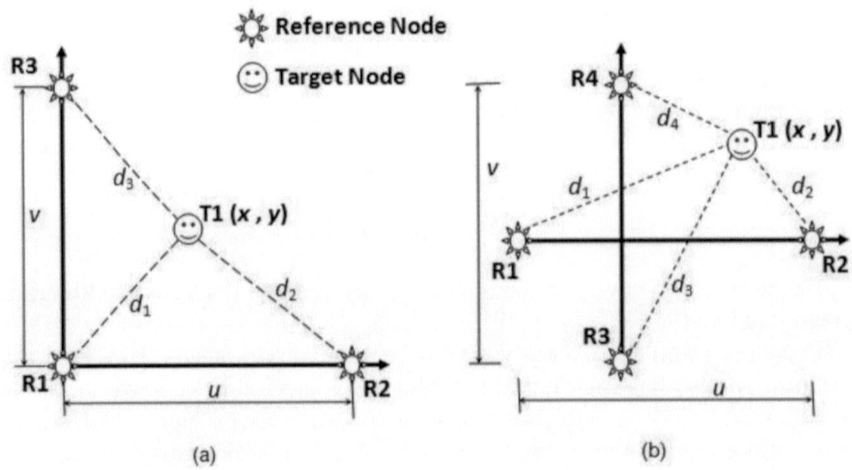

Fig. 15. Locations for Simplified Trilateration (Pu, 2009).

In Fig. 15(a), the reference sensor nodes are located at the corners of the rectangular area. This approach only requires three reference nodes for trilateration. To estimate the location coordinate, two reference sensor nodes R1 and R2 along the x-axis are sufficient to provide inputs for calculating x. Since reference node R1 is aligned with R3 along the y-axis, R1 also can be used together with R3 to provide inputs for calculating y.

In Fig. 15(b), the reference sensor nodes are located at the edges of the rectangular area. This approach requires four reference nodes for trilateration. To estimate the location coordinate of target node, two reference nodes R1 and R2 are used to provide inputs for calculating x while R3 and R4 are used to provide inputs for calculating y.

The distances among sensor nodes (d_1, d_2, d_3, and d_4) are obtained using log-distance path loss model to convert RSSI values to distances. The distances (d_1 and d_2) can be used to determine x as shown in the following expression (Pu, 2009):

$$x = \frac{u^2 + \left(d_1^{\,2} - d_2^{\,2}\right)}{2u} \tag{21}$$

In the first approach, the distances (d_1 and d_3) can be used to determine y as shown in the following expression (Pu, 2009):

$$y = \frac{v^2 + \left(d_1^{\ 2} - d_3^{\ 2}\right)}{2v} \tag{22}$$

In the second approach, the distances (d_3 and d_4) can be used to determine y as shown in the following expression (Pu, 2009):

$$y = \frac{v^2 + \left(d_3^{\ 2} - d_4^{\ 2}\right)}{2v} \tag{23}$$

3.2 Network Implementation

After the flow of location information processing was decided, the next step is to investigate the current technologies available and choose the most suitable solution to implement the operation network. Among many alternatives, WSN technology has the capability to perform such indoor location system works and it provides many advantages for ubiquitous implementation.

These advantages include: low power consumption, devices are not expensive, small size, software configurable and flexible, wide radio coverage, good processing ability, sufficient I/O for sensing and actuating, and etc. Most important factor is that WSN has been well established in various fields of research. Therefore, many resources and good algorithms are available from other research efforts. Hence, WSN was chosen as the main operation network to implement indoor location system.

3.2.1 Network Structure

The construction of the operation network for indoor location system based on WSN is related to the source of raw data and the sink of useful information. Thus, the characteristics of the WSN implementation for indoor location system are investigated and shown in Fig. 16 and the following points:

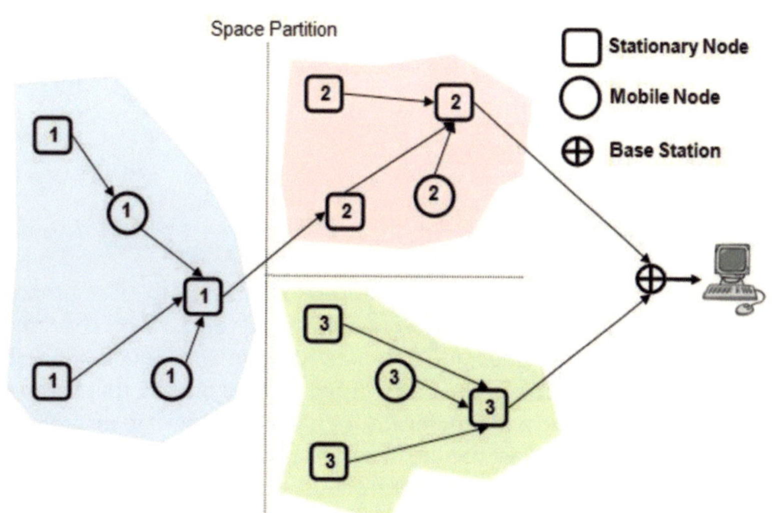

Fig. 16. Network Structure (Pu, 2009).

1. Network is constructed to support monitoring all the time, thus all sources of information send data constantly to a base station.
2. The network is multi-source single sink data network.
3. The data direction is from source to sink, thus no query service is available.
4. According to the movement status of sensor nodes, there are two types of network nodes: stationary and mobile nodes
5. All sensor nodes including stationary and mobile nodes can be an intermediate node for routing packets to base station.
6. The sensor nodes located in the same indoor area can be organized together as a cluster of the network.
7. A cluster consists of both stationary and mobile nodes. Cluster with only stationary nodes is possible but cluster with pure mobile nodes does not exist.

3.2.2 Interaction and Scheduling

For network implementation, communication signals are initiated from mobile nodes. This is to make sure that when mobile node enters a new zone, it is able to wake up all reference nodes. When a reference node cannot hear any mobile node for more than ten seconds, the reference node will be automatically switched to inactive mode. To save power consumption, an accelerometer can be installed into the sensor node. Whenever there is motion, the accelerometer is able to activate mobile node, and the mobile node activates other reference nodes. The communication paths are shown in Fig. 17.

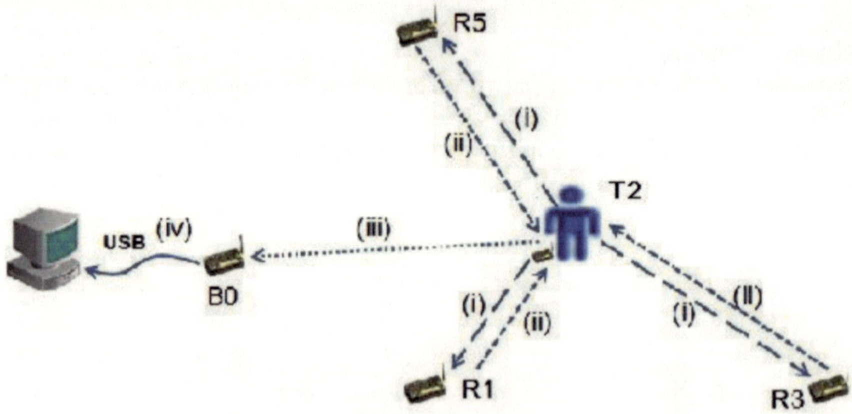

Fig. 17. Interaction and Communication Paths (Pu, 2009).

For communication path (*i*), target node T2 broadcasts a message to all reference nodes (R1, R3, R5). Reference nodes are awaked and reply to T2 with (*ii*). T2 then collects the IDs and RSSI values from all reference nodes and estimate location coordinate of the target node. The resultant location information is then forwarded to base station (B0) through path (*iii*). Base station forwards the data to a computer through USB (*iv*) for display and monitoring.
To save power consumption and last the life of batteries in the sensor nodes, reference nodes are in inactive mode when there is no target node in the area. When a target node moves into the area, the movement of the target node causes motion sensor to generate activation signal. The activation signal is broadcasted to activate all reference nodes in the area.

A problem exists in this interaction among sensor nodes. When the number of reference nodes is increased, the problem becomes more serious. This problem arises because all reference nodes receive the activation signal from target node at the same time. In this case, all reference nodes are synchronized and send estimation signal for RSS ranging at the same time. Therefore, the target node receives all the estimation signals to measure RSSI at the same time. Inevitably, packet loss happens, leading to operation failure.

To solve this problem, transmission scheduling must be considered in the reference nodes. There are three kinds of transmission scheduling can be considered in indoor location tracking system implementation:

1. Use a random number generator to produce time delay t_d for the first estimation signal. The duration of delay can be obtained using the random number n_r (ranged from 0 to 1) as shown in the following expression (Pu, 2009):

$$t_d = T \times n_r \tag{24}$$

2. Use a fixed number n_{id} obtained from the node ID or address to produce time delay t_d for the first estimation signal. The duration of delay can be obtained using the following expression (Pu, 2009):

$$t_d = T \times \frac{n_{id}}{N} \tag{25}$$

3. Use a fixed number n_g obtained from the group ID to produce time delay t_d for the first estimation signal. Group ID is used to differentiate the sensor nodes within the same indoor area or cluster assigned by cluster head. Thus, the duration of delay can be obtained using the following expression (Pu, 2009):

$$t_d = T \times \frac{n_g}{G} \tag{26}$$

where T represents the transmission period of the estimation signal broadcasted from reference nodes, N is the total number of sensor nodes used in the indoor location system network, and G is the total number of member nodes in a cluster.

The first kind of transmission scheduling may still have signal collision problem as two reference nodes generate the same random number. However, the advantage is the ease of implementation. The second kind of transmission scheduling may have problem when the number of total sensor nodes is large and the transmission period T is short. This causes the divided delay time duration too short. In addition, expansion of network increases the total number of nodes, leading to unnecessary reinstallation to all sensor nodes. The third kind of transmission scheduling is a good choice, but it depends on the good clustering result of network.

3.2.3 In-network Processing

Wireless sensor network is formed by spatially distributed wireless sensor motes that are able to work independently or cooperatively with other sensor motes. Due to the size constraint, the individual device in wireless sensor network is normally limited in processing capability, storage capacity, communication bandwidth, and battery power supply (Culler, et al., 2004). The battery life-time and the communication bandwidth usage are generally treated higher priority than the rest since in most applications, battery may not be frequently recharged or replaced. Saving bandwidth or reducing the data transmission among sensor nodes also means reducing power consumption used in communication. Therefore, various algorithms such as collaborative signal processing, adaptive system, distributed algorithm, and sensor fusion were developed for low power and bandwidth applications.

Recently, a new trend of study is focused on in-network processing and intelligent system such as (Tseng, et al., 2007) and (Yang, et al., 2007). For the applications of location tracking, (Liu, et al., 2003) develop the initial concept of collaborative in-network processing for target tracking. The focus is on vehicle tracking using acoustic and direction-of-arrival sensors. (Lin, et al., 2004, 2006) presents in-network moving object tracking. The way of tracking object is based on detection in a mass deployment of sensor nodes.

In general, the received RSSI values from reference nodes are sent to base station immediately. The based station is an interface between WSN and computer, which collects sufficient RSSI values and forwards them to the computer. In this case, location estimation task is performed and stored in the computer.

Besides the monitoring of user's activities, location information also can be used to support the needs of network routing, data sensing, information query, self-organization, task scheduling, field coverage, and etc. If the sensor nodes need the resultant location information for decision making, the computer has to send the computed location estimation result back to sensor nodes through the network. In this way, location estimation does not consume processing power in the sensor nodes but this greatly increases the wireless data transmission traffic for multi-user condition.

For a compromise, it is better to let the sensor nodes to collect all RSSI values and estimate location coordinates locally within the WSN. The estimated location information is then forwarded to a computer for monitoring or display. This approach also provides fast location update rate due to short packets used. If the location information can be updated immediately, the response and operation sensing tasks can be active, and the time taken for decision making is short. The architectures of estimating location coordinate in a computer and in sensor nodes are shown in Fig. 18.

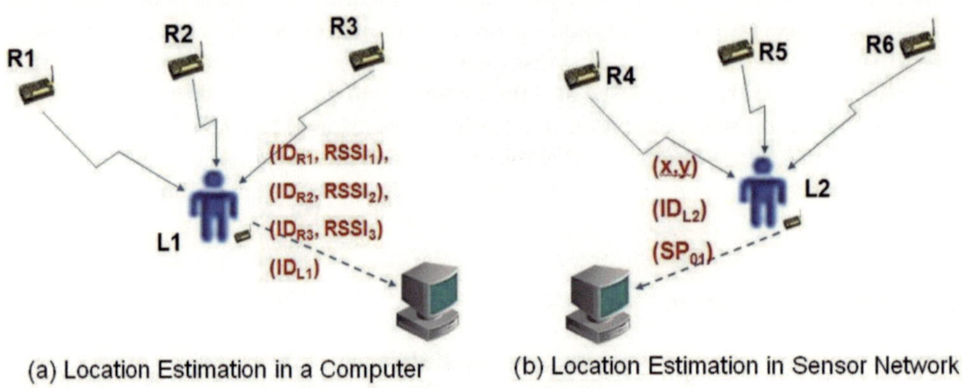

Fig. 18. Two Scenarios of Location Estimation (Pu, 2009).

In Fig. 18(a), R1 to R3 are reference nodes in the area. A mobile node L1 is hold by a user and moving around the area. L1 collects data from all reference nodes, and forwards them to a computer. The packet includes the ID of each reference nodes (ID_{R1}, ID_{R2}, ID_{R3},), RSSI values from each reference node ($RSSI_1$, $RSSI_2$, $RSSI_{3}$,), and the ID of the mobile node (ID_{L1}). If the number of reference node increases, the packet size would be large. This largely increases network traffic and load.

In Fig. 18 (b), R4 to R6 are reference nodes in the area. A mobile node L2 is hold by user and moving around the area. L2 collects data from all reference nodes, and perform location estimation locally. The resultant packet is then forwarded to computer. Hence, the packet only includes the coordinate (x, y), space ID (SP_{01}), and the ID of the mobile node (ID_{L2}). If the number of reference node increases, the packet size does not increase but still remains small and constant because only the estimation result is forwarded to computer.

Wireless sensor network have substantial processing capability in the aggregate, but not individually. For most of the low-power mobile device such as wireless sensor motes, the processors or microcontrollers are limited in computational capability. For this reason, indoor location estimation algorithms must be simple and ease of implementation.

For ensuring light-weight processing and tool-independent programming, it is necessary to consider carefully that algorithms, mathematical calculations and processing are simple and programmable to any low-power mobile devices which have limitation and constraints. The main computational loads are in RSSI-distance conversion step and in trilateration step. Computation using trilateration can be simplified by carefully planning the locations of reference nodes at strategic locations and applying equations (21) to (23).

However, the computation of RSSI-distance conversion is not easy to be implemented in a resource and computational power limited sensor node. This is because the computation of exponential function is required in the equation (20), which generates large number if the input data is not stable. To solve this problem, Taylor series can be used to avoid exponential computation and simplify the calculation by selecting appropriate length of expression L as shown in the following expression (Pu, 2009):

$$d = d_0 \times \left(1 + \frac{x^1}{1!} + \frac{x^2}{2!} + \frac{x^3}{3!} + \ldots \frac{x^L}{L!}\right) = d_0 \times \left(1 + \sum_{i=1}^{L} \frac{x^i}{i!}\right) \tag{27}$$

where

$$x = \ln(10) \times \left(\frac{P_{r(d0)} - P_{r(d)}}{10n}\right) \tag{28}$$

4. Conclusions

This chapter is to provide essential knowledge on the development of a location awareness system for location monitoring in ubiquitous applications. The location system must be able to estimate fine-grained location in indoor environment. Wireless sensor network was selected as the main body of the system. All data from wireless sensor network are sent to a base station for centralized operation and management.

Based on the way of ranging, location system can be time measurement or signal measurement. Time measurement can be achieved using the combination of RF and ultrasound for time difference of arrival (TDOA). Signal measurement can be achieved by converting received signal strength indicator (RSSI) to distance. Since RSSI does not need additional dedicated devices for ranging, and the power consumption is much lower than other distance measurement methods, it was selected as the ranging method in this research. With the existing technology, RSSI ranging is still not a perfect solution for fine-grained location tracking because of inaccurate and uncertain input data when it is used in indoor environment. Therefore, it is required to be improved through research studies. Three important processes of indoor location tracking can be studied to improve the performance. First, the signal quality of RSSI in indoor environment must be studied for accuracy and precision improvement. Second, the methods used for environmental characterization need to be re-investigated so that a convenient and effective calibration method or procedure can be developed to obtained accurate environmental parameters. Third, the positioning algorithm must be reconsidered to exploit an innovative way of location estimation that may provide advantages additional to traditional positioning algorithm.

5. References

Abdalla, M.; Feeney, S. M. & Salous, S. (2003). Antenna Array and Quadrature Calibration for Angle of Arrival Estimation, SCI, Florida, July 2003.

Bulusu, N.; Heidemann, J. & Estrin, D. (2000). GPS-less Low Cost Outdoor Localization for Very Small Devices, *IEEE Personal Communications Magazine*, vol.7, no.5, pp.28–34.

Cong, T.-X.; Kim, E. & Koo, I. (2008). An Efficient RSS-Based Localization Scheme with Calibration in Wireless Sensor Networks, *IEICE Trans. Communications*, vol.E91-B, no.12, pp.4013–4016.

Culler, D.; Estrin, D. & Srivastava, M. (2004). Guest Editors's Introduction: Overview of Sensor Networks, *IEEE Computer Society*, vol. 37, no. 8, pp.41–49.

Eltahir, I. K. (2007). The Impact of Different Radio Propagation Models for Mobile Ad hoc NETworks (MANET) in Urban Area Environment, AusWireless, pp. 30–38, Sydney, Australia, Aug 2007.

Favre-Bulle, B.; Prenninger, J. & Eitzinger, C. (1998). Efficient Tracking of 3D-Robot Positions by Dynamic Triangulation, MTC, pp.446–449, St. Paul, Minnesota, May 1998.

He, J. (2008). Optimizing 2-D Triangulations by the Steepest Descent Method, PACIIA, pp.939–943, Wuhan, China, December 2008.

He, T.; Huang, C.; Blum, B. M.; Stankovic, J. A. & Abdelzaher, T. F. (2005). Range-Free Localization and Its Impact on Large Scale Sensor Networks, *ACM Trans. Embedded Computing Systems*, vol.4, no.4, November 2005, pp.877–906.

Hightower, J. & Borriello, G. (2001). Location Systems for Ubiquitous Computing, *IEEE Computer*, vol.34, no.8, August 2001, pp.57–66.

Kamath, S.; Meisner, E. & Isler, V. (2007). Triangulation Based Multi Target Tracking with Mobile Sensor Networks, ICRA, pp.3283–3288, Roma, Italy, April 2007.

Li, X.-Y.; Calinescu, G.; Wan, P.-J. & Wang, Y. (2003). Localized Delaunay Triangulation with Application in Ad Hoc Wireless Networks, *IEEE Trans. Parallel and Distributed Systems*, vol.14, no.10, pp.1035–1047.

Li, X.-Y.; Wang, Y. & Frieder, O. (2003). Localized Routing for Wireless Ad Hoc Networks, ICC, pp.443-447, Anchorage, Alaska, USA, May 2003.

Lin C.-Y. & Tseng, Y.-C. (2004). Structures for In-Network Moving Object Tracking in Wireless Sensor Networks, BROADNET, pp.718–727, San Jose, California, USA, 2004.

Lin, C.-Y.; Peng, W.-C. & Tseng, Y.-C. (2006). Efficient In-network Moving Object Tracking in Wireless Sensor Network, *IEEE Transactions on Mobile Computing*, vol.5, no.8, pp.1044–1056.

Liu, J.; Reich, J. & Zhao, F. (2003). Collaborative In-Network Processing for Target Tracking, *EURASIP Journal on Applied Signal Processing*, vol.4, pp.378–391.

Mak, L. C & Furukawa, T. (2006). A ToA-based Approach to NLOS Localization Usiong Low-Frequency Sound, ACRA, Auckland, New Zealand, December 2006.

Najar, M. & Vidal, J. (2001). Kalman Tracking based on TDOA for UMTS Mobile Location, PIMRC, pp.B45-B49, San Diego, California, USA, September 2001.

Nakajima, N. (2007). Indoor Wireless Network for Person Location Identification and Vital Data Collection, ISMICT, Oulu, Finland, December 2007.

Niculescu, D. & Nath, B. (2003). DV Based Positioning in Ad hoc Networks. *Journal of Telecommunication Systems*, vol.22, no.1-4, pp.1018–4864.

Phaiboon, S. (2002). An Empirically Based Path Loss Model for Indoor Wireless Channels in Laboratory Building, IEEE TENCON, pp.1020–1023, vol.2, October 2002.

Pu, C.-C. (2009). *Development of a New Collaborative Ranging Algorithm for RSSI Indoor Location Tracking in WSN*, PhD Thesis, Dongseo University, South Korea.

Rao, S.V.; Xu, X. & Sahni, S. (2007). A Computational Geometry Method for DTOA Triangulation, ICIF, pp.1-7, Quebec, Canada, July 2007.

Rice, A & Harle, R. (2005). Evaluating Lateration-based Positioning Algorithms for Fine-grained Tracking, DIALM-POMC, pp.54–61, Cologne, Germany, September 2005.

Satyanarayana, D. & Rao, S. V. (2008). Local Delaunay Triangulation for Mobile Nodes, ICETET, pp.282-287, Nagpur, Maharashtra, India, July 2008.

Savvides, A.; Han, C.-C. & Mani, B. (2001). Strivastava. Dynamic Fine-Grained Localization in Ad-Hoc Networks of Sensors, MobiCom, pp.166–179, Rome, Italy, July 2001.

Sklar, B. (1997). Rayleigh Fading Channels in Mobile Digital Communication Systems: Characterization and Mitigation, *IEEE Communications Magazine*, vol. 35, no. 7, pp. 90–109.

Smith, A.; Balakrishnan, H.; Goraczko, M. & Priyantha, N. (2004). Tracking Moving Devices with the Cricket Location System, MobiSYS, pp.190–202, Boston, USA.

Thomas, F. & Ros, L. (2005). Revisiting Trilateration for Robot Localization, *IEEE Robotics*, vol.21, no.1, pp.93–101.

Tian, H.; Wang, S. & Xie, H. (2007). Localization using Cooperative AOA Approach, WiCOM, pp.2416–2419, Shanghai, China, September 2007.

Tseng, Y.-C; Chen, C.-C.; Lee, C. & Huang, Y.-K. (2007). Incremental In-Network RNN Search in Wireless Sensor Networks, ICPPW, pp.64–64, XiAn, China, September 2007.

Yang, H.-Y.; Peng, W.-C. & Lo, C.-H. (2007). Optimizing Multiple In-Network Aggregate Queries in Wireless Sensor Networks, *LNCS*, vol.4443, pp.870–875.

Zhao, F.; Liu, J.; Liu, J.; Guibas, L. & Reich, J. (2003). Collaborative signal and information processing: an information directed approach, *Proc. IEEE*, vol.91, no.8, pp.1199–1209.

Zhao, F. & Guibas, L. J. (2004). *Wireless Sensor Networks: An Information Processing Approach*, Elsevier: Morgan Kaufmann Series.

12

Mobile Location Tracking Scheme for Wireless Sensor Networks with Deficient Number of Sensor Nodes

Po-Hsuan Tseng, Wen-Jiunn Liu and Kai-Ten Feng
Department of Communication Engineering, National Chiao Tung University
Taiwan, R.O.C.

1.Introduction

A wireless sensor network (WSN) consists of sensor nodes (SNs) with wireless communication capabilities for specific sensing tasks. Among different applications, wireless location technologies which are designated to estimate the position of SNs (Geziciet al., 2005) (Haraet al., 2005) (Patwari et al., 2005)have drawn a lot of attention over the past few decades. There are increasing demands for commercial applications to adopt location tracking information within their system design, such as navigation systems, location-based billing, health care systems, and intelligent transportation systems. With emergent interests in location-based services (Perusco & Michael, 2007), location estimation and tracking algorithms with enhanced precision become necessitate for the applications under different circumstances.

The location estimation schemes have been widely proposed and employed in the wireless communication system. These schemes locate the position of a mobile sensor (MS) based on the measured radio signals from its neighborhood anchor nodes (ANs). The representative algorithms for the measured distance techniques are the Time-Of-Arrival (TOA),the Time Difference-Of-Arrival (TDOA), and the Angle-Of-Arrival (AOA). The TOA scheme measures the arrival time of the radio signals coming from different wireless BSs; while the TDOA scheme measures the time difference between the radio signals. The AOA technique is conducted within the BS by observing the arriving angle of the signals coming from the MS.

It is recognized that the equations associated with the location estimation schemes are inherently nonlinear. The uncertainties induced by the measurement noises make it more difficult to acquire the estimated MS position with tolerable precision. The Taylor Series Expansion (TSE) method was utilized in(Foy, 1976) to acquire the location estimation of the MS from the TOA measurements. The method requires iterative processes to obtain the location estimate from a linearized system. The major drawback of the TSE scheme is that it may suffer from the convergence problem due to an incorrect initial guess of the MS's position. The two-step Least Square (LS) method was adopted to solve the location estimation problem from the TOA (Wanget al., 2003), the TDOA (Chen& Ho, 1994), and the hybrid TOA/TDOA(Tseng & Feng, 2009) measurements. It is an approximate realization of the Maximum Likelihood (ML) estimator and does not require iterative processes. The two-step LS scheme is advantageous in its computational efficiency with adequate accuracy for location estimation.

In addition to the estimation of a MS's position, trajectory tracking of a moving MS has been studied. The Extended Kalman Filter (EKF) scheme is considered the well-adopted method for location tracking. The EKF algorithm estimates the MS's position, speed, and acceleration via the linearization of measurement inputs. The Kalman Tracking (KT) scheme (Nájar& Vidal,2001) distinguishes the linear part from the originally nonlinear equations for location estimation. The linear aspect is exploited within the Kalman filtering formulation; while the nonlinear term is served as an external measurement input to the Kalman filter. The Cascade Location Tracking(CLT) scheme (Chen &Feng, 2005) utilizes the two-step LS method for initial location estimation of the MS.The Kalman filtering technique is employed to smooth out and to trace the position of the MS based on its previously estimated data.

With the characteristics of simplicity and high accuracy, the range-based positioning method based on triangulation approach is considered according to the time-of-arrival measurements. The location of a MS can be estimated and traced from the availability of enough SNs with known positions, denoted as anchor nodes ANs. In general, at least three ANs are required to perform two-dimensional location estimation for an MS. However, enough signal sources for location estimation and tracking may not always happen under the WSN scenarios. Unlike the regular deployment of satellites or cellular base stations, the ANs within the WSN are in general spontaneously and arbitrarily deployed. Even though there can be high density of SNs within certain area, the number of ANs with known position can still be limited. Moreover, the transmission ranges for SNs are comparably shorter than both the satellite-based (Kuusniemi et al., 2007) and the cellular-based (Zhao, 2002) systems. Therefore, there is high probability for the node deficiency problem (i.e., the number of available ANs is less than three) to occur within the WSN, especially under the situations that the SNs are moving. Due to the deficiency of signal sources, most of the existing location estimation and tracking schemes becomes inapplicable for the WSNs.

In this book chapter, a predictive location tracking (PLT) algorithm is proposed to alleviate the problem with insufficient measurement inputs for the WSNs. Location tracking can still be performed even with only two ANs or a single AN available to be exploited. The predictive information obtained from the Kalman filtering technique (Zaidi & Mark, 2005) is adopted as the virtual signal sources, which are incorporated into the two-step least square method for location estimation and tracking. Persistent accuracy for location tracking can be achieved by adopting the proposed PLT scheme, especially under the situations with inadequate signal sources. Numerical results demonstrate that the proposed PLT algorithm can achieve better precision in comparison with other location tracking schemes under the WSNs.

2. Preliminaries

2.1 Mathematical Modeling

In order to facilitate the design of the proposed PLT algorithm, the signal model for the TOA measurements is utilized. The set $\mathbf{r}_k$contains all the available measured relative distance at the k^{th}time step, i.e., $\mathbf{r}_k = \{ r_{1,k}, r_{2,k}, \ldots, r_{i,k}, \ldots, r_{N_k,k} \}$, where N_k denotes the number of available ANs. The measured relative distance ($r_{i,k}$) between the MS and the i^{th}AN(obtained at the k^{th}time step) can be represented as

$$r_{i,k} = c \cdot t_{i,k} = \zeta_{i,k} + n_{i,k} + e_{i,k} \qquad (1)$$

Where $t_{i,k}$ denotes the TOA measurement obtained from the i^{th}AN at the k^{th}time step, and c is the speed of light. $r_{i,k}$ is contaminated with the TOA measurement noise $n_{i,k}$and the NLOS error $e_{i,k}$. It is noted that the measurement noise $n_{i,k}$is in general considered as zero mean with Gaussian distribution. On the other hand, the NLOS error $e_{i,k}$is modeled as exponentially-distributed for representing the positive bias due to the NLOS effect (Lee, 1993). The noiseless relative distance $\zeta_{i,k}$in (1) between the MS's true position and the i^{th}AN can be obtained as

$$\zeta_{i,k} = [(x_k - x_{i,k})^2 + (y_k - y_{i,k})^2]^{1/2} \qquad (2)$$

where $\mathbf{x}_k = [x_k y_k]$ represents the MS's true position and $\mathbf{x}_{i,k} = [x_{i,k} y_{i,k}]$ is the location of the i^{th}AN for i = 1 to N_k. Therefore, the set of all the available ANs at the k^{th}time step can be obtained as $\mathbf{P}_{AN,k} = \{ \mathbf{x}_{1,k}, \mathbf{x}_{2,k}, \ldots, \mathbf{x}_{i,k}, \ldots, \mathbf{x}_{N_k,k} \}$.

2.2Two-Step LS Estimator

The two-step LS scheme (Chen& Ho, 1994) is utilized as the baseline location estimator for the proposed predictive location tracking algorithms. It is noticed that three TOA measurements are required for the two-step LS method in order to solve for the location estimation problem. The concept of the two-step LS scheme is to acquire an intermediate location estimate in the first step with the definition of a new variable β_k, which is mathematically related to the MS's position, i.e., $\beta_k = x_k^2 + y_k^2$. At this stage, the variable $\beta_k$is assumed to be uncorrelated to the MS's position. This assumption effectively transforms the nonlinear equations for location estimation into a set of linear equations, which can be directly solved by the LS method. Moreover, the elements within the associated covariance matrix are selected based on the standard deviation from the measurements. The variations within the corresponding signal paths are therefore considered within the problem formulation.

The second step of the method primarily considers the relationship that the variable $\beta_k$is equal to $x_k^2 + y_k^2$, which was originally assumed to be uncorrelated in the first step. Improved location estimation can be obtained after the adjustment from the second step. The detail algorithm of the two-step LS method for location estimation can be found in (Chen& Ho, 1994) (Cong & Zhuang, 2002) (Wang et al., 2003).

3. Architecture overview of proposed PLT algorithm

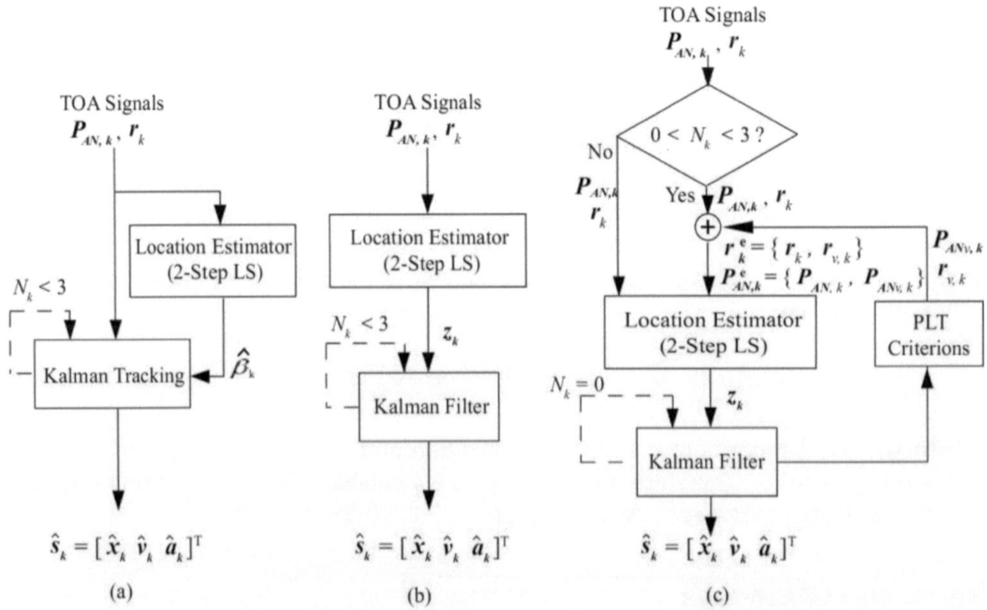

Fig. 1.The architecture diagrams of (a) the KT scheme; (b) the CLTscheme; and (c) the proposed PLT scheme.

The objective of the proposed PLT algorithm is to utilize the predictive information acquired from the Kalman filter to serve as the assisted measurement inputs while the environments are deficient with signal sources. Fig. 1 illustrates the system architectures of the KT(Nájar& Vidal,2001), the CLT (Chen & Feng, 2005) and the proposed PLT scheme. The TOA signals ($\mathbf{r}_k$as in (1)) associated with the corresponding location set of the ANs ($\mathbf{P}_{AN,k}$) are obtained as the signal inputs to each of the system, which result in the estimated state vector of the MS, i.e.$\hat{\mathbf{s}}_k = [\,\hat{\mathbf{x}}_k \hat{\mathbf{v}}_k \hat{\mathbf{a}}_k]^T$where $\hat{\mathbf{x}}_k = [\,\hat{x}_k \hat{y}_k]$ represents the MS's estimated position, $\hat{\mathbf{v}}_k = [\,\hat{v}_{x,k} \hat{v}_{y,k}]$ is the estimated velocity, and $\hat{\mathbf{a}}_k = [\,\hat{a}_{x,k} \hat{a}_{y,k}]$= denotes the estimated acceleration.
Since the equations (i.e., (1) and (2)) associated with the location estimation are intrinsically nonlinear, different mechanisms are considered within the existing algorithms for location tracking. The KT scheme (as shown in Fig. 1.(a)) explores the linear aspect of location estimation within the Kalman filtering formulation; while the nonlinear term (i.e.,$\hat{\beta}_k = \hat{x}_k^2 + \hat{y}_k^2$) is treated as an additional measurement input to the Kalman filter. It is stated within the KT scheme that the value of the nonlinear term can be obtained from an external location estimator, e.g. via the two-step LS method. Consequently, the estimation accuracy of the KT algorithm greatly depends on the precision of the additional location estimator. On the other hand, the CLT scheme (as illustrated in Fig. 1.(b)) adopts the two-step LS method to acquire the preliminary location estimate of the MS. The Kalman Filter is utilized to smooth out the estimation error by tracing the estimated state vector $\hat{\mathbf{s}}_k$of the MS.

The architecture of the proposed PLT scheme is illustrated in Fig. 1.(c). It can be seen that the PLT algorithm will be thesame as the CLT scheme while $N_k \geq 3$, i.e. the number of available ANs is greater than or equal to three. However, the effectiveness of the PLT schemes is revealed as$1 \leq N_k < 3$, i.e. with deficient measurement inputs. The predictive state information obtained from the Kalman filter is utilized for acquiring the assisted information, which will be fed back into the location estimator. The extended sets for the locations of the ANs (i.e., $\mathbf{P}^e_{AN,k} = \{\mathbf{P}_{AN,k}, \mathbf{P}_{AN_v,k}\}$) and the measured relative distances(i.e.,$\mathbf{r}^e_k = \{\mathbf{r}_k, \mathbf{r}_{v,k}\}$) will be utilized as the inputs to thelocation estimator. The sets of the virtual ANs' locations$\mathbf{P}_{AN_v,k}$and the virtual measurements $\mathbf{r}_{v,k}$are defined asfollows.

Definition 1 (Virtual Anchor Nodes). Within the PLT formulation, the virtual Anchor Nodes are considered as the designed locations for assisting the location tracking of the MS under the environments with deficient signal sources. The set of virtual ANs $\mathbf{P}_{AN_v,k}$ is defined under two different numbers of N_k as

$$\mathbf{P}_{AN_v,k} = \begin{cases} \{\mathbf{x}_{v1,k}\} & \text{for } N_k = 2 \\ \{\mathbf{x}_{v1,k}, \quad \mathbf{x}_{v2,k}\} & \text{for } N_k = 1 \end{cases} \tag{3}$$

Definition 2 (Virtual Measurements). Within thePLT formulation, the virtual measurements are utilized to provide assisted measurement inputs while the signal sources are insufficient. Associating with the designed set of virtual ANs $\mathbf{P}_{AN_v,k}$, the corresponding set of virtual measurements is defined as

$$\mathbf{r}_{v,k} = \begin{cases} \{r_{v1,k}\} & \text{for } N_k = 2 \\ \{r_{v1,k}, \quad r_{v2,k}\} & \text{for } N_k = 1 \end{cases} \tag{4}$$

It is noticed that the major task of the PLT scheme is to design and to acquire the values of $\mathbf{P}_{AN_v,k}$and $\mathbf{r}_{v,k}$for the two cases (i.e. $N_k = 1$ and2) with inadequate signal sources. In both the KT andthe CLT schemes, the estimated state vector $\hat{\mathbf{s}}_k$can onlybe updated by the internal prediction mechanism of the Kalman filter while there are insufficient numbers of ANs (i.e.,$N_k < 3$ as shown in Fig. 1.(a) and 1.(b) with the dashed lines). The location estimator (i.e., the two-step LS method) is consequently disabled owing to the inadequate number of the signal sources. The tracking capabilities of both schemes significantly depend on the correctness of the Kalman filter's prediction mechanism. Therefore, the performance for location tracking can be severely degraded due to the changing behavior of the MS, i.e., with the variations from the MS's acceleration.

On the other hand, the proposed PLT algorithm can still provide satisfactory tracking performance with deficient measurement inputs, i.e., with $N_k = 1$ and 2. Under these circumstances, the locationestimator is still effective with the additional virtual ANs $\mathbf{P}_{AN_v,k}$and the virtual measurements$\mathbf{r}_{v,k}$, whichare imposed from the predictive output of the Kalman filter (as shown in Fig. 1.(c)). It is also noted that the PLT scheme will perform the same as the CLT method under the case with no signal input, i.e., under$N_k = 0$. The virtual ANs' location set $\mathbf{P}_{AN_v,k}$andthe virtual measurements $\mathbf{r}_{v,k}$by exploiting the PLTformulation are presented in the next section.

4. Formulation of PLT algorithm

The proposed PLT scheme will be explained in this section. As shown in Fig. 1.(c), the measurement and state equations for the Kalman filter can be represented as

$$\mathbf{z}_k = \mathbf{M} \cdot \hat{\mathbf{s}}_k + m_k \tag{5}$$

$$\hat{\mathbf{s}}_k = \mathbf{F} \cdot \hat{\mathbf{s}}_{k-1} + p_k \tag{6}$$

where $\hat{\mathbf{s}}_k = [\,\hat{\mathbf{x}}_k \hat{\mathbf{v}}_k \hat{\mathbf{a}}_k]^T$. The variables m_k and p_k denotethe measurement and the process noises associated withthe covariance matrices R and Q within the Kalman filtering formulation. The measurement vector $\mathbf{z}_k = [\,\hat{\mathbf{x}}_{ls,k} \hat{\mathbf{y}}_{ls,k}]^T$ represents the measurement input whichis obtained from the output of the two-step LS estimatorat the kth time step (as in Fig. 1.(c)). The matrix M and the state transition matrix F can be obtained as

$$\mathbf{M} = \begin{bmatrix} 1 & 0 & 00 & 0 & 0 \\ 0 & 1 & 00 & 0 & 0 \end{bmatrix} \tag{7}$$

$$\mathbf{F} = \begin{bmatrix} 1 & 0 & \Delta t & 0 & 0.5\Delta t^2 & 0 \\ 0 & 1 & 0 & \Delta t & 0 & 0.5\Delta t^2 \\ 0 & 0 & 1 & 0 & \Delta t & 0 \\ 0 & 0 & 0 & 1 & 0 & \Delta t \\ 0 & 0 & 0 & 0 & 1 & 0 \\ 0 & 0 & 0 & 0 & 0 & 1 \end{bmatrix} \tag{8}$$

whereΔtdenotes the sample time interval. The mainconcept of the PLT scheme is to provide additional virtual measurements (i.e.,$\mathbf{r}_{v,k}$as in (4)) to the two-step LS estimator while the signal sources are insufficient. Two cases (i.e. the two-ANs case and the single-AN case) are considered in the following subsections.

4.1Two-ANs case

As shown in Fig. 2, it is assumed that only two ANs (i.e., $AN_1$and AN_2) associated with two TOA measurements are available at the time step k in consideration. The main target is to introduce an additional virtual AN along with its virtual measurement (i.e., $\mathbf{P}_{AN_v,k} = \{\,\mathbf{x}_{v1,k}\,\}$and $\mathbf{r}_{v,k} = \{\,r_{v1,k}\,\}$) by acquiring the predictive output information from the Kalman filter. Knowing that there are predicting and correcting phases within the Kalman filtering formulation, the predictive state can therefore be utilized to compute the supplementary virtual measurement $r_{v1,k}$ as

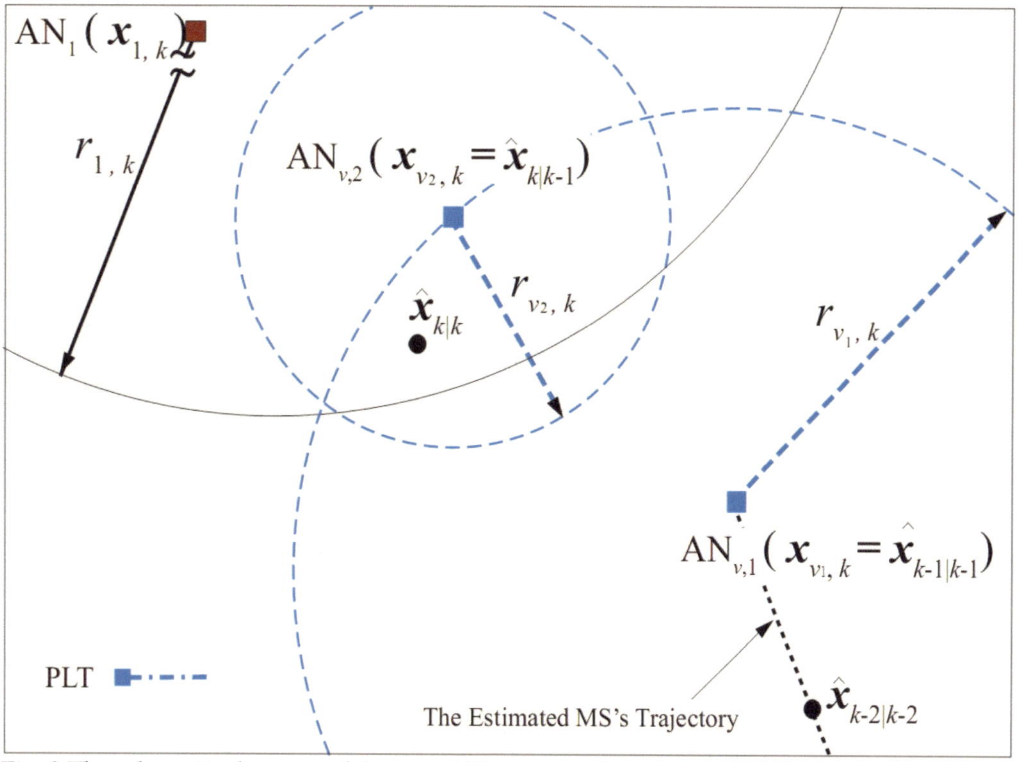

Fig. 2.The schematic diagram of the two-ANs case for the proposed PLT scheme.

$$\begin{aligned} r_{v1,k} &= \left\|\hat{\mathbf{x}}_{k\,|\,k-1} - \hat{\mathbf{x}}_{k-1\,|\,k-1}\right\| \\ &= \left\|\, M \cdot F \cdot \hat{\mathbf{s}}_{k-1\,|\,k-1} - \hat{\mathbf{x}}_{k-1\,|\,k-1}\right\| \end{aligned} \tag{9}$$

where $\hat{x}_{k\,|\,k-1}$ denotes the predicted MS's position at time step k; while $\hat{x}_{k-1\,|\,k-1}$ is the corrected (i.e., estimated) MS's position obtained at the (k - 1)th time step. It is noticed that both values are available at the (k - 1)th time step. The virtual measurement $r_{v1,k}$ isdefined as the distance between the previous locationestimate ($\hat{x}_{k-1\,|\,k-1}$) as the position of the virtual AN (i.e., AN$_{v,1}$: $x_{v1,k} \triangleq \hat{x}_{k-1\,|\,k-1}$) and the predicted MS's position($\hat{x}_{k\,|\,k-1}$) as the possible position of the MS as shown in Fig. 2. It is also noted that the corrected state vector$\hat{s}_{k-1\,|\,k-1}$is available at the current time step k. However, due to the insufficient measurement input, the state vector $\hat{s}_{k\,|\,k}$is unobtainable at the kth time step while adopting the conventional two-step LS estimator. By exploiting $r_{v1,k}$ (in (9)) as the additional signal input, the measurement vector z_k can be acquired after thethree measurement inputs $r_k^e = \{r_{1,k}, r_{2,k}, r_{v1,k}\}$and thelocations of the ANs $P_{AN,k}^e = \{x_{1,k}, x_{2,k}, x_{v1,k}\}$have beenimposed into the two-step LS estimator. As $\mathbf{z}_k$has beenobtained, the corrected state vector $\hat{s}_{k\,|\,k}$can be updatedwith the implementation of the correcting phase of the Kalman filter at the time step k as

$$\hat{\mathbf{s}}_{k|k} = \hat{\mathbf{s}}_{k|k-1} + \mathbf{P}_{k|k-1}\mathbf{M}^T\left[\mathbf{M}\mathbf{P}_{k|k-1}\mathbf{M}^T + \mathbf{R}\right]^{-1}(\mathbf{z}_k - \mathbf{M}\hat{\mathbf{s}}_{k|k-1}) \tag{10}$$

where

$$\mathbf{P}_{k|k-1} = \mathbf{F}\mathbf{P}_{k|k-1}\mathbf{F}^{T} + \mathbf{Q} \tag{11}$$

and

$$\mathbf{P}_{k-1|k-1} = [\mathbf{I} - \mathbf{P}_{k-1|k-2}\mathbf{M}^{T}(\mathbf{M}\mathbf{P}_{k-1|k-2}\mathbf{M}^{T} + \mathbf{R})^{-1}\mathbf{M}] \cdot \mathbf{P}_{k-1|k-2} \tag{12}$$

It is noted that $\mathbf{P}_{k|k-1}$ and $\mathbf{P}_{k-1|k-1}$ represent the predicted and the corrected estimation covariance within the Kalman filter. **I** in (12) is denoted as an identity matrix. As can been observed from Fig. 2, the virtual measurement $r_{v1,k}$ associating with the other two existingmeasurements $r_{1,k}$ and $r_{2,k}$ provide a confinedregion for the estimation of the MS's location at the time step k, i.e.,$\hat{\mathbf{x}}_{k|k}$.Based on (9), the signal variation of $r_{v1,k}$ isconsidered as the variance of the predicted distance$\|\hat{\mathbf{x}}_{k\,|\,k-1} - \hat{\mathbf{x}}_{k-1\,|\,k-1}\|$between the previous (k -1) time steps. Therefore, the variance of virtual noise $n_{v1,k}$ is regarded as $\sigma^2_{n_{v1,k}}$ = Var ($\|\hat{\mathbf{x}}_{k\,|\,k-1} - \hat{\mathbf{x}}_{k-1\,|\,k-1}\|$).

4.2One-AN case

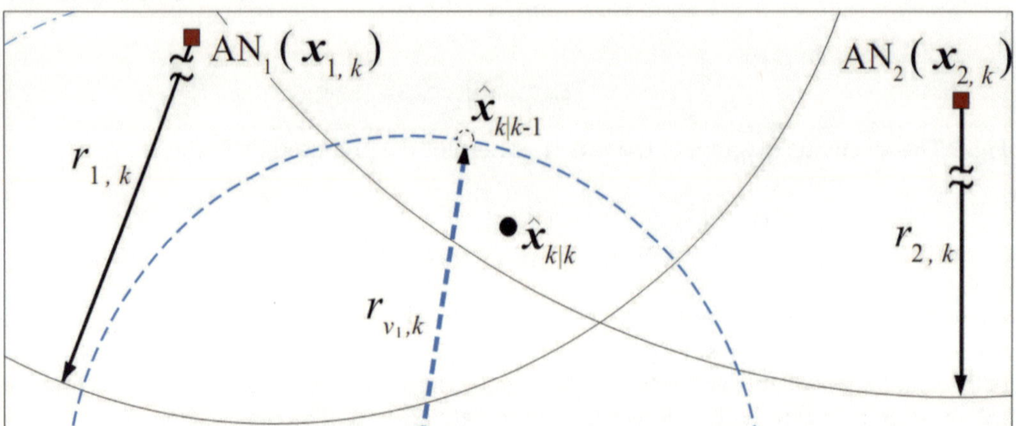

Fig. 3.The schematic diagram of the one-AN case for the proposed PLT scheme.

In this case, only one AN (i.e.,AN$_1$) with one TOA measurement input is available at the kth time step(as shown in Fig. 3). Two additional virtual ANs and measurements are required for the computation of the two-step LS estimator, i.e., $\mathbf{P}_{AN_v,k} = \{\mathbf{x}_{v1,k}, \mathbf{x}_{v2,k}\}$ and $\mathbf{r}_{v,k} = \{r_{v1,k}, r_{v2,k}\}$. Similar to the previous case,the first virtual measurement $r_{v1,k}$ is acquired as in(9) by considering $\hat{x}_{k-1|k-1}$ as the position of the firstvirtual AN (i.e.,$\mathbf{x}_{v1,k} = \hat{x}_{k-1|k-1}$) with the predicted MS'sposition (i.e.,$\hat{x}_{k|k-1}$) as the possible position of the MS.On the other hand, the second virtual AN's position i sassumed to locate at the predicted MS's position (i.e., $\mathbf{x}_{v2,k} \triangleq \hat{x}_{k|k-1}$) as illustrated in Fig. 3. The corresponding second virtual measurement $r_{v2,k}$ is defined as the averageprediction error obtained from the Kalman filtering formulation by accumulating the previous time steps as

$$r_{v2,k} = \frac{1}{k-1}\sum_{i=1}^{k-1}\left\|\hat{\mathbf{x}}_{i|i} - \hat{\mathbf{x}}_{i|i-1}\right\| \tag{13}$$

It is noted that $r_{v2,k}$ is obtained as the mean predictionerror until the (k - 1)th time step. In the case while the Kalman filter is capable of providing sufficient accuracy in its prediction phase, the virtual measurement $r_{v2,k}$ may approach zero value. Associating with the singlemeasurement $r_{v1,k}$ from AN_1, the two additional virtual measurements $r_{v1,k}$ (centered at $\hat{x}_{k-1|k-1}$) and $r_{v2,k}$ (centered at $\hat{x}_{k|k-1}$) result in a constrained region (as in Fig. 3) for location estimation of the MS under the environments with insufficient signal sources. Similarly to two-ANs case, the variance of virtual noise $n_{v1,k}$ is regarded as $\sigma^2_{n_{v1,k}}$ = Var $\left(\left\|\hat{\mathbf{x}}_{k|k-1} - \hat{\mathbf{x}}_{k-1|k-1}\right\|\right)$. On the other hand, the signal variation of the second virtual measurement $r_{v2,k}$ is obtained as the variance of the averaged prediction errors as

$$\begin{aligned} n_{v2,k} &= r_{v2,k} - \zeta_{v2,k} \\ &= \frac{1}{k-1}\sum_{i=1}^{k-1}\left\|\hat{\mathbf{x}}_{i|i} - \hat{\mathbf{x}}_{i|i-1}\right\| - \left\|\hat{\mathbf{x}}_{k|k} - \hat{\mathbf{x}}_{k|k-1}\right\| \end{aligned} \tag{14}$$

The associated variance of virtual noise $n_{v2,k}$can also be regarded as $\sigma^2_{n_{v2,k}}$ = Var $(r_{v2,k})$. It is noted that the variances will be exploited as the weighting coefficients within the formulation of the two-step LS estimator.

5. Performance evaluation

Simulations are performed to show the effectiveness of the proposed PLT scheme under different numbers of ANs, including the scenarios with deficient signal sources. The noise models and the simulation parameters are illustrated in Subsection 5.1. The performance comparison between the proposed PLT algorithm with the other existing location tracking schemes, i.e., the KT and the CLT techniques, are conducted in Subsection 5.2.

5.1 Noise model

Different noise models (Chen, 1999) for the TOA measurements are considered in the simulations. The model for the measurement noise of the TOA signals is selected as the Gaussian distribution with zero mean and 5meters of standard deviation, i.e. $n_{i,k} \sim N(0,25)$.On the other hand, an exponential distribution $p_{e_i,k}(\tau)$is assumed for the NLOS noise model of the TOAmeasurements as

$$p_{e_{i,k}}(v) = \begin{cases} \frac{1}{\lambda_{i,k}} \exp\left(-\frac{v}{\lambda_{i,k}}\right) & v > 0 \\ 0 & \text{otherwise} \end{cases} \tag{15}$$

where $\lambda_{i,k} = c \cdot \tau_{i,k} = c \cdot \tau_m (\zeta_{i,k})^{\varepsilon} \rho$. The parameter $\tau_{i,k}$is the RMS delay spread between the ith AN to the MS.τ_m represents the median value of $\tau_{i,k}$, which is selectedas 0.1in the simulations. ε is the path loss exponentwhich is assumed to be 0.5. The shadow fading factor ρ is a log-normal random variable with zero mean andstandard deviation $\sigma_\rho$chosen as 4 dB in the simulations.The parameters for the noise models as listed in thissubsection primarily fulfill the environment while theMS is located within the rural area in (Chen,1999). It is noticed that the reason for selecting the rural area as the simulation scenario is due to its similarity to the channel condition of WSNs. The transmission range of the AN is set as 100 meter. Moreover, the sampling timeΔt is chosen as 1 sec in the simulations.

5.2 Simulation Results

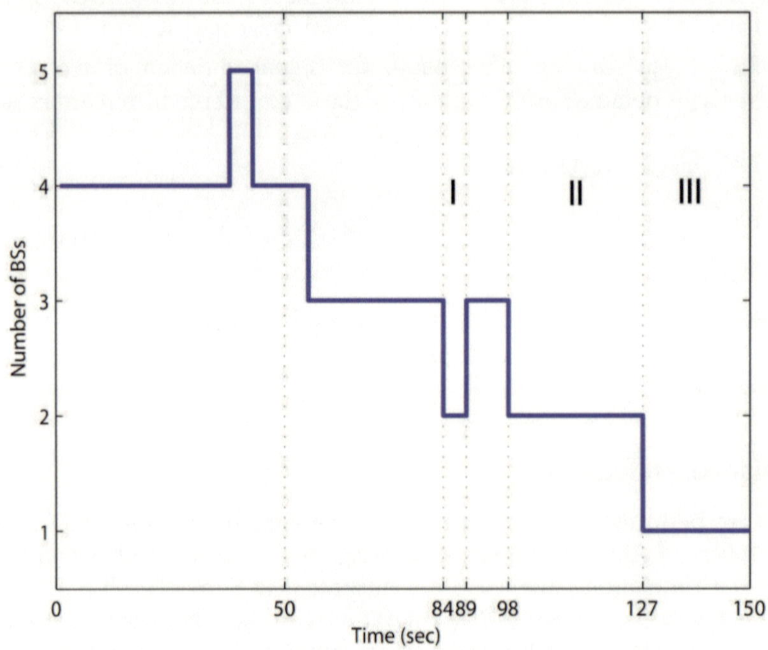

Fig. 4.Total number of available ANs (N_k) vs. simulation time (sec).

The performance comparisons between the KT scheme, the CLT scheme, and the proposed PLT algorithm are conducted under the rural environment. Fig. 4 illustrates the scenario with various numbers of ANs (i.e. the N_k values) that are available at different time intervals. It can be seen that the number of ANs becomes insufficient (i.e. N_k<3) from the time interval of t = 84 to 89 and t=98 to 150 sec. The region I marked in Fig. 4 denotes for the time period t=84 to 89 when the number of available AN is two (i.e., N_k= 2); the region II represents for the time period t=98 to 126 when N_k= 2; while the region III stands for t =127 to 150 when N_k= 1. The total simulation interval is set as 150 seconds.

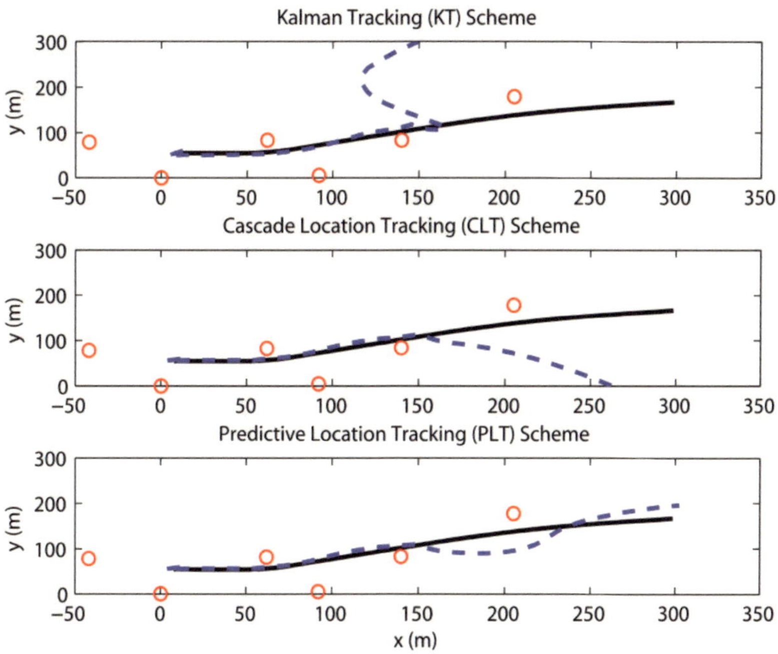

Fig. 5.Performance comparison of MS tracking. (Dashed lines: estimated trajectory; Solid lines: true trajectory; Red empty circles: the position of the ANs).

Fig. 5 illustrates the performance comparison of the trajectory using the three algorithms. The estimated values obtained from these schemes are illustrated via the dashed lines; while the true values are denoted by the solid lines. The locations of the ANs are represented by the red empty circles as in Fig. 5. The acceleration is designed to vary at time t = 1, 40, 55, 100, and 120sec from $\mathbf{a}_k$= ($\mathbf{a}_{x,k}$, $a_{y,k}$) = (0.05, 0), (-0.01, 0.075), (0, 0), (0.025,0), to (0.05, -0.1) m/sec^2. The corresponding velocity of MS is lied between [0,5] m/sec. It is noted that the MS experiences third (i.e., region I and II), fourth (i.e., region II) and fifth (i.e. region III) acceleration change when the number of ANs becomes insufficient.

By observing the starting time interval between t = 0and 83 sec (where the number of ANs is sufficient), the three algorithms provide similar performance on location tracking as shown in the x-y plots in Fig. 5.During the time interval between t = 98 and 150 sec with inadequate signal sources, it can be observed that only the proposed PLT scheme can achieve satisfactory performance in the trajectory tracking. The estimated trajectories obtained from both the KT and the CLT schemes diverge from the true trajectories due to the inadequate number of measurement inputs.

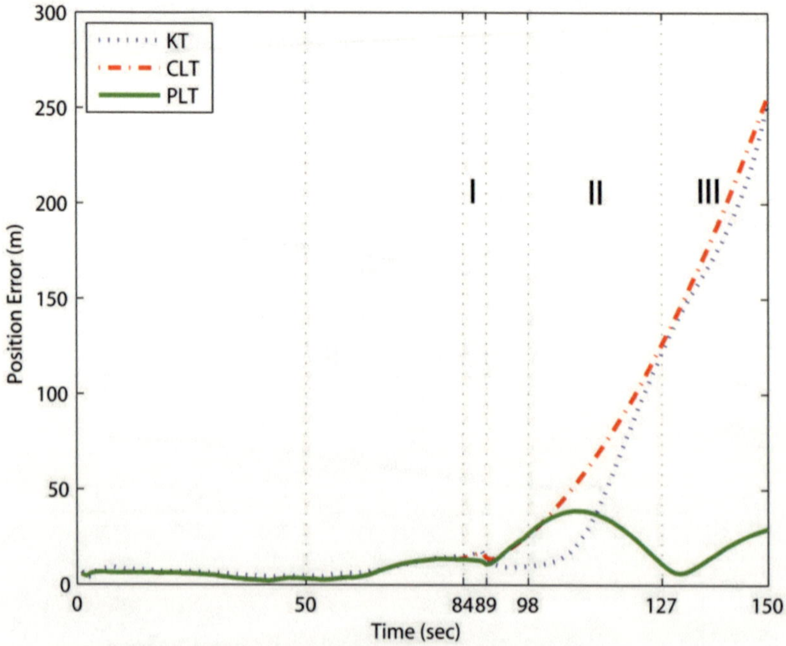

Fig. 6.The position error(m) vs. the simulation time (sec)

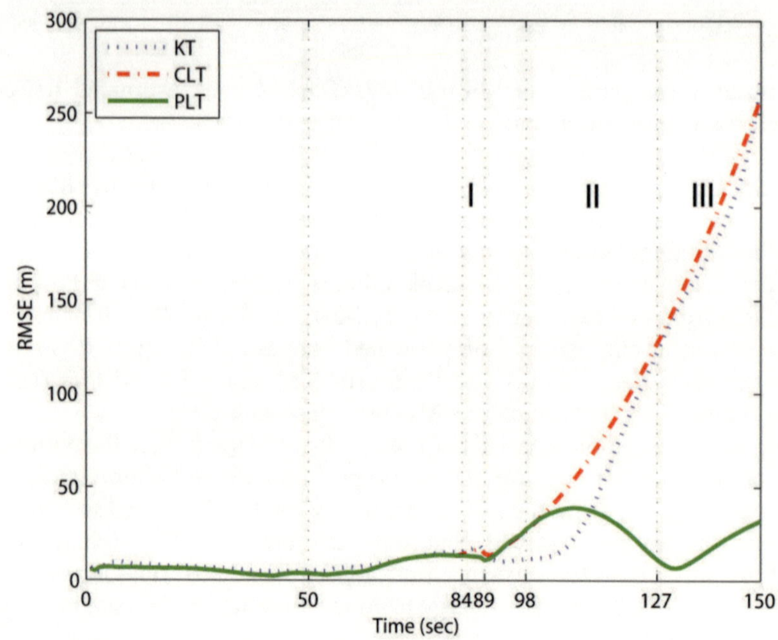

Fig. 7.The RMSE (m) vs. the simulation time (sec).

Moreover, Figs. 6 and 7 illustrate the position error and the Root Mean Square Error (RMSE)(i.e., characterizing the signal variances) for location estimation and tracking of the

MS. It is noted that the position error (Δx_k) are computed as: $\Delta x_k = [||\hat{x}_k - x_k||]/N_r$, where N_r= 100 indicates the number of simulation runs. On the other hand, it is noted that the RMSE is computed as: RMSE= $\{[\sum_{i=1}^{N_r} ||\hat{x}_k - x_k||^2]/N_r\}^{1/2}$.The three location tracking schemes are compared based on the same simulation scenario as shown in Fig. 5. It can be observed from both plots that the proposed PLT algorithms outperform the conventional KT and CLT schemes. The main differences between these algorithms occur while the signal sources become insufficient within the region I, II, and III. The proposed PLT schemes can still provide consistent location estimation and tracking; while the other two algorithms result in significantly augmented estimation errors. The major reason is attributed to the assisted information that is fed back into the location estimator while the signal sources are deficient.

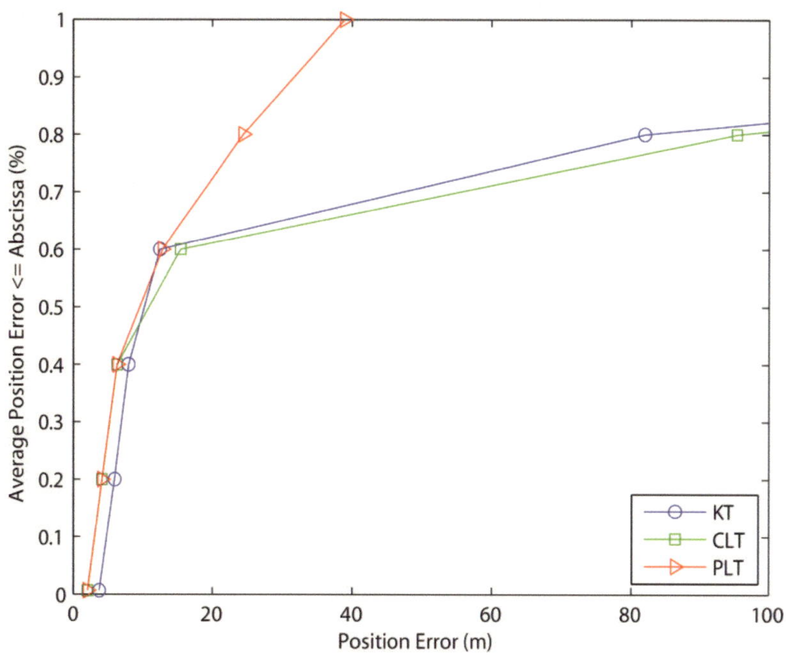

Fig. 8.Performance comparison between the location tracking schemes.

Fig. 8 shows the sorted position errors based on the same simulation results as shown in Fig. 6. Since the PLT algorithm is essentially the same as the CLT scheme while the number of ANs is adequate, both schemes perform the same under 50% of position errors. The performance of the CLT scheme becomes worse after 60% of position errors due to the deficiency of signal sources; while the proposed PLT algorithm can still provide feasible performance for location tracking. Moreover, the performance obtained from the KT scheme is similar to the CLT which is comparably worse than the PLT algorithm.

6. Conclusion

In this book chapter, the Predictive Location Tracking (PLT) scheme is proposed. The predictive information obtained from the Kalman filtering formulation is exploited as the additional measurement inputs for the location estimator. With the feedback information, sufficient signal sources become available for location estimation and tracking of a mobile device. It is shown in the simulation results that the proposed PLT scheme can provide consistent accuracy for location estimation and tracking even with insufficient signal sources.

7. References

Chen, C.-L. & Feng, K.-F. (2005). Hybrid Location Estimation and Tracking System for Mobile Devices, *Proceedings of IEEE Vehicular Technology Conference*, pp. 2648–2652, Jun. 2005

Chen, P. C. (1999). A Non-Line-of-Sight Error Mitigation Algorithm in Location Estimation, *Proceedings of IEEE Wireless Communications Networking Conference*, pp. 316–320, Sep. 1999

Chen, Y. T. & Ho, K. C. (1994).A Simple and Efficient Estimator for Hyperbolic Location. *IEEE Trans. Signal Processing*, Vol. 42, Aug. 1994.pp.1905–1915

Cong, L. & Zhuang, W. (2002).Hybrid TDOA/AOA Mobile User Location for Wideband CDMA Cellular Systems. *IEEE Trans. Wireless Commun.*, Vol. 1, Jul. 2002, pp. 439–447

Foy,W. H. (1976).Position-Location Solutions by Taylor-Series Estimation, *IEEE Trans. Aerosp. Electron. Syst.*, vol. 12, pp. 187–194, Mar.1976.

Gezici, S.; Tian Z.; Giannakis, G. B.; Kobayashi, H.; Molisch, A. F.; Poor, H. V.& Sahinoglu, Z. (2005). Localization via Ultra-Wideband Radios: A Look at Positioning Aspects for Future Sensor Networks. *IEEE Signal Processing Mag.*, Vol. 22, Jul. 2005, pp. 70–84

Hara, S.; Zhao, D.; Yanagihara, K.; Taketsugu, J.; Fukui, K.; Fukunaga, S. & Kitayama, K. (2005). Propagation Characteristics of IEEE 802.15.4 Radio Signal and Their Application for Location Estimation, *Proceedings of IEEE Vehicular Technology Conference*, pp. 97–101, Jun. 2005

Lee, C. Y. (1993). *Mobile Communications Engineering*, McGraw-Halls, ISBN: 978-0070370395

Kuusniemi, H.; Wieser, A.; Lachapellea, G. & Takala, J. (2007).User-level reliability monitoring in urban personal satellite-navigation. *IEEE Trans. Aerosp. Electron. Syst.*, Vol. 43, Oct. 2007, pp. 1305–1318

Nájar, M. & Vidal, J. (2001).Kalman Tracking Based on TDOA for UMTS Mobile Location, *Proceedings of IEEE International Symposium on Personal, Indoor and Mobile Radio Communications*, pp. 45–49, Sep. 2001

Patwari, N.; Ash, J. N.; Kyperountas, S.; Hero III, A. O.; Moses, R. L. & Correal, N. S. (2005). Locating the Nodes: Cooperative Localization in Wireless Sensor Networks. *IEEE Signal Processing Mag.*, Vol. 22, Jul. 2005, pp. 54–69

Perusco, L. & Michael, K. (2007). Control, Trust, Privacy, and Security: Evaluating Location-based Services. *IEEE Technol. Soc. Mag.*, Vol. 26, Jul. 2007, pp. 4–16

Tseng, P.-H. & Feng, K.-F.(2009).Hybrid Network/Satellite-Based Location Estimation and Tracking Systems for Wireless Networks,*IEEE Trans. Veh. Technol.*, vol.58, issue 9, pp.5174-5189, Nov. 2009

Wang, X.; Wang Z. & O'Dea, B. (2003).A TOA-Based Location Algorithm Reducing the Errors Due to Non-Line-of-Sight (NLOS) Propagation. *IEEE Trans. Veh. Technol.*, Vol. 52, Jan. 2003, pp. 112–116

Zaidi, Z. R. & Mark, B. L. (2005) Real-time mobility tracking algorithms for cellular networks based on Kalman filtering. *IEEE Trans. Mobile Comput.*, Vol. 4, Mar. 2005, pp. 195–208

Zhao, Y. (2002). Standardization of Mobile Phone Positioning for 3G Systems. *IEEE Commun. Mag.*, Vol. 40, Jul. 2002, pp. 108–116